The fifth edition of *The Reflective Educator's Guide to Practitioner Inquiry* has me eager to work alongside teachers as they engage in inquiry! Its progression is sequenced in such a way that allows for teachers to inquire independently or within a community of practitioners. I highly recommend *The Reflective Educator's Guide to Practitioner Inquiry* to anyone who is looking to address difficult (and sometimes contested) issues in the classroom while also developing in professional practice.

—Lisa Vojacek
School-Based Instructional Coach
Valley Middle School, Grand Forks Public Schools, North Dakota

What Your Colleagues Are Saying . . .

The fifth edition of *The Reflective Educator's Guide to Practitioner Inquiry* offers a compelling framework for identifying persistent, contextualized challenges and using systematic, intentional investigation to drive continuous improvement in teaching and learning. Packed with practical tools, real-world examples, and reflections on the inquiry process, this book empowers teachers to approach their work with a mindset of curiosity, adaptability, and lifelong professional growth.

—Jill Perry
Professor of Practice and Executive Director
University of Pittsburgh; Carnegie Project on the Education Doctorate

The fifth edition is more than an update. Dana, Yendol-Hoppey, and Rutten's latest is a manifesto for teacher inquiry: laying out its history, describing the dramatic changes to the contexts of teaching since the fourth edition, and providing the purpose for teacher inquiry as a tool to create more just and more equitable schooling experiences. I predict this edition will become a seminal work in our field.

—Rachelle Meyer Rodgers
Past President of the Association of Teacher Educators and
Clinical Professor, Baylor University

This book, coupled with its extensive online resources for each chapter, makes coaching, facilitating, and teaching inquiry a truly enriching experience. I have used this book with teacher candidates, teacher leaders, administrators, and graduate students because it provides step-by-step guidance on planning an inquiry and walks readers through the process, providing real-world examples and guides for all audiences.

—Jamey B. Burns
Director, Jacksonville Teacher Residency
University of North Florida

This fifth edition of *The Reflective Educator's Guide to Practitioner Inquiry* is poised to make a lasting impact on the field of education as it reframes classroom research to practitioner inquiry, adding agency prominently into the role and practice of reflective educators. Emphasizing the process of inquiry as central to the purpose of practitioner inquiry, Dana, Yendol-Hoppey, and Rutten highlight the interplay of inquiry as a process, a product, and a stance toward knowledge and practice for the education profession. This revised edition provides a framework for engaging the process of inquiry, using the product of inquiry to make an impact on education practice, and living an inquiry stance toward teaching to enable a way of being for reflective educators and transformative educational work.

—Jenn Snow
Professor and Program Area Coordinator
Boise State University

The fifth edition of *The Reflective Educator's Guide to Practitioner Inquiry* highlights the transformative power of practitioner inquiry in education, serving as both a guide and inspiration for educators seeking to deepen their impact. By fostering curiosity, reflection, and action, it equips teachers to navigate complexities, elevate their practice, and champion equity in classrooms and communities.

—**Frannie Tunseth**
Classroom Teacher and Teacher Educator
May-Port CG School District; University of North Dakota

As an instructional coach, I've used *The Reflective Educator's Guide to Practitioner Inquiry* to guide my own action research as well as facilitate the professional development of others. Learning how to systematically investigate my own practice through inquiry has been transformative. A powerful and impactful learning experience always results.

—**Kerri Bartholomew**
Instructional Coach
Ketchikan Gateway Borough School District, Alaska

Since its first edition, I have relied on *The Reflective Educator's Guide* as my essential resource for guiding teachers through the inquiry process. Dana, Yendol-Hoppey, and Rutten masterfully scaffold this process, using vivid examples to illuminate each phase of the inquiry cycle and bring it to life. These examples demonstrate how practitioner research can seamlessly integrate into teachers' daily practice. I am especially thrilled that this edition introduces new content on developing a research plan, offering a detailed roadmap to help teachers navigate inquiry planning stages with greater depth and purpose. The updated examples, addressing timely topics like artificial intelligence, make this edition particularly relevant to today's educators. At a time when external forces increasingly diminish teachers' autonomy, classroom research offers a powerful means of reclaiming agency and ensuring effective teaching practices for their students.

—**Jennifer Jacobs**
Associate Professor and Director
Office of Clinical Education, University of South Florida

The Reflective Educator's Guide to Practitioner Inquiry is a masterful bridge between research and practice, equipping educators with the tools and mindset to cultivate continuous, data-driven improvements that elevate student-centered teaching.

—**Aimee H. Barber**
Assistant Professor
College of Education & Human Development
University of Louisiana at Lafayette

The Reflective Educator's Guide to Practitioner Inquiry

Fifth Edition

For teacher inquirers everywhere, who keep our passion for reforming teaching and teacher education alive

The Reflective Educator's Guide to Practitioner Inquiry

Fifth Edition

Nancy Fichtman Dana
Diane Yendol-Hoppey
Logan Rutten

A Joint Publication

CORWIN

FOR INFORMATION:

Corwin

A SAGE Company

2455 Teller Road

Thousand Oaks, California 91320

(800) 233-9936

www.corwin.com

SAGE Publications Ltd.

1 Oliver's Yard

55 City Road

London EC1Y 1SP

United Kingdom

SAGE Publications India Pvt. Ltd.

Unit No 323-333, Third Floor, F-Block

International Trade Tower Nehru Place

New Delhi 110 019

India

SAGE Publications Asia-Pacific Pte. Ltd.

18 Cross Street #10-10/11/12

China Square Central

Singapore 048423

Vice President and
   Editorial Director: Monica Eckman

Acquisitions Editor: Megan Bedell

Content Development
   Manager: Lucas Schleicher

Senior Editorial
   Assistant: Natalie Delpino

Project Editor: Amy Schroller

Copy Editor: Talia Greenberg

Typesetter: C&M Digitals (P) Ltd.

Proofreader: Lawrence W. Baker

Cover Designer: Candice Harman

Marketing Manager: Melissa Duclos

Copyright © 2025 by Corwin Press, Inc.

All rights reserved. Except as permitted by U.S. copyright law, no part of this work may be reproduced or distributed in any form or by any means, or stored in a database or retrieval system, without permission in writing from the publisher.

When forms and sample documents appearing in this work are intended for reproduction, they will be marked as such. Reproduction of their use is authorized for educational use by educators, local school sites, and/or noncommercial or nonprofit entities that have purchased the book.

All third-party trademarks referenced or depicted herein are included solely for the purpose of illustration and are the property of their respective owners. Reference to these trademarks in no way indicates any relationship with, or endorsement by, the trademark owner.

No AI training. Without in any way limiting the author's and publisher's exclusive rights under copyright, any use of this publication to "train" generative artificial intelligence (AI) or for other AI uses is expressly prohibited. The publisher reserves all rights to license uses of this publication for generative AI training or other AI uses.

Library of Congress Cataloging-in-Publication Data

Names: Dana, Nancy Fichtman, 1964- author | Yendol-Hoppey, Diane author | Rutten, Logan author

Title: The reflective educator's guide to practitioner inquiry / Nancy Fichtman Dana, Diane Yendol-Hoppey, Logan Rutten.

Description: Fifth edition. | Thousand Oaks, California : Corwin, [2025] | Previous edition: 2019. | Includes bibliographical references and index.

Identifiers: LCCN 2025003310 | ISBN 9781071966655 paperback | ISBN 9781071966662 epub | ISBN 9781071966679 epub | ISBN 9781071966686 pdf

Subjects: LCSH: Action research in education | Teachers—In-service training | Action research in education

Classification: LCC LB1028.24 .D35 2025 | DDC 370.72—dc23/eng/20250326

LC record available at https://lccn.loc.gov/2025003310

This book is printed on acid-free paper.

25 26 27 28 29 10 9 8 7 6 5 4 3 2 1

DISCLAIMER: This book may direct you to access third-party content via Web links, QR codes, or other scannable technologies, which are provided for your reference by the author(s). Corwin makes no guarantee that such third-party content will be available for your use and encourages you to review the terms and conditions of such third-party content. Corwin takes no responsibility and assumes no liability for your use of any third-party content, nor does Corwin approve, sponsor, endorse, verify, or certify such third-party content.

Contents

List of Resources	xv
Preface	xix
Acknowledgments	xxiii
About the Authors	xxv
How to Use the Inquiry Books	xxix
Inquiry Facilitation Tools	xxxi

Chapter 1. Teacher Inquiry Defined — 1

What Is Teacher Inquiry?	2
What Evidence Exists That Teacher Inquiry Is Worth Doing?	4
What Are the Origins of Teacher Inquiry?	7
How Is Teacher Inquiry Changing With the Times?	13
What Is the Relationship Between Teacher Inquiry and AI?	18
How Is Teacher Inquiry Different From What I Already Do as a Reflective Teacher?	19
Why Inquire? Inquiry as a Pathway to Equity	21
What Are Some Contexts Ripe for Teacher Inquiry?	22
Professional Development/Learning Programs	23
Professional Learning Communities	24
Teacher Candidate Clinical Experiences/Residencies	26
Professional Development Schools	27
Professional Practice Doctoral Programs	28

How Does My Engaging in Teacher Inquiry Help Shape the Profession of Teaching?	29
What Is Ahead in This Book, and How Do I Use It?	30

Chapter 2. The Passions That Drive Your Journey: Finding a Wondering — 35

Where Do I Begin?	35
Where Do I Find My Wonderings?	37
Passion 1: Helping an Individual Child	39
Passion 2: Desire to Improve or Enrich Curriculum	47
Passion 3: Focus on Developing Content Knowledge	54
Passion 4: Desire to Improve or Experiment With Teaching Strategies and Teaching Techniques	57
Passion 5: Desire to Explore the Relationship Between Your Beliefs and Your Classroom Practice	61
Passion 6: The Intersection of Your Personal and Professional Identities	62
Passion 7: Advocating for Equity and Social Justice	71
Passion 8: Focus on Understanding the Teaching and Learning Context	81
What Are the Next Steps in Wondering Development?	86

Chapter 3. Data Collection: Making Inquiry a Part of Your Teaching Practice — 95

What Is Data Collection?	96
What Do Data Look Like, How Do I Collect Them, and How Do They Fit Into My Work as a Teacher?	96
Strategy 1: Student Work and Other Instructional Artifacts	96
Strategy 2: Field Notes	104
Strategy 3: Interviews	114
Strategy 4: Focus Groups	117

Strategy 5: Digital Pictures	118
Strategy 6: Video as Data	120
Strategy 7: Reflective Journals/Blogs	121
Strategy 8: Surveys	126
Strategy 9: Quantitative Measures of Student Achievement (Standardized Test Scores, Assessment Measures, Grades)	138
Strategy 10: Colleague Feedback	146
When Do I Begin Data Collection?	153

Chapter 4. Developing a Research Plan: Mapping Out Your Inquiry Journey — 159

Inquiry Planning Stage 1: Identify the Problem	160
Understand Your Context	162
Exercise 1. Understanding Your Context	163
Define Your Topic	163
Exercise 2. Defining Your Topic	163
Clarify Your Purpose and Rationale	164
Exercise 3. Clarifying Your Purpose and Rationale	164
Craft and Claim Your Wondering	165
Exercise 4. Crafting and Claiming Your Wondering	168
Consult the Literature	168
Exercise 5. Consulting the Literature	172
Inquiry Planning Stage 2: Develop an Implementation Plan	178
Articulate a Theory of Action	181
Exercise 6. Developing a Theory of Action	185
Describe Your Actions/Interventions	186
Exercise 7. Describing Your Actions	186
Select Data Collection Strategies	187
Exercise 8. Selecting Data Collection Strategies	187

Inquiry Planning Stage 3: Establish an Inquiry Timeline	189
Consider Timing and Duration of Data Collection	189
Exercise 9. Considering Timing and Duration of Data Collection	190
Consider How Data Will Be Stored, Displayed, and Analyzed	190
Exercise 10. Considering How Data Will Be Stored, Displayed, and Analyzed	191
Develop a Weekly Calendar	192
Exercise 11. Developing Your Weekly Calendar	192
Inquiry Planning Stage 4: Create an Inquiry Brief	193
Collaborate	193
Exercise 12. Grounding Your Inquiry in Collaboration	198
Write	199
Exercise 13. Writing Your Inquiry Brief	200
Tune	206
Exercise 14. Tuning Your Brief	206
Inquiry Planning Stage 5: Consider the Ethical Dimensions of Your Work	206
Contemplate Ethics in General	208
Check Out School District Research Policies	213
Look Into University Institutional Review Boards	215
Exercise 15. Considering the Ethical Dimensions of Your Work	219
Your Inquiry Plan	220

Chapter 5. Finding Your Findings: Data Analysis — 231

What Is Formative Data Analysis?	232
Conducting Formative Data Analysis: A Four-Step Approach	233
An Example of Formative Data Analysis With Quantitative Data: Megan Hefner	234

    *An Example of Formative Data Analysis
With Qualitative Data: May Steward* — 240

  What Is Summative Data Analysis? — 244

  What Might Summative Analysis Look Like? — 273

Chapter 6. Sharing Your Inquiry Journey: Presenting and Publishing — 287

  Why Is It Important to Share My Work With Others? — 288

  How Do I Present My Work? — 294

  How Do I Write About My Work? — 304

  What Might My Writing Look Like? — 304

    Step 1: Providing Background Information — 315

    *Step 2: Sharing the Design of the Inquiry
(Procedures, Data Collection, and Data Analysis)* — 320

    *Step 3: Stating the Learning and Supporting
the Statements With Data* — 322

    Step 4: Providing Concluding Thoughts — 340

Chapter 7. Contributing to the Creation of More Equitable Schools and Classrooms: The Why of Inquiry — 345

  Coming to View Inquiry as a Pathway to Equity:
A Teacher Researcher's Story (Mickey MacDonald) — 346

  Informing Thinking, Teaching, and Teacher Education: The Power of Equity-Focused Inquiry (Paige Bildstein, Mikhayla Kruse-Meek, Jillian Pohland, Nicole Snitkey, and Hilarie Welsh) — 354

Chapter 8. On Your Way: Becoming the Best Teacher and Researcher You Can Be — 369

  How Can Inquiry Be Three Things in One (Process, Product, and Stance)? — 370

    Inquiry as a Process — 370

    Inquiry as a Product — 370

Inquiry as a Stance	370
The Interconnectedness of Process, Product, and Stance	371
Why Is It Important to Assess the Quality of My Work?	375
What Is the Difference Between Generalizability and Transferability?	376
How Do I Go About Assessing Teacher Research Quality, and Why Is It So Difficult to Do?	378
What Are Some Quality Indicators for Teacher Research?	387
Quality Indicator 1: Context for Inquiry	387
Quality Indicator 2: Wonderings and Purpose	388
Quality Indicator 3: Inquiry Design	388
Quality Indicator 4: Data Collection	389
Quality Indicator 5: Data Analysis	390
Quality Indicator 6: Statements of Learning (Findings)	391
Quality Indicator 7: Implications for Practice	392
What Are Some Ways to Enhance Inquiry Quality?	393
Where Do I Go From Here?	393

References   **397**

Index   **411**

List of Resources

Chapter 1

Figure 1.1	Inquiry Cycle	4
Table 1.1	Competing Paradigms: The Multiple Voices of Research	8
Table 1.2	University-Based Research and Teacher Inquiry Comparison	12

Chapter 2

Figure 2.1	Inquiry Cycle: Develop a Wondering	36
Figure 2.2	Developing Your Research Question	38
AI Moment	Using a Chatbot to Expand Your Thinking and Uncover New Perspectives Related to Your Wonderings	89

Chapter 3

Figure 3.1	Inquiry Cycle: Collect Data	97
Figure 3.2	Ted—Random Writing Samples From Children at the Writing Center	98
Figure 3.3	Ted—Writing Samples When Working With Best Friend	99
Figure 3.4	Canvas and Google Docs Graphic Organizer	102
Figure 3.5	Scripted Field Notes by Darice and Beth	105
Figure 3.6	Scripted Notes Taken for Julie	110
Figure 3.7	Priya's Field Notes	111
Figure 3.8	Cheryl's Field Notes	113
Figure 3.9	Bridge-Building Project—Early Stage in Group 3's Work	119
Figure 3.10	Bridge-Building Project—Completed Bridge by Group 3	119
Figure 3.11	Wendy's Blog Entry	124
Exhibit 3.1	Journal Entry	122

Exhibit 3.2	Parental Survey 1	133
Exhibit 3.3	Parental Survey 2	134
Exhibit 3.4	Chemistry "Help Session" Student Survey	136
Exhibit 3.5	Mickey's Critical Friends Group Feedback	147
Table 3.1	Mickey's Spreadsheet	140
Table 3.2	Debbi's DIBELS Data	142
AI Moment	Using AI-Generated Student Work as a Form of Data	100
AI Moment	Inquiring Into Teaching About AI to My Middle School Students: The Use of Surveys	128

Chapter 4

Figure 4.1	Planning Your Inquiry	161
Figure 4.2	Take Action	178
Figure 4.3	Guidance for the Action Component of Your Inquiry Cycle	182
Figure 4.4	Teacher Research Blogging Site	194
Exhibit 4.1	Inquiry Brief Tuning Protocol—Six Steps to a Fine-Tuned Plan for Inquiry	207
Exhibit 4.2	Sample Consent Form for an IRB Application	215
Exhibit 4.3	Inquiry Brief Example 1	221
Exhibit 4.4	Inquiry Brief Example 2	222
Table 4.1	In What Ways Do Science Talks Enhance Student Understandings of Science Concepts?	188
AI Moment	Reflections on Partnering With ChatGPT in the Development of an Inquiry Brief	200
AI Moment	The Ethics of AI and Inquiry	211

Chapter 5

Figure 5.1	Inquiry Cycle: Data Analysis	231
Figure 5.2	Formative Data Analysis Step by Step	235
Figure 5.3	Letter Recognition	239
Figure 5.4	Sound Recognition	239
Figure 5.5	Summative Data Analysis Step by Step	247
Figure 5.6	Poster Examples	265
Figure 5.7	Amy's List of "Inquiry—What I'm Noticing"	275
Figure 5.8	Amy's Index Card Denoting Pattern Symbols Used for Coding	276
Figure 5.9	Example of Coded Data—Field Notes Scripted by Supervisor	277
Figure 5.10	Example of Coded Data—Journal	278

Figure 5.11	Example of Coded Data—Field Notes Taken by Amy	281
Exhibit 5.1	RtI Design Worksheet	238
Table 5.1	Examples of Organizing Units	261
Table 5.2	Student Interview Codes	263
Table 5.3	Strategies for Illustrating Your Findings	268
AI Moment	Using "Lex" as a Thought Partner in Data Analysis	270

Chapter 6

Figure 6.1	Inquiry Cycle: Share With Others	286
Figure 6.2	Inquiry Conference Program	297
Figure 6.3	Inquiry Poster	300
Figure 6.4	PowerPoint Slides From Debbi's Presentation	301
Figure 6.5	Debbi Hubbell Presents Her Inquiry at the Fourth Annual Teaching, Inquiry, and Innovation Showcase at the University of Florida's P. K. Yonge Developmental Research School	303
Figure 6.6	Inquiry Brochure Example	307
Figure 6.7	Inquiry Brochure Example 2	308
Figure 6.8	Inquiry Template Example	310
Figure 6.9	Critical Features for Presenting and Writing Up Your Inquiry	311
AI Moment	Preparing to Share an Inquiry With Some Assistance From AI	312

Chapter 7

Figure 7.1	Mickey's Data Analysis Posters	351
Figure 7.2	Mickey's "What I See" Poster	352
Figure 7.3	Mickey's Student Completes Vocabulary Sort Activity	353
Figure 7.4	Popplet	358
Figure 7.5	Finished Book	358
Figure 7.6	Loras College Teacher Education Conceptual Framework	363
Figure 7.7	Loras Teacher Candidates Present Their Inquiry	364

Chapter 8

Figure 8.1	Inquiry Cycle	374
Table 8.1	Inquiry as Process, Product, and Stance	371
Table 8.2	Quality Indicators for Assessing Practitioner Inquiry	383

Preface

We (Nancy and Diane) have had the joy of reading about, studying, writing about, doing, and facilitating others' learning through inquiry since the late 1980s. We have long recognized that as we age as inquiry authors, scholars, and advocates, the power of inquiry will endure well beyond the time we have left to contribute to the movement that we love. For this reason, for the fifth edition, we wished to invite a junior scholar, who is as passionate about inquiry as we have always been, to join our writing team and carry this work forward. We were delighted when Logan Rutten, assistant professor at the University of North Dakota, accepted our invitation, and we proudly introduce the reader to the third member of our authorship "we" (Nancy, Diane, and Logan).

Working together as an authorship trio has greatly enhanced the ways we present the inquiry experience to the reader in the fifth edition, which followers of our book will recognize has had a slight title adjustment from *The Reflective Educator's Guide to Classroom Research: Learning to Teach and Teaching to Learn Through Practitioner Inquiry* (a mouthful) to a shorter, simpler title: *The Reflective Educator's Guide to Practitioner Inquiry*. We believe this modification for the fifth edition better represents the book as a whole as well as who the book is for, as while many of the examples we use in the text emanate from teachers' classrooms, other educational professionals who do not have their own classrooms such as principals, other district administrators, librarians, professors, and the like, have used this book to learn about and guide their own inquiries. Furthermore, we use the terminology *practitioner inquiry* throughout the book, rather than *classroom research*, so we thought it made sense to bring these words from the subtitle into the main title itself.

While there has been a slight title change, the core of the fifth edition has remained the same, while simultaneously offering updated examples, a reorganization, and new material we believe will enhance the reader's inquiry experience. Our fifth edition renovations include an expanded discussion of inquiry as stance and repositioning of the inquiry cycle diagram from the final chapter to the book's first few pages. This expanded discussion and repositioning will set readers on their inquiry journeys with a clear understanding of the ultimate goal of engagement in the process of inquiry described in the chapters ahead.

Speaking of inquiry journey, for the fifth edition we have worked hard to elevate the journey metaphor throughout the book. With the inquiry cycle illustration now positioned at the start of the book, we repeat the illustration throughout the text with a "You are here" notation, echoing a map where you find a "You are here" marker to help orient you as you chart your course. We have also improved our discussion of the circuitous nature of inquiry, both directly in our writing and with a new text feature that invites the reader to skip ahead and circle back to different parts of the book as needed throughout their inquiry journey.

In Chapter 1, we also added two new sections, "How Is Inquiry Changing With the Times?" and, as one of the most impactful changes of the times is the emergence of AI on the educational landscape, "What Is the Relationship Between Teacher Inquiry and AI?" You will note in this section that we introduce the reader to a textbox feature in the book called "AI Moments." We, or inquirers with whom we have worked, have written seven of these textboxes that appear throughout the book, adding a modern take on both the topics relevant for educators to inquire into and the use of AI to enhance each component of one's inquiry journey.

Chapter 4 is a brand-new chapter that we believe makes an important addition to the text. This chapter focuses on planning your inquiry and takes the reader step-by-step through the planning process. In previous editions, the chapters on wondering development and data collection ended with exercises that helped the reader plan their inquiry, but that approach pretty much left the reader on their own to apply what they had learned in those chapters to the design of their work. This new chapter takes the reader by the hand and helps them apply what they learned about inquiry thus far in the book to the creation of their own inquiry plan. This approach also enabled us to streamline the chapter structure from the fourth edition by subsuming the content of three short fourth-edition chapters (Chapter 3—Learning With and From the Literature; Chapter 4—Learning With and From Your Colleagues; and Chapter 5—Considering the Ethical Dimensions of Your Work as an Inquirer) into the new chapter on planning.

The chapters on data collection and data analysis have also been updated, with an explicit definition of data collection presented at the start of Chapter 3 and seven new exercises, designed to help inquirers practice and refine their data collection skills, ending the chapter. In this edition, we have provided a more detailed description of the formative data analysis process, capturing it with a new figure that guides the reader step-by-step through analysis of data as they are collected. Furthermore, we streamlined our discussion of summative data analysis, better integrating summative analyses with quantitative and qualitative data sources.

Finally, in our last chapter, we offer a new discussion of inquiry as process, product, *and* stance, defining each as well as illustrating the interconnectiveness among these three constructs. Reflecting new material in this edition, we have also expanded our presentation of quality indicators in this chapter to assess the products of inquiry with a total of seven indicators now presented, up from five in our previous editions. We hope our careful work updating these quality indicators will truly help teacher researchers everywhere continue to grow not only as practitioners but as researchers as well.

In addition to these chapter changes and other updates, this fifth edition continues to integrate the previous material we had available on the book's accompanying website with the text of the book itself by presenting discussion questions at the end of each chapter. After the discussion questions, we also print a summary of the online materials available to teach each chapter (many of which have been updated or added to), continuing to make the connection between the book's text and website more fluid.

The fifth edition emerges from our understanding of the literature in the areas of professional learning, action research, teacher research, qualitative research, quantitative research, and the process of change as well as our collective experience working with practicing and teacher candidates engaged in inquiry for more than 30 years. Over those 30 years, we have seen how inquiry both endures through the times and shifts in response to the times. To reflect the simultaneously enduring and shifting nature of inquiry, we have purposefully left some of the initial examples of teacher inquiry from the first edition published in 2003 that remain relevant today but also replaced some examples from the first four editions that were outdated with new examples gathered from teachers since the publication of the fourth edition in 2020. What we have learned from all the many teacher inquirers we have worked with over the past 30 years about how and why they inquire provides insights into the power that teacher inquiry holds to transform classrooms and schools to places where teachers' voices contribute to the knowledge generated about teaching and learning.

Acknowledgments

We have had the honor and privilege to work with many tremendous teachers throughout our careers, and it is through these teachers' work that we have witnessed the process of inquiry and the power of inquiry as a tool for professional learning. Throughout our careers, we have also always been passionate about raising the voices of teachers in educational reform, teaching, and teacher education. In an effort to raise teacher voices, we weave within this text many rich examples of these teachers' inquiries as we describe the process step-by-step. Hence, this book would not have been possible without the inquiries that only prospective and practicing teachers can provide. We are grateful to all of the practicing teachers and teacher candidates with whom we have worked. Their time, dedication, and contribution to teacher inquiry and the education profession are immeasurable. We continue to admire their devotion and are grateful for their dedication to the profession of teaching and their support in writing this book.

We are also grateful to numerous colleagues who helped us conceptualize and enact our work with inquiry and have pushed our thinking about the process over time. We also thank the great people at Corwin, specifically Megan Bedell, Lucas Schleicher, and Mia Rodriguez for their support of the fifth edition, as well as Kirsten Bennett (Nancy's daughter) for her work on new figures introduced in this edition. We wish to thank all of our children (Greg, Kirsten, Caran, Billy, and Kevin), who were in elementary school when the first edition of this book was published, served as our initial inquiry inspirations, and are now awesome adults who continue to support our work.

Finally, we thank our incredible spouses. Heather Rutten, at The Pennsylvania State University, became a champion for practitioner inquiry upon first witnessing its impacts on Logan's teaching in Montana. Heather's artistic vision, strengths-based perspective on rural communities, and steadfast encouragement have all been instrumental in this journey of inquiry. David Hoppey, at the University of North Florida, has spent the last decade helping practitioners understand how to enact an inquiry stance that can transform the experiences of struggling learners and educational leaders. His work serves as an example to all interested in high-quality special education teacher education, job-embedded professional learning, and educational change. And Tom Dana, at the University of Florida, continues to lay the foundation for the spread of teacher inquiry that we began at Penn State with his unselfish support and encouragement in the early stages of our work. The many conversations we had as all five editions of this book were taking shape were invaluable to each book's completion. He served as our IT helper, editor, idea bouncer, AI consultant, and friend. We are grateful for and admire his dedication to rethinking teacher education and building an inquiry stance toward teaching, as well as his awesome administrative talent that makes these things happen.

About the Authors

Nancy Fichtman Dana is professor of education and distinguished teaching scholar at the University of Florida, Gainesville. She began her career in education as an elementary school teacher in Hannibal Central Schools, New York. Since earning her PhD from Florida State University in 1991, she has been a passionate advocate for teacher inquiry and has worked extensively in supporting schools, districts, and universities in implementing powerful programs of job-embedded professional development through inquiry across the United States and in several countries, including Belgium, China, Estonia, the Netherlands, Portugal, Slovenia, South Korea, and Spain. She has published 12 books and more than 100 articles in professional journals and edited books focused on her research exploring teacher and principal professional development and practitioner inquiry. Dana has received many honors for her teaching, research, and writing. Among them are the Association of Teacher Educators Mentoring and Distinguished Research in Teacher Education awards, the Carnegie Project on the Education Doctorate's David G. Imig Distinguished Service Award, and the National Staff Development Council (now Learning Forward) Book of the Year Award, and she was one of three finalists in Baylor University's prestigious Robert Foster Cherry Award for Great Teaching 2020 competition. Before joining the faculty at the University of Florida in 2003, she worked at The Pennsylvania State University for 11 years, creating and launching its award-winning inquiry-based Professional Development School program with the State College Area School District. At the University of Florida, she worked to embed inquiry as a signature pedagogy into the undergraduate teacher education program, as well as developed and taught three popular classes on inquiry at the master's and doctoral levels. In partnership with the Lastinger Center for Learning, Dana led the development and implementation of inquiry-based professional development for teachers across the state that included several of the nation's largest school districts. Furthermore, she was instrumental in the development of UF's Teacher Leadership for School Improvement Program and Professional Practice Doctorate in Teachers, Schools, and Society, both national award-winning programs that highlight inquiry as a signature program feature and have been recognized by *U.S. News & World Report* as the #1 Online Graduate Education Programs in the nation.

Diane Yendol-Hoppey is professor of teacher education in the College of Education and Human Services at the University of North Florida. She has served as dean, associate dean of educator preparation and partnerships, department chair, and center director. She taught for many years at the University of Florida where she was the evaluator of numerous district, state, and national professional development efforts. Before beginning her work in higher education, Yendol-Hoppey spent 13 years as an elementary school teacher in Pennsylvania and Maryland. She holds a PhD in curriculum and instruction from The Pennsylvania State University. Yendol-Hoppey's current work explores national and international research focusing on teacher education clinical practice, job-embedded professional learning, and teacher leadership. Yendol-Hoppey has received the AERA Division K Early Career Research Award and the ATE Distinguished Teacher Educator Award for her ongoing commitment to researching innovative approaches to teacher learning. She has published six books, more than 60 articles in professional journals, and secured $20 million in external funding to support teacher learning.

Logan Rutten is assistant professor in the College of Education & Human Development at the University of North Dakota, where he studies and teaches practitioner inquiry as a form of educator professional learning. A graduate of the Bismarck Public Schools and Concordia College, Rutten began his career as a teacher of Latin and music in Minnesota, Montana, and Pennsylvania. He later earned his PhD at The Pennsylvania State University and received the Robert F. Schuck Distinguished Dissertation in Teacher Education Award from the Association of Teacher Educators for his research about inquiry stance among teacher candidates in a Professional Development School. His current scholarship is rooted in sustained collaborations with educators serving K–12 students in rural and Indigenous communities. Rutten is associate editor of *The Cambridge Handbook of School–University Partnerships* and presently serves as co-chair of the Research Committee for the National Association for School–University Partnerships. His recent publications appear in journals such as the *Journal of Teacher Education, Action in Teacher Education, Teaching and Teacher Education, Teacher Development, Journal of Curriculum Theorizing*, and *School–University Partnerships*.

How to Use the Inquiry Books

This table summarizes the books we have authored or coauthored related to inquiry and describes their focus, differentiating the texts and delineating their use.

BOOK	AUTHORS	FOCUS
The Reflective Educator's Guide to Practitioner Inquiry, 5th edition (2025)	Nancy Fichtman Dana Diane Yendol-Hoppey Logan Rutten	This book provides an in-depth introduction to teacher inquiry for both prospective and practicing teachers, taking the reader step-by-step through the process, including developing a wondering, reading literature, collaborating with others, collecting data, analyzing data, sharing one's work, and assessing the quality of inquiry. With an explicit equity focus, this is a great first book on teacher inquiry.
The PLC Book (2016)	Nancy Fichtman Dana Diane Yendol-Hoppey	This book embeds inquiry into a professional learning community model, renewing and energizing the ways this common model for professional development plays out for teachers in schools.
The Reflective Educator's Guide to Professional Development: Coaching Inquiry-Oriented Learning Communities (2008)	Nancy Fichtman Dana Diane Yendol-Hoppey	This book focuses on coaching the inquiry process within professional learning communities. In addition to tips on the establishment of healthy learning communities, it contains numerous coaching resources to take teachers through each stage of the inquiry process.
Leading With Passion and Knowledge: The Principal as Action Researcher (2009)	Nancy Fichtman Dana	This book takes administrators through the process of inquiry step-by-step, offering rich examples of principals engaged in each step of the process. It is a perfect resource for districts to provide powerful professional development for principals as well as university professors to help their students enrolled in educational leadership programs write an action research thesis or dissertation.

(Continued)

(Continued)

BOOK	AUTHORS	FOCUS
Powerful Professional Development: Building Expertise Within the Four Walls of Your School (2010)	Diane Yendol-Hoppey Nancy Fichtman Dana	This book provides a bird's-eye view of numerous job-embedded professional development strategies. In addition to a chapter on inquiry, chapters focus on book studies, webinars and podcasts, coteaching, conversation tools, lesson study, culturally responsive and content-focused coaching, and professional learning communities.
Inquiry: A Districtwide Approach to Staff and Student Learning (2011)	Nancy Fichtman Dana Carol Thomas Sylvia Boynton	This book describes the ways engagement in inquiry fits together for all constituencies within a district—principals, teachers, students, and coaches. This systems overview of inquiry and the ways the process can connect improved practice to student achievement enables the reader to enhance learning for adults and students across an entire district.
Digging Deeper Into Action Research: A Teacher Inquirer's Field Guide (2013)	Nancy Fichtman Dana	This book takes off where other introductory texts on action research leave the reader, providing teacher inquirers tips for each part of the inquiry process as they are in the midst of doing it (i.e., developing a wondering, developing an inquiry plan, analyzing data, and presenting one's work). A perfect complement to *The Reflective Educator's Guide to Practitioner Inquiry*, this book can also be used as a short, succinct, stand-alone text to guide teachers through the inquiry process in a very targeted and specific way. It may also be used as a text in any university course (whether or not the course focuses on action research) to help students complete a required inquiry-based assignment.
Inquiring Into the Common Core (2013)	Nancy Fichtman Dana Jamey Bolton Burns Rachel Wolkenhauer	This book tells the story of Woodson Elementary School and the ways the teachers and administrators in this building used the process of inquiry to better understand their implementation of the Common Core State Standards (CCSS). In addition, teachers engaged their students in inquiry to actualize the CCSS in classroom practice. Examples of teacher inquiry and student inquiry provide insights for the reader into their own pathway to accelerating achievement with the CCSS as their guide.

Inquiry Facilitation Tools

[online resources] Visit the companion website at **https://resources.corwin.com/ReflectiveEducatorsGuide** for downloadable resources to facilitate and coach the inquiry process.

Activity 1.1: Block Party. This activity provides 12 short quotes from Chapter 1 that can be distributed for paired discussions to introduce readers to the chapter.

Activity 1.2: Save the Last Word for Me. This activity asks readers to highlight the passages that are most significant to them and provides steps to discuss their selected passages in groups of four.

Activity 1.3: Hopes and Fears. This activity asks readers to brainstorm several hopes and fears for studying their own practice, placing each individual hope and fear on a different sticky note for analysis in small groups.

Activity 2.1: The Great Wondering Brainstorm. This activity asks readers to brainstorm one to two wonderings that were sparked by each passion. It provides a structure for narrowing down the list created to select the final wondering for exploration (a handout is provided at the end of the activity).

Activity 2.2: Passion Jigsaw. This activity structures group exploration of the chapter's content by assigning each passion to a different small group to discuss and subsequently present to the whole group.

Activity 2.3: Passions Protocol. This activity provides paragraph descriptions of each passion rewritten in relation to choosing a career as an educator. Readers choose the passion that best represents why they chose a teaching career and discuss general wonderings that emerge for educators who hold this passion.

Activity 3.1: Open-Ended Sentences. This activity provides seven sentence stems that readers complete to capture and discuss how they feel about data collection.

Activity 3.2: Semi-Structured Interview Template. This resource provides a basic template to guide the development of a protocol for a semi-structured interview. The resource includes a suggested opening script, opening questions, fill-in-the-blank spaces to write questions, follow-up probes, and closing questions.

Activity 4.1: Wondering Refinement Partner Talk. This activity provides a structure for conversation between two partners as they help each other refine the focus and working of their wonderings.

Activity 4.2: Developing Equity-Focused Wonderings. This activity presents questions with an emerging equity focus, developed by teacher candidates in the Teacher Research Collaborative (Friedrich & McKinney, 2010) and University of South Carolina teacher preparation program, for discussion and analysis.

Activity 4.3: Triad Literature Chat. This activity asks readers to respond to three question prompts individually to help them synthesize literature they have read related to the topic of their inquiry and subsequently discuss their response to the literature in groups of three. (A handout is provided at the end of this activity.)

Activity 4.4: Four Corners. This activity helps readers examine their beliefs about collaboration as they respond to a series of statements on the topic by physically moving to a corner of the room designated as "Strongly Agree," "Agree," "Disagree," and "Strongly Disagree" after each individual statement is read aloud.

Activity 4.5: Coaching Inquiry Brief Development. This activity provides a sample inquiry brief completed by Daniella Suárez, a secondary mathematics teacher who wished to use the process of inquiry to adjust her statistics units to foster social justice. Comments embedded by her inquiry coach, Gage Jeter, provide insights into how to provide supportive feedback to strengthen an inquiry.

Activity 4.6: Three Levels of Text: Considering Ethical Dimensions for My Work as an Inquirer. The activity asks readers to consider ethical dimensions of their work as inquirers by identifying one passage in this chapter they believe has important implications for their research and discussing this passage in small groups by (1) reading the passage aloud, (2) stating personal thoughts/interpretations of the passage, and

(3) stating what they see as the implications of the passage for their work as inquirers.

Activity 5.1: Data Analysis Memo. This example of a memo written by a teacher researcher in the early stages of summative data analysis with feedback provided by one of the authors both exemplifies the construction of a data analysis memo and illustrates how readers can provide feedback to one another as they work on data analysis.

Activity 5.2: Data Analysis Summary Sheet and Data Analysis Protocol. This activity provides a series of timed steps to scaffold discussion as readers share what they are learning from an initial read of their entire data set for feedback in small groups.

Activity 6.1: Chalk Talk. This activity structures small-group discussion about the importance of sharing inquiry with others by engaging readers in a silent conversation on paper.

Activity 6.2: All About Conference Proposals. This activity provides a brief overview of the process of writing a proposal to present at a conference along with two examples of successful conference proposals written by the teacher researcher featured in the next chapter, Mickey MacDonald, for readers to analyze and discuss.

Activity 6.3: Writer's Workshop. This activity structures writing and feedback time for small groups of readers as they draft their inquiries.

Activity 6.4: Write-Up Tutorial. This activity takes readers through eight simple steps to create an executive summary write-up of their work, aided by suggestions for cutting and pasting from their inquiry brief (if completed earlier in the inquiry process) as well as the completion of sentence stems. A writing template is provided.

Activity 6.5: Writing Up Inquiry: Model Exploration. To complement examples of inquiry write-up models provided in this chapter, an additional model of an inquiry write-up by teacher candidate Cara Dore from The Pennsylvania State University is presented along with an analysis table to help readers analyze this and other models for inquiry write-ups.

Activity 7.1: Equity Chalk Talk. This activity structures small-group discussion with others about using inquiry as a pathway to equity by engaging readers in a silent conversation on paper.

Activity 7.2: Inquiry for Equity Triad Discussion. This activity asks readers to respond to three question prompts to foster reflection on the contents of this chapter in groups of three, with order of question response by members of the triad shifting for each question posed.

Activity 8.1: The 4 A's Protocol: Understanding the Complexity of Inquiry Stance and Assessing Teacher Inquiry. This activity structures small-group discussion as readers share self-selected quotes from the chapter that represent a point they would like to **A**gree with, **A**rgue with, and **A**spire to, as well as articulate **A**ssumptions about the inquiry process made throughout this chapter.

Activity 8.2: Self and Peer Evaluation. A downloadable form based on the quality indicators is provided for self and peer evaluation.

Teacher Inquiry Defined   1

Teaching involves a search for meaning in the world. Teaching is a life project, a calling, a vocation that is an organizing center of all other activities. Teaching is past and future as well as present, it is background as well as foreground, it is depth as well as surface. Teaching is pain and humor, joy and anger, dreariness and epiphany. Teaching is world building, it is architecture and design, it is purpose and moral enterprise. Teaching is a way of being in the world that breaks through the boundaries of the traditional job and in the process redefines all life and teaching itself.

—William Ayers (1989, p. 130)

Whether you are a beginning or veteran teacher, an administrator, or a teacher educator, when you think of teaching, learning to teach, and continuing your growth as a teacher, you cannot help but be struck by the enormous complexities, paradoxes, and tensions inherent in the act of teaching, captured so eloquently in the quote from William Ayers. With all of these complexities, paradoxes, and tensions, a teacher's work shapes the daily life of his or her classroom. In addition to responding to the needs of the children within the classroom, a teacher is expected to implement endless changes advocated by those outside the four walls of the classroom—administrators, politicians, policymakers, and researchers. While teachers have gained insights into their educational practice from these groups, teachers' voices have typically been absent from larger discussions about educational change and reform. Historically, teachers have not had access to the tools that could have brought their knowledge to the table and raised their voices to a high-enough level to be heard in these larger conversations.

Teacher inquiry is a vehicle that can be used by teachers to untangle some of the complexities that occur in the profession, raise teachers' voices in discussions of educational reform, and ultimately transform assumptions about the teaching profession itself. Transforming the profession is really the capstone of the teacher inquiry experience. Let's begin our journey into the what, why, and how of teacher inquiry with a brief overview of this very complex, rewarding, transformative, provocative, and productive process.

What Is Teacher Inquiry?

First and foremost, inquiry is a stance—an intentional, enduring way of approaching your teaching. Working from an inquiry stance entails a commitment to addressing all the great complexity inherent within teaching while continuously growing your ability to enhance the learning and life chances of every student you teach. An inquiry stance is rooted in curiosity, always remaining open to and inquisitive about your students and teaching by actively noticing and subsequently wondering about your day-to-day teaching practices. For example, when you teach from an inquiry stance, you might notice that some of your students seem engaged and thriving during a lesson while others seem simultaneously disengaged and not yet understanding. This noticing might lead you to wonder: Why do some of my students seem to grasp the concept being taught in this lesson while others seem to struggle? The important questions, or wonderings, that emerge when you approach your teaching through an inquiry stance can be addressed through an inquiry process that entails:

- systematically capturing the thinking and experiences relevant to your wondering that occur as a part of your everyday work (data collection);

- intentionally reflecting on what you have captured and the meaning it holds for your own learning and the learning of your students (data analysis);

- making informed changes to improve the learning and life chances of your students (action); and

- communicating what you have learned through inquiring with others (sharing).

The term *inquiry stance,* or *inquiry as stance,* was first coined by Marilyn Cochran-Smith and Susan Lytle. When these scholars began writing about inquiry as stance in the 1990s, they described it as follows:

> In everyday language, "stance" is used to describe body postures, particularly with regard to the position of the feet, as in sports or dance, and also to describe political positions, particularly their consistency (or lack thereof) over time. . . . In our work, we offer the term "inquiry as stance" to describe the positions teachers and others who work together in inquiry communities take toward knowledge and its relationships to practice. We use the metaphor of stance to suggest both orientational and positional ideas, to carry allusions to the physical placing of the body as well as to intellectual activities and perspectives over time. In this sense the metaphor is intended to capture the ways we stand, the ways we see, and the lenses we see through. Teaching is a complex activity that occurs within webs of social, historical, cultural, and political significance. Across the life span, an inquiry stance provides a kind of grounding within the changing cultures of school reform and competing political agendas. (Cochran-Smith & Lytle, 1999, p. 288–289)

Since then, Cochran-Smith and Lytle (2009) have authored an entire book entitled *Inquiry as Stance,* carefully choosing these words for their title to suggest that inquiry is more than the sum of its parts (i.e., developing questions, collecting and analyzing data, taking actions for change based on what was learned through the process, and sharing that learning with others). While inquiry does, indeed, involve a systematic and intentional process of investigating one's teaching, working from an inquiry stance is truly about "a worldview and a habit of mind—a way of knowing and being in the world of educational practice that carries across educational contexts and various points in one's professional career and that links individuals to larger groups and social movements intended to challenge the inequities perpetuated by the educational status quo" (Cochran-Smith & Lytle, 2009, p. vii). This stance can provide both early-career and veteran educators a firm foundation for a career in education—and a way of responsibly navigating continuous change and complexity (e.g., Rutten & Wolkenhauer, 2023a, 2023b, 2024). In sum, inquiry is both a process for investigating one's teaching—and a consistent, principled way of living one's life as an educator to maximize impact. This way of living entails making life and learning conditions

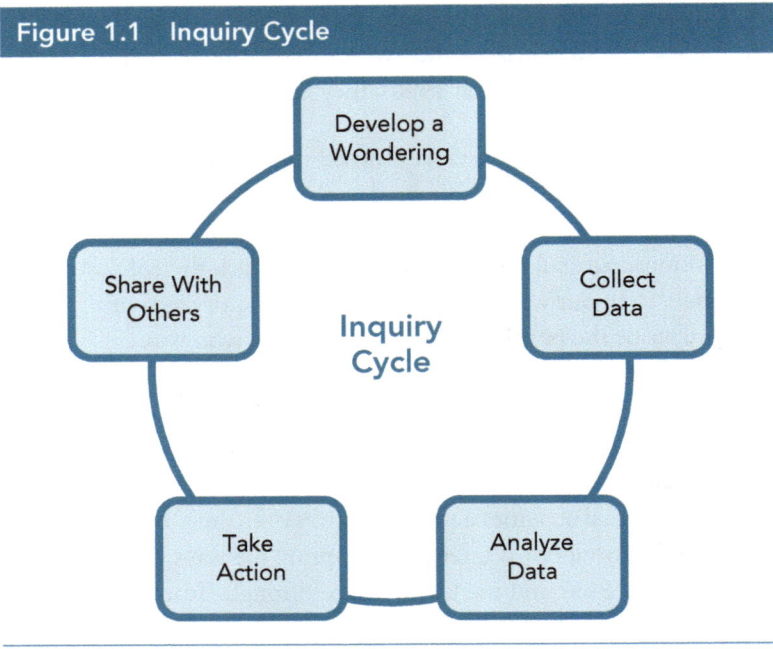

Figure 1.1 Inquiry Cycle

Source: Dana (2013).

better for *all* the children we teach by cycling through the five components illustrated in Figure 1.1, either in shorter daily bursts, entire school-year investigations, or anywhere in-between. The culmination of this reflective, inquiry stance and the iterative, systematic process results in the generation of new understandings, which are the true products of the inquiry that empower teachers to strengthen their practice.

What Evidence Exists That Teacher Inquiry Is Worth Doing?

Now that we have defined inquiry, you may be thinking that it sounds okay in theory but have developed a healthy skepticism. The everyday work of teaching is challenging, and teachers are constantly asked to do more and more with less and less. If teachers are to incorporate the process of inquiry illustrated in Figure 1.1 into their very full days, it's important to know what evidence exists that it is truly worth doing.

Fortunately, evidence abounds that teachers' engagement in inquiry is indeed worth the effort. The first set of evidence comes from teachers themselves who have published their work. There are numerous collections of teacher research, and from reading and analyzing the work of actual teacher researchers that appear in these collections, it is clear that engagement in inquiry can have a powerful impact on the professional learning of teachers and the lives of the students in their classrooms. Some of our favorite collections of teacher research include the following:

- *Creating Equitable Classrooms Through Action Research* (Caro-Bruce et al., 2007). This book shares the research of 10 educators from the Madison (Wisconsin) Metropolitan School District, whose inquiries focused on making their school district a more equitable place for all learners.
- *Empowering the Voice of the Teacher Researcher: Achieving Success Through a Culture of Inquiry* (Brindley & Crocco, 2009). This book shares the research of six teacher researchers from a single school in Florida, whose inquiries focus on better meeting the needs of middle school children.
- *Engaging in Educational Change: Voices of Practitioner Inquiry* (Fleet et al., 2016). This book contains real-life cases of several teachers across various classroom contexts in Australia, capturing their stories of inquiry to improve their practice and ultimately the outcomes for the children they teach.
- *Our Inquiry, Our Practice: Undertaking, Supporting, and Learning from Early Childhood Teacher Research(ers)* (G. Perry et al., 2012). This book shares the research of six early childhood professionals, working in both primary grades and preschool, as well as reviews of some of the finer points of the inquiry process and how it is particularly suited for early childhood contexts.
- *Promising Pedagogies for Teacher Inquiry and Practice: Teaching Out Loud* (Crawford-Garrett & Carbajal, 2023). This book contains five chapters written by teachers in New Mexico who participated in a multigenerational teacher inquiry group over a two-year period during the COVID-19 pandemic, exploring what it means to teach for social justice in politically contentious times.
- *Taking Action With Teacher Research* (Meyers & Rust, 2003). This book shares the research of six teacher researchers from the Teacher Network Leadership Institute in New York, whose inquiries focused on political action.
- *Teachers Engaged in Research* (Langrall, 2006; Masingila, 2006; S. Z. Smith & Smith, 2006; Van Zoest, 2006). This four-volume series published by the National Council of Teachers of Mathematics (NCTM) shares the inquiries of several teachers into their mathematics teaching in Grades K–2, 3–5, 6–8, and 9–12, respectively.

The second set of evidence that teacher inquiry is worth doing comes from university-based researchers. There is a large body of university-based research conducted on both teacher candidates and practicing teachers engaged in the inquiry process to better understand the impact of their work. One of the most extensive studies of impact was published by Sue Nichols and Phil Cormack in the text *Impactful Practitioner Inquiry: The Ripple Effect on Classrooms, Schools, and Teacher Professionalism* (2017). These University of South Australia faculty began their research on the process of inquiry by developing a database of 339 educators who had participated in inquiry projects with them in various capacities over the course of a 10-year timespan and successfully made contact with 290 of the individuals amassed in their database. To understand inquiry impact, Nichols and Cormack collected data from these educators in three ways: a survey, interviews with the inquirers, and interviews with the inquirers' colleagues. Among other impacts, teachers reported that engagement in inquiry enabled them to:

- view the curriculum differently;
- develop new resources;
- see new connections between practice and theory;
- increase the diversity of learning activities offered to students;
- modify existing resources to benefit student learning;
- view students from a strengths-based rather than deficit-based perspective;
- increase their use of technology to enhance learning;
- incorporate more student choice into lessons;
- increase range of assessment practices; and
- integrate inquiry as a pedagogical approach to their own teaching of students. (Nichols & Cormack, 2017, p. 14)

Complementing the work of Nichols and Cormack, several studies have also reported on the influence of practitioner inquiry on both teacher candidates' and practicing teachers' learning, concluding that practitioner inquiry can:

- enable a safe, collaborative environment to pose questions (Adams, 2016; Rutten et al., 2024; Willegems et al., 2018);
- promote growth and change in teaching practice (Dresser, 2007; Ermeling, 2010; Levin & Rock, 2003; Rock & Levin, 2002) and enhance teacher identity (Taylor, 2017);

- increase research skills and data literacy (Athanases et al., 2013; Davis et al., 2018);
- bring issues and systems of inequity into sharper focus (Rutten et al., 2022; Weisberg et al., 2024);
- facilitate meaningful changes toward educational equity (Butville et al., 2021; Crawford-Garrett et al., 2015);
- support incorporation of instructional technology (Clayton & Meadows, 2013);
- lead to increased teacher efficacy and confidence (Capobianco & Ní Ríordáin, 2015; Kinskey, 2018; Rutten et al., 2023); and
- foster both individual and collective teacher empowerment and transformation (Rutten et al., 2024).

While we share some studies on the impact of inquiry above, it is beyond the scope of this book to review *all* of the empirical studies completed by academics focused on teachers' engagement in inquiry. Many additional studies are reviewed and referenced in Marilyn Cochran-Smith and Susan Lytle's book *Inquiry as Stance: Practitioner Research for the Next Generation* (2009). It is clear from the studies we reviewed here as well as the extensive review of research on teacher inquiry in the Cochran-Smith and Lytle text that engaging in the inquiry process results in several benefits for both teacher candidates who conduct inquiry as a part of their studies in teaching at the university and practicing teachers who conduct inquiry as part of their everyday work in schools.

The publications by teachers of their own inquiries as well as publications by university-based researchers that report research efforts to understand the impact of teachers' engagement in the process attest to the important role inquiry can play in the lives of teachers and the children they teach. An additional source of evidence of the value inherent in engagement in inquiry comes from the fact that inquiry has been around for a long time, has endured through changing times, and remains relevant today. Teachers who have taught for years often report seeing many new ideas come and go over time, reducing them to educational fads. As the next sections will demonstrate, this is not the case with inquiry, providing further evidence that inquiry is, indeed, worth doing.

What Are the Origins of Teacher Inquiry?

Reviewing the history of teacher inquiry helps to make the case that inquiry is not a new educational fad that will come and go. Our history lesson begins by looking closely at three educational research traditions:

process-product research, qualitative or interpretive research, and teacher inquiry (see Table 1.1).

Table 1.1 Competing Paradigms: The Multiple Voices of Research

	RESEARCH PARADIGMS		
	PROCESS-PRODUCT	**QUALITATIVE OR INTERPRETIVE**	**TEACHER INQUIRY**
Teacher	Teacher as technician	Teacher as story character	Teacher as storyteller
Researcher	Outsider	Outsider	Insider
Process	Linear	Discursive	Cyclical
Source of research question	University researcher	University researcher	Teacher
Type of research question	Focused on control, prediction, or impact	Focused on generating descriptions or explanations of a process or phenomenon	Focused on gaining insight into a teacher's own classroom practice in an effort to make changes that will ultimately improve student learning
Example of research question	Which culturally responsive instructional strategies demonstrate the most significant impact on student motivation?	How do children experience culturally responsive instruction?	How can I use culturally responsive instruction to support my ESL students at the kindergarten writing table?

Two paradigms have historically dominated educational research on schooling, teaching, and learning. In the first paradigm, process-product research (L. Shulman, 1986) portrays teaching as a primarily linear activity and depicts teachers as technicians. The teacher's role in the process-product paradigm is to implement the research-based recommendations of outside experts, almost exclusively university researchers, who are distant from the local happenings of teachers' real-world classrooms. In this paradigm, teachers are not expected to act as professional problem posers or problem solvers. Rather, teachers are tasked with implementing approaches or interventions developed by others, such as teaching with fidelity a curriculum designed by expert researchers outside of their classrooms.

Based on their experiences with research from the process-product paradigm, many teachers have learned that it is sometimes best not to question or problematize their classroom experiences and first-hand observations because to do so may mean an admittance of failure to implement a curriculum as directed. In fact, the culture of many schools has demonstrated that teachers can suffer punitive repercussions when teachers identify current practices as problematic. Pointing out problems has often resulted in teachers being subjected to retraining or remediation. In the process-product paradigm, an educational community does not encourage active solution-seeking by professional classroom teachers but rather passive, technical implementation of other people's ideas.

In the second paradigm—educational research drawn from qualitative or interpretative studies—teaching is portrayed as a highly complex, context-specific, interactive activity. A goal of the research is often to generate a vivid description or compelling explanation of some phenomenon or process of interest. In addition, the qualitative or interpretive paradigm emphasizes investigations of important differences across classrooms, schools, and communities. While acknowledging the value of research from the qualitative or interpretive paradigm, Clark (1995) problematizes this paradigm's tendency, over time, to ignore important contextual differences as follows: "Description becomes prescription, often with less and less regard for the contextual matters that make the description meaningful in the first place" (p. 20).

Although qualitative or interpretive research does attend to issues of context, most of the studies emerging from this research paradigm are still conducted by university researchers and are intended primarily for academic audiences. Such university research can provide valuable insights into the connections between theory and practice, but, like the process-product research, the qualitative or interpretive approach limits teachers' roles in the research process. In fact, the knowledge about teaching and learning generated through university study of theory and practice is still defined and generated primarily by outsiders to the school and classroom. While both the process-product and qualitative research paradigms have generated valuable insights into the teaching and learning process, they have too often excluded the voices of the people closest to children—classroom teachers.

Hence, a third research paradigm—teacher inquiry—has emerged to showcase the vital role classroom teachers play as knowledge generators. This paradigm is often referred to as "teacher research," "teacher inquiry," "classroom research," "action research," "practitioner inquiry," or "practitioner research." In general, the teacher inquiry movement focuses on the concerns of teachers (not outside researchers) and engages teachers in the design, data collection, and interpretation of data around a locally framed question. Termed *action research* by Carr and Kemmis (1986), this paradigm for approaching educational research has many benefits, among them: (1) theories and knowledge are generated from research grounded in the realities of day-to-day educational practice; (2) teachers become collaborators in educational research by investigating their own problems; and (3) teachers play an integral part in the research process, which makes them more likely to facilitate change based on the knowledge they create.

Although the terms *teacher research, teacher inquiry,* and *action research* are comparatively new, the underlying conceptions of teaching as inquiry and the role of teachers as inquirers are not. Early in the 20th century, John Dewey (1933) called for teachers to engage in reflective action that would transition them into inquiry-oriented classroom practitioners. More recently, teacher educator Ken Zeichner (1996) traced and summarized more than 30 years of research, calling for cultivating an informed practice as illustrated in such descriptors as "teachers as action researchers," "teacher scholars," "teacher innovators," and "teachers as participant observers" (p. 3). Similarly, scholar Donald Schön (1983, 1987) also depicted teacher professional practice as a cognitive process of posing and exploring problems or dilemmas identified by the teachers themselves. In doing so, teachers ask questions that other researchers may not perceive or deem relevant. In addition, teachers often discern patterns that outsiders may not be able to see. Today, *action research* usually refers to research intended to bring about a desired change of some kind, usually with a social justice focus, whereas *teacher research* quite often has the goal of generating insights into a teacher's classroom practice in order to improve teaching or to better understand what works.

As these varying examples illustrate, while some of the terms have been used interchangeably, they do have somewhat different emphases and histories (Cochran-Smith & Lytle, 2009). For the purposes of this text and to streamline our discussion of research traditions, we have grouped all of these related processes together to represent teachers' systematic study of their own practice. Yet we use the term *inquiry* most often because, in our coaching of teachers' systematic studies of their own practices, we became discouraged by the baggage that the word *research* in the term *action research* carried with it when the concept was first introduced to teachers. The images that the word *research* conjures up come mostly from the process-product paradigm and include "a controlled setting," "an experiment with control and treatment groups," "an objective scientist removed from the subjects of study so as not to contaminate findings," "long hours in the library," and "crunching numbers." Teachers, in general, weren't overly enthused by these images, and it took a good deal of time for us to deconstruct these images and help teachers see that those images were antithetical to what teacher/action research was all about. So, over time, we began replacing the terms *action research* and *teacher research* with one simple word that carried much less baggage with it—*inquiry*—and we will continue this tradition both in this section on research traditions and throughout the remainder of this text.

To help unpack some of the baggage the word *research* carries with it, it is important to further explore the difference between research conducted in a university setting (stemming from the process-product and interpretive paradigms) and inquiry conducted by classroom teachers. First and foremost, in general, the purpose of research conducted by academics and classroom teachers is quite different. The general focus of university-based research is to advance a field. Professors are required to publish their work in journals read by other academics and present their work at national and international venues to their peers at other institutions as evidence of their ability to impact the field broadly. In fact, professors' value within many institutions is measured largely by their publication record and the number of times their publications are cited by others. In contrast, the purpose of engagement in inquiry by classroom teachers is to improve classroom practice. The point of doing inquiry is for identifying and implementing changes that lead to real improvements in student learning and life outcomes, not for impact in scholarly literature or theory (although this can happen, too).

The focus of university-based researchers and teacher inquirers is also different. In general, university-based researchers working in the process-product paradigm focus their efforts on control, prediction, and impact, while university-based researchers working in the qualitative or interpretive paradigm focus their efforts on description, explanation, and understanding of various teaching phenomena. In contrast, teacher inquirers focus on providing insights into teaching in an effort to make change, working tirelessly to unpack all of the complexities inherent in the act of teaching to become the very best teachers they can be for every individual student.

A final difference between research conducted at the university and inquiry conducted by classroom teachers into their own practice is ownership. While the research generated by university researchers is critically important to teachers, it is university researchers who make the decisions about what is important to study and how to go about studying it based on a careful and critical analysis of a broad and extensive body of literature related to the topic of study. In contrast, teacher inquirers make decisions about what is important to study and how to go about studying it based on a careful and critical analysis of what is happening at a local level in their own classrooms, schools, and districts. The work of university-based researchers informs the inquiries of teachers, but ownership of the classroom-based investigation resides with classroom teachers themselves.

To help distinguish between research produced at a university and inquiry done in classrooms and schools (summarized in Table 1.2), we often invoke the words of Lawrence Stenhouse, who noted, "The difference between a teacher researcher and the large-scale education researcher is like the difference between a farmer with a huge agricultural business to maintain and the 'careful gardener' tending a backyard plot" (Hubbard & Power, 1999, p. 5).

> In agriculture the equation of invested input against gross yield is all: it does not matter if individual plants fail to thrive or die so long as the cost of saving them is greater than the cost of losing them. . . . This does not apply to the careful gardener whose labour is not costed, but a labour of love. He wants each of his plants to thrive, and he can treat each one individually. Indeed he can grow a hundred different plants in his garden and differentiate his treatment of each, pruning his roses, but not his sweet peas. Gardening rather than agriculture is the analogy for education. (Ruddock & Hopkins, 1985, p. 26)

Table 1.2 University-Based Research and Teacher Inquiry Comparison

	UNIVERSITY RESEARCH	TEACHER RESEARCH (INQUIRY)
PURPOSE	Advance a field	Improve classroom practice
FOCUS	Control/Prediction/Impact/Explanation	Provide insight into teaching in an effort to make change
OWNERSHIP	Outsider	Insider
IMPACT	Broad	Local

This image of the university-based researcher as a farmer with a huge agricultural business and the teacher inquirer as a gardener helps to encapsulate the differences between the university-based research you are likely most familiar with and the research you can generate from within the four walls of your own classroom. It is of value to note that the work of both farmers and gardeners is important and somewhat related but also quite different. Such is the case with university-based researchers and teacher inquirers. The work of both is important and somewhat related but quite different. As we discuss each component of the inquiry process in depth throughout this book, you will continue to uncover the importance of both types of research, including the relationship and differences between them.

How Is Teacher Inquiry Changing With the Times?

As we learned in our brief history lesson, teacher inquiry traces its origins to the writings of John Dewey in the 20th century. Although its antecedents are decades old, contemporary understandings of teacher inquiry (as both a process and a stance) continue to evolve in tandem with rapid changes in schools and society. In fact, teacher inquiry has been consistently "remodelled" across different times and contexts (Dana, 2016; Somekh & Zeichner, 2009)—and yet, for many teacher inquirers, the pace of change has seemed to accelerate in recent years.

Since the last edition of this book, teachers have confronted the dual pandemics of COVID-19 and systemic racism (J. M. Jones, 2021). The global COVID-19 pandemic that spread rapidly in the year 2020 turned schooling upside down, with teachers, students, and communities scrambling as they shifted to emergency remote teaching. Many teachers had to figure out, in the span of just days, how to teach via Zoom, Microsoft Teams, or Google Meet. Teachers and students reported feelings of isolation and mental health challenges (Baker et al., 2021; Kush et al., 2022). For some teachers, the significant inequities that had long been embedded in school systems—such as assumptions about students' access to high-speed internet connections, or the role of school meal programs in nourishing students—were laid bare for the first time (Rutten et al., 2022).

Also in 2020, teachers across the United States and in other countries grappled with how to teach responsibly and equitably in the wake of killings by White police officers of Black people, including Breonna Taylor in Kentucky and George Floyd in Minnesota, which many understood as high-profile, public manifestations of systemic racism. As we write the fifth edition of this book, the impacts of these events on teachers and students are still being investigated—yet they have also increased many educators' sense of urgency in pursuing inquiries that meaningfully enhance equity and social justice (e.g., Grace et al., 2024), illustrating the enduring relevance of teacher inquiry to change with the times.

For example, in some school districts and teacher education programs where teacher inquiry had long served as an anchor for professional learning, the familiar stance and process of inquiry furnished a powerful mechanism for navigating even the significant challenges of the dual pandemics (Dana & Kilgore, 2021). At the P. K. Yonge Developmental Research School at the University of Florida, teachers lived out their inquiry stances through a Remote Learning Inquiry (RLI), in which they investigated how remote learning tools could help them reestablish caring relationships and classroom communities when their school transitioned to emergency remote learning necessitated by COVID-19 (E. Davis et al., 2021). In a teacher education program at The Pennsylvania State University, teacher interns rapidly claimed new identities as emergent teacher leaders by asking critical questions of veteran teachers and school administrators and using insights from their inquiries to push school administrators to consider issues of equitable access to technology (Rutten et al., 2022). And in a public school district in central Minnesota, where expiring American Rescue Plan Act (ARPA) federal funds were about to precipitate significant budget cuts, a veteran elementary teacher inquired into how she could support the well-being and mental health of her teacher colleagues; Kelly Herrera's impactful inquiry is highlighted in Chapter 2.

In other school districts, the creation of new inquiry communities, where teachers met in support of one another throughout the COVID-19 and systemic racism pandemics, served to renew connection and collaboration through the stance, process, and products of inquiry. These communities reduced the sense of professional isolation many were experiencing. For example, in one semirural school district, where teachers had been grappling with issues of racial injustice, one teacher reflected on the powerful role of an inquiry community in helping her reconnect with colleagues as she navigated these issues:

> I had really been feeling like an island. Part of the experience for me was learning that I can find common ground with people who seem so opposite and so different from me—and

finding the language that would help me communicate with them. . . . If I hear how other people in the inquiry community are approaching different things, it helps me also to understand how other people in my building might be approaching things. . . . You're learning new ideas. You're like, "Well, I never thought about it that way!" (Rutten et al., 2024, p. 298)

Another teacher from the same community shared:

It's that collaboration and supportive environment where you can explore ideas and not feel silly, or somebody can build on what you start with, or you can, you know, help them back-and-forth. There's not a lot of time for that anymore. But we're finding that place to respect concerns in a real way, and really delve into them and come to a common ground on them. (Rutten et al., 2024, p. 300)

And a third teacher shared the impacts of engaging in inquiry in the wake of COVID-19:

There's started to be dialogue between the admin and teachers that has never, ever, happened before. That allowed for more collaboration in our building, so maybe that's the piece that has been the most powerful, is that the inquiry community actually created a space for that difficult interaction to start happening. . . . That's some of the most powerful learning that there is. (Rutten et al., 2024, p. 299)

As these examples illustrate, teacher inquiry and inquiry communities are flexible, yet durable, ways of working and learning together—serving as both a road map for improving teaching across a career span, and a compass for navigating uncertain terrain such as COVID-19.

In addition to the dual pandemics, many teachers presently face heightened challenges stemming from the political contexts that frame their professional practices. The political nature of curriculum and teaching is nothing new for teacher inquirers, whose inquiries have long engaged head-on with competing visions for society and divergent understandings of justice (Cochran-Smith & Lytle, 2009, p. 151). Still, in recent years, political polarization and partisanship have fueled a uniquely turbulent context for teaching (Hallman et al., 2022) where teachers find their day-to-day professional practices under unprecedented scrutiny by parents, caregivers/guardians, and community members (Journell, 2022).

For many educators, a steady stream of divisive national headlines, heated local debates about school board policies, social media posts, and controversial state legislation has contributed to a climate of fear surrounding the work of teaching (Carter Andrews et al., 2018; Pace, 2022). In particular, teachers whose curriculum or standards require them to teach about difficult topics such as race and racism, slavery, human rights abuses, or issues of privilege and oppression may fear community backlash (Ranschaert, 2023). Controversies over both domestic and foreign affairs such as presidential elections, international conflicts, immigration, abortion, or gender compound an already turbulent context for teaching (Rutten et al., 2023, 2024). Furthermore, teachers from any grade level or content area may find that classroom discussions of difficult or contested topics may "bubble up" unexpectedly during their day-to-day work—from sources such as student issues, professional issues, curriculum issues, community issues, and teachers' own identities (Rutten et al., 2025). As one teacher who recently participated in an inquiry community focused on learning to address difficult topics shared:

> As a math teacher, I didn't really think I had difficult topics. But now I also understand LGBTQ issues, and issues like abuse in the home, and all kinds of things that are not necessarily *what* I'm teaching—but when those are the issues that are walking in my door, I've realized that I need to address it and not pretend like it's not here. . . . These difficult topics aren't going away. (Rutten et al., 2024, p. 300)

While it is understandable that some teachers may be inclined to "shy away" from the difficult topics or contested issues they face within their schools, many teachers decide to "lean in" to such topics (Rutten et al., 2024) because they recognize potential educational value for their students such as the possibility of fostering empathy (Haas, 2020), civic discourse (McAvoy & Hess, 2013), or critical-analytic thinking (Middaugh, 2019; Woolley, 2011). In particular, adopting an inquiry stance and intentionally leaning into potentially difficult topics such as race and racism (D. Harris, 2023) can assist teachers in enhancing the learning of every student.

The challenges of "leaning in" to difficult topics and contested issues are many, yet both the process and stance of teacher inquiry can support teachers in making informed decisions about whether, and how, to engage with such topics. Teachers in urban, suburban, and rural communities alike are adapting inquiry, and collaborating within new kinds of inquiry communities, to assist them in engaging with difficult topics in their schools and communities (Rutten et al., 2024). By grounding their approach in an inquiry stance, teachers and students alike are learning, together, how to discuss difficult topics and contested issues. As one teacher shared:

> Our inquiry community has made me a different kind of teacher. I'm more open to hearing from students, and that affects every minute of every day—that I'm more open to hearing what students have to say. You may be teaching in one way, and then you're going to find this whole new way of thinking. Inquiry is about giving students a voice and making them feel like they matter in the classroom, and to me that is just a completely different mindset. This is intentionally giving everyone a voice, and I love it. And with inquiry, it never stops. We're setting them up to be thinkers and to be inquirers. (Rutten et al., 2024, p. 301)

In addition to investigating difficult topics in their professional practices, the process and stance of inquiry provide an anchor for teaching difficult topics within the curriculum. Fifth-grade teacher inquirer Wendy Lane Smith described living in a county in the Eastern United States that had been "in the national spotlight for proposed school board policies related to classroom and school library books, many of which were written by or featured the stories of people of color" (Rutten et al., 2023, p. 9). She joined an inquiry community of other teachers who wanted to use inquiry to navigate difficult topics and, over time, introduced inquiry to her students—first as a way of building their classroom community, and later as a way of learning curricular content together. Wendy described the challenges she sometimes faced in her community when teaching about slavery and the Civil War, but rooting her approach in inquiry—rather than in a "sage on the stage" approach—supported her in teaching responsibly. She shared how, in the past, she had "used the textbook to lay out facts" but that, in a recent year,

> I decided to use the inquiry cycle to structure the Civil War unit. As I began to explain the inquiry cycle to my students, I was able to present myself as a co-learner and let them know that I did not know all the outcomes of our

inquiries, but that we would learn together. . . . Each student had to support their ideas with evidence from individual research. They also worked in groups to create their own representations of the factors that helped the Union to win the war. I guided and coached them in finding their conclusions but only intervened if there was misinformation involved. Given the previous problems we had with students being unkind to each other, it was gratifying to watch them sort through, debate, and discuss tough issues in a supportive way. (Rutten et al., 2023)

As Wendy's example illustrates, teaching from both the stance and process of inquiry can offer a responsible, respectful, and hopeful way of addressing difficult topics and contested issues—illustrating how an inquiry stance is both an enduring professional posture and a way of changing with the times.

What Is the Relationship Between Teacher Inquiry and AI?

One of the most riveting changes currently happening in education is the proliferation of artificial intelligence (AI). AI refers to the broad research/development field that targets the creation of machines to perform tasks that ordinarily require human intelligence (i.e., problem solving and reasoning). The development and rapid advancement of AI tools such as chatbots, computer programs that use AI to imitate human conversation and writing, lead to problems of practice teachers everywhere now face, such as:

- In what ways might AI best support our work as educators?
- How do we integrate AI into instructional practice?
- What are the ethical implications of student and teacher use of AI tools?

Inquiry can serve as a powerful mechanism to explore uses of AI in the classroom and the relationship between these uses and student learning.

In addition to AI being a topic of inquiry for educators, it can also enhance the inquiry process. In particular, AI tools can aid in each of the components of inquiry introduced in Figure 1.1, as well as in the design of inquiry itself. Many teacher researchers are already using AI as integral aspects of their inquiries. According to Florida teacher researcher Jon Mundorf:

As I pursued an inquiry into AI in education, "Lex," as the chatbot ChatGPT now asked to be called, has become a key collaborator in the research process. From helping design the research questions to reflecting on AI's impact in classrooms, Lex has provided valuable insight. Though my inquiry work is my own, Lex has significantly shaped my study, helping me explore the evolving relationship between AI, teaching, and learning. Having Lex as a thought partner has transformed my approach to teaching and research, allowing me to focus on what truly matters—connecting with my students and enhancing their learning experiences.

As Jon's quotation illustrates, AI can be used throughout the process of practitioner inquiry. It might serve as the topical focus of your inquiry, a "key collaborator" as you design your plan for inquiry, or a means of supporting your data collection and analysis activities.

For this reason, throughout this book, we will continually suggest some ways AI might enhance the various components of inquiry. Look for the special AI Moment textboxes, noted by this icon, in the chapters ahead:

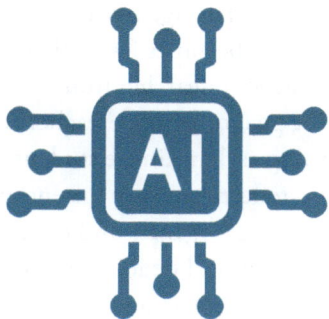

How Is Teacher Inquiry Different From What I Already Do as a Reflective Teacher?

All teachers reflect. They reflect on what happened during previously taught lessons as they plan lessons for the future. They reflect on their students' performance as they assess their work. They reflect on the content and the best pedagogy available to teach that content to their learners. They reflect on interactions they observed students having, as well as on their own interactions with students and the ways these interactions contribute to learning. Teachers reflect all day, every day, *on* the act of teaching while *in* the act of teaching—and long after the school day is over. Reflection is important and critical to good teaching

(Körkkö et al., 2016; Loughran, 2010; Schön, 1987; K. M. Zeichner & Liston, 1996). In addition, reflection is a key component of teacher inquiry. Yet teacher inquiry is different from daily reflection in and on practice in three important ways.

First, teacher inquiry is less happenstance. The very definition of teacher inquiry includes the word *intentional.* We do not mean to suggest that reflection is never intentional, but in the busy, complex life of teaching, reflection is something that frequently occurs in an unplanned or spontaneous way, such as on the way to the teachers' room for lunch, during a chat with a colleague during a special, when students are engaged in an independent activity, on the drive home, in the shower, or during dinner—wherever and whenever a moment arises. Unfortunately, few teachers have a planned reflection time. Teacher inquiry invites intentional, planned reflection, heightening your focus on problem posing.

Second, teacher inquiry is more visible than reflection. The daily reflection teachers engage in is not observable by others unless it is given some form (perhaps through talk or journaling). As teachers engage in the process of inquiry, their thinking and reflection are made public for discussion, sharing, debate, and purposeful educative conversation, and teaching becomes less isolated and overwhelming. Gail Ritchie, veteran teacher researcher from Fairfax County Schools, Virginia, notes that the goal of being a teacher researcher is to facilitate teaching and learning and maximize student potential. As teacher researchers engage in reflection, they intentionally ask questions about teaching and learning, organize and collect information, focus on a specific area of inquiry, and benefit from ongoing collaboration and support of critical friends (Lassonde et al., 2008).

Finally, teacher inquiry requires identifying, collecting, and making sense of data to inform decision-making and practice. Reflection is often based on personal observations, experiences, and judgments, which are valuable but not always systematically grounded in evidence. In contrast, inquiry goes further by demanding a deliberate process of gathering and analyzing data that surround and inform the teacher researcher. These data might include student work, assessment results, classroom observations, or other artifacts that help the teacher explore a specific problem or question more deeply and systematically. By grounding their reflections in evidence, teacher researchers can move beyond intuition to develop actionable insights that drive meaningful changes in teaching and learning.

Why Inquire? Inquiry as a Pathway to Equity

Up to this point in Chapter 1 we have introduced you to inquiry by defining it, providing evidence of its value, discussing its history and evolution (including AI's recent appearance to this movement), and distinguishing inquiry from everyday reflective practice that is the foundation of good teaching. Yet we have not yet addressed the most important question. As a part of your introduction to inquiry, it is imperative to ask, "Inquiry for what purpose? What do teachers inquire for?"

One reason why it is critical to pose this question is, as already stated in this chapter, inquiry is not a fad—teachers have been researching their own practice for decades. As inquiry has evolved through the years, it has been "shaped and reshaped in relationship to the era within which it has existed" (Dana, 2016, p. 1). As a process evolves and shape-shifts "both *through* time and *in response to* the times, those who engage in the process can easily lose sight of *why* they are doing it in the first place" (Dana & Currin, 2017, p. 1). Hence, the "why" of inquiry is not always made explicit when the process is first taught to teacher candidates as a part of their teacher education programs or to practicing teachers as a mechanism for professional learning.

To answer the "Why inquire?" question, we turn to the most pervasive problem of practice that all educators face today—the persistent achievement gaps in America's schools. People of color and those living in poverty routinely encounter an educational system that inadequately supports their chances for achievement. The term *achievement gap* is still used widely by educators to reflect the disparities that exist, as measured by standardized test scores, in academic achievement between minoritized groups, primarily African Americans, Hispanics, and Native Americans, and the dominant group, primarily White people, as well as variance in performance by students based on socioeconomic status (J. V. Clark, 2013; Darling-Hammond, 2013). While educators still broadly use the term *achievement gap* to discuss the schooling experiences of different groups of students throughout the nation, several educational scholars have noted the need to reframe the discussion with the term *opportunity gap* to reflect the fact that the inequalities that exist in schools are a direct consequence of the inequalities that exist within our society, encompassing systemic disparities in health care, wealth, education, affordable housing, quality childcare, school funding, teacher quality, and curricula (Boykin & Noguera, 2011; G. Ladson-Billings, 2007; Milner, 2010; Welner & Carter, 2013).

Hence, understanding and correcting the inequalities that exist in schools and society are of critical importance to all educators. Engagement in inquiry can be a powerful pathway to the creation of more equitable classrooms. In fact, echoing back to our definition of inquiry as stance earlier in this chapter, distinguished scholars of the practitioner research movement, Marilyn Cochran-Smith and Susan Lytle, maintain that the ultimate goal of practitioner inquiry "always and in every context" is to enhance "students' learning and life chances for participation in and contribution to a diverse and democratic society" (Cochran-Smith and Lytle, 2009, p. 146). Teachers engage in inquiry for equity to increase the learning and life chances of every student with whom they work, regardless of factors (e.g., race, socioeconomic status, gender, sexuality, and ability) that often inhibit students in an educational system that was not designed to meet their needs. Returning to one of the largest research studies undertaken on the impact of inquiry we introduced earlier in this chapter, educational researchers Sue Nichols and Phil Cormack reported, "Practitioner research was at its most powerful when it served [teachers'] ethical commitments to struggling students" (Nichols & Cormack, 2017, p. 20), reinforcing the importance of inquiry undertaken for more equitable learning and schooling experiences for all.

Whereas the creation of more just and more equitable schooling experiences is the ultimate goal of engagement in the process of inquiry, not all teachers first come to inquiry with an equity focus, but rather discover this underlying problem of practice through time and several cycles of the inquiry process. For this reason, in this text, as we teach about each component of the inquiry process in Chapters 2 through 6, we will highlight many examples of inquiry related to the creation of more equitable learning experiences, but we will also share examples of the process that may not be directly related to issues of equity, but nonetheless, did serve as powerful professional learning experiences for teachers and teacher candidates at the start of their inquiry journeys. We will return to the ultimate equity goal of practitioner inquiry in Chapter 7, where we share the story of a prolific teacher researcher who came to see inquiry as a pathway to equity over time, as well as teacher candidates who are beginning their teaching careers with a passion for using inquiry to examine issues of equity.

What Are Some Contexts Ripe for Teacher Inquiry?

With an understanding of what teacher inquiry is and the ultimate reason for engaging in the process, let us consider the kinds of professional and collaborative contexts that can support teacher inquiry.

As previously discussed, teaching is full of enormous complexities, and hence, teaching itself invites inquiry. However, even as inquiry beckons each and every teacher, becoming a lone inquirer is difficult! For this reason, we explore five particularly ripe contexts for developing your inquiry stance: (1) professional development/learning programs, (2) professional learning communities, (3) teacher candidate clinical experiences/residencies, (4) Professional Development Schools, and (5) professional practice doctoral programs. You may already be engaged with one or more of these five contexts—or you may wish to get involved as you begin or continue your teaching career.

Professional Development/Learning Programs

Throughout their careers, teachers have a wide variety of opportunities to grow their professional practices. Many teachers seek out professional growth by enrolling in professional development/learning programs. Participation in such programs can frequently also be used to fulfill requirements for maintaining your state teaching credential, earning a graduate degree, or advancing on your school district's salary schedule. As a teacher, you are likely to spend many hours each year engaged in professional development/learning. These programs can be among the most promising contexts for growing your inquiry stance.

The types of programs you join may take the form of traditional professional development programming, which has historically focused on acquiring new knowledge or skills through one-size-fits-all workshops planned by external experts. Such one-shot programs typically feature minimal follow-up, customization, or support for classroom application—and they may or may not be meaningfully connected to your day-to-day teaching experiences. In contrast, a change in both terminology and approach to emphasize professional learning represents a shift away from professional development and toward an ongoing, collaborative, and contextually specific process in which teachers take an active role in their own growth. As agents of their own learning, teachers who engage in sustained, high-quality professional learning intentionally contribute to shaping their own learning, their students' learning, and educational change.

Significant professional learning requires that teachers be supported with sufficient professional time and autonomy to engage in deep collaboration as they tackle shared, locally defined problems of practice. Although many school districts in the United States still emphasize professional development, other districts are restructuring their yearly calendars, daily bell schedules, and overarching philosophies to weave time and space throughout the school year for sustained professional learning to occur. To aid in enacting this important shift from professional *development* (PD) to professional *learning* (PL), we highly recommend the organization appropriately named Learning Forward (https://learningforward.org). Reflecting the goals of this outstanding organization and the ongoing shift from "PD" to "PL," throughout the rest of this book we intentionally use the term *professional learning* as a way to acknowledge the roles of teachers as lifelong professional learners who are active in propelling their own growth.

Inquiry is a powerful approach to designing a professional learning program. It can be coupled with traditional professional development approaches, serve as a stand-alone professional learning design, or be seamlessly integrated with innovative school calendars for professional learning. In each of these ways, inquiry can assist you in connecting your learning about content and pedagogy with your classroom practice. For instance, the University of Florida's Prime Online program uses inquiry to support teachers in integrating research-based mathematics teaching methods with their classroom practices (Dana et al., 2017). Similarly, the University of North Florida's Project InTERSECT (**In**quiry to **T**ransform **R**eadiness for **S**TEM+C **E**arly **C**hildhood **T**eaching) uses inquiry to support early childhood educators' abilities to implement STEM+C project-based learning (Robinson-Wilson et al., in press), and Tiger Academy (a school in Duval County, Florida) offers inquiry-based professional learning programming focused on responding to the literacy needs of PK–5 students. You may be able to locate these kinds of professional learning programs through a partnership with a university in your area, or you might work with colleagues and administrators to build a local, inquiry-based professional learning program within the walls of your own school.

Professional Learning Communities

While there are many types of professional learning programs, professional learning communities (PLCs) are among the most widespread. PLCs serve to connect and network groups of professionals to do just what their name entails—to *learn* from practice. PLCs meet on a regular basis, and their time together is often structured by the use of protocols to ensure focused, deliberate conversation and dialogue by teachers about student work and student learning. Protocols for educators provide a script or series of timed steps for how a conversation among teachers on a chosen topic will develop (Dana & Yendol-Hoppey, 2016).

A variety of protocols has been developed for use in PLCs by a number of noteworthy organizations such as Learning Forward (e.g., Lois Brown Easton's *Powerful Designs for Professional Learning*, 2004), School Reform Initiative (www.schoolreforminitiative.org), and the National School Reform Faculty (www.nsrfharmony.org), which developed one version of a PLC called Critical Friends Groups (CFGs). In their work conceptualizing CFGs, the National School Reform Faculty laid much of the groundwork for shifting the nature of the dialogue between and among teachers about their practice in schools, and is responsible for training thousands of teachers to focus on developing collegial relationships, encouraging reflective practice, and rethinking leadership in restructuring schools. The CFGs provide deliberate time and structures dedicated to promoting adult professional growth that is directly linked to student learning.

By their own nature, then, PLCs enhance the possibilities for conducting an inquiry and cultivating a community of inquirers. In fact, in our companion book to this text, *The Reflective Educator's Guide to Professional Development* (Dana & Yendol-Hoppey, 2008a), as well as in our book simply titled *The PLC Book* (2016), we describe a model for school-based professional development that combines some of the best of what we know about action research and PLCs and, in the process, address a weakness that has been defined in traditional professional development practices. We name this new entity the "inquiry-oriented PLC" and define it as a group of six to twelve professionals who meet on a regular basis to learn from practice through structured dialogue and engage in continuous cycles through the process of action research (articulating a wondering, collecting data to gain insights into the wondering, analyzing data, making improvements in practice based on what is learned, and sharing learning with others). The book *Inquiry: A Districtwide Approach to Staff and Student Learning* illustrates inquiry-oriented learning communities of teachers and principals and how they can be set up across an entire district (Dana et al., 2011).

Teacher Candidate Clinical Experiences/Residencies

Like PLCs, clinical experiences, internships, student teaching, or teacher residences offer rich contexts for professional learning. If you are a veteran teacher, you likely recall your own student teaching experience as an important feature of your preservice education. Similarly, if you are a teacher candidate, you have likely looked forward to your clinical experiences with great anticipation. According to a 2018 report prepared by the American Association of Colleges for Teacher Education (AACTE), a paradigmatic shift in teacher preparation is needed that places a greater emphasis on the clinical experience and learning within the field. Similarly, the Association of Teacher Educators published their standards for clinical experiences (2023). The standards emphasize inquiry as a pedagogical tool by highlighting how clinical educators engage teacher candidates in data-driven conversations to critically reflect on and systematically inquire into improving their teaching practices. The goal is to prepare teachers who are simultaneously content experts and innovators, collaborators, and problem solvers. According to the AACTE's recent report:

> Clinical practice offers a lens through which to understand the problems of practice that currently face the profession, stemming from factors such as demographic changes, poverty, and teacher shortages. The problematizing of these issues allows for creative thinking and innovation by the many players engaged in the clinical practice space. (AACTE, 2018, p. 8)

Within the report, teacher inquiry is highlighted as an important tool for strengthening clinical practice, and an inquiry stance is an orientation believed to strengthen teacher preparation. Mounting evidence suggests that field experiences that include engagement in teacher inquiry enhance the quality of teacher preparation (see, e.g., Dana & Silva, 2001; D. C. Delane et al., 2017; Rutten, 2021, 2022; Yendol-Hoppey & Franco, 2014). The reason why inquiry has become so much a part of quality teacher preparation is quite logical. Given that the act of teaching is an enormously complex endeavor, learning to teach in any brief, simple, and step-by-step way is impossible. As a teacher candidate, you are immersed in the complexities of teaching for the first time in clinical experiences. Immersion in this complexity naturally encourages engagement in inquiry, since questions about teaching, schools, and schooling abound. As you student teach, inquiry can help you learn to identify the complexities and problems inherent in teaching and tease these complexities apart to gain insights into your work with children. Given the comprehensive nature of teaching, identifying complexities and striving to understand them is a process that lasts an entire career. Engagement in teacher inquiry as an integral component of field preparation enhances the power of the field experience. As you simultaneously learn to teach and to inquire into teaching, these two processes become intricately intertwined. When teaching and inquiry become synonymous, you have cultivated an inquiry stance toward teaching that will serve you, your students, and the field of education well for the duration of your career!

Professional Development Schools

Since the late 1980s, a specialized setting for student teaching and other field experiences has emerged—the Professional Development School (PDS). A PDS is a learning community that intentionally fosters collaboration and mutual learning among pre- and in-service P–12 practitioners, university-based teacher educators, and scholars (National Association for Professional Development Schools [NAPDS], 2021). According to Darling-Hammond (1994), PDSs

> aim to provide new models of teacher education and development by serving as exemplars of practice, builders of knowledge, and vehicles for communicating professional understanding among teacher educators, novices, and veteran teachers. They support the learning of teacher candidates and beginning teachers by creating settings in which novices enter professional practice by working with expert practitioners, enabling veteran teachers to renew their own professional development and assume new roles as mentors, university adjuncts, and teacher leaders. They allow school and university educators to engage jointly in research and rethinking of practice, thus creating an opportunity for the profession to expand its knowledge base by putting research into practice—and practice into research. (Darling-Hammond, 1994, p. 1)

In a PDS, then, teacher inquiry is a central part of the professional practice of all members—practicing teachers, teacher candidates, administrators, and university teacher educators. This transition to inquiry is the mechanism for reinventing schools as learning organizations. Hence, a PDS culture supports and celebrates the engagement of teachers and other PDS professionals in constructing knowledge through intentional, systematic inquiry and using that knowledge to continually reform, refine, and change the practice of teaching (Dana, 2017; Wolkenauer et al., 2022; Yendol-Hoppey, 2011; Yendol-Hoppey & Dana, 2008).

Beginning in 2005, PDSs organized themselves through a national network referred to as the National Association for Professional Development Schools (NAPDS). Given the success and expansion of partnership work, in 2024 the organization changed its name to the National Association for School University Partnerships (NASUP) as a way of expanding their reach and forming more inclusive conversations about partnerships committed to improving teaching and learning. The mission of this new organization is to advance the education profession by providing leadership, advocacy, and support to create and sustain school–university partnerships such as Professional Development Schools to function as learning communities to improve student learning, prepare educators through clinical practice, engage in reciprocal professional learning, and conduct shared inquiry. Specific examples illustrating how inquiry is central to the work of PDSs can be found in the Fall 2017 special themed edition of *School–University Partnerships* entitled "Teacher Inquiry in Professional Development Schools: How it Makes a Difference." The work of teacher inquiry remains a vital component of NASUP, and teacher inquirers from PDSs and similar school–university partnerships regularly share their work at the annual NASUP conference.

Professional Practice Doctoral Programs

In recognition of the need to cultivate leaders and change agents who will not leave their practice contexts to become *professional researchers* in institutions of higher education but remain in their schools and districts and function as *researching professionals,* well positioned to tackle the most pervasive problems our education system faces, a new focus on professional practice doctoral programs has emerged (L. S. Shulman et al., 2006). Led by the Carnegie Project on the Education Doctorate (CPED) (D. G. Perry & Imig, 2008), the professional practice doctorate is a national movement. The goal of the professional practice doctoral degree is to meet the unique needs of practitioners who do not wish to leave their positions on the front lines to enter higher education, but want to earn their doctorates to develop the skills to lead informed change and improvements from within their schools and classrooms. Termed *scholarly practitioners* by CPED, these professionals use "practical research and applied theory as tools of change" (J. A. Perry, 2013, p. 3) as they "direct their research to the improvement of practice, based in the needs of the organizations that they seek to help and blend research methods with problems of practice" (Barnett & Muth, 2008, p. 12). Since the work of the practitioner scholar targets "empirical inquiry that is more closely tied to practice settings than to theoretical questions" (McClintock, 2004, p. 4), engagement in inquiry/action research has been adopted as a signature pedagogy in many professional practice doctoral programs as they have been launched across the nation (Buss, 2018; Dana et al., 2016; Wetzel & Ewbank, 2013), culminating with the Dissertation in Practice, a study that uses practitioner inquiry as the primary research methodology (Ma et al., 2018). Hence, several advanced practitioners working on their doctorates are using the process of inquiry introduced in this book to earn the terminal degree in the field, seamlessly weaving into their career trajectory the centrality of taking an inquiry stance toward their practice to transform the schooling experience from the inside out, rather than from the outside in.

How Does My Engaging in Teacher Inquiry Help Shape the Profession of Teaching?

Regardless of your method of inquiry, the subject of your inquiry, or the context of your inquiry, what is most important is that you *do* inquire! For decades, scholars of teaching and teacher education, such as Aronowitz and Giroux (1985), Greene (1986), and Zeichner (1986), have argued that "teachers are decision makers and collaborators who must reclaim their roles in the shaping of practice by taking a stand as both educators and activists" (Cochran-Smith, 1991, p. 280). These calls continue today as educators engage in inquiry to change, enhance, and challenge their practices (Butville et al., 2021; Rutten et al., 2024). Inquiry is a core tool that teachers use when making informed and systematic decisions. Through the inquiry process, teachers can support with evidence the decisions they make as educators and, subsequently, advocate for particular children, changes in curriculum, and/or changes in pedagogy. Inquiry ultimately emerges as action and results in change.

As a teacher candidate, practicing teacher, mentor teacher, and/or doctoral student interested in problematizing your professional practice, you have committed to simultaneous renewal and reform of the teaching profession and teacher education. Teacher inquiry is the ticket to enact this reform! Cochran-Smith and Lytle (1993) claim that in any classroom where teacher inquiry is occurring, "there is a radical, but quiet kind of educational reform in process" (p. 101). Your individual engagement in teacher inquiry is a contribution to larger educational reform, a transformation of the teaching profession . . . so, let us begin the journey.

What Is Ahead in This Book, and How Do I Use It?

Using a journey metaphor, in this text we take you through inquiry step by step, beginning in Chapter 2. This chapter, appropriately titled "The Passions That Drive Your Journey: Finding a Wondering," gets you started on an inquiry by engaging you in a series of exercises to help you explore all of the intricacies and complexities of teaching from different vantage points. This exploration serves to jump-start your development of an inquiry question that will guide your journey. The passions you will explore for this purpose are inquiring into an individual child's academic, social, and/or emotional needs; a desire to improve or enrich curriculum; a desire to enhance content knowledge; a desire to improve or experiment with teaching strategies and teaching techniques; a desire to explore the relationship between your beliefs and your classroom practice; an investigation of the intersection between your personal and professional identities; advocating for issues of equity and social justice; and understanding the learning context. As we explore each passion, we use examples from teacher inquirers we have worked with to illustrate the ways their inquiry questions emerged from the intersection of their real-world problems of practice and one of the particular passions defined in Chapter 2.

In Chapter 3, we discuss 10 common strategies for data collection used by teacher inquirers (student work and other instructional artifacts, field notes, interviews, focus groups, digital pictures, video, reflective journals/blogs, surveys, standardized test scores and other assessment measures, and colleague feedback). Throughout our discussion, we point to the ways each of these strategies connects to what you already do in your life and work as a teacher. We do this because we want you to see how teacher inquiry is *a part of* and not *apart from* the work you do as a teacher.

With the start of possible wonderings to drive your journey completed in Chapter 2 as well as the knowledge you develop about data collection strategies in Chapter 3, you will be ready to plan your first cycle of inquiry, a topic explored in Chapter 4. This chapter takes you through five stages of designing an inquiry cycle that will help you fine-tune your wondering, select relevant data collection strategies to gain insights into it, and consider additional pertinent topics associated with inquiry design such as developing a theory of action, collaborating with others, and the ethical dimensions of inquiry.

In Chapter 5, we explore what we have found to be one of the most difficult steps for teacher inquirers—data analysis. We discuss and illustrate the ways you analyze data *as* you are collecting them as well as *after* collection is complete. If you enjoy jigsaw puzzles, you will particularly enjoy your journey through this chapter, since we fully develop this metaphor to describe the summative data analysis process step by step. In addition, we use the work of one teacher inquirer to illustrate what data analysis might actually look like in practice.

To extend the learning that happens during data analysis, in Chapter 6 we look closely at sharing your inquiry with others through both oral presentation and writing up your work. One teacher inquirer's work is shared in its entirety to illustrate four basic components of any teacher's inquiry write-up.

In Chapter 7, we return to the question posed earlier in this chapter, "Inquiry for what purpose?" by further making the case that the ultimate goal of engagement in inquiry is to create more democratic, equitable, and socially just schooling experiences for all children. We illustrate this purpose through two stories: one of a longtime teacher researcher and one of four teacher candidates and their professor embarking on inquiry for the first time.

Finally, in Chapter 8, we return to and discuss stance again in greater detail, positioning it alongside a discussion of inquiry as process and inquiry as product. One part of enacting stance is reflecting on the quality of the teacher research you produce. Hence, Chapter 8 offers seven quality indicators and questions you can ask yourself as you reflect on your own and your colleagues' research, preparing you for a lifetime of professional learning through inquiry.

While we organize the chapters of this book using a journey metaphor and promise to take you on this journey step by step, we do need to qualify this promise before moving forward. As you saw in Figure 1.1, each inquiry component is depicted in the shape of a circle with the individual components connected to one another. We illustrate inquiry in this way in order to reflect its cyclical, rather than linear, nature. Hence, in some ways it is insincere to promise that we will take you through this process "step by step," which suggests that inquiry progresses in a forward motion with a clear beginning, middle, and end. Yet we must find some way to discuss each component within the linear sequencing of a book. As such, we artificially tease apart the cyclical process of inquiry and order it in the chapters ahead, but we do so with the qualifying statement that your journey will likely not unfold in the step-by-step progression laid out in this book. Rather, you may step into one part of the process and feel the need to leap multiple steps ahead or take a sidestep to consider another part of the process as your journey unfolds. Furthermore, you may find yourself multiple steps into the process but needing to circle back to the beginning of your inquiry path to review and/or reconsider an earlier step you made. For this reason, we utilize a call-out feature, an example of which appears below, that suggests places in the book you might wish to skip ahead or circle back to as you work on each individual component of inquiry presented in the chapters ahead.

Across the nation, prospective and practicing teachers vary greatly in their experience with teacher inquiry. Perhaps you are brand-new to teacher inquiry. Perhaps you have been engaged in inquiry for years and wish to further the development of teacher inquiry in your school or as part of your graduate program to earn a master's or doctoral degree. Perhaps you wish to make teacher inquiry a more visible or meaningful part of your teacher education program. Perhaps you seek to mentor other professionals in their first inquiries. Wherever you may be in your inquiry journey, we hope this text provides the impetus for you to take the next steps along the pathway of simultaneous renewal and reform, and to improve life and learning outcomes for *all* of the children you serve. Happy inquiring!

CHAPTER 1 EXERCISES

1. Look at some examples of teacher research published in the collections we mentioned in this chapter or that you may find in journals such as *Journal of Practitioner Research*, *Journal of Teacher Action Research*, *Voices of Practitioners*, *Action Research*, and *Networks: An Online Journal for Teacher Research*. What are some things you notice about the process of inquiry you will explore in this book from looking at actual examples of teachers' research?

2. Start an inquiry journal to trace your learning journey as you proceed through this book. For your first entry, capture the excitement and enthusiasm you may be feeling for the inquiry process after reading Chapter 1, as well as any apprehension or trepidations you feel about the process. Use these sentence starters as your journal prompts:

    - My greatest hopes for engaging in the inquiry process include . . .
    - My greatest fears for engaging in the inquiry process include . . .

    Discuss your responses with colleagues and continue to use your journal throughout the text to respond to the exercises provided in each chapter. When you actually begin your own inquiry, your journal can evolve into a way to collect data (covered in Chapter 3).

DISCUSSION QUESTIONS

1. What role does teacher inquiry play in educational reform?

2. The authors state, "Teacher inquiry is a vehicle that can be used by teachers to untangle some of the complexities that occur in the profession, raise teachers' voices in discussions of educational reform, and ultimately transform assumptions about the teaching profession itself." What are some common assumptions the general public holds about teaching and learning that you would like to see challenged? How can your engagement in inquiry help to challenge these assumptions?

3. What conceptions about educational research did you hold prior to beginning this book? To articulate your prior conceptions, consider the following:

    - Who does educational research?
    - Where is educational research done?
    - When is educational research done?
    - Why is educational research done?
    - How is educational research done?
    - What do you see as the strengths and weaknesses of educational research?

(Continued)

(Continued)

- Do you think teachers value educational research? Why or why not?
- Is there anything missing from educational research as you see it?
- In what ways might engagement in inquiry address what is missing?

4. How does engagement in teacher inquiry differ from traditional models of professional development?

5. Which ripe contexts for teacher inquiry professional development/learning programs, PLCs, teacher candidate clinical experiences/residencies, PDSs, or professional practice doctoral programs) are most pertinent to your current position? How can/will engagement in inquiry become a part of your current work as an educator?

6. What difficult topics or contested issues do you face in your context? How might the process and stance of inquiry support you to address these issues?

7. How can inquiry be a powerful tool in creating more equitable classrooms?

8. What excites you about the teacher inquiry movement? What concerns you?

9. How do you feel about embarking on your personal teacher inquiry journey?

ONLINE MATERIALS

The following materials designed to facilitate the exploration of inquiry are available for download at **https://companion.corwin.com/courses/ReflectiveEdsGuide5e**:

- **Activity 1.1: Block Party.** Discuss 12 provocative quotes about inquiry from Chapter 1.
- **Activity 1.2: Save the Last Word for Me.** Share and discuss your selection of the most significant passage from Chapter 1.
- **Activity 1.3: Hopes and Fears.** Name and discuss your hopes and fears generated by the prospect of studying your own professional practice.

The Passions That Drive Your Journey

Finding a Wondering

Where Do I Begin?

In Chapter 1, we welcomed you to teacher inquiry by defining the process, discussing inquiry as professional learning, and exploring the relationship between inquiry and educational reform. Our welcome to inquiry intentionally places you, as teacher candidates and practicing teachers, in charge of your own professional growth and learning.

Taking an active role in your professional learning is likely quite different from many of your past experiences with preservice and inservice teacher education. If you are a teacher candidate, up to this point you have likely engaged in coursework where professors have specified learning objectives for you in course syllabi, chosen the texts you will read, and defined assignments that you must complete to be eligible for graduation and initial certification. If you are a veteran teacher, you have likely attended inservice sessions covering topics selected for you by administrators or curriculum specialists in your district or perhaps topics mandated by your state. Hence, by taking charge of your own professional learning, you may be beginning a journey into uncharted territory! Charting new territory, when you are unfamiliar with both the terrain and your final destination, can be exciting but also somewhat intimidating. Beginning your journey becomes less daunting after you do some initial preparation and take your first steps.

Just as hikers gather certain equipment before starting a hike, as a teacher inquirer you will need maps and a compass before you embark on your first inquiry journey—and you, yourself, are responsible for drafting your map and constructing your compass. You begin to draw the map for an inquiry journey when you adopt what Charles Kettering refers to as the welcoming attitude toward, and active seeking of, change: "Essentially research is nothing but a state of mind . . . a friendly, welcoming attitude toward change . . . going out to look for change instead of waiting for it to come" (Kettering, in Boyd, 1961, p. 91). This welcoming attitude provides a basis for mapping out the first steps of your inquiry journey. The compass that provides the direction or question for your inquiry comes from reflection in and on your own teaching practice.

As teachers seek out change and reflect on practice, the first step of their journey begins with brainstorming questions for exploration—then deliberately honing, refining, and wordsmithing these initial questions into intentionally worded wondering(s) that serve to frame, focus, and anchor the inquiry. We distinguish "wonderings" from fleeting curiosities, and from initial reflective brainstorms of tentative questions, by defining them as *intentionally refined questions that frame and focus an inquiry*. In this chapter, we'll begin the process of wondering or question development by helping you examine your practice systematically with an eye toward brainstorming possible questions to drive the investigation into your practice, and then return to these developing questions later in the text to reconsider and refine them.

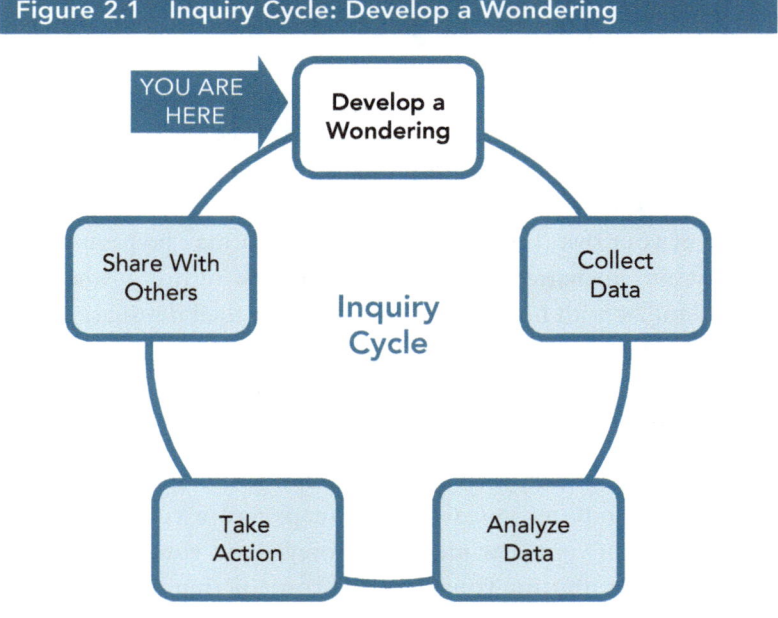

Figure 2.1 Inquiry Cycle: Develop a Wondering

Where Do I Find My Wonderings?

As you begin to brainstorm your own questions about teaching, it's essential to recognize that these questions are not just abstract ideas but are deeply rooted in the everyday experiences and naturally occurring data you encounter in your teaching environment. The questions you formulate should emerge from what you observe in your classroom—the interactions, challenges, successes, and subtle patterns that arise during your daily practice. These naturally occurring data are your most authentic source of inspiration and direction. For instance, you might notice a recurring issue with student engagement during certain lessons, or perhaps you observe that specific teaching strategies yield varying results with different groups of students.

These kinds of noticings can be defined as problems of practice—the intriguing real-world issues, tensions, dilemmas, and felt difficulties that are a natural and normal part of teaching, given all the rich complexity inherent within it. Problems of practice are not setbacks, hindrances, obstructions, or obstacles *to* good teaching. Rather, they are puzzling fascinations that invite the exploration and reflection that are necessary *for* good teaching, and when carefully honed into powerful questions, can lead to a focused, meaningful, and impactful inquiry.

In fact, in his book entitled *A More Beautiful Question: The Power of Inquiry to Spark Breakthrough Ideas,* Warren Berger (2014) describes problem finding as a necessary precursor to question development and refinement, describing good questions as "engines of the intellect—cerebral machines that convert curiosity into controlled inquiry" (p. 15). Additional metaphors he notes to describe the surprising power that questions can have include "flashlights that shine a light on where you need to go," "spades that help to unearth buried truths," and "levers used to pry open the stuck lids on paint cans" (p. 15).

Hence, by grounding your wonderings in problems of practice, you ensure that your inquiry is not only relevant but also practical and immediately applicable to improving your practice—converting your curiosities into actionable explorations, illuminating promising directions to take, unearthing assumptions that may impede innovation, and/or moving past a place of "stuckness" in your teaching. As you set out on your inquiry journey, then, let the rich tapestry of your daily teaching experiences and all the great complexity inherent within it, as well as the data that naturally surround you and the problems these data invite, be your guides to shaping the questions that will drive your professional growth and ultimately lead you to more informed, intentional, and impactful teaching.

After working with thousands of teacher inquirers, we believe that a teacher's wonderings begin to materialize through an examination of one's professional passions. Figure 2.1 represents how these passions are located at the nexus of a teacher's work—his or her problems of practice that arise within the complexity of classroom teaching.

Figure 2.2: Developing Your Research Question

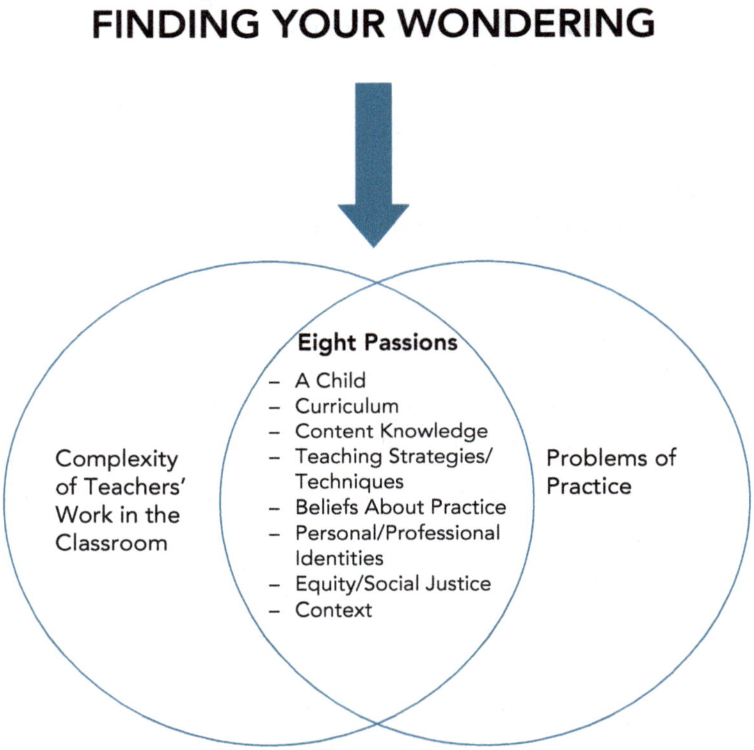

FINDING YOUR WONDERING

Complexity of Teachers' Work in the Classroom

Eight Passions
- A Child
- Curriculum
- Content Knowledge
- Teaching Strategies/Techniques
- Beliefs About Practice
- Personal/Professional Identities
- Equity/Social Justice
- Context

Problems of Practice

In the sections that follow, we map out the eight passions named in Figure 2.2 that emerged from our analysis of more than 100 teacher inquiries (Dana et al., 2006). In many ways, the eight passions overlap—but we present them as distinct entities in order to help you explore an array of possibilities for finding and defining your first wondering. Each passion is illustrated with the work of one or more teacher inquirers. As we share excerpts from the work of these teacher candidates and practicing teachers, we analyze the thought processes they used to derive their first wondering. In so doing, we offer you practical suggestions and guidance as you progress through a similar process. Finally, we end each section with exercises designed to help you explore areas ripe for the development of your wonderings. You may wish to pause at the end of each section to complete these exercises before reading further.

As you interact with this chapter to ignite the process of wondering development by exploring your passions, it is important to note that the passions we present (A Child, Curriculum, Content Knowledge, Teaching Strategies/Techniques, Beliefs About Practice, Personal/Professional Identities, Equity/Social Justice, and Context) are not meant to be separate topics or categories for wonderings but rather sparks to kindle more nuanced explorations of dilemmas that may be surfacing in your teaching practice from which important questions may emerge. As sparks rather than as topics or categories, the exercises you engage in related to one passion might lead you to develop a question that seems to fit within another. It matters not what passion your inquiry seems to fit within. In fact, as you will see in the examples we provide in this chapter, a single inquiry question may overlap with several passions. What matters as you read this chapter is that you use the passions to conduct a careful and critical analysis of your teaching and explore many possibilities for great wonderings you might choose to pursue.

As you use these passions to examine your own teaching, observe the ways teachers' interactions with several of the passions unearthed wonderings that related in some way to the ultimate "Why?" of teacher inquiry discussed in Chapter 1—the creation of more equitable classrooms and schools. Take note of the ways the birth of wonderings related to the creation of more equitable schooling experiences often occur even when the passion explored may not appear to be directly related to issues of equity at the start, and keep this ultimate goal of engagement in inquiry in mind as you read, reflect, and wonder.

Passion 1: Helping an Individual Child

You are likely familiar with a common saying proudly displayed by many teachers:

> *A hundred years from now, it will not matter what my bank account was, the sort of house I lived in, or the kind of car I drove. But the world may be different because I was important in the life of a child.*

In fact, you may very well have entered the teaching profession on the basis of your passion for children, your talent for connecting with them, and your willingness to commit yourself to positively impacting children's lives.

Each year, teachers encounter children who stand out for a variety of reasons—perhaps a child in your class has already progressed far beyond the expectations for your grade level and could benefit from intentional enrichment; is struggling with a particular concept in the curriculum; is experiencing great successes or challenges in social interactions; or behaves in ways that are not conducive to a positive classroom learning environment. These learners can be understood as intriguing puzzles that teachers try to understand as they strive to make a meaningful difference in each child's life.

A puzzling child can be a wonderful spark for your first wondering. If you are a beginning teacher, this is a common, comfortable, and developmentally appropriate place to develop your inquiry stance toward teaching. If you are a practicing teacher, you may also find that studying a particular student can enhance the child's experience both within your classroom and the wider school community. This process also informs your own ability to adapt your instruction to meet the needs of each learner and to track student growth. Each year we work with numerous teacher candidates and practicing teachers who inquire to gain insights into learners who stand out to them as intriguing puzzles. A few examples follow.

Amy Ruth, an intern in a kindergarten classroom, did not have a difficult time generating a large number of curiosities and wonderings for her first inquiry. In fact, Amy ended each of her professional journal entries with questions that emerged from her daily practice. As she brainstormed, she realized that many of her wonderings focused on student growth, and she eventually narrowed her inquiry to focus on an English as a Second Language (ESL) learner in her classroom. As you read the following excerpt from Amy's inquiry, note how she describes the process of finding her wondering:

> It was not hard for me to come up with a huge number of curiosities or wonderings that I have within my classroom. As I began to narrow down the wonderings, I began to notice that many of them centered around topics that held things in common, particularly the following areas: peer interactions, peer influence, ESL students, and the kindergarten writing center. Out of the list that I narrowed down, I asked myself, "What is it that really fascinates me?," "What am I passionate about?," and "Why am I a teacher?" The answer to all three of these questions for me is "student growth." It fascinates me to see the enormous growth students have over time.

I am passionate about setting up a learning environment that fosters growth. I am a teacher because teaching represents the challenge of finding ways to help a child grow, the excitement in the student growth as it is taking place, and the joy I feel of seeing that growth has and is taking place within my classroom!

My inquiry project became more apparent as I began to take over at the writing center during language arts time. Since the beginning of the year, I had watched one ESL student's language develop and grow right before my eyes. His forceful nature, strong personality, and undying energy had at times exhausted me, while at the same time it empowered me. He instilled a challenge in me to find ways to facilitate his entrance into our school, our classroom community, and our language. For being a child who came to school knowing very little of the English language, he is extremely outgoing and eager to be accepted by his teachers and his peers.

It was not long after I began working with the students at the writing center that I decided that my inquiry would focus on this ESL student, who I will refer to as Adam. As an intern in a kindergarten classroom, from the beginning of the year I had been amazed by the growth students show in their illustrating and drawing. I am always full of wonder and amazement as children's one-page illustrations develop into seven- or eight-page detailed stories.

The first time that Adam's group came to the writing center, I was blown away to see how he interacted with his peers. Immediately after sitting down with his writing folder, he handed a new sheet of paper to a peer, Kevin, and told him to draw a fish. "Fish!" he said. "Big fish!" I was amazed at the request. The thought that Adam would ask Kevin, a well-known artist in our room, seemed so clever to me. Where would this request lead Adam in his writing? Was this interaction/request going to be typical of Adam at the writing center? Would this help Adam's written language develop, as his spoken language had recently?

Now I had found my initial inquiry wondering: How does peer interaction facilitate Adam's writing at the kindergarten writing center? (Ruth, 1999)

To find her first wondering, Amy began by raising questions as she journaled about her classroom each day. Then, she began listing broad categories of areas that fascinated her—peer interactions, ESL students, the writing process. She found a common theme that connected all of her current fascinations in her teaching—student growth. Finally, an observation of an interaction between two of her learners during a writers' workshop sparked the final focus of her inquiry wondering. This incident provides a fine illustration of what Hubbard and Power (1993) refer to as inquiry resulting from real-world observations. Wonderings also come from dilemmas or felt difficulties. In the next example, note how intern Quinn Garman encountered a very common dilemma faced by many beginning teachers—she actually began to fear a student who challenged her directions:

> Imagine that you are a teacher candidate in a kindergarten room during the third day of your experience. At her request, all of the students join your mentor teacher on the rug for a story . . . all except one child, "Suzy." After I remind Suzy several times that it is time to stop her project and join the others on the rug, she continues to color using just one more marker, to sprinkle glitter in just one more place, and to put on just one more piece of sequin. Then, instead of quietly joining the group, she decides it would be more exciting to also sprinkle glitter on the worktable, pour glue on the carpet, and use marker wherever there is room on the floor, the table, and even her hands. The more she ignores my reminders, the more frustrated and agitated I become. Finally, with a stern face and voice, I stoop down to Suzy's eye level and give her a choice: Either she can quietly meet Mrs. Brown and the others at the rug or she can have a time-out. Just as those seemingly harmless words spill off the tip of my tongue, Suzy raises her right hand and with all her might, grazes my cheek with a mixture of pure anger and fear while yelling, "No!" Her unexpected reaction immediately stuns my words and freezes me like a popsicle. My numb legs can barely hold my paralyzed body up straight. Unaware of the situation, Mrs. Brown gently reminds Suzy that her place is at the rug. Immediately, Suzy bolts from the scene and finds a cozy spot right in front of the story, as if she had been there from the start. For a few minutes afterward, I can't move or think. I stand in a daze wondering what has just happened. Is this how this innocent five-year-old usually reacts to situations? Or is this just her way of reaching out?

> Unfortunately, this was not just an imagined scenario for me, but rather a serious slap in the face. As absurd as this may sound, I actually began to fear Suzy. She was the first person I thought of in the morning and the last person I thought of at night. In fact, I found myself trying to avoid contact with her whenever possible. As horrible as this may sound, I sometimes felt more comfortable working with someone who I knew would not hurt me rather than risk having a confrontation with Suzy. With all of this happening, I knew that I needed to develop a better relationship with Suzy during my student-teaching experience.
>
> During this time of my student teaching, I began attending seminars on teacher inquiry and reading books on teacher research. This research led me to question my own teaching beliefs and practices. This skepticism about my teaching, coupled with Suzy's slap, led me to complete a systematic study of our relationship. Therefore, the purpose of my study was to understand the behavioral patterns of one student, Suzy, in relation to my behavior as the teacher.
>
> The following research question guided my inquiry: "How do the structure and management of my classroom encourage or deter a particular student's behavior?" (Garman, 1997, p. 1–4)

Like Amy's, Quinn's question was sparked by a specific incident in the classroom that led her to focus on a particular child. In contrast to Amy's critical incident, where she observed two learners interacting with each other, Quinn's critical incident was characterized by her own interaction with a learner. Out of this particular interaction a dilemma developed—a desire to avoid a five-year-old whom she was responsible for teaching each day. Her wondering or felt difficulty was born out of the combination of her own interaction with a learner, subsequent reflection on that interaction, and desire to confront the dilemma she faced.

While you, like Amy and Quinn, note observations of particular learners and interact with individual learners hundreds of times each teaching day, sometimes a wondering about a particular child is not spawned by one observation or critical incident but emerges from what you notice and are learning about a particular child over time. In the following example, note how Jenn Thulin's (1999) interest in a particular first-grade child emerged after many months of discussion and observation between Jenn and her mentor teacher:

Meg is an imaginative child who stood out to my mentor teacher and me from the beginning of the year when she told us her stories of castles, princesses, and talking dogs. She told these stories with the enthusiasm and excitement of an actress who was on stage. We knew that she was very creative, but did not know the extent of her talent until she sang to us one day. Meg sang with the most incredible voice and perfect pitch. She not only enjoyed singing songs but also enjoyed making up her own songs.

While it was clear from the first day of school that Meg was a very talented and creative young girl, she also stood out in the classroom because of extreme language difficulties. At first, we noticed problems with her speech. Many of her syllables were reversed and she would often substitute incorrect sounds. For example, she would say "bery" instead of "very." She also had a hard time processing auditory information such as questions and directions. From the beginning of the year Meg struggled with all subjects but was especially discouraged and falling behind in reading.

In contrast to most of her peers, she did not know many sounds and confused many letters of the alphabet. We struggled for many months to help her learn the alphabet and sounds. She would make progress, but it was inconsistent. Just because Meg knew a sound one day did not automatically guarantee she would know it the next day. To help her achieve consistency, it was necessary to give Meg a great deal of individual instruction.

Therefore, Meg was recommended as a candidate for instructional support, which led to observation and testing by a team of educators. Through this process, we discovered that Meg had very poor auditory processing skills and auditory memory. It was very hard for her to comprehend and remember things that were told to her orally. Meg scored extremely low on auditory processing, but she scored exceptionally high in visual processing. If Meg saw a picture or a visual representation it was easy for her to understand. Because of the processing and memory difficulties, reading was a challenge for Meg. If you read Meg a passage from a book, she may not understand a word of it. However, if you showed her an illustration associated with that passage, she could tell you what the passage was about.

After witnessing the instructional support process and observing Meg struggle throughout the year with reading, I wanted to find a way to help her. The first thing that came to my mind was music. I noticed not only that Meg was a wonderful singer but also that she remembered songs very easily, so I hoped that music might work well with her auditory memory and processing difficulties. I hoped there was some way I could connect music to reading. I wondered, "In what ways could I use music to help Meg become a better reader?" and "How might music help her combat some frustrations when reading and boost her self-esteem?" (Thulin, 1999)

Jenn's long-term commitment to understanding and supporting an individual child provides a fertile foundation for the cultivation of this inquiry and relates to the ultimate goal of inquiry as a pathway to equity, providing every child what they need to be successful rather than treating every child the same.

In this example, Jenn used the process of inquiry to differentiate reading instruction for Meg to build intentionally on her strength with visual processing and her remarkable musical ability, rather than take a deficit view by categorizing Meg as a slow reader in need of remediation to fix a problem with her auditory processing. Jenn's framing of her wondering related to Meg's strengths reveals an important lesson for teachers committed to equitable schooling experiences for every child they teach—taking a strengths-based, rather than a deficit, view of students. In studying what teachers do in urban schools to create more equitable school experiences for students, Lisa Delpit (2006) notes the challenges teachers encounter in finding and focusing on student strengths, particularly when a teacher is not from the same cultural or class background as the student. Delpit asserts that teachers "must have the means to discover what the children are able to do outside of school"—for example, "in church, at community centers, and as caretakers for younger siblings"—in order to connect the kinds of skills and knowledge students possess to school learning (Delpit, 2006, p. 226). In this example, Jenn discovers a strength of Meg's and frames her wondering in relation to it.

PASSION 1 EXERCISES

1. Create a list of all the children in your class (elementary teachers) or a list of all the students in one period you teach each day (middle and high school teachers). As you add each student's name to the list, think about what makes that particular individual unique. Focus on identifying attributes that your students exhibit and factual observations of students rather than judgments or critiques about student performance or personality. Jot down one question next to each student's name that would provide you with insights into this particular learner. The following example is inspired by a real high school teacher and department chair:

   I have 100 students in four sections. Below is a listing of the students who most intrigue me because of their background, performance, or personality.

   Erick: Seems to have strong verbal skills but experiences challenges with writing. Larger concepts seem challenging to comprehend and apply to real-life situations in his writing. How can I help him to process the ideas and apply them to his writing?

   Lupita: Bright, very quiet, demanding parents, kind, gets upset when she does not do well. What are ways I can help her to understand that getting the right answer is not the point but that learning is the point?

   Gail: Low performing, but no known learning disability, extremely quiet, painfully shy. How can I create a classroom environment where Gail can feel more free to contribute?

   Rahila: A joy, smiles all the time, messy, difficult for her to keep track of things, father concerned about this. Should I take time to work with Rahila on developing organizational skills? How can I empower her to take ownership?

   Minori: Very quiet and kind, hasn't turned in assignments since the beginning of the semester, grade in the class is 11 out of 100!, mother does not know what to do about her, many meetings with counselor and administration, will procrastinate, is failing in other classes also. How can I be there for her when there are deeper psychological issues at play here? This is the one student I agonize over.

Sean: Sincere, honest, caring, slower than the rest of the students, not afraid to raise his hand in class, takes many rewrites to get papers up to where they need to be, hard worker. How can I keep him motivated and make sure that he does not get frustrated with himself?

2. Thinking back over the course of the school year, create a Top 10 list of critical incidents or intriguing observations that have occurred with particular learners in your classroom. Create a chart by generating a column next to each critical incident or observation that notes the student or students who were involved. Finally, in a third column, add a few words that describe the essence of the experience or observation. After you have completed your chart, look for themes across incidents, such as, "Does one student appear on my chart consistently?" and "What are the commonalities among each of the incidents or observations I listed?"

Passion 2: Desire to Improve or Enrich Curriculum

Just as you interact with and observe children every day, during each day of teaching you interact with the curriculum you are expected to teach. You work diligently to develop lessons and units of study that engage your students with meaningful content designed to actualize your objectives. Sometimes, for different reasons, teachers become dissatisfied with a curriculum unit and particular lessons they have delivered in the past.

Locating your inquiry within the development or enrichment of curriculum is a ripe area for the development of your first wondering. Curriculum development inquiries are popular for veteran teachers, since they often emerge from the teacher's dissatisfaction of "what was" the last time the unit was taught. In addition, veterans can reap the benefits of revising and enriching curriculum when they return to the same units or lessons year after year. Inquiry into student learning as a result of teaching a particular chunk of curriculum can also provide the point of entry for inquiry for teacher candidates. This kind of inquiry allows teacher candidates to systematically explore and critique existing curriculum that can lead to changes in their own use or conception of curriculum. Teacher candidates often teach curriculum for the first time in their field experience and study what student learning occurred through the curriculum.

We now share three examples of veteran teacher inquiries motivated by the desire to improve curriculum. Judi Kur, a first-grade teacher, finds her initial wondering in the tension between the required teaching of an outdated dinosaur curriculum unit that is focused on the acquisition of facts, and the specific topic that is highly motivating for her primary school–aged children:

> I first thought about my inquiry project about the same time I began contemplating my upcoming responsibilities as the chair of a unit titled "Prehistoric Life and Fossils." In my district, teachers are organized into teams that collaborate to teach four thematic, literature-based units each school year. As the unit chair, it was my responsibility to organize activities, orchestrate the sharing of books and materials among the teachers on my team, and lead the development of a culminating activity at the close of the unit.
>
> I had been dissatisfied with most of the science units in the primary curriculum since I began teaching first grade. I enjoy science and am fascinated with teaching science. However, to me science curriculum should focus on topics that children can experiment with, and topics where the students can use the scientific process to ask and answer questions. This had not been my experience with the dinosaur unit. Yes, the children love the topic, and they are motivated to learn, but I didn't feel that I was taking advantage of the children's and my enthusiasm. This unit as it was written didn't help me. In addition, a survey of the primary teachers in the district showed that most teachers thought the unit was extremely outdated. The science curriculum focuses on fossils, and the objectives can be covered in about a week. To top it off, we were being told that we cannot use the word *theories* in our teaching of the unit, due to concerns expressed by parents that the dinosaur unit was teaching evolution and that was contrary to their religious beliefs.
>
> Is it any wonder that when I last taught the dinosaur unit, the learning the children did was reading about other people's discoveries, not making their own? My students, similar to those mentioned by Craig Munsart in his book *Investigating Science With Dinosaurs* (1993), "easily memorized names and dimensions of dinosaurs but learned little about the science that surrounds them." And yet I agreed with a statement that

> I read by Don Lessem in an article in the *New York Times* (1991): "Dinosaurs are often a child's first introduction to science. As such, they could be the key to engendering a lifelong interest in all science."
>
> And so, I wondered, "How can I take a science unit that is heavy on content, and make it more science inquiry based?" After reading the book *Organizing Wonder: Making Inquiry Science Work in the Elementary School* (1998) by Jody Hall and talking with Carla Zembal-Saul, a professor in science education at the university, I embarked on developing lessons for this unit framed around the question, "How do scientists know so much about dinosaurs?" Once my lessons were developed and implemented, I pondered an additional research question: "What evidence exists that my newly developed inquiry-based lessons on dinosaurs help children develop the abilities advocated by the National Science Standards in the section that discusses science as inquiry?" (Kur, 2000)

In sum, Judi's inquiry question emerged from her dissatisfaction with the existing curriculum and her own commitment to providing primary-grade students the opportunity to experience scientific inquiry. As a result of these interacting conditions (students, curriculum, and teacher beliefs), Judi sought outside support in the form of human and other resources to further refine her question.

Like Judi, fourth-grade teaching colleagues Amy Jones and Diane Reed collaborated on an inquiry, finding their first wondering in a social studies unit on explorers. As you read the excerpt from Amy and Diane's inquiry, note that, once again, they articulate a dilemma or felt difficulty in the curriculum's existing approach to teaching. In this case, the unit covers Christopher Columbus:

> "In 1492, Columbus sailed the ocean blue." Most elementary students early in their education learn this traditional verse. A less familiar verse, which comes to us from native peoples, is, "In 1493, Columbus stole all that he could see." This striking difference between the two quotes offers a glimpse at the task that we, as educators, are trying to accomplish by meshing two different perspectives in the teaching of the "true discovery" of America. This idea led to our collaboration, as two fourth-grade teachers, to investigate other possibilities for teaching a unit on explorers in our district.

Teaching the explorer unit presented several dilemmas that needed to be addressed prior to the implementation of the unit. First, we struggled with the fact that we had four weeks to instruct the children with the material. The question was raised, "Should we spend the four weeks highlighting several explorers, or should we focus on Columbus and do an in-depth study of his encounter with the native people?"

After reviewing the materials and discussing the time limitations together, we felt that our time and our students' time were better served by focusing on Columbus's encounter. With that decided, the next dilemma revolved around another concern: Are fourth-grade students able to look at multiple perspectives and accuracy of historical events? This question initiated our framework for our inquiry.

When we began working on this project, we first had to find our focal point. In *Rethinking Columbus* (Bigelow & Peterson, 1998), we found the following quote that would navigate our curriculum writing:

> Our goal is not to idealize native people, demonize Europeans, or present a depressing litany of victimization. We hope to encourage a deeper understanding of the European invasion's consequences, to honor the rich legacy of resistance to the injustices it created, to convey some appreciation for the diverse indigenous cultures of the hemisphere, and to reflect on what this all means for us today. (Bigelow & Peterson, 1998, p. 11)

We also needed to enhance our own background knowledge of this historical event. *Lies My Teacher Told Me: Everything Your American History Textbook Got Wrong* (Loewen, 1995) presented a more historically accurate account of Columbus's arrival. *The Tainos: The People Who Welcomed Columbus* (Jacobs, 1992) provided specific information on the lifestyle of the Tainos, both before and after the arrival of Columbus. Neither resource was developmentally appropriate for fourth graders, but they provided us with the essential background knowledge needed to teach this unit.

As we began to review the literature for the unit, as well as additional resources, several questions emerged that became the basis for our inquiry project: "How can the story of the 'true discovery' of America be taught to fourth graders in a developmentally appropriate way?" and "What changes occur in students' knowledge/understanding of the 'true discovery' of America as a result of the lessons we constructed?"

Subquestions targeted at change emerged, including, "What changes occur in students' knowledge/understanding of Columbus?," "What changes occur in students' knowledge/understanding of the Taino people?," "What changes occur in students' knowledge/understanding of authors' bias regarding the depiction of this historical event?," and "What changes occur in students' knowledge/understanding of the meaning of the word *discovery*?" (A. Jones & Reed, 2000)

Amy and Diane's inquiry reflected their belief that their elementary students were indeed capable of understanding multiple perspectives on the same content. In light of this belief, they sought to enrich curriculum by providing a more historically accurate, nuanced portrayal of Christopher Columbus's arrival in North America.

Like Amy and Diane, third-grade teacher Carissa Johnson experienced a felt difficulty with the existing curriculum. In Carissa's case, however, her felt difficulty with curriculum began to emerge in light of a deepened historical understanding developed through a graduate course:

> I teach at the Tate Topa Tribal School of the Spirit Lake Nation in Fort Totten, North Dakota. My school enrolls a 100 percent Indigenous student population and, during a graduate course at the University of North Dakota focused on leading curriculum and instruction in K–12 schools, I extended my understandings of how the Western institution of school has historically been utilized to eliminate Indigenous peoples' languages, cultures, and traditions, and how culturally revitalizing and sustaining curricula can support the thriving and academic success of Indigenous youth, through course readings such as Tarajean Yazzie-Mintz's (2011) articulation of Sustaining Indigenous Traditions as a culturally based way of approaching curriculum theory. As I reflected on these readings in relationship to the current culture of my school, I realized that students' engagement with Dakota language and culture tended to be isolated to a weekly lesson with a Dakota language and culture teacher. I also realized that my

own curriculum for teaching reading and writing could be reimagined to support Indigenous lifeways, while meeting all applicable standards and school expectations. Therefore, I wondered: "How can I incorporate Dakota Oyate culture, traditions, and language into my literacy curriculum?"

To investigate this question, I took the following actions: (1) I created a recurring meeting with my school's Dakota language and culture teacher; (2) I began to incorporate Dakota language into the day-to-day routine of my classroom; (3) I identified a list of community members and elders willing to share their stories and practice the Dakota language with my students; and (4) I expanded my classroom library to include more books written by Indigenous people or featuring accurate information about Indigenous peoples and, specifically, important Dakota Oyate leaders. I also registered for additional professional learning offered by the Fort Totten State Historic Site to support me with responsible teaching of truthful histories of Indigenous peoples in North Dakota. Exploring my inquiry question through these actions truly empowered me to make curricular change.

Notice that Carissa's inquiry around curriculum started with a "How can I?" question: *How can I incorporate Dakota Oyate culture, traditions, and language into my literacy curriculum?* Likewise, Amy, Diane, and Judy's inquiries began with "How can I?" questions as well: *How can we teach the story of the true discovery of America to fourth graders in a developmentally appropriate way?* and *How can I take a science unit that is heavy on content and make it more inquiry based?* While "How can I?" questions are wonderful starting points for curriculum development inquiries, if a teacher inquirer stops here, his or her work may become purely the development of lesson plans without systematic study. Although the development of new lesson plans and implementing these plans are important work, focusing on what is learned as a result of the curriculum development makes the work teacher inquiry. Hence, if you begin with a "How can I . . ." wondering, also formulate a companion wondering that leads you beyond the lessons you developed to what you have learned about children, curriculum, and/or yourself as a teacher as a result of developing and implementing these new lessons. These companion questions are often generated by engaging in adult-level research about the content as well as the teaching strategies you are about to use. In the earlier examples, Judi turned to Hall's (1998) *Organizing Wonder: Making Inquiry Science Work in the Elementary School,* whereas

Amy and Diane read *Lies My Teacher Told Me: Everything Your American History Textbook Got Wrong* (Loewen, 1995) and *The Tainos: The People Who Welcomed Columbus* (Jacobs, 1992), and Carissa read *Cultures of Curriculum* (Joseph, 2011), which served as part of the spark for her inquiry. In each of these cases, content area reading becomes an essential component of wondering development.

PASSION 2 EXERCISES

1. Browse through your textbooks, your district's curriculum documents, and your old plan books. As you browse, generate a list of the topics you teach each school year that you felt uncomfortable teaching in the past or wished to enrich in some way. Next to each entry on your list, jot down a few words that describe how the unit might be enhanced or revised. Select one item from your list on which to focus a potential inquiry and begin the process of brainstorming questions related to the teaching of this curriculum.

2. In light of Carissa Johnson's inquiry example, take a second look at the same curricular materials you browsed through to complete Exercise 1. This time, consider how the materials do or do not offer your students "mirrors, windows, and sliding glass doors" (Bishop, 1990)—opportunities to see their identities and closely held perspectives reflected, extended, and challenged. Consider whether the materials are culturally responsive or sustaining for your students and whether any changes may be warranted based on how your students responded to the materials the last time you taught them.

3. Visit the websites of the leading national organizations for teaching of specific subject matter, such as the National Council of Teachers of Mathematics (NCTM; www.nctm.org), National Science Teachers Association (www.nsta.org), National Council for the Social Studies (www.ncss.org), and National Council of Teachers of English (www.ncte.org). View each organization's standards for best practice in that field. How does the delivery of your curriculum mesh with best teaching practice as advocated by these associations?

(Continued)

(Continued)

4. Meet with the curriculum specialist or administrator in your building. Find out what changes he or she is anticipating in the curriculum. Identify an interest area and question connected to these changes. By studying the new implementation or change process, you are likely to have some influence regarding what develops!

Passion 3: Focus on Developing Content Knowledge

In Passion 2, inquiry focused on developing curriculum with new alternative instructional approaches and objectives to shape curriculum. As indicated in all three inquiries shared in this section, a precursor to this kind of curriculum development was a focus on developing deeper teacher content knowledge and then identifying the developmentally appropriate content knowledge for the children within each teacher's classroom. In this case, the inquiry wondering emerges as teachers identify areas of the curriculum they teach that provoke a content-related felt difficulty. For example, Diane and Amy's inquiry into "How can we teach the story of the 'true discovery' of America to fourth graders in a developmentally appropriate way?" provoked them to inquire into the underlying content of the curriculum they were planning. They needed to understand the voices represented in alternative stories. This required substantive, adult-level content reading and research.

Inquiry or research into content requires multiple phases of teacher activity. First, the inquiry begins as teachers pose a question about the content they are teaching—for example, "What do I know about the 'true discovery' of America?," "What do I know about the Holocaust?," or "How do airplanes fly?" Next, teachers obtain multiple resources and perspectives that can help them respond to that inquiry. For example, teachers may explore reference materials, review primary documents, conduct an oral history, or delve into artifacts that inform their inquiry question. One teacher shared the following:

> You know, as an elementary teacher, I really don't have the time to be an expert on anything. I felt really fortunate to have the time to investigate one content area in depth and figure out a way to make sense of it for my young students. The Holocaust is a particularly sensitive issue. I am always

> wondering what my first through fourth graders should know about it and what I can teach them that is really at their level of understanding. After spending a good month reading everything that I could about the Holocaust and really trying to get an adult-level understanding of the events and atrocities that happened, I finally felt prepared to teach. (Field notes, Alachua County Teacher)

By exploring multiple sources, the teacher constructs a stronger understanding of the various perspectives on the content she needs to teach.

Once the teachers have developed adult-level content knowledge, they begin the third step of the inquiry, which focuses on defining what is believed to be the developmentally appropriate content for the students within the classroom. This is a teacher activity, because it requires teachers to investigate their own students' cognitive, physical, social, and emotional levels regarding the content area investigated. One example of investigating students' cognitive, physical, social, and emotional levels regarding the content area investigated emerged as elementary teachers considered the students' readiness for the content of the Holocaust as follows:

> We talked to a lot of people about how to share the Holocaust with young children. We spoke to our administrator, guidance counselor, and a slew of parents. We met with the media specialist, too, and some local experts on the Holocaust. We even talked to members of the Jewish community within our town. I think the most important information came from interviews with our students. Although most of them knew nothing about the Holocaust themselves, which wasn't surprising to us, we realized through analyzing our data that certain content specific to the Holocaust should be incorporated into the elementary curriculum and that, in addition, certain democratic dispositions or underpinnings for addressing and understanding issues of the Holocaust were missing from our current curriculum. (Field notes, Alachua County teacher)

After a great deal of background research, this elementary teacher and her inquiry partner decided that it was more developmentally appropriate to structure the elementary students' learning around key ideas underpinning the Holocaust, as follows:

> By the time we finished digging into our own understanding of the Holocaust, we realized that our students needed to understand some fundamental ideas. We focused on helping our students develop themselves in moral and responsible ways by promoting a caring and accepting nature toward others. . . . We also worked on helping our students understand that change is necessary in the world if we are to survive and that prejudice, discrimination, and stereotyping are unproductive activities if we strive to reach the goal of survival. (Field notes, Alachua County teacher)

Interestingly, these teachers decided that these were the important concepts for their students to learn in regard to the content of the Holocaust.

Because the teacher is key to student learning, it is a legitimate and worthy task to spend time constructing content knowledge and transforming that knowledge into developmentally appropriate content for children. You will not only become much more familiar with the content, but you will also become clearer about what you do not know. Exploring content and determining its relevance to the students within your classroom is a powerful way to enhance your teaching and the learning process.

In addition to using the process of inquiry to enhance your own adult-level content knowledge and translate that knowledge into your teaching practice, a teacher's own dilemma related to adult-level content knowledge on a subject might lead to designing and implementing creative instructional approaches. For example, Kathryn Janicke, in the role of support teacher for students in grades 10–12, reflects on the challenge she faced in teaching when she did not have the subject-matter knowledge necessary to support some of her learners:

> One dilemma I face is developing supports for students who are struggling to master the content of the chemistry honors class. Struggling students often need direct support with the content and reteaching of classroom concepts to master the material. Unfortunately, I often do not have the content knowledge and/or resources to support students in this fashion because I do not have a science education background. One strategy that offers promise to circumvent my limited chemistry subject matter knowledge and meet the needs of my students is the creation of a peer-tutoring environment. This strategy has led me to my wondering: In what ways does

organizing and enacting a high-school honors chemistry peer-tutoring program improve the academic achievement of the students I support in this class? (Janicke, 2018)

Kathryn's inquiry once again reflects an equity focus, since she uses the process of inquiry to find the supports necessary for students with disabilities to be successful in an honors course, even if the supports that are needed lie outside the realm of services she herself, due to limited content knowledge in a subject area, has the ability to provide.

PASSION 3 EXERCISES

1. Make a list of topics you teach for which deeper content knowledge would enhance your classroom practice. On this list, circle the topics that you believe require substantive transformation or adaptation if you are to teach the content area to children.

2. Evaluate the materials you currently use to teach content within each subject area and unit you teach. Do these resources represent diversity of perspectives and multiple voices? Whose voices are present or missing?

Passion 4: Desire to Improve or Experiment With Teaching Strategies and Teaching Techniques

In Passions 2 and 3, wonderings are located around a particular topic and content area. The work of the teacher also encompasses applying generic teaching strategies (e.g., cooperative learning, role play, simulation, lecture, and discussion) and specific teaching techniques (e.g., questioning, assessing student learning, and integrating technology into instruction) throughout the teaching day. Similar to the desire to improve or enhance a particular piece of curriculum as discussed in Passion 2, you may have a desire to gain insights into, improve, and/or experiment with new or routine teaching strategies and techniques. In the following example, intern Nancy Sunner is intrigued with learning more about the questions she poses to students in her daily teaching:

> Questioning is an enormously powerful and important skill in productive teaching. For decades, teacher questioning has been a topic of study. Researchers had found that teachers rely on questioning as an essential element of their teaching

repertoire. On an average, elementary school teachers ask 348 questions during a typical school day (Acheson & Gall, 1997). Through the process of effective questioning, teachers can stimulate thought, help students reinforce basic skills, involve shy or quiet students, draw in the attention of a student who has drifted off, and promote self-esteem and success in the classroom.

The skill of effective questioning requires teachers to constantly balance several things at once. During questioning, teachers must remember their lesson goals, monitor their communication with the students, assess the students' verbal and nonverbal responses (nods, raised hands, shrugs, and downcast eyes), and think about the next question. This impressive and sometimes overwhelming aspect of teaching sparked my curiosity about my own questioning techniques in the classroom.

As a beginning teacher, I have experienced great satisfaction when I asked a student a question and received a correct response. I feel as though the students get it and that I am somehow responsible for this accomplishment. On the other hand, I have had experiences this year when a lesson is falling apart and it seems that no matter what questions I ask, the students cannot follow my line of questioning. This is the ultimate frustrating experience for everyone.

Therefore, the focus of my inquiry is to better understand my questioning behavior as a teacher. The questions I will address through this inquiry are "What type of questions do I ask?" and "How does questioning change with the subjects I am teaching?" (Sunner, 1999)

Of the examples of teachers' wonderings we have explored thus far, note that Nancy's wonderings are perhaps the most straightforward and technical. They emerge at the intersection of her professional readings and her felt difficulty regarding her use of questioning. Straightforward and technical wonderings are often powerful in that they lead to teachers' discoveries that their beliefs, philosophies, and desires are not always congruent with their practice. For example, through scripting the questions posed throughout different lessons and sorting each question into one of five categories (higher order/thought questions, recall/narrow questions, managerial/behavioral questions, procedural questions, and probing questions) as her inquiry unfolded, Nancy discovered that the majority of her questions were fact/recall questions. This discovery was inconsistent with her desire to teach for conceptual understanding and led to keener attention to her questioning efforts as well as changes in her questioning.

There is an old proverb, "A fish would be the last creature to discover water." In teaching, generic strategies and techniques can become so routine and ingrained in our practice that we do not notice significant ways in which our routines interface with the goals of our teaching. In addition, we can become so immersed in strategies and routines that have worked in the past that we fail to try new strategies that could potentially enhance our teaching. Systematically studying teaching strategies and techniques can lead to discoveries that would not have become apparent in the absence of systematic study, and these discoveries ultimately lead to new and significant changes in teaching practice.

Inquiring into teaching strategies and techniques can also have an explicit equity focus. For example, Melanie Harris, a middle school performing arts teacher and high school choral director for a K–12 school, used the process of inquiry to apply pedagogy associated with the teaching of music to boost the achievement of her African American female students in their math and science classes. She reflects on the foundation of her wondering:

> As my students moved from eighth to ninth grade, I continually observed the difficult transition from middle school to high school math and science for many of the African American students in my women's ensemble choral group. Their musical ability and talent placed them in an elite high school music performance ensemble, but the opportunity gap continued to affect their other academic classes (most drastically in biology and geometry). I wondered if there was something that could be done to support the learning of students who displayed a high degree of musical talent and commitment, but who struggled to be successful in their math and science classes. (M. Harris, 2015, p. 13)

And so Melanie turned to the process of inquiry to explore the ways that she, as a music teacher, could support academic teachers in meeting the science and mathematics learning needs of the African American female learners they all taught. Melanie wondered, "In what ways can I, as a music educator, use my knowledge of music and the students I teach to support the math and science learning of my students through collaborative work with their academic teachers within a Professional Learning Community?" A subquestion Melanie explored was, "In what ways might the teaching strategies I employ to teach music be used to support student learning in science and math?" Recognizing the opportunity gap discussed in Chapter 1, Melanie Harris frames her wondering to investigate the role that particular teaching strategies might play in mitigating societal factors that have contributed to the ways her African American female students were performing in math and science classes at her school.

PASSION 4 EXERCISES

1. Brainstorm a list of teaching strategies you would like to try. Next to each entry on your list, jot down a few words that describe your reasoning for wanting to try this strategy. Formulate a question that connects the strategy and your reasoning for trying to use that strategy. For example,

    a. Cooperative learning: My students are very talkative. Cooperative learning could fulfill their need to talk and focus their talking on academic learning simultaneously. How can I use my children's social skills to enhance their learning and instruction at the same time?

    b. Integrating a SMART Board into instruction: After seeing a SMART Board demonstrated at a conference recently, I was intrigued by the power this technology might hold to enhance instruction. I was reluctant to try a SMART Board, though, because my prior teaching experiences suggest that integrating technology into instruction can be intimidating and frustrating. How can a team of teachers work through problems together and support each other to overcome hurdles when using new technologies?

2. Brainstorm a list of the most frequent strategies and/or techniques you draw on in your teaching. After brainstorming your list, place a star next to the strategies that are most intriguing to you. Jot down a few sentences or phrases next to your starred strategies that capture why these techniques are intriguing. Then formulate a question that connects the strategy and your intrigue with it. For example:

a. Questioning: Sometimes students don't answer the questions I am asking. How do the ways I phrase questions contribute to how learners interpret them?

b. Facilitating discussions: During my literature circles, it feels like the students never talk to each other when discussing a book. The conversations feel like they resemble ping-pong matches as the dialogue goes back and forth between me and my students: teacher → student → teacher → student → teacher → student. I'd prefer the students talk to each other. What are some strategies I could use to facilitate better literature discussions?

Passion 5: Desire to Explore the Relationship Between Your Beliefs and Your Classroom Practice

In the example used to illustrate Passion 4, Nancy's wondering led to her conclusion that her teaching desires and her practice were inconsistent with each other. While Nancy's inquiry *ended* with this discovery, many teachers *begin* their inquiry with the realization that the relationship between their beliefs and practice are incongruent. Exploring the relationship between your beliefs and practice provides another possibility for generating your first wondering. In the example that follows, Holly Niebauer Jones finds her first teacher inquiry wondering as she discovers that her implementation of a classroom management plan does not match her philosophy.

> I was fortunate to be a part of an experimental student-teacher-as-researcher program at Penn State designed to focus on learning about and doing teacher research during the student teaching experience. Class discussions about teacher research and three books titled *The Art of Classroom Inquiry* (1993) by Ruth Shagoury Hubbard and Brenda Miller Power, *Inside/Outside: Teacher Research and Knowledge* (1993) by Marilyn Cochran-Smith and Susan L. Lytle, and *Teachers as Researchers: Qualitative Inquiry as a Path to Empowerment* (1991) by Joe Kincheloe helped give me a strong background for pursuing research.
>
> As I progressed through the semester, I thought of numerous projects that were possibilities for teacher research projects. The topic that consistently surfaced, however, was that I noticed inconsistencies between my philosophy of education

and my actions as a teacher, particularly as they related to classroom management. The idealistic components in my philosophy were not always practiced. I pondered over this daily and wanted to find reasons for the inconsistencies.

In order to focus my data collection for research, I generated two questions: (1) In what ways do my classroom management and practices detract from my philosophy of teaching and my beliefs about how children learn? and (2) What are my underlying/suppressed beliefs about teaching and learning and children and schooling that cause or contribute to the gaps between my beliefs and my actions? (Niebauer, 1997)

As you can see, Holly found her inquiry at the intersection of her espoused teaching philosophy and her ability to critically self-reflect on her own classroom management.

PASSION 5 EXERCISES

1. Write a series of philosophy statements that describe your general teaching philosophy; your philosophy of teaching science, social studies, reading/language arts, mathematics; and/or creating a classroom learning environment conducive to instruction. (If you are a teacher candidate, you may have already completed essays such as these in your prior teacher preparation coursework.) Once it is committed to paper, share your philosophy with a colleague or friend. Discuss the ways you are and are not enacting your philosophies of teaching in your classroom practice.

2. Keep a teaching journal for one week. Each night, reflect on one happening in the classroom that you wish you had the opportunity to repeat and react to in a different way. Note what beliefs you hold that led you to react as you did, as well as how you would react differently if able to turn back time. What beliefs undergird your alternative reaction?

Passion 6: The Intersection of Your Personal and Professional Identities

Just as wonderings may be found at the intersection of your beliefs and practice, they may also be found at the intersection of your personal and professional identities. According to William Ayers (1989), who you are as a teacher and who you are as a person are intricately intertwined. In his study of six exemplary preschool teachers, he came to the following conclusion:

> "teaching as identity" is the clearest theme to emerge in this inquiry, and "teaching as identity" is the frame through which each portrait makes sense. In these portraits, there is no clear line delineating the person and the teacher. Rather, there is a seamless web between teaching and being, between teacher and person. Teaching is not simply what one does, it is who one is. (Ayers, 1989, p. 130)

Hence, a wonderful place to find your first wondering is by focusing on who you are as a person and a teacher and further exploring one of your own personal passions and the ways that passion plays out in your teaching.

An example of personal passion translating to teaching is found in the work of intern Julie Russell. In the example of Julie's inquiry, note how her personal passion for writing led to her first wonderings:

> I can still remember every detail of the moment when I became a writer. The warm August air sticks to my skin, powdery chalk dust tickles my nose, and the comforting sounds of my mother making dinner fill my ears whenever I begin to put words on a page. I found my voice as a writer the summer before second grade. I was six years old, and my older sister had suddenly decided that she was too mature to play with me. She would disappear with her friends, and I was left to fill the long, summer days without her. One afternoon, I wandered into the basement and started to draw on an old chalkboard that my sister and I used when we were playing school. After a while, I stopped drawing and began writing poetry. When my mother called me for dinner, she saw my poems and became my first audience. She encouraged my efforts and gave me a small, yellow notebook so I could continue to write. My passion for writing grew as I continued to read quality literature and experienced the powerful ways in which expert authors manipulate language and develop engaging stories. Throughout my life, I have turned to written words to express my thoughts and ideas.
>
> As I developed a teaching philosophy, I realized that my passion for teaching is intertwined with my passion for

writing. My goal as a teacher is to help children become lifelong learners who can think critically about the world around them and create and articulate their own ideas. I hope that, by sharing my love for writing with my students, I can help them express the thoughts and opinions that are important and meaningful to them. Therefore, when I pictured my future classroom, I always seemed to arrive during writer's workshop. I assumed that I would be an effective, engaging writing teacher simply because I enjoyed writing. I imagined a classroom filled with eager students who loved writing and could not wait to commit their ideas to paper. I was thrilled to be an intern in a second-grade classroom because I could remember the wonderful writing experiences I had during my own second-grade year.

As I began my internship experience, I helped provide writing instruction for a group of second graders with differing strengths, needs, and interests. I quickly realized that teaching writing is extremely complicated. Some children wrote independently and produced several pages of text during each workshop. Others wrote one sentence at a time and frequently approached me to ask, "Am I done yet?" I often sat with a small group of students who struggled to get their thoughts down on paper. As I tried to keep these children on task and encourage them to continue writing, I asked questions and made story maps. At the end of many writing sessions, I felt uncomfortable with the amount of support I was giving to some young writers. Several children who were quite capable of writing independently often came to me and asked, "Can I write with you?" I worried that I was allowing some children to become too dependent on my help and that my influence was hindering the flow of their ideas.

As I studied children's writing development, I realized that the range of writing behaviors in my classroom was common for second graders. I felt relief when I read the experts' descriptions of second-grade writers and realized they mirrored my feelings about the young writers in my classroom. Some children write "fluently" and approach writing with "carefree confidence" (Calkins, 1986, p. 67). These children write long, detailed narratives with ease. Other children seem to erase more than they write. Second graders are beginning to become "aware of an audience" for their writing, and the "easy confidence" they felt as first graders often turns into their first cases of "writer's block" (Calkins, 1986, p. 68). They are concerned about approaching tasks in the "right way"; that vulnerability makes writing a difficult and painstaking process for many children (Calkins, 1986, p. 69). Therefore, writing instruction in second grade must address this wide range of writing behaviors.

During the students' goal-setting conferences in the beginning of the school year, my mentor, Linda Witmer, spoke to many of the children about working toward meeting the district's benchmark for writing by the end of the year. According to this benchmark, the students must be able to write stories with beginnings, middles, and endings. These stories should be understandable and must include characters, settings, and major events. The students are also expected to include some descriptive language, use some punctuation and capitalization, and spell the district benchmark words correctly. The students must complete the writing assessment independently. After winter break, Linda and I were both concerned about our students' writing. As I looked through the students' work, I noticed that extremely capable children were often scoring below the benchmark. Many of the children were still writing incomplete stories, and endings were particularly difficult for many students. Although our students had wonderful, creative ideas, we worried that several of them would not meet the district's benchmark for writing because they did not take the reader on a complete journey from beginning to middle to end.

My initial experiences as a writing teacher were frustrating. After years of imagining myself as an effective writing teacher, I was dismayed when I realized that my efforts were not helping my students meet their writing goals. In some cases, I worried that I was doing more harm than good because my attempts to help often became persistent prompting that drowned out the students' voices in their own writing. I was heartbroken when students resisted writing, because I was so eager to share my passion for stories and language. When I conducted a survey to collect data about the students' attitudes toward writing, I was concerned when I realized that many children thought that they were good writers because of neat handwriting, good spelling, or using time wisely.

Although those skills are important, I noticed that most children did not mention that they were proud of their ability to create stories. Gradually, I began to doubt my ability to provide my students with writing instruction that would help them meet the district's writing goals and that would inspire them to enjoy writing. My passion for writing, which I believed would be an asset in the classroom, actually hindered my progress as a writing teacher because I struggled to relate to and communicate with students who resisted writing. As I studied writing instruction, I learned that teachers' personal experiences with the subject matter influence the way they teach their students (Frank, 1979). I realized that, because I had positive writing experiences as a child, I had naively assumed that all of my second graders would react to writing with similar enthusiasm.

My passion for writing and teaching, as well as my frustrations with the realities of teaching writing, led me to my wonderings. I wanted to do a project that would focus on my students' development as writers and would also help me develop as a writing teacher. Therefore, I began my project with the following wonderings: "Will my second graders write more complete stories if the elements of a story are broken down into a series of mini-lessons?," "Will my second graders become more independent writers and gain confidence in their writing abilities if my expectations for their writing are more explicit?," "Will collaborating with other learners help my students grow as writers?," "Will my students grow as writers if the lessons include opportunities to make connections between children's literature and their own stories?," and "Will these changes in writing instruction improve the way my students feel about themselves as writers and the way I feel about myself as a writing teacher?" (Russell, 2002)

As indicated, Julie's wonderings developed from her own personal interest in writing and her identity as a writer. Similarly, in the following example, Algebra I teacher Carlee Escue finds that her prior life experiences in architecture played a big role in the ways she approached the teaching of high school mathematics:

My college BA is in architectural design. I chose to become a teacher, and I am very happy with my decision, although there are times that I feel I have an interesting background for a math teacher and I would like to share it more with my students. In my teaching experience the most common question from students is "When am I going to use this in the real world?" For at least a handful of math concepts I teach, I am able to answer that I have actually experienced having to use these skills in the real world. I have also experienced in architectural business that we do not work alone. Every project I did consisted of more than four people contributing to the final outcome. Everyone depended on one another to do their job accurately and on time. So, over the past three years, I've been engaged in a continuous cycle of inquiry to address the question, "How can I share my love of architecture, demonstrate real-world mathematics skill application to high schoolers, and provide them with real-world experience in working together?"

My quest to explore this wondering translated into my assignment of a cooperative learning project to design a playground in the spring to my ninth-grade Algebra I students. It lasts about two months from introduction to the final group presentation. Students work in groups of four with each group member being assigned one of the following specified roles: project manager, designer, accountant, and technician. Each group is responsible for taking site measurements and designing a playground for two different age groups (ages 2–5 and ages 5–12) with an outside classroom that can accommodate 60 seated adults. They then need to consult with real playground equipment companies to purchase the materials. Their budget is $80,000. The project culminates with presentation of their playground proposals to a fictitious investor, Escue Enterprises. They must incorporate technology into this presentation. It is a detailed project with many checkpoint grading periods to keep the students on track.

Because I find this project to be very interesting, and because it relates to my background and real-world experiences, I want to improve on it constantly. I have modified my approach every year. For the past three years most of my modifications have involved organization, real-world accuracy, and ease of application and delivery on my part. I find it is time to approach the problems that have been more difficult to solve. Facilitating effective cooperative learning groups has been one of these challenges. I need to address group dynamics, positive confrontation skills, parental involvement, and understanding of the project.

Although these issues were present in the past three years, students struggling with cooperative learning were more apparent to me this year. It proved to be an issue I needed to address immediately. Although the nuts and bolts of the project were addressed and refined, I discovered the problem with collaboration when I had my first large grading cycle. I have designed the grading to have little checkpoints throughout the two months. The grading period that addressed the rough draft and site plan revealed to me which groups were functional and which were dysfunctional.

I addressed each group and discussed the expectations I had for them, as well as why their work was appropriate or unacceptable.

After these grades were posted and my group discussions were concluded, I received emails from parents who were hearing for the first time about this project. They were not pleased with what was going on in their child's group and/or with their child's grade. At first, I found myself getting defensive because I had thought I had been thinking ahead. For example, I had allotted time in my class for work. Giving half the class period to work in their groups, I gave each student a job description form and a sign-up sheet. I had allowed the students to pick their top two job choices, and then I put students into the group with their top choice position. Each group had a portfolio that I reviewed with the classes when I presented my PowerPoint introduction to the project with sample drawings and models. But what seemed to support my argument most was that I had groups that were working very effectively. I found myself defending my project and not addressing the concerns. I couldn't understand how there was an issue when I had done so much to prevent the issue from occurring.

After I relaxed and started to face the fact that there was a problem with dysfunctional groups, I decided that I would pick my two most dysfunctional groups and try to figure out what went wrong. The reason I chose these two groups is they were my most dysfunctional in the aspect that they had the least amount of work turned in. In addition, when they met with me, they demonstrated through their comments and body language that they were miserable, confused, angry, and frustrated. These groups consisted of one group from my Honors Algebra class and the other from my regular Algebra I class. My inquiry questions for this year became, "What can I learn about how to group ninth graders for my yearly playground design project by closely examining the group dynamics of low-functioning groups?" and "What action can I take as a teacher to help dysfunctional cooperative learning groups ascertain the difficulties they are having in working together and become functional?" (Escue, 2006)

In this example, by weaving her prior life experiences in architecture with her teaching, Carlee was able to breathe new, creative life into the Algebra I curriculum that went beyond traditional textbook coverage for her students each year. However, because teaching is so complex, it is natural and normal for issues to surface as teachers try out new pedagogy and projects with their students. While our first instinct may be to become defensive or to pretend problems don't exist, taking an inquiry stance toward teaching means we celebrate problems by naming them and systematically studying them to gain insights into practice, as Carlee did in this case. As a result of this inquiry, Carlee was able to name three main issues that she would address in the future: (1) the teaching of positive confrontation skills, (2) providing practice in cooperative learning, and (3) remaining in constant contact with parents.

The intersection of one's personal and professional identities can also lead a teacher to target issues of equity through inquiry. For example, similar to Carlee Escue who entered the profession of teaching after years of experience in architecture, Gary Boulware was drawn to high school teaching after retiring from a successful career in business. As a business executive, Gary was well aware of the challenges inherent in advancing diversity and inclusion in the workplace. Hence, once he secured his first teaching position as an advanced placement (AP) Economics teacher, he quickly noticed that almost all of the students in his courses were White, and noted the inequalities in curricula intensity occurring when most White students were receiving a rigorous AP curriculum and most students of color were receiving a watered-down general curriculum.

To entice a more diverse population of students to enroll in AP classes, Gary decided to offer a guaranteed C to all students:

- If you attend class regularly,
- if you are not a pain in my backside,
- if you earn a minimum of 70% on every notebook check,
- if you take every test/quiz, and
- if you complete points make-up after every test . . .
- . . . you will earn at least a C in my classes.

The intent was to provide a safety net for students new to the rigors of an AP environment and to take some of the risk out of taking an AP course. Gary's background in the business world led him to believe the success of the next generation of future leaders and economic engine of our country depended on setting high expectations for *all* students while they were still in high school. Furthermore, Gary hoped his actions might serve in some capacity to level the playing field for students who were tracked into a general curriculum, because he learned from readings that a strong relationship existed between taking AP classes and college admission and graduation rates (Dougherty et al., 2006). With this in mind, Gary wondered, "What are the implications for my students of offering a guaranteed C for completing assigned work, regardless of quiz and test performance in the AP classes I teach?"

The exercises at the end of this section help you explore, like Gary, Carlee, and Julie did, who you are as a person and teacher. They will serve as precursors to the development of wonderings that might emerge from your prior life experiences and intersect your personal and professional identities.

PASSION 6 EXERCISES

1. Write your own autobiography. Discuss the development of your own interests and passions. Finally, discuss the factors that led to your chosen career field as a teacher.

2. Design a timeline of your growth and development as a person and a teacher, beginning with your birth and noting years and dates of critical incidents that impacted your personal and professional life.

3. Follow the guide provided to design a teacher's coat of arms. In Space 1, draw a real or mythical animal that best describes the teacher you want to be. In Space 2, choose a real symbol, or create your own design, for an insignia that best describes the teacher you want to be. In Space 3, choose one color in any shade—or a rainbow effect—that best describes the teacher you want to be. In Space 4, draw one character, real or fictional, that best describes the teacher you want to be. In Space 5, choose one word that best describes the teacher you want to be. How you write that word should also help to describe the teacher you want to be.

Exhibit for Exercise 3

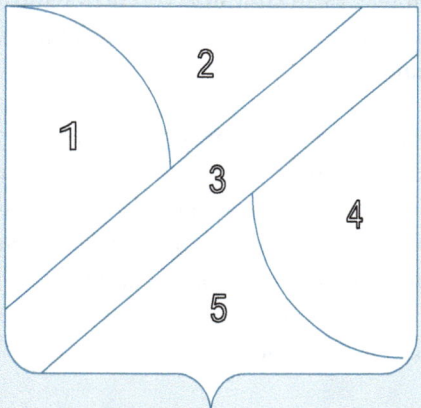

Passion 7: Advocating for Equity and Social Justice

Up until this point in the chapter, the six passions we have explored led many teachers to develop a wondering related to the creation of more equitable schooling and learning experiences for the children they teach. A concept that is very closely related to equity is social justice, a construct commonly defined as "principles of fairness and equality for all people and respect for their basic human rights" (Sensoy & DiAngelo, 2017, p. xix). Scholars Ozlem Sensoy and Robin DiAngelo (2017) point out that while most people agree with this common definition, a gap exists between the ideals and practice of social justice. For this reason, these educational leaders introduce a critical approach to social justice that illuminates the connection between social justice and equity:

> A critical approach to social justice refers to specific theoretical perspectives that recognize that society is *stratified* (i.e., divided and unequal) in significant and far-reaching ways along social group lines that include race, class, gender, sexuality, and ability. Critical social justice recognizes inequality as deeply embedded in the fabric of society (i.e., as structural) and actively seeks to change this. (Sensoy and DiAngelo, 2017, p. xx)

Many teacher researchers begin the process of wondering development with a critical social justice lens. This lens is related to the notion explored in Chapter 1 that engaging in inquiry is a responsibility you accept as a teacher that enables you to take a stand and effect educational change. By generating data and evidence to support the decisions and positions you take as an educator, you help reform classrooms and schools, which results in the promotion of social justice. According to Cochran-Smith and Lytle:

> When teachers research their own practice . . . they begin to envision alternative configurations of human and material resources to meet the needs of culturally diverse groups of students, teachers, and administrators. And they are willing to invest more of their own resources and professional energy in larger efforts to reform classrooms and schools. (Cochran-Smith & Lytle, 1993, p. 80)

Your first teacher inquiry wondering may come from your desire to effect social change by exploring questions of race, class, gender, sexuality, or ability. In fact, effecting social change in regard to issues of social justice may indeed become the focus for your entire teaching career. Inquiry can be a powerful vehicle that begins your journey working toward this goal.

Entire school districts have used the action research process to focus on equity, race, and closing gaps in opportunity and academic achievement between groups of students. For example, as mentioned in Chapter 1, the Madison (Wisconsin) Metropolitan School District has published a collection of teacher research authored by teachers within their district focused on creating equitable classrooms through action research (Caro-Bruce et al., 2007). These excellent examples range in scope "from a close study of one child and how his elementary teacher adapted instructional practices to ensure school success to a study of how a high school science department changed inclusive practices in an effort to eliminate tracking" (Caro-Bruce et al., 2007, p. 3). We highly recommend this text, as well as a special issue of *Journal of Practitioner Research* (https://scholarcommons.usf.edu/jpr/vol2/iss2/) that celebrated the 10-year anniversary of the publication of this book with updated examples of teachers using the process of inquiry to uncover and disrupt inequitable schooling practices (Dana & Currin, 2017). These readings illuminate the significance of the student and teacher learning that can occur when teachers use action research to better understand issues of social justice and educational equity from inside classrooms and schools.

In addition to the insightful pieces of teacher research published in this book and journal, in this chapter we provide three examples from elementary, middle, and high school contexts, respectively, that illustrate teachers beginning their inquiry journeys motivated by addressing complex questions derived from a critical social justice perspective.

In the first example, teaching intern Andrea Hosfeld begins her journey toward exploring questions related to teaching for social justice by reflecting on her own childhood experiences:

> As a child growing up in the 1980s, I believed that the world was a place where anyone with an aspiration could succeed with determination. It was a time when poverty and racism were covered by a thick haze of rhetoric. Men and women of every race and nationality need only believe that their dreams would be realized and it would be so. In high school I began to see, for the very first time, that the world was not so fair and just as I had always assumed. I found myself experiencing feelings of powerlessness and vulnerability. As a female, in particular, I felt boxed in by society's expectations and constraints.
>
> Upon escaping from high school, I began to replace my pessimism with passion. I started to conduct research and read interesting books that spoke of the hopelessness and hatred pervading our world. For the past four years, I have spent a great deal of time educating myself and grappling with difficult issues involving race, class, and gender. Part of my decision to become a teacher was influenced by my desire to introduce children to these issues. It was my hope that while portraying an honest though sometimes grim picture of humanity, I might also replace blind acceptance with a sense of empowerment and a hunger for change.

> I knew very early on in the year that I wanted to engage my students in antibias activities and lessons that would build on each other throughout the year. Identifying the question I was seeking to answer, however, proved to be a very long and searching process. Although I'd read multiple theorists that suggested children were capable of engaging in lessons of this nature, I didn't really have any first-hand experience. I was comforted by the words of Louis Derman-Sparks, who stated, "We know enough not to underestimate the power of children to perceive the negative messages in their world or the power of those messages to harm them" (Derman-Sparks, 1989, p. 10).
>
> Initially, I had many questions: Are third graders capable of discussing difficult and controversial issues? How do I begin to engage them in this process? Which activities lend themselves to such an exploration? I answered several of these questions in the first few months of my inquiry and my original queries were replaced by more complex questions. I wanted to know the role of developmentally appropriate practice in implementing an antibias curriculum approach as well as the role of the district curriculum in determining the events and issues I could introduce. It was only in analyzing and reflecting on the data I'd collected that I realized the wondering I was pursuing. What began as a project primarily geared toward the thoughts and ideas of children became an inquiry into my own evolution as a teacher of antibias curriculum. (Hosfeld, 2000)

Andrea's commitment to issues of social justice emerged out of her own political stance and ideology demonstrating the intersection between the role of teacher beliefs and inquiry into issues of social justice.

Andrea's work presents another important lesson about finding and developing your first wondering. She notes that her questions changed and emerged over time. This is a very common occurrence in teacher research. Therefore, understand that as you work diligently to find, refine, and study your first inquiry question, your question(s) may change and emerge. This is a totally natural part of the inquiry process. Consequently, as you proceed with your inquiry you may find that the question you originally developed no longer suits your work or captures the most powerful components of what you are learning. Remember, you may still be finding your question. Be prepared to recognize and embrace an emerging question by remaining calm and flexible. You can return to your original questions and modify or change them throughout the duration of your inquiry.

In our second example, middle school teacher and reading coach Joan Thate finds her first inquiry question by reflecting on populations that historically have not performed well on academic achievement tests at her school:

> The achievement gap: the problem is nationally pervasive and perennially stubborn and the questions are numerous and enormous. Our school is no exception. For as many years as records have been available, our school has had two populations that have not performed well on our state standardized tests in reading or math: Exceptional Student Education (ESE) students and African American students, particularly males. My concern was with Black males who were not identified as ESE, and therefore shouldn't have (theoretically, at least) any physical reason why they can't read perfectly well.
>
> We know that many students at our school come from backgrounds where reading was not modeled or materially supported. We also know that many come from circumstances where scarcity and lack of variety of parent–child verbal interactions left them linguistically well behind their peers the first day they appeared at school. Obviously, these things we cannot change. Looking into and working on some of the things we might try, things we *can* change, was where I needed to begin. We must break the cycle, and I see the middle school years as offering our last likely chance.
>
> In such a short time span as the inquiry provided, the major questions needed to be pared down to monitoring one action that might help at least point to a direction we might take at the middle school level to begin to turn some of these students into less-reluctant, more-resilient, and more-comprehending readers—the kind of readers who cannot only survive our state's standardized reading test with some skill and confidence, but also emerge as people who pick up and read a book because they choose to, not because they must. Until a reader reads by choice, I do not believe we can accurately say they are readers, even though they may decode and comprehend adequately.

Our school storage areas are littered with the debris of unsuccessful attempts to address and remedy the problem, concrete proof that many advertised panaceas simply did not work—and in some cases, apparently aggravated the problem. I have read a considerable amount of opinion and research on this subject (see, e.g., Allington, 2006; Fashola, 2005; Lesesne, 2003; Tatum, 2005). The most consistent finding of all reading research is that the most valuable contribution schools can make to their developing readers is providing the right books and the time for students to read them. One of the points that many writers and researchers make is that much of what reluctant readers, most particularly adolescent Black males, are asked or required to read in school is neither engaging nor culturally relevant for them.

Now, I am not a proponent of the idea that everything one reads should mirror his own experiences and life. As a matter of fact, one of the most important reasons to read is to expand the experience and understanding of people, places, times, and cultures that are different from what is known. But perhaps, if virtually *no* reading matter is ever introduced that does relate to the reader's life, reading can seem dry, alien, irrelevant—a school thing that can't and doesn't and won't ever touch what is closest to him. And we all know that we return to and practice what brings us some joy, some satisfaction, some meaning.

Therefore, I started looking for lists of reading that featured African American males as central characters, or had been written by African American males, or biographical stories, books, or articles based on famous or not-so-famous African Americans who had made significant contributions in some way. From the writings of Alfred Tatum (2005) and others came some good suggestions. We also had experienced some positive responses to a series of books from Townsend Press, the Bluford Series. This series of (currently) thirteen books is set in an urban high school named after the first Black astronaut. The plots are based on the kinds of problems all kids face: peer pressure to participate in illegal activities, family problems such as divorce, difficulties with friends or girlfriend/boyfriend relationships, and school problems, including bullying. The books are thin, written on a sixth-grade level, and feature minority faces on the covers. The two sets we had brought into the school from a reading conference last year had caught on immediately with struggling readers in one class. I now had some ideas for books to start ordering.

Thus, my question became, "In what ways will offering more culturally relevant materials improve the relationship of this constituency with reading?" Collateral questions also emerged: "Will these nonreaders read more and less reluctantly because they have such material to read?," "Can we provide enough books to test the theory?," "Is providing, presenting, and promoting culturally relevant materials a direction we should explore in more depth as a means of enticing this group to read more and therefore become better readers?" And, "What might be some effective ways of introducing and incorporating this material?" (Thate, 2007)

Joan's work presents yet another important lesson regarding finding your wondering. Note that in framing her wonderings, Joan drew on literature in the field of reading research (Allington, 2006; Fashola, 2005; Lesesne, 2003; Tatum, 2005). Joan's knowledge of the reading research literature helped her craft her inquiry question to target reluctant African American middle school male readers in order to get the right books to them at the right time. The core concept of Joan's inquiry (providing the right books and the time to read them) came directly from research on reading and therefore situated Joan's inquiry in the larger knowledge base on learning to read. When teacher researchers do not connect and situate their studies to what is already known, we risk powerful and meaningful teacher research becoming an unsystematic piling up of accounts of learning that have occurred in individual classrooms. While it can be powerful for individual teachers, such research does not contribute to the larger discussion in the educational literature. We also risk missing some important knowledge that may contribute to the way we frame our research questions and subsequently design our research. For this reason, we suggest that all teacher researchers draw on the literature in the finding and framing of their wondering (as illustrated by Joan in the example earlier) as well as throughout the entirety of the inquiry process. We'll further discuss the role of literature in Chapter 4.

In our final example, high school assistant principal Dana Schmidt was participating in a schoolwide inquiry community focused on learning to address difficult topics and issues (Dvir et al., 2023; Rutten et al., 2023, 2024). The community's focus naturally lent itself to the examination of practice using a social justice lens. Dana reflects on her experience being a member of this community and the discoveries she made as her wondering transformed throughout the inquiry process:

> In the wake of the COVID-19 pandemic during which time systemic racism was being further illuminated, I was fortunate to be offered a professional development opportunity to participate with colleagues in an inquiry learning community. Serving as one of three assistant principals, the responsibility for student discipline positioned me uniquely in this space to explore something I noticed that was troubling not only to me, but the teachers in our inquiry community as well. At our school, the number of students skipping class and being referred to the office for disciplinary action had increased dramatically since the onset of the pandemic, which often led to exclusionary actions such as detentions or suspensions. Hence, from the very start of my work in this inquiry community, I contemplated and pitched a collaborative, building-wide inquiry to my colleagues. My wondering, as it initially read, was "How can we reduce class cuts and office referrals in our building?"
>
> Working with colleagues throughout my building, especially with our Positive Behavior Interventions and Supports (PBIS) team, we gathered quantitative data from our school district's PBIS tracking system, examined recent office referral data, and looked at attendance records. My initial action was to meet with a group of teachers on our Professional Growth Team (PGT) and share my insights. In that meeting, consensus was built that hall passes should be used consistently. We introduced clearer expectations to students, implemented our plan, and over 85 percent of students showed a decrease in this behavior.
>
> Thankfully, however, my colleagues both inside and outside of the inquiry community pushed me to ask more questions about the remaining 15 percent. I reframed my question to ask, "Why do students cut class and get referred to the office—and why are traditional consequences ineffective?" With a new question, the inquiry community also pushed me to consider qualitative sources of insight in addition to the quantitative data I had already explored and to integrate an asset-based lens as my inquiry proceeded. In response, I started walking through the school hallways to observe, finding it to be a valuable source of qualitative data. As I got

out into the hallways more frequently, I started to notice the places where kids cutting class tended to congregate—such as under stairwells and near vending machines. I mapped those places, then, rather than referring them to the office, conducted mini-interviews with the students I encountered.

Through conducting mini-interviews with students, I gained valuable insights into equity within our school. Analyzing student demographics revealed a concerning trend: A disproportionate number of students were referred to the office for class cuts and disrespect due to teachers addressing dress code violations. Further investigation, through building stronger relationships with students, revealed that many of these "class cuts" were not intentional. Students were often avoiding class to escape confrontations stemming from nondisruptive dress code violations, such as wearing hats or hoods.

This led to the discovery that our school's current discipline policy—regardless of its original intentions—was disproportionately punishing students, resulting in significant loss of opportunities-to-learn due to nondisruptive behavior such as a dress code violation. When I presented these data back to my teacher colleagues, the consensus was quick to emerge that a policy change was needed. I reframed my inquiry yet again to ask the question, "How can I, as assistant principal, collaborate with teachers to update the school's discipline policy to eliminate the 'hats and hoods' restriction for students who were not disrupting anyone's opportunity to learn?" When the inquiry was brought to the administrative team, my principal acknowledged that the dress code policy was inadvertently causing a discipline problem due to confrontations between students and staff yet did not have any impact on instruction. As I delved deeper, my initial questions evolved, leading to a deeper understanding of the issues and ultimately, a positive change within our school. I may not have had the perfect question or the perfect inquiry, but it's led to real progress in my school. I am currently collecting data to see how our policy change is impacting students and can't wait to see what the next iteration of my question will be.

Dana's inquiry reiterates the important lesson about wondering development gleaned from the first example of Andrea Hosfeld in this section: A question can modify and change as an inquiry cycle unfolds. Although refining a question is important, as noted in the definition of a wondering itself we introduced at the start of this chapter (*A wondering is an intentionally refined question that frames and focuses an inquiry*), the point of inquiry is not to define a single question, refined to perfection, and then answer it. In fact, if a question is well formed through the refinement process, it will likely not lead to a single, definitive answer anyway, as the question will honor all the great complexities inherent in the act of teaching. Rather, teachers inquire to *gain insights* into their questions, act on those insights, and develop new (and perhaps better) questions to explore. In Dana's case, the evolution of her questions reflects the ways inquiry can unearth hidden assumptions and issues about teaching and learning that pervade schools. In so doing, inquiry becomes a catalyst for social change.

Dana's inquiry offers two new additional lessons as well. First, Dana inquired as a part of a community, collaborating with other teachers on her inquiry. Collaboration plays an important role in the inquiry process, a point to which we will return in Chapter 4. Second, question development and the collection and analysis of data are often intricately intertwined with one another. We will also return to this point in the chapters ahead.

PASSION 7 EXERCISES

1. Look closely at the demographics of the students you teach. Pick a subset of them (e.g., gender, race, class, or ability) and pay particular attention to them during the day. Record in a journal your general observations and emerging questions. Do these children all experience schooling in a similar way?

2. Brainstorm a list of units/topics you teach. Investigate the content of the resources you are using to teach these units. What perspectives seem to be present or missing (e.g., gender, race, class, or ability)? Then analyze each unit by asking yourself how these resources and activities support diversity, democracy, and literacy opportunities for all students.

3. Write down your philosophy of how you prepare your students to become democratic citizens. What role does teaching children about democracy play in your classroom? To what extent does your classroom encourage the development of participation and character traits central to a democratic citizen?

Passion 8: Focus on Understanding the Teaching and Learning Context

An important feature of teacher inquiry is that inquiry occurs within a specific context. That context represents a particular classroom within a particular school, within a particular community, within a particular state or province, within a particular country, and within a particular moment in time. Context is so important to the development of your question that we will return to your consideration of it later in the text. However, context as the final passion in this chapter, represents the fact that some teachers' felt difficulties emerge as a result of contextual characteristics that influence their teaching. Once again, we present three examples from elementary, middle school, and high school, respectively, that illustrate how three teachers' wonderings were generated by contextual factors. As you read the examples, note that while reflection on context sparked their wondering development, you will find elements that relate to the definition of critical social justice and equity defined in the previous section.

Kelly Herrera is a second-grade teacher and doctoral student at the University of North Dakota. As in many school districts, the COVID-19 pandemic created significant disruptions to existing routines of teaching and learning in her public school district in west central Minnesota. In the pandemic's wake, the United States Congress passed American Rescue Plan Act (ARPA) emergency pandemic relief legislation, which included Elementary and Secondary School Emergency Relief (ESSER) funding. In Kelly's district, an influx of federal funding, at least during the height of COVID-19, provided enhanced support to meet students' immediate needs, but new challenges arose as the funds ran low.

During the 2023–2024 school year, teachers in Kelly's school were charged with implementing a new literacy curriculum and a new approach to restorative disciplinary practices. At the same time, they faced an acute and growing shortage of well-qualified substitute teachers and paraprofessionals, and a reduction of student support by social workers and behavioral specialists. An August 2023 district survey indicated that a metric of teachers' overall well-being was slipping. By 2024, the ESSER funds had run out, and Kelly's school district began to prepare for budget cutbacks, which entailed reductions in teachers' professional preparation time and layoffs in the educator workforce—all while teachers were navigating a state-mandated series of trainings on a new approach to literacy instruction.

There was no one, single contextual factor that sparked Kelly's inquiry. However, as she described the seemingly endless waves of change and stress that were affecting the context for teaching and learning in her district, Kelly shared, "all of these felt, real-world tensions led me to wonder, 'How can I support the well-being of my colleagues?'"

While there were several contextual factors associated with Kelly's school context that led to her wondering, sometimes it is a single factor, such as the makeup of the students in a classroom or school, that leads teachers to develop wonderings related to their community context. These wonderings relate to understanding the diverse cultures within the classroom and school community in order to provide better instruction, enhance communication, or develop stronger relationships.

In our second example, seventh-grade civics teacher Darby Delane and her teaching colleagues at Kanapaha Middle School began noticing changes to their student population as the first ripples of the school choice movement became real in their area, followed by the housing and banking crisis of the 2000s. At Darby's school, the number of students living in poverty was increasing, and their more economically privileged students were leaving for private schools, charter schools, and magnet programs. In tandem with the demographic shift in student population, teachers also noticed more student misconduct, which frequently ended in the exclusion of students from their classrooms. Most of the repeatedly excluded students were Black and brown, and most of them lived in economically distressed neighborhoods.

Faculty and administration were troubled over the new pattern they saw forming: They were excluding mostly Black students and perpetuating the kinds of inequitable practices that were already so pervasive in other schools throughout the United States. And so they wondered, "What is going on here?" Looking at classic literature on middle school education, they were reminded that relationships with students are critical to the success of early adolescents, and from the literature they also learned that a key to developing relationships with one another was understanding each other as cultural beings. Darby reflected:

> You see, our school's educators were mostly White, female, and middle class, while our chronically disciplined students were mostly Black or brown and living in poverty. We had

to have the courage to make relationships our first priority once again, and learn with and from each other about our different cultures, and how they impact the ways we behave as teachers and students in the classroom. As a team consisting of teachers, administrators, and—here's the twist—our most chronically disciplined students themselves, we engaged in a collaborative inquiry to explore the question, "How can sustained lunchtime conversations about culture between teachers, students, and administrators improve educator–student relationships?" (Dana et al., 2017)

A close look at a changing school demographic context led Darby, her colleagues, and her students to engage in a collaborative inquiry to purposefully examine and fix the *exclusion* of students from classroom learning experiences. Sometimes an examination of context can also shape what teachers *include* in the curriculum, and the process of inquiry can be used to help them untangle the complexities of creating an inclusive environment for *all* learners in their classrooms. For example, in response to research documenting schools as unwelcoming and unsafe places for most LGBT students (Kosciw et al., 2015), Jill Hermann-Wilmarth and Caitlin Ryan (2015) discuss the role context plays for teachers considering ways to address LGBT topics in language arts curricula:

> When we tell our preservice teacher students that they can address lesbian, gay, bisexual, and/or transgender (LGBT) topics in language arts curricula, we watch the questions and protests forming in their heads create unsure looks on their faces. A few are eager, but many others have serious concerns: Would administration allow it? Aren't those books banned? Is it appropriate for kids to talk about those topics in schools? And, most emphatically, what about the parents? These questions and concerns stem from fear and perhaps their own discomfort with LGBT topics, but also from the knowledge that, when it comes to teaching, especially about identity and difference, *context matters*. (Hermann-Wilmarth & Ryan, 2015, p. 436)

In our last example, ninth-grade language arts teacher Cody Miller uses the process of inquiry to introduce LGBTQ literature into his classroom context as well as examine contextual factors that impact how students respond to it. Over a five-year period, Cody worked with a team of teachers to weave Young Adult Literature (YAL) into the fabric of the English language arts (ELA) curriculum at their school. Cody and his colleagues reflected:

> YAL offers students opportunities to read about experiences and characters that are different from their own and see themselves in their ELA curriculum. In other words, YAL provides what Bishop (1990) calls "mirrors [and] windows," literature that allows students to see themselves in what they read as well as gain perspective from people different from themselves. Bishop's clarion call has been vital to our own ELA curriculum as have more recent calls to expand the definition of multicultural literature to include religious and sexual minorities as well as people with disabilities and people living outside the United States (Temple et al., 2014). Our school has a diverse student population extend[ing] beyond state indicators: we have students who identify as LGBTQ, students who are immigrants or whose parents are immigrants, students who practice a minority religion, and students who are adopted. We believe it would be unethical to create and implement curriculum that does not include the voices of people like our students. Therefore, we believe that curriculum should be treated as a living and evolving entity that should be nurtured and revised as student populations shift. Many classic texts are Eurocentric and reflect a limited worldview. Fortunately, YAL provides an opportunity for our curriculum to be as diverse as our student body. (Colantonio-Yurko et al., 2017, p. 4)

To actualize his colleagues' and his own commitment to creating a curriculum as diverse as their student body, among other texts, Cody introduced to his ninth-grade students the reading of YAL with LGBTQ characters such as Sara Farizan's *If You Could Be Mine* (2013) and *Tell Me Again How a Crush Should Feel* (2015). With the Supreme Court decision *Obergefell v. Hodges* occurring shortly after texts featuring LGBTQ characters were placed in the hands of his students, as well as topics such as transgender students' access to bathrooms in schools being featured in the news, Cody was interested in exploring the ways his students were making sense of LGBTQ literature in relation to current events and how he might adjust his teaching in light of what he learned. And so, Cody wondered, "How do students respond to LGBTQ texts in our current political climate?" (Miller, 2018). Through this inquiry, Cody worked to create a classroom "where his students felt they belonged and could reach their full potential," while acknowledging the act of doing so "will depend on teachers themselves, their students, their curriculum, and their context" (Hermann-Wilmarth & Ryan, 2015, p. 442).

In addition to the examples related to context shared from elementary, middle school, and high school classrooms, one final note on how context can be the source of an inquiry question emerges across all grade levels as teachers respond to state and national accountability pressures and policy. Many teachers in states where pressure from high-stakes testing seems to dominate the culture of the district and schools wonder, "How can we make learning relevant and motivating in a context where testing seems to dominate curriculum and scheduling?" and "How can I maintain an inclusive classroom when high-stakes testing seems to encourage noninclusive practices?" As teachers recognize the role of context and its impact on their teaching, they can use inquiry to identify ways to accommodate, merge, or deflect contextual influences that affect their work in the classroom. Teacher inquirers can also use their research as an "important means through which to expose the various sources of tension between policy and teaching, as well as to elucidate the impact of education policies on teachers' practice" (Rust & Meyers, 2006, p. 69). Teacher inquiry provides context-sensitive tools to accomplish these tasks.

PASSION 8 EXERCISES

1. Make a three-column list.

CHALLENGE WITHIN YOUR CONTEXT	FELT DIFFICULTY	WONDERING

After brainstorming a list of contextual challenges, identify the frustrations that you can potentially influence at either a student, classroom, or school level.

As indicated, these eight passions are not discrete entities, and as noted early in this chapter, any single wondering one develops within the exploration of one passion can end up relating to another passion or multiple passions. We offer these eight passions not to classify wonderings but instead as lenses for looking at your own teaching. As you use the passions as lenses, think about each passion as a pair of glasses you try on. For example, if you try on the "social justice glasses," you analyze your classroom by looking at issues of race, class, gender, sexuality, or ability. If you try on the "child glasses," you analyze your teaching from the perspective of the students you teach. It may be that as you analyze your teaching from the perspective of the children you teach, you uncover issues of race, class, gender, sexuality, or ability in your classroom, and your wondering emerges related to social justice. Developing an inquiry stance toward teaching relies on teachers becoming active in problematizing each of the lenses or passions and understanding the interrelations between them, while simultaneously keeping in mind the underlying goal of engagement in inquiry: making schools a more equitable place for *all* learners. These multiple lenses provide teacher candidates and practicing teachers with a framework for systematically examining their daily work.

What Are the Next Steps in Wondering Development?

The examination of your daily work through the eight passion lenses generates multiple possibilities for the direction of your inquiry and the wonderings you may wish to explore. At this point you are probably thinking, "How will I narrow down the possibilities and ultimately zero-in on *the* question I wish to explore?" In Chapter 4, we will address this question as we guide you through the creation of an all-inclusive plan for your inquiry that involves intentionally honing in on, refining, and wordsmithing the question that will serve to frame, focus, and anchor your inquiry. In the meantime, however, we invite you to begin the honing in process by discussing the exploration of the eight passions completed in this chapter with one or more colleagues, as the exploration of these passions can become more provocative if you collaboratively discuss them with others. For example, if you are a veteran teacher, you might discuss the passions with your teammates, resource teachers, administrators, or university partners. You might also use AI as a critical friend to dialogue with, as illustrated in this chapter's AI Moment textbox, "Using a Chatbot to Expand Your Thinking and Uncover New Perspectives Related to Your Wonderings," located at the end of this chapter. The following excerpt, where intern Lisa Malaggese describes how the dialogue she had with her mentor teacher related to the development of her question, indicates how talking with others can help move the development of your wondering forward:

> "What are you planning to do for your inquiry project?" As my mentor, Christina, asked me this question, my mind was pretty blank. It was something I had thought about numerous times before, but I had not found anything that had jumped out at me. When the inquiry project had been initially described to us, it sounded as though the topic for my inquiry would be as obvious as a blinking neon sign. For some people, I am sure that this is how they come upon the topics for their inquiries. I saw no such blinking sign. When I searched my brain, looking for possible wonderings, nothing really stood out as something that I desperately wanted to find the answers to.
>
> So, when Christina asked me this question, I told her I honestly did not know. She mentioned that something she had always been interested in was taking a more in-depth approach to teaching fractions to first graders. At first I said that could be interesting, but that I was not sure what I wanted to do yet. Christina made it clear that it was my decision and that she would help me with whatever I decided to do. I was still waiting for my neon sign. As our classes devoted to inquiry started, with my neon sign nowhere in sight, I started thinking more about Christina's fraction idea.
>
> "Teaching fractions to first graders could be interesting," I thought. The mathematics education course I had taken had left me with a lot of unanswered questions about how to teach mathematics. Even though there is a big focus in my mentor's classroom on the children's understanding of mathematical concepts, I still did not feel confident with my ability to teach math. I decided that the questions I had and my lack of confidence could best be addressed through the actual teaching and designing of math lessons. I hoped that the information I learned about teaching mathematics would also hold true for other subject areas. That way, I could improve my teaching, and thereby my confidence in teaching in all subject areas.
>
> After much consideration, I decided to go ahead with exploring fractions. All right, I had a topic. Now what? What was it *really* that I was trying to find out? After brainstorming

with Christina, we came up with our overall question: "Can fractions be taught conceptually to primary students?" I was very proud of that question until it was pointed out to me that it could be a question that could be easily answered with a simple "yes" or "no." I reworked the question; and my official wonderings became, "How do I teach fractions conceptually, and what are the impacts of that teaching on the different learners in my classroom?"

At that point, I would not say I was exactly jumping with excitement about my topic. However, I knew it was something that would prove to be interesting and challenging. I think some of my initial lack of excitement stemmed from my disappointment that my neon sign had never come. Little did I know that it really was there; I just had not turned on the switch yet! (Malaggese, 2001)

Lisa's excerpt presents two final important lessons that serve as a preview to the work you will do in Chapter 4 to finalize your question. First, note how Lisa reframed her first wondering from a dichotomous yes/no question (e.g., "Can fractions be taught conceptually to primary students?") to an open-ended "How do I?" and accompanying companion question (e.g., "How do I teach fractions conceptually, and what are the impacts of that teaching on the different learners in my classroom?"). As foreshadowed through the examples in this chapter, teacher researchers do not eloquently state their wonderings immediately. It takes time, brainstorming, and actually playing with your question, something through which we will guide you in Chapter 4. As we end this chapter, then, we learn from Lisa that it is important to be patient with careful articulation of your wondering(s). By playing with the wording of your question, you often fine-tune and discover more detail about the subject you are really passionate about understanding.

Finally, notice in Lisa's case that sometimes a passion for your work will not independently develop from the outset of your inquiry journey. Yet, based on our years of experience helping teacher candidates and practicing teachers engage in inquiry for the first time, we are confident that, as in Lisa's case earlier, a passion for your work will develop.

Sometimes that passion comes from the examination of data. Classroom teachers have access to a wealth of naturally occurring data that can serve as a rich resource for identifying their inquiry wonderings. As you interact with your students daily, you gather observations, assessments, and reflections that provide insights into their unique needs, strengths, and challenges. These data aren't always formal; they can be found in casual conversations, student work samples, behavior patterns, or even the way a student approaches a task. By paying close attention to these naturally occurring data, you can begin to identify patterns or recurring issues that might inform your wonderings. For instance, are there particular students who struggle consistently with certain types of tasks? Does a specific teaching strategy seem to resonate well with some students but not others? These observations can help you formulate inquiry questions that are grounded in the real-world context of your classroom, making your inquiry more relevant and actionable. Hence, in the next chapter, we take an intentional sidestep in the development of your wondering by exploring another component of the inquiry process—data collection.

Using a Chatbot to Expand Your Thinking and Uncover New Perspectives Related to Your Wonderings

AI MOMENT

As computer programs designed to simulate human-like conversation with users via AI and natural language processing, chatbots can become valuable virtual assistants for the teacher inquirer during the initial wondering development stage. Many chatbots are available, such as ChatGPT and Microsoft Copilot, as the development of these virtual assistant applications continues to advance at a rapid pace. Whatever application you choose to use, a chatbot can be enormously helpful to expand your thinking and uncover new perspectives related to your wondering.

Teaching can often feel like an isolating endeavor, especially when facing persistent challenges and trying to innovate your practice through the development of an inquiry question. Sometimes you just need a fresh perspective or a way to get "unstuck." This is where a chatbot can step in as a helpful tool. What if you shared your current passion(s) and related problems of practice with a chatbot and asked it to offer new questions or a different perspective on the issue? A chatbot can act as a "friend," helping you to think more deeply or explore an area from a fresh angle.

For example, if you're a veteran teacher, you may have already discussed the passions presented in this chapter with teammates, resource

(Continued)

(Continued)

teachers, administrators, or university partners. If you're a teacher candidate, you may have already chatted about the passions with your peers, your mentor teacher, and/or your professors. And if you are a masters or doctoral student, you may have already conversed about the passions throughout your program experiences. However, by using a chatbot as a dialogue partner, you can expand the range of ideas and questions that shape your inquiry. An added bonus is that chatbots are always safe and trusted friends—you don't have to worry about a chatbot judging you, and conversations are always confidential. AI can offer perspectives that might otherwise remain unexplored and help you refine your thinking as you develop and work through an inquiry question.

For example, let's imagine a teacher who is passionate about understanding how to support an individual student with a different cultural background and promote more social interaction between this student and their peers (Passion 1). Here's a simulation (drawn from an actual chatbot interaction) of how a chatbot might support the teacher in expanding their thinking:

Teacher: I have a fourth-grade student from a different cultural background than the other students in my class, and I'm passionate about finding ways to promote social interaction between this student and their classmates. I want to integrate the student's cultural traditions into the classroom more effectively. What can I do? Please ask me some questions to help me think about this student and my teaching. I am seeking help expanding my thinking and not just looking for a list of teaching strategies.

Chatbot: That's an important and thoughtful focus! How do you think your student currently feels about their place within the classroom? Are there specific interactions or behaviors you've noticed from the student or their peers that might give you insight into what barriers exist?

Teacher: The student is often quiet and doesn't initiate much with peers. I've introduced some cultural elements like their holidays and language, but I'm not sure it's had a real impact on building social interactions.

Chatbot: It might help to explore how your student's peers perceive these cultural elements. Could you create opportunities for the class to engage in more interactive activities around the

	student's cultural traditions? How could these activities spark curiosity and encourage deeper connections between the student and their classmates?
Teacher:	I like the idea, but I don't think a big project will work. I'm more focused on making small, meaningful changes in daily routines—like incorporating the student's traditional music or greetings into the morning circle. A large project might feel overwhelming or even isolating for the student.
Chatbot:	That's a great point! Small, consistent changes could definitely create more natural integration of the student's culture into the classroom environment. How do you think incorporating these elements into daily routines might change how the student interacts with their peers?
Teacher:	I think it would make the student feel more included and make the cultural practices feel like a regular part of the class, rather than something special that stands out. But I also want to make sure the other students understand why we're doing this. I'm not sure how to approach that without making it seem forced.
Chatbot:	That's a valid concern. How about introducing a conversation about cultural diversity as part of your classroom's regular discussions on respect and community? You could frame it in a way that encourages curiosity and appreciation, without singling out the student. What do you think?
Teacher:	I don't know. I worry about explicitly talking about one student's culture. It might make the student feel more self-conscious. I'm leaning toward a more subtle approach, where cultural elements just naturally become part of the classroom routine, without a big discussion.
Chatbot:	That's completely understandable. A subtle approach can also be effective in fostering inclusion. Maybe you can gauge how the students are responding over time and adjust if necessary. Do you think integrating some reflective activities—like journaling about their experiences discussing culture—could help students process these changes in their own way without making it a formal discussion?
Teacher:	I like that idea. Journaling could give students a way to think about cultural differences privately, without putting anyone

(Continued)

(Continued)

> on the spot. I think I'll try that as a quiet, personal reflection piece. I am planning to study my actions through practitioner inquiry and will now develop a wondering, defined as an intentionally refined question that frames and focuses an inquiry. Can you now push me more on my wondering? What potential downsides could there be to my current plan to subtly integrate learning about a student's cultural traditions into existing classroom routines? Please identify important factors I might be overlooking in this situation.

At this point in the conversation, the chatbot provided a lengthy response, helping the teacher approach the development of their wondering from a more critical angle. This AI-generated response noted and explained three potential downsides to the teacher's current approach (superficial integration, unintentional signaling out, limited peer engagement), three overlooked factors (student agency and comfort, peer readiness, whole-class cultural learning), and additional considerations the teacher might wish to contemplate as wondering development continues.

The above private conversation demonstrates how chatbots can serve as a sounding board and critical friend, helping teacher inquirers consider different strategies while respecting their preferences and concerns, even when there is chatbot–teacher inquirer disagreement and a teacher wants to go in a different direction. The teacher's initial hesitation to adopt the chatbot's guidance leads this teacher to a more nuanced understanding of the complexity inherent in the problem of practice from which the wondering was emerging, resulting in the teacher proceeding to develop a rich inquiry question that focuses on both subtle cultural integration and reflective activities that align with the teacher's goals and the classroom's needs. By engaging in this judgment-free back-and-forth with the chatbot, this teacher began the process of refining an emerging wondering, staying grounded in their passion for understanding students and promoting social interaction in a way that feels right for their classroom.

As you end this chapter, consider engaging in a chatbot dialogue like the one shared in this first AI Moment textbox. You can save your chat and return to it later in the book as you continue to develop your wondering.

For more on wondering development, skip ahead to Chapter 4, Inquiry Planning Stage 1, on page 160.

DISCUSSION QUESTIONS

1. What are some common real-world dilemmas teachers face each day? What types of initial questions do these dilemmas raise?

2. Which of the eight passions (A Child, Curriculum, Content Knowledge, Teaching Strategies/Techniques, Beliefs About Practice, Personal/Professional Identities, Equity/Social Justice, and Context) do you feel will serve as the most important spark to explore potential wonderings at this point in your professional lifetime? Why?

3. Which of the eight passions (A Child, Curriculum, Content Knowledge, Teaching Strategies/Techniques, Beliefs About Practice, Personal/Professional Identities, Equity/Social Justice, and Context) do you feel will serve as the least important spark to explore potential wonderings at this point in your professional lifetime? Why?

4. Which examples presented within the passion exploration related to equity and social justice did you most connect with? Why? How might an exploration of equity and social justice, informed by data as in the case of Dana Schmidt, naturally emerge from a wondering within each of the passions?

ONLINE MATERIALS

The following materials designed to facilitate wondering development are available for download at **https://companion.corwin.com/courses/ReflectiveEdsGuide5e:**

(Continued)

(Continued)

- **Activity 2.1: The Great Wondering Brainstorm.** Brainstorm possible wonderings related to your passions.

- **Activity 2.2: Passion Jigsaw.** Divide and conquer learning about the passions that can fuel your inquiry with others.

- **Activity 2.3: Passions Protocol.** Discuss the passion most associated with selecting education as your career.

Data Collection

Making Inquiry a Part of Your Teaching Practice

3

The wondering you began to develop in the previous chapter will become the north star for your inquiry journey, guiding every step you take and illuminating the various pathways that will help you arrive at your destination—the development of informed knowledge and insights into the question you pose. As teacher inquirers explore their passions in search of a wondering, it is also useful to consider different types of data that might be collected and used to inform the wondering. Considering different types of data you can collect now will help you decide later which of the many available alternative routes you might take to explore the wondering you are carefully crafting. Hence, in this chapter, we explore data collection strategies you might decide to incorporate into your inquiry journey.

As we explore these strategies, it is important to keep in mind that meaningful teacher inquiry should not occur *apart from* the daily work of classroom teachers but instead should become *a part of* their daily work. When we discuss data collection strategies, then, first and foremost, it is important to consider naturally occurring data in your classroom. To do this will require thinking about life in your classroom/school and the ways in which day-to-day happenings might be naturally captured as data. In the sections ahead, we explore 10 different ways you might naturally capture life in your classroom/school as it unfolds: (1) Student Work and Other Instructional Artifacts, (2) Field Notes, (3) Interviews, (4) Focus Groups, (5) Digital Pictures, (6) Video, (7) Reflective Journals/Blogs, (8) Surveys, (9) Quantitative Measures of Student Achievement (Standardized Test Scores, Assessment Measures, Grades), and (10) Colleague Feedback. To help you develop an understanding of these strategies and how they might fit into your work as a teacher, we begin this chapter first with a simple definition of data collection for the teacher researcher.

What Is Data Collection?

Those who choose a life of teaching know that it is extremely demanding work. One reason why the work of teaching is so demanding is that schools and classrooms are busy places, jam-packed with action, learning, and thinking. Data collection for the teacher researcher refers to the process of capturing the action, learning, and thinking that is occurring in the classroom so it can be returned to by the teacher researcher at a later date and time (Dana, 2013). Because the work of teaching is so busy, if teachers don't find some intentional way to capture the actions and learning that transpire, as well as the thinking of our students and ourselves that occurs in relationship to that action and learning, we will simply forget much of it by the end of the day. Intentionally capturing classroom action, learning, and thinking as data allows the teacher researcher to systematically analyze and reflect on the outcomes of teaching and learning to create new insights and understandings in relationship to the research wondering. For the teacher researcher, one obvious form of data is student work, but there are also many additional powerful ways that teacher researchers capture action, learning, and thinking in their classrooms.

What Do Data Look Like, How Do I Collect Them, and How Do They Fit Into My Work as a Teacher?

We turn now to ten common strategies teacher researchers use for capturing the data of life in schools. We demonstrate each strategy through the work of one or more teacher inquirers. Some examples come from teachers you have already met in previous chapters, while others introduce new teachers and their inquiries as examples for illustrating particular types of data collection. As we share excerpts from these teachers' work, we point to lessons learned about data collection to offer you practical suggestions and guidance about this component of inquiry.

Strategy 1: Student Work and Other Instructional Artifacts

Schools and classrooms naturally generate a tremendous paper trail that captures a great deal of daily classroom activity. Although paperwork remains central to teachers' work, teachers do not just deal with paperwork. Digital tools offer many new ways to easily capture students' work and other related documents. For example, emails, electronic parent/

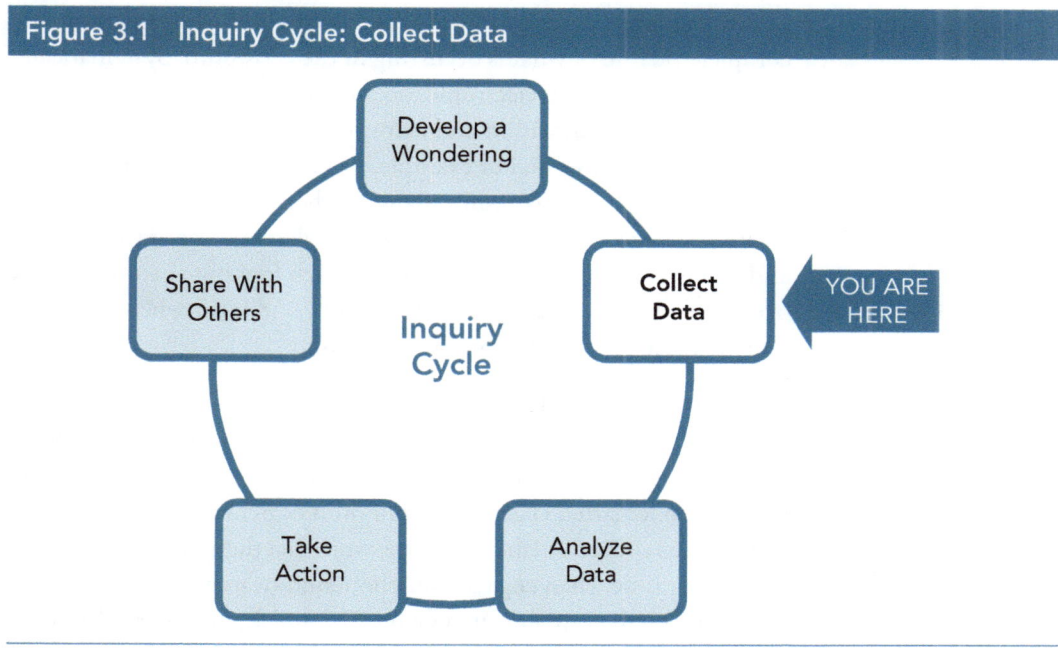

Figure 3.1 Inquiry Cycle: Collect Data

caregiver communication tools, screenshots, student files, online work, Zoom recordings, and smartphone photographs of student work can offer insight. Learning Management Systems (LMSs) such as Google Classroom, Blackboard, Canvas, Moodle, or Microsoft Teams are virtual treasure troves of student work. Additionally, curriculum guides, textbooks, teacher manuals, children's literature, individualized education plans (IEPs), district memos, progress reports, teacher plan books, written lesson plans, and correspondence to and from parents/caregivers, the principal, and specialists also help capture action, learning, and thinking.

The amount of paper and electronic documents that cross a teacher's desk can make any teacher bleary eyed. Often, patterns from the naturally occurring paper or electronic documents that teachers view are difficult to identify when read in isolation or when read quickly during a planning period or after school hours in order to be able to hand back student work as soon as possible. Teachers often feel the need to move quickly through examinations of student work and related documents simply to keep up.

Yet, when viewed through the perspective of your wondering, student work and related artifacts become a potentially insightful form of data and take on new and often deeper meaning. When collected and saved over time, these data can be reviewed together to offer a more complete picture of what is occurring in the classroom. Systematically collecting paper and electronic documents provides you with the opportunity to look within and across documents to analyze them in new and different ways. For example, as a method of tracking student productivity in the classroom, many teachers save student work and create electronic portfolios that note the date and context of when and where the work was produced. Through looking at student work over time, they can make claims that could not occur when they view a single piece of student work in isolation.

An illustration of student work as data appears in an inquiry into the developing phonemic awareness of two students completed collaboratively by mentor teacher Darice Hampton and intern Beth Schickel, in their kindergarten classroom (Hampton & Schickel, 2002). As one form of data collection, they saved the work that these two children produced over time when engaging in phonemic awareness activities. Two pieces of their data are shown in Figures 3.2 and 3.3 on pages 98 and 99.

Figure 3.2 Ted—Random Writing Samples From Children at the Writing Center

Source: Used with permission of Beth Schickel and Darice Hampton.

Figure 3.3 Ted—Writing Samples When Working With Best Friend

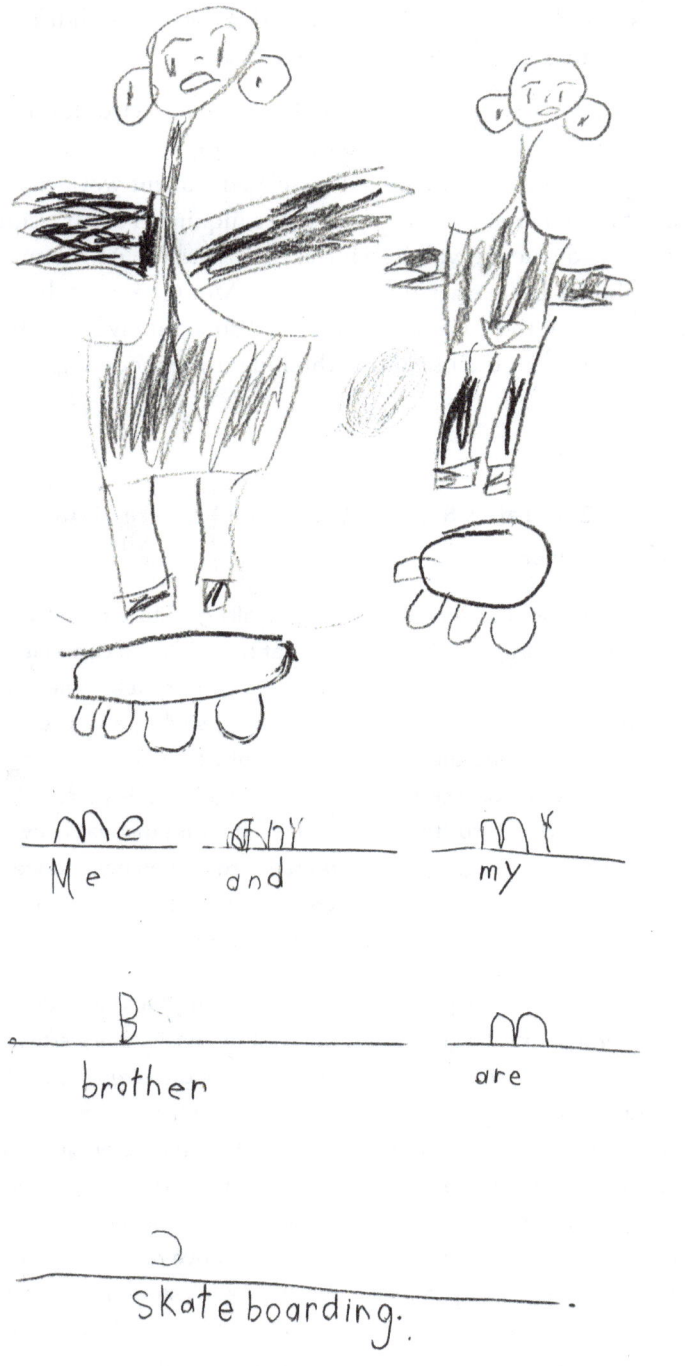

Source: Used with permission of Beth Schickel and Darice Hampton.

Through comparing these two artifacts, as well as other data produced during their study, Darice and Beth were able to conclude that when Ted was in the company of friends, his illustrations were more detailed and his sound spelling more developed than when Ted didn't strongly connect with other children at his table.

As indicated, classrooms are filled with print and electronic documents that are naturally occurring forms of data. More recently, student work is being generated via AI, and AI-generated student work can also be a valuable source of data for the teacher inquirer. For an example of AI-generated student work serving as data, read the AI Moment textbox authored by teacher researcher Sara Montgomery, who studied the ways using the AI image generator Adobe Firefly could help her students represent their scientific thinking using modeling.

AI MOMENT

Using AI-Generated Student Work as a Form of Data
Sara Montgomery

As a middle school science teacher, I naturally gravitated toward practitioner inquiry when it was offered at my school to continue my professional learning. During the 2023–2024 school year, a new unit on Newton's Laws of Motion was added to my sixth-grade science curriculum, presenting the perfect opportunity to try (and inquire into) something new. Having completed several inquiry cycles through the years, I decided to focus this cycle on investigating the ways new AI technologies could help solve a persistent problem in my science classroom: students' being able to create models that both look good and show deep conceptual understanding of the content.

Although we make many models throughout the year, my students often struggle with hand-drawn models. Some students, who are artistic, focus on the "art" of creating the model, working to create a perfect drawing at the expense of why they are creating the model in the first place. Other students, who don't feel confident in their artistic abilities, are paralyzed by their perceived inability to draw. Their insecurities about art cause them to be overly focused on the mechanics of model creation, and they struggle with their own creative representation of phenomena. After years of trying to convince my students that I was not concerned with the quality of their drawings, that I *really* was interested in how they *explained* the model, I decided to change tactics.

Enter AI. Instead of creating hand-drawn models, as in previous units, I wanted to use the process of inquiry to investigate what would happen if I introduced students to Adobe Firefly (an AI image generator) to create an AI-generated image representing one of Newton's Laws of Motion. I developed the following wonderings, "How can the use of AI-generated images provide a framework for middle school students' annotation of scientific models to demonstrate their understanding of scientific phenomena?" and "How does the use of Adobe Firefly impact student engagement with the scientific modeling process?"

Once introduced to Adobe Firefly, students would use the following graphic organizer, sent via Canvas and Google Docs, to keep track of their model's progression and as a place for self-reflection and peer feedback.

My theory of action, an "*If . . . , Then . . . , So That*" statement that helps teacher inquirers establish a clear connection between their intentions and the anticipated impact they hope to have, was as follows:

> *If* the modeling process is not focused on students' individual abilities in art, *Then* they will be able to focus on the science content, *So that* they can articulate the relationship between their model and the scientific phenomena it was created to demonstrate.

For more on how the development of a theory of action can assist in the planning of your inquiry, skip ahead to Chapter 4, Inquiry Planning Stage 2, Articulate a Theory of Action, on page 181.

By using an AI tool as an assistive technology and removing the barrier of being either overly focused on or afraid of art, the students could demonstrate mastery of the concept without anxiety.

While teaching about and completing these models, I collected multiple forms of data. Although data in all forms were useful, the students' collected graphic organizers and completed models provided exceptional insight into how the ways I structured student use of Adobe Firefly to create scientific models was playing out in my science classroom.

(Continued)

(Continued)

Figure 3.4 Canvas and Google Docs Graphic Organizer

MODELING NEWTON'S LAWS

Part 1:

- **Using Adobe Firefly,** (sign in with your school email and password, NOT Google), **create an image that represents one of Newton's Laws.**
- As you tell the tool what to create, keep track of your prompts and the images it creates. Copy and paste them in the graphic organizer.
- Reflect on the image created. Is it what you wanted? How can you make it better? Record your thoughts in the graphic organizer.
- Ask your partners to help you brainstorm new prompts based on changes you want to make.

WHICH LAW DID YOU CHOOSE:

PROMPT	IMAGE	REVIEW
		- Were you surprised by the result? Why? - How can you make your prompt better?
		- Were you surprised by the result? Why? - How can you make your prompt better?
		- Were you surprised by the result? Why? - How can you make your prompt better?
		- Were you surprised by the result? Why? - How can you make your prompt better?

WHICH LAW DID YOU CHOOSE:

PROMPT	IMAGE	REVIEW
		- Were you surprised by the result? Why? - How can you make your prompt better?

Part 2:

- After choosing your best image, **add annotations** to explain how it illustrates one of Newton's Laws by opening your image in **Adobe Express** and adding words, arrows, numbers, etc.
- After adding your annotations, copy your image and paste it below.
- **Paste Image Here:**

Part 3:

- Write a paragraph explaining how your image illustrates one of Newton's Laws.

For example, in my graphic organizer, the first reflection question asked, "Were you surprised by the results?" From analyzing my students' response to this question, I saw that it is possible to simply answer "no" and move on. After some coaching, however, most students were able to reflect on their attempts and make changes as necessary. The following two examples show the variety of responses, on each end of the spectrum:

PROMPT	IMAGE	REVIEW
People in a kayak	Photo 3.1: Painting of people in a kayak (AI Example) 	**Were you surprised by the result? Why?** • No, not really **How can you make your prompt better?** • I want it to look less realistic and more cartoony

PROMPT	IMAGE	REVIEW
A guy pushing his foot across the ground while on a scooter	Photo 3.2: Painting of a man on a scooter (AI Example) 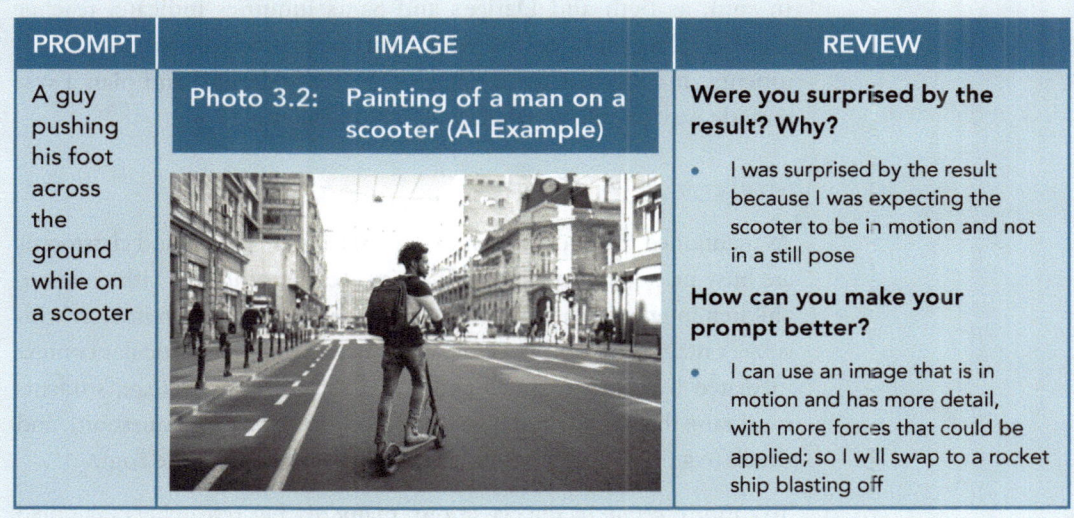	**Were you surprised by the result? Why?** • I was surprised by the result because I was expecting the scooter to be in motion and not in a still pose **How can you make your prompt better?** • I can use an image that is in motion and has more detail, with more forces that could be applied; so I will swap to a rocket ship blasting off

(Continued)

(Continued)

I learned from my analysis of AI-generated student work, and other sources of data, that many students were initially frustrated with creating an image that showed their thinking. This was partially due to the students using the prompt, "Create an image that shows Newton's 2nd law." The students who used this prompt initially were frustrated to find an image of the "scales of justice." After discussing why this might happen (the image generator focusing on the word *law*), students came to the realization that they needed to make a better plan about what they wanted to portray and ask for that instead. As students worked with Adobe Firefly, their prompts improved. Eventually, students were able to engineer their prompts to create an image that displayed the images in their head, and represented their conceptual understanding of Newton's Laws.

In sum, the use of AI-generated images embedded within graphic organizers provided not only a new instructional strategy for my science classroom, but also a novel type of student work as data for my inquiry. Weaving together student work samples with my other data sources and my own reflections, I gained new insights into the role of generative AI for reducing barriers to students' engagement with modeling their understandings of scientific phenomena. AI was simultaneously integrated into my teaching practice and served as an insightful source of data for my inquiry.

In sum, as Beth and Darice's and Sara's inquiries indicate, teacher inquirers need only decide which naturally produced artifacts, documents, and student work relate to their wonderings and plan a systematic way to collect, label, and organize them.

Strategy 2: Field Notes

As mentioned in the definition of data collection, schools and classrooms are busy places, jam-packed with *action*. Teachers inter*act* with children, children inter*act* with each other, and teachers and children inter*act* with subject matter. All of these inter*actions* occur within a particular context mediated by values (e.g., all children can learn), norms (e.g., students must raise their hands and be called on before answering a question), and rituals (e.g., each morning the class pledges allegiance to the flag).

To capture *action* in the classroom, many teacher researchers take field notes as they observe. Field notes can come in many shapes, forms, and varieties. Some of these include scripting dialogue and conversation, diagramming the classroom or a particular part of the classroom, noting what a student or group of students is doing at particular time intervals (e.g., every two minutes), and recording every question a teacher asks. Field notes do not interpret but rather focus on capturing what is occurring without commenting as to why the action might be occurring or how one judges a particular act.

The forms your field notes take depend on your wondering. For instance, in Nancy Sunner's study of her questioning techniques, her field notes listed every question she asked during selected lessons. The connections between your wondering and the forms your field notes take will become more apparent in subsequent examples of field notes shared throughout this section.

You may take field notes as you engage in the teaching act or have them taken for you by others. An example of field notes taken by teachers as they inquired comes once again from the work of intern Beth Schickel and mentor teacher Darice Hampton referenced in the previous section. Recall that Beth and Darice were interested in the development of phonemic awareness in two of their kindergarten learners, collecting student work generated as one source of data. As they worked with these children, another way they captured the action, learning, and thinking was by taking field notes, scripting the responses the children had to different phonemic awareness activities. One activity they developed for these learners involved finding pictures with the same initial phonemes. To illustrate scripting a student's response, an excerpt from their scripted field notes that was collected during this activity is shared in Figure 3.5.

Figure 3.5 Scripted Field Notes by Darice and Beth

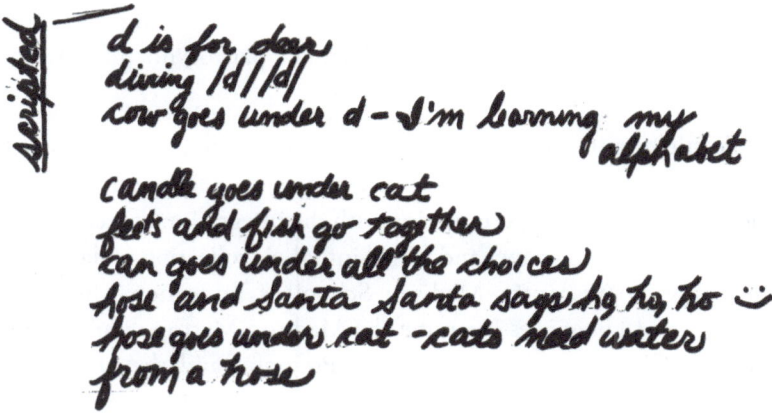

Source: Used with permission of Beth Schickel and Darice Hampton.

Scripting as a form of field notes simply involves writing down verbatim (or as close to verbatim as possible) what your learners are saying. The first time you script notes for yourself, it may feel awkward or unnatural. Some of the teacher inquirers we know have found tricks to help in the process. For example, when Amy Ruth was scripting at the kindergarten writing table, she found the children were more interested in what and why she was writing than in completing their own work. Frustrated after her first attempt to collect data by scripting, since it seemed to interfere more with her teaching than help her inquire into her teaching, she found a way to fold data collection unobtrusively into her teaching in the following way: Amy constructed a red folder that looked just like the red folders all of her kindergarteners worked with at their writing center. The cover of the red folder Amy constructed for herself was marked in big black magic marker: "Miss Ruth's Writing Folder." She shared the folder with her students, telling the children that over the next few weeks, "Miss Ruth is going to be writing at the writing center just like you! When you do your writing, I will be doing mine." Amy used that folder when engaged in scripting, and the children understood that Miss Ruth was working just like they were and never questioned her about it again.

Similarly, another kindergarten teacher inquirer we know, Lynn Dobash, became frustrated when she discovered that important actions she wanted to capture never occurred in a single sitting but rather were sprinkled throughout her day. It was not practical for Lynn to run to her desk to grab her field notebook each time she wanted to make a note. To solve this problem, she began wearing a very fashionable necklace—a yellow sticky notepad with a pen attached. When a child said or did something that she wished to capture, she simply jotted it down on a sticky note and continued teaching. At the end of the day, she stuck each sticky in her notebook. A little ingenuity can go a long way when making data collection a part of, not apart from, your teaching.

While sticky notes are a wonderful invention that can help teacher inquirers with field noting and other phases of their research, many teacher inquirers are experimenting with the integration of technology that doesn't require a paper and pencil into their collection of data. The University of Wisconsin–Madison School of Education Literacies, Cultures and Languages Institute; the Madison Metropolitan School District's Classroom Action Research Program; and the University of Wisconsin Office of Educational Outreach introduced a program entitled "The iPad as a Teacher Research Tool for Literacy Educators Program" to teacher inquirers in their vicinity, which advertised the opportunity as follows:

> Knowing your students' literacy strengths and reflecting on their literacy practices are keys to excellent literacy instruction. This summer/fall course is designed for novice and experienced teacher researchers who are interested in literacy learning and exploring the role iPads can play in data collection and analysis. iPads provide portable, flexible, and multifaceted tools that teacher researchers can use in their classrooms to explore instructional issues. iPads can record audio and video, take photographs, and store data. They can easily be used to take anecdotal notes in busy classrooms as well as store electronic copies of student work or class projects. Finally, books and articles that support research can be stored and accessed through the iPad.

The program filled quickly and had an enormous waiting list.

Sometimes, unlike Amy and Lynn or teacher inquirers from the Madison Metropolitan Area School District who are excitedly experimenting with iPads to take field notes and support other aspects of their research, some teacher inquirers just cannot find a comfortable way to take field notes for themselves, or they want to capture action when they are an integral part of that action (e.g., giving directions, leading a discussion, asking questions). In these cases, it is impossible to record in writing your own directions as you are giving them or your own questions as you pose them. If this is the case for you, other options are available: (1) audio record yourself or (2) find a colleague to help script the observation for you. If you are recording, you will make the recording, listen to it later, and transcribe what has occurred by taking notes or enlisting another person to script notes from the recording for you. Given the intensity of transcribing large amounts of data, some teachers use their cell phone audio recorder to notate critical events occurring as they teach. Much like the note approach, the immediate recording allows them to capture critical points they believe may be important data related to their study without having to fully transcribe the situation.

Although listening to yourself through audio recordings can be extremely insightful, many teacher inquirers we know find it difficult to make this a part of their teaching and opt for having others take notes for them instead. For example, intern Gail Romig and mentor teacher Brian Peters were engaged in a shared inquiry project to investigate the ways they might use science talks to enhance student understanding of science concepts. Early in their inquiry, they recorded the science talks as they occurred but changed to taking turns scripting the talks for each other as follows:

> Throughout our inquiry process, we took turns facilitating the talks and gathering data. While one person sat with the group and helped to guide the conversation, the other person sat outside the circle and kept track of who was talking and what kind of information they were sharing. The person who collected data sat outside the circle so as to not distract or intimidate the students. If the students thought their ideas were being judged or scrutinized, perhaps they would not have been as likely to share. This seemed to be the reaction of some children when they knew they were being audio-recorded.
>
> Early on we tape-recorded a few of our Science Talks. It seemed, however, that some students were reluctant to talk when they saw the microphone. During one of our small group talks later in the marking period, one child asked why we don't record the talks anymore. Gail told him that it seemed like people were afraid to talk if they thought they were being recorded. The student said that he didn't like to talk when we recorded because he thought his voice "sounded dumb" on recordings.
>
> In addition to students being uncomfortable with audio recording, we found that listening to the tapes in the evening after school was insightful but too time consuming and not worth the time it was taking to rehash the entirety of the Science Talk discussion. Audio recording captured more than we needed to capture. To gain insights into our wondering, we just needed to know who was talking and what type of talk it seemed to be. Consequently, we developed a system for taking field notes that involved noting who was talking, paraphrasing what was said, and coding the comment with one of four different codes: "S" for simple, "D" for detailed, "R" for repeat, and "0" for no response. Along with this

system we also made notes of what we observed happening during the talks, for example, if students were sharing with a child next to them. (Peters & Romig, 2001)

As with Amy and Lynn, it took some time for Gail and Brian to find a comfortable way to capture the classroom action in their field notes. For two sound reasons (i.e., some students feeling self-conscious and the time-consuming nature of listening to the recordings), they moved from audio recording as a form of data collection to taking field notes for each other. If you choose field notes as one of your data collection strategies, realize that it might take some time and experimentation to find a form of note taking that works for you and for your inquiry, and as with the teacher inquirers in the Madison Metropolitan School District, you may wish to experiment with technology to find what works for you.

If you are completing your first inquiry as a teacher candidate currently in a clinical experience, a logical note taker for you may be your university supervisor or mentor teacher. Over time, traditional visits by your university supervisor can move from the supervisor taking charge of the direction of the observation and providing evaluative feedback to you, to you taking charge of the direction of the observations by sharing with your supervisor the nature of your inquiry question and asking him or her to script certain lessons for you. For example, one way that Julie Russell collected data for her study of teaching writing to second graders was by asking her supervisor to make data collection around her inquiry a priority during her weekly observations (see Figure 3.6).

If you do not have another adult readily available in your classroom to take field notes for you and want to collect data in this way, you may need to get a bit more creative. For example, you might adjust your schedule to teach the lesson you would like scripted during the time a fellow teacher friend has a scheduled special or planning period and ask your teacher friend to come in and take notes for you. Fourth-grade teachers Cheryl McCarty and Priya Poehner exemplified this type of creativity and flexibility in their study of peer coaching and the ways engaging in this process could give them insights into questions they held about their teaching. The following excerpts from Cheryl and Priya's inquiry share each of their thought processes that led them to a particular form of field noting, plus an example of that field note form (McCarty & Poehner, 2002).

Figure 3.6 Scripted Notes Taken for Julie

PENN STATE — COLLEGE of EDUCATION
Office of Pre-Service Teaching
p. 1

INQUIRY NOTES:
TARGET 2 areas:
• Rubric
• Brainstorming

NAME Julie Russell
DATE/DAY 3/27/02
SUBJECT/GRADE 2
TIME 9:15
NO. OF STUDENTS 22
OBSERVER N Dana
SCHOOL MV
DISTRICT SCASD

What's this check list for?
  To help us write complete stories.
What does a beginning need?
  C - reads
  D - makes your story that people want to read more.
    - characters
  C - dazzling action words
What did endings need?
  E - happy ending
      solve problem
  H - you have a problem that makes sense to your story
Are we allowed to use happily ever after?
No - why not?
  K - They need to know more
We're going to read Babbage Rose. Look at your rubric. How would you score writer?
Look at this rubric. How did the author do?
  D - can you grab the book and read the first sentence?
  A - I'd give it a star
Why?
  Because the sun paints the world
  K - What would you give it?
    A work hard on it because it sounds like a research book and I don't like research books

Source: Used with permission of Julie Russell.

PRIYA'S NARRATIVE

My inquiry question focused on one of my lower-ability reading groups and their use of the discussion strategies that I had taught them. I was often frustrated that these students were unable to carry on a conversation without me being there to keep them on task and keep the conversation flowing. I was interested in seeing whether this was really the case, and if it was, to get some ideas on how to improve the situation.

CHAPTER 3: DATA COLLECTION   111

I sat down with Cheryl after school one day and talked about the layout and the focus of the observation that she was about to perform. I told her my frustrations with this literature group and mentioned that they were unable to have discussions without books. This was an area of concern:

Figure 3.7   Priya's Field Notes

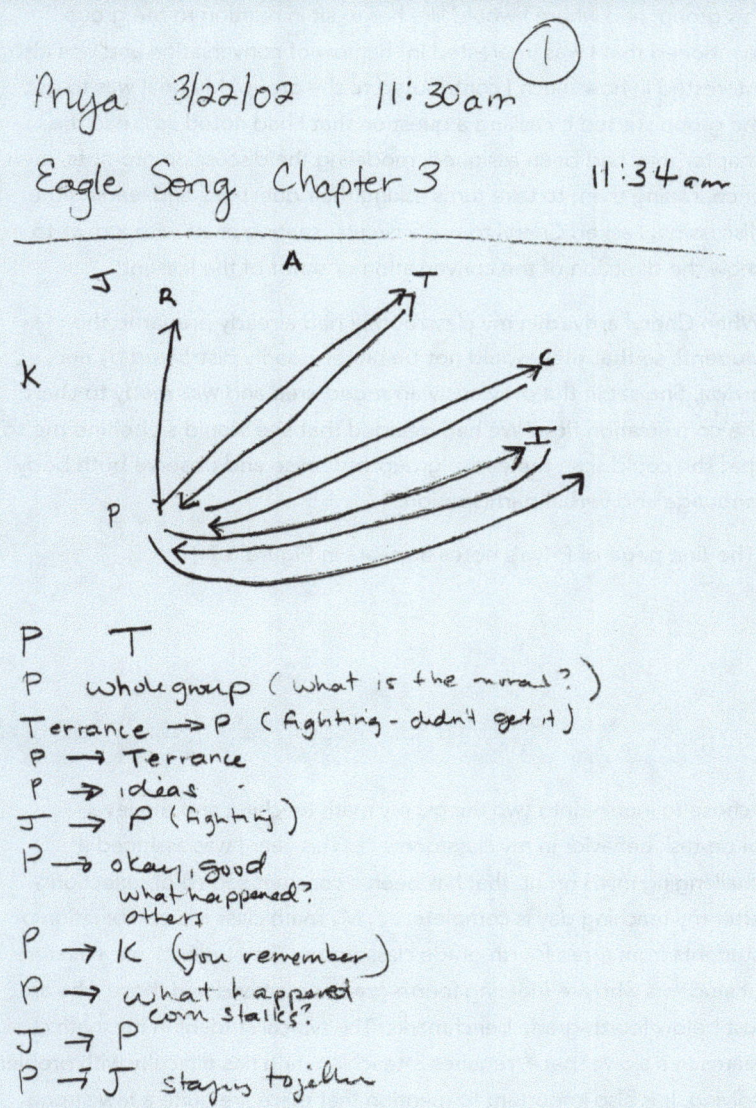

Source: Used with permission of Priya Poehner.

(Continued)

(Continued)

more advanced groups understood and enjoyed the books we were reading at a deeper level as a result of their group discussions. During our discussion, I described and talked about the students in this group so that Cheryl could identify them easily. We talked about where the group usually met, where each of the students sat, my placement within this group, and where I would like her to sit in relation to the group. I mentioned that I was interested in the flow of conversation and was also interested in how much I contributed to the group. My goal was to get the group started by asking a question that I had noted as I read the chapter they had been assigned, modeling the discussion prompts, then encouraging them to take turns asking their questions and leading the discussion. I asked Cheryl to use a circular seating chart with arrows to show the direction of the conversation or script of the lesson.

When Cheryl arrived in my classroom, I had already prepared the students so that they would not be unnecessarily distracted by her arrival. She sat in the previously arranged area and was ready to chart the conversation flow. We had decided that she would sit behind me so that she could scan the entire group with ease and observe both body language and verbal participation.

[The first page of Priya's notes appears in Figure 3.7.]

CHERYL'S NARRATIVE

I chose to inquire into two things: my math teaching and the level of on-task behavior in my classroom. . . . This year I was assigned a challenging math group that has been a constant source of reflection after my teaching day is complete. . . . My math class is a combination of students from three fourth-grade classrooms. The students are a mixture of students who are meeting fourth-grade objectives and those who are just below fourth-grade benchmarks. The typical student in my math class learns at a slower pace, requires reteaching, and has difficulty with problem solving. It is also important to mention that there are quite a few strong personalities in my class and, as a group, they are difficult to manage.

Wanting to collect data on a lesson on fractions in my class, I asked Priya to observe me. Since Priya and I work very closely, she was completely aware of the makeup of my math class as well as my teaching style and philosophies for teaching this particular math group. We agreed on a form for field notes and her location while in my classroom. Noting my concerns that my class was often off task and not attending to my teaching, Priya would take two-minute sweeps of the room and watch the class as a whole for on-task behavior.

I explained that my math lesson would consist of four different parts: problem solving, fraction concept review, addition of fractions using number lines, and classwork and homework. We decided the best way for her to note on-task behavior would be to use a seating chart in which she would mark her observations of each student. [Figure 3.8 shows how Cheryl coded her observations for different parts of the lesson.]

Figure 3.8   Cheryl's Field Notes

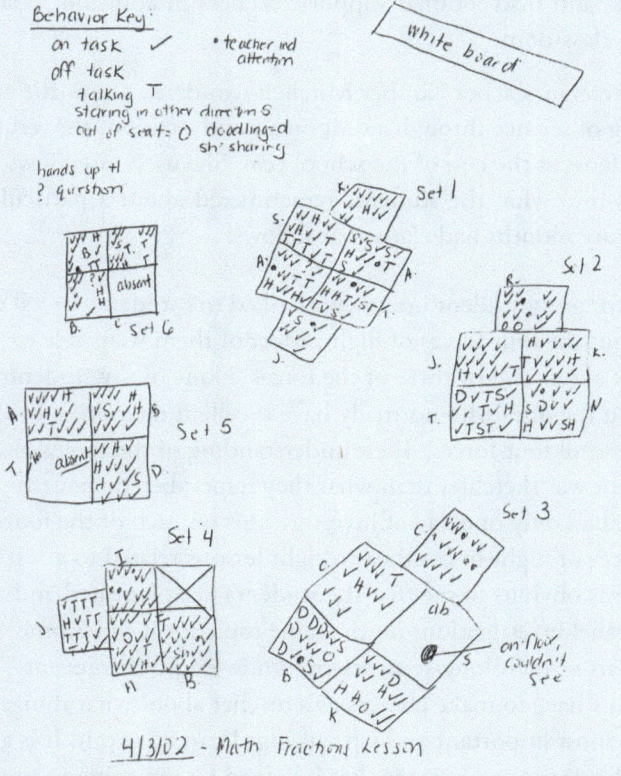

Source: Used with permission of Cheryl McCarty.

(Continued)

(Continued)

By looking across each field note example shared here, we demonstrate that field notes can be as different and varied as the individuals who take them. Most important is to select or create a system that works for you in practice and that collects data that inform your wondering.

Strategy 3: Interviews

When they take the form of scripting, field notes are one way to capture talk that occurs during classroom activities. Because talk is crucial to the teaching and learning process, some teacher inquirers go one step farther by conducting individual interviews. Interviewing can be informal and spontaneous or more thoughtfully planned and structured. Depending on your wondering, you might interview adults such as parents/caregivers, administrators, other classroom teachers, and instructional support teachers in addition to students in your classroom.

When veteran teacher Kimber Mitchell wondered about the effective teaching of science through a unit on air and aviation, she returned to her students at the end of the school year. She used interviews to gain insights into what the students remembered about a particular unit after many months had elapsed as follows:

> During my student interviews I asked my students to tell me about the four forces of flight. Most of them were able to talk about two or three of the forces. None of my students, even the ones who normally have excellent memories, could name all four forces. Their understanding of the forces of flight was sketchier than what they remembered about air. We had only one day of investigations on each of the four forces of flight in contrast to eight lessons related to air. It seems obvious to me that the students need repeated and parallel investigations on the same topic for it to become a part of their long-term science knowledge. This means that I have to make choices as a teacher about what things are most important and what things I can leave out. It is a difficult process but one that is helped by returning to one of my original questions: Which investigations help the children to understand how airplanes fly? In an interview, one of my students summed it up this way: "If you do a lot

of experiments about one thing and do the experiments over and over (many trials), it will explain things." (Emily Dong in Mitchell, 2000)

Interviewing students in the classroom can be a rich source of data, but for this to happen, it is important not to get hung up on the word *interview* or to imagine that the act of interviewing as it relates to inquiry is anything different from what great teachers, like Kimber, do on a regular basis. Asking students about their thinking and their learning is a natural part of lessons and instructional activities, and when related to an inquiry question, naturally occurring conversations with students can automatically become interviews.

In the example of interviewing that follows, the teacher was inquiring into ways to teach mathematics conceptually rather than just procedurally. To garner initial understandings of her students' conceptual knowledge, she circulated as students in her class worked on a fraction problem and asked them to explain their thinking.

Teacher: Can you explain to me how you're finding an equivalent fraction here?

Student: Well, there's a fraction law that says you have to do the same thing on the bottom and the top, so I'm multiplying by two on the top and multiplying by two on the bottom.

Teacher: Do you know why you have to multiply by the same number on the top and the bottom?

Student: Because that's what the fraction law tells me to do.

Teacher: But there has to be a reason for the law. Do you know what it is?

Student: No.

She used interviews such as these as data to track the development of her students' conceptual understandings of fractions over time. Later, after introducing manipulative materials and working with students on concrete representations of a problem, an interview with the same student revealed his developing ability to approach a problem conceptually.

Teacher: Using the fraction bars, can you show me the first fraction, $\frac{1}{2}$?

Student: (*pulls out the two half pieces and points at one of them*)

Teacher: Good. You have shown me one half piece. You found earlier that $\frac{2}{4}$ was an equivalent fraction to $\frac{1}{2}$. Can you show me $\frac{2}{4}$ with the fraction bars?

Student: (*pulls out fourth pieces and points at two of them*)

Teacher: So what makes those fractions equivalent?

Student: Well, they take up the same amount of space.

Teacher: Great! So then how did you get from $\frac{1}{2}$ to $\frac{2}{4}$?

Student: Oh! I get it now! I couldn't explain it before without the fraction bars, but now I see that the one half piece turned into two fourth pieces. It multiplied by two. And the total number of pieces in $\frac{1}{2}$ is two. The total number of pieces in $\frac{1}{4}$ is four. It multiplied by two. That's why the fraction law says I have to do the same thing on the bottom and on the top.

Teacher: What would happen if you multiplied by different numbers on the top and bottom?

Student: (*after thinking for a minute*) Can I use the fraction bars to figure it out?

Teacher: Sure!

Student: (*works through the process by showing two different fractions with the fraction bars*) Well, if I multiplied the top number by two then I get two like I did before. If I multiply the bottom number by three instead of two, then I get six. (*uses the sixth pieces to show $\frac{2}{6}$ and puts it next to the $\frac{1}{2}$ tiles*) These fractions aren't equivalent because they don't take up the same amount of space.

Interviewing as a form of data collection can be as simple as circulating during instruction and asking students about their learning. What makes the instructional activity of asking students questions into an interview is that this act relates directly to the wondering you are exploring for your inquiry. In the former case, the teacher was inquiring into building conceptual understandings of fractions with her fourth-grade learners.

Strategy 4: Focus Groups

Focus groups offer teachers another vehicle for collecting the talk and thoughts of children in the classroom. In many ways, focus groups occur daily in the form of whole-class or small-group discussion. The focus-group discussion can serve as a tool for understanding students' perceptions. For example, a focus group can provide insight into how students experience a new instructional strategy. Teacher researcher Marisa Ramirez conducted an inquiry into differentiating mathematics instruction in her first-grade classroom through the design and implementation of Challenge Baskets, a system of tiered activities built from previously introduced skills. Each of these baskets contained a variety of activities for the students to complete independently, providing them with extra practice or enrichment in previously introduced skills and an individualized schedule of which activities to complete from which basket based on their ability level and needs. Marisa writes:

> I could tell from the beginning that my students were excited when it was Challenge Basket time, but I wanted to hear from them the reasons why they liked it. I also wanted to know what their dislikes and suggestions for improvement would be. We held a class meeting to discuss their thoughts and feelings. I charted their comments on three large pieces of paper labeled, "Reasons Why We Like Challenge Baskets," "Things We Don't Like," and "Ideas or Suggestions," as they shared them in class. The students took this meeting very seriously and were glad to share their suggestions. This made the Challenge Baskets even more exciting to them since I asked for their opinions and even implemented some of their suggestions. (Ramirez, 2007, p. 104)

In essence, Marisa's use of the class meeting served as a focus-group interview. Many teacher researchers also use focus-group interviews to ascertain what prior knowledge students possess about a particular content area. Teachers who use graphic organizers such as What We Know, What We Want to Know, What We Learned (K-W-L) strategies are conducting a form of focus group that can serve as a source of data that can inform inquiry. Although focus groups can serve as a quick way to obtain data, they have some limitations. For example, focus groups are more likely to capture breadth of opinion because the goal is often to understand the group's perspective. In addition, due to the presence of diverging opinions, less confident focus-group members might refrain from sharing their thoughts.

Strategy 5: Digital Pictures

Interviews and focus groups can capture words as data. A very old proverb you are likely familiar with is, "A picture is worth a thousand words." Another wonderful way to capture action that occurs in the classroom as data is through digital photography.

For example, when taking a University of Florida course entitled Integrating Technology in the Elementary Classroom, which included a heavy field experience component requiring engagement in teacher inquiry (Dawson & Dana, 2007), one teacher candidate studied the ways a toothpick bridge-building project stimulated student thinking in a fourth-grade math and science gifted classroom. These fourth-grade students were assigned to groups to build a bridge out of toothpicks. Simulating an actual bridge-building corporation, students in each group selected the jobs of architect, accountant, materials manager, carpenter, or project manager. With a fictional budget of $5 million to start, the accountant managed the money, writing checks and keeping a balance of money expended using a Microsoft Excel spreadsheet. When the bridges were finished, the students created a video and PowerPoint presentation to document their progress from the start of the project through the final bridge construction.

For her inquiry, the teacher candidate in this classroom wished to capture and understand the ways working in a group contributed to the thinking of these young, gifted learners at each step in the process. How did the group members negotiate? How did their interactions with one another contribute to these learners' individual knowledge construction during this project? To gain insights into these wonderings, teacher observations were captured as field notes, weekly reflections were written by the students and the teacher candidate, student interviews were conducted, and digital pictures were taken. The digital pictures served two purposes: First, they documented group progress over time, and second, they were subsequently used during the student interviews as prompts to ask each group of students to describe the ways their group collaborated to complete each phase of this bridge-building process. Figures 3.9 and 3.10 illustrate two of these digital photos taken at an early stage in bridge construction and when the bridge was completed.

Figure 3.9 Bridge-Building Project—Early Stage in Group 3's Work

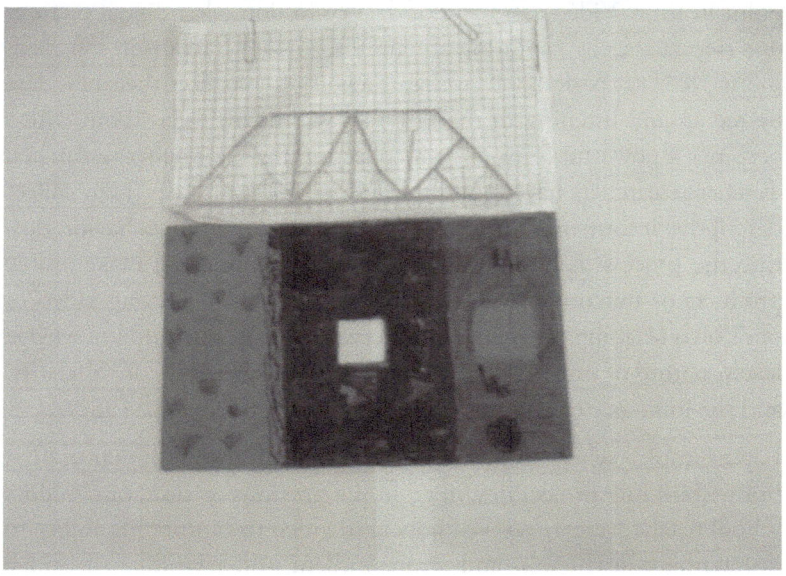

Source: Used with permission of Kara Dawson.

Figure 3.10 Bridge-Building Project—Completed Bridge by Group 3

Source: Used with permission of Kara Dawson.

Strategy 6: Video as Data

Digital pictures capture a single snippet of action in the classroom at one point in time. Video as a form of data collection takes digital pictures one step farther by capturing an entire segment of action in the classroom over a set period. Given that teachers often collect their best data by seeing and listening to the activities within their classroom, video becomes a powerful form of data collection for the teacher researcher. Teacher researchers have found that using video can help them collect descriptive information, better understand an unfolding behavior, capture the process used, study the learning situation, and make visible products or outcomes. More specifically, through observing video of one's own teaching, teachers can observe attitudes, skill and knowledge levels, nature of interactions, nonverbal behavior, instructional clarity, and the influence of physical surroundings (Cloutier et al., 1987).

For example, when implementing a unit of study similar to the bridge-building project described in the previous section, one middle school teacher researcher we know used video to capture his ability to differentiate instruction and create student understanding of bridge construction. The video work captured the instruction, group work, content exploration, presentation, and product. The unique part of this teacher research was that the teacher researcher involved his students in the video work in three ways. First, his students often served as videographers and took turns filming. Their choice of what to film also was an information source. Second, the students reviewed portions of the video with their teacher to provide their own insight and analysis of the learning process. By engaging the students in the analysis, they became meta-cognitively aware of the components that facilitated or inhibited their learning. Third, the teacher used the video to capture and document participant perspectives. By carefully interviewing his students on video, this teacher researcher was able to more completely understand his students' experiences.

In a similar fashion, high school chemistry teacher Stephen Burgin (2007a) used video in an interesting way to gain insights into his wondering, "How can I better use demonstrations in a way that empowers my students' learning of high school chemistry?" In this inquiry, Stephen developed a month-long curriculum that consisted of a discrepant event demonstration for each time his class met. Because his school was on a block schedule, his classes met three times a week, for a total of 13 demonstrations used in the teaching unit. During the unit, students video-recorded Stephen performing each of the 13 demonstrations. Students were then quizzed and tested on the content of the Demo-A-Day unit. During these assessments, the videos were played back for the students to help stimulate their thought processes and remind them of what they had previously observed in class. Used in this way, the videos both captured the events for Stephen as a teacher researcher and aided his students in reconstructing the discrepant event demonstrations and the chemistry behind them during a quiz.

Following these assessments, Stephen then placed his students in groups of four. Each group selected 1 of the 13 demonstrations they had previously observed in the Demo-A-Day unit. Groups then prepared the necessary solutions, planned a script to present their demonstration to a group of local elementary students, and practiced their demonstrations in front of their peers. Once again, Stephen enlisted video at this point in his inquiry. Groups were video-recorded as they performed their demonstration shows for the elementary students. Following the show, students were asked to write a reflective paper on both the Demo-A-Day unit and the demonstration show. Stephen again shared excerpts of the videos with his students to spawn their reflections prior to writing their papers. In this way, Stephen's use of video once again served two purposes:

1. Video captured his students' performance of the demonstrations for elementary students, so Stephen could use video excerpts to stimulate his own reflections on what occurred during this portion of the inquiry and provide documentation for his own teacher research.

2. Video was used as a precursor to students' writing of a reflective paper to help them be more articulate and thoughtful in their reflections.

Given that video can be used as both an observation tool and a tool to capture the experiences of students and stimulate their thought processes, video is an underused but powerful form of technology for documenting the work of teacher researchers.

Strategy 7: Reflective Journals/Blogs

Thus far, we have discussed ways to make data collection a part of your teaching by capturing what naturally occurs in your teaching day—student progress in your classroom through document analysis; action in the classroom through field notes, digital pictures, and video; and talk in the classroom or school through interviews and focus groups. One of the ways that interviewing and focus groups serve as powerful data collection strategies is through the *talk* of interviewing, because a teacher inquirer gains access into the *thinking* of the child or adult being interviewed.

Capturing thinking is a challenge for any researcher. One way a teacher researcher captures the thinking that occurs in the school and classroom and within his or her own mind is through journaling. Journals provide teachers a tool for reflecting on their own thought processes and can also serve as a tool for students to record their thinking related to the project at hand. An example of a journal entry from Julie Russell's inquiry is presented here.

Exhibit 3.1 Journal Entry

Julie Russell

February 22, 2002

Inquiry Lesson #3

This week's lesson was really exciting for me because I am really beginning to see that my efforts are making a difference. I always imagined creating a writing atmosphere in which my students felt comfortable and confident about presenting their work alongside that of published, established authors. In my classroom library, I am going to have a section for "Classroom Authors." When one of my students publishes a story, they will get a copy to take home and will make another copy to leave in the library. As we went around the circle and the students named their own characters, I felt so excited for these children. They are in an incredibly powerful creative space right now in which they feel capable. I can remember writing my own chapter book with no hesitation when I was eight years old. Now, I would be terrified to tackle that sort of job. I suppose that is the source of my passion for developing writing instruction for primary students. My dream is to help my children see themselves as "real" authors and feel proud of their work before they begin to doubt their abilities. I would be so proud to make a difference in that way.

I think this inquiry project has taught me a very important lesson about pacing. One of my biggest weaknesses is expecting way too much. I know what those expectations can do to me, and I never want to put that kind of pressure on my children. Honestly, I think I would have done more harm than good if I continued to push so hard. Before the writing segment of my second inquiry lesson, the children were so excited to begin writing. When I started my third lesson, C. actually asked, "Do we have to write a WHOLE story AGAIN?" I felt horrible! I was so glad that we had lightened the work load. I think the whole flow of the lesson felt better. I am a much better teacher when I do not feel rushed and overwhelmed. I have noticed how incredibly sensitive the children are to how I am feeling. Do you remember when I scolded them and they apologized during that reading group? They do that often lately. They seem to want to behave and achieve to please me, and they get upset if they think I am not pleased. It's a big responsibility to have someone care that much about your opinion. It becomes a constant process of reflection and negotiation, because their sensitivity to my expectations makes me really sensitive to whether or not my expectations are appropriate. I think that breaking the writing into more manageable chunks made a huge difference. The children did not get burned out, and I was able to relax and really enjoy the lesson. Part of my goal for this project was to share my passion for writing, and I can't do that if I am not enjoying the writing lesson.

> I think that the connection to literature is very effective. Many of the children—even those for whom writing is a struggle—are starting to include beautiful literary language in their stories. I saw this emerge particularly during this lesson. I think the students have more time to write and I had more time to emphasize the literature. Their comments as we discussed both their fairy tales and the published fairy tales indicate that they are becoming more aware of the strategies that good authors use. One of the central ideas in my philosophy as a writing teacher is that even very young children can recognize what they like so they can begin to apply it in their own writing. It's exciting for me to see my role in writing instruction emerge, because that was one of the things I was questioning.

Source: Used with permission of Julie Russell.

Electronic journals are often referred to as weblogs, or simply blogs. Blogs are another excellent way teacher researchers can capture their thinking as an inquiry unfolds. Will Richardson defines a weblog, or blog, in its most general sense as "an easily created, easily updateable Web site that allows an author (or authors) to publish instantly to the Internet from any Internet connection" (Richardson, 2006, p. 17). Because blogs consist of a series of entries arranged in reverse chronological order, they can serve as a sort of online diary where teacher researchers can post commentary or news about the research they are currently engaged in. Unlike the journal as a form of data collection, the teacher researcher who blogs can combine text, images, and links to other blogs as well as post comments in an interactive format. The comment feature of blogs provides the opportunity for teacher researchers to receive feedback from anyone in the world (in an open blog community) or other teacher researchers (in a closed community).

For example, third-grade teacher Wendy Drexler used a blog both to capture her own reflection throughout the duration of an inquiry and to serve as the object of her inquiry when she investigated a K–12/university blogging collaboration between preservice teachers and her third-grade students. Wendy gained insight into her wondering, "What happens to third-grade students' attitude toward writing, quality of the final writing product, and motivation to write when they participate with preservice teachers in a blogging project related to the study of Native American culture?" by collecting data in the following ways: writing survey, student blogs, interviews, student concept maps, and student five-paragraph presentations. In addition, Wendy kept a teacher's reflective blog to capture details that were taking place on a daily basis as well as her feelings as the project evolved. Sample entries from Wendy's blog appear in Figure 3.11 on page 124.

Figure 3.11 Wendy's Blog Entry

October 14, 2006

Wendy

[Logged in users] Narrowing Topics and Concept Maps
Posted by Wendy | 0 comment(s) | Edit | Delete | Trackback URI

The children blogged on Monday about the three topics on which the research essay will focus. The university partners responded with good comments and some additional resources. On Friday, each child created an Inspiration concept map to help visualize where more content was needed to round out the research. This was an excellent exercise for the students. Previously, they were having difficulty organizing long lists of facts. Ultimately, the Inspiration concept map will be viewed in outline form to help the students organize the actual paper. One very valuable aspect of this type of project is allowing those students who excel and enjoy the research process to include as much detail in the paper as can be found. The students who work more slowly or those who struggle are still able to work with more simplistic topics. It was also interesting to observe one student who is notoriously slow on most assignments. He often appears distracted and requires a lot of verbal cues to pull him back in. In this case, he was engrossed in the content, specifically focused on the language of his tribe. Again, time is the greatest challenge in these types of projects. As a teacher, I am encouraged by his focus and desire to learn more. However, there is only so much time available. We decided to change one of his three topics to language. But, I still had to scoot him along to make sure he completed enough of the assignment to keep him from falling further behind. Since all of the children have Internet access at home, they can continue most aspects of the project outside of school. However, at this age (third grade), they are not accustomed to taking that kind of responsibility for out-of-school learning. Most still require very concrete, specific instructions for homework assignments. I'm going to think more about this. How wonderful it would be for each student to have as much time as needed to approach the learning process in his or her own way without always being hurried. Next week, we will finish the concept maps and post them on the website for the university partners to see.

Keywords: educational technology, hurried child, Integrating technology with social studies, Native American Projects, special projects

Source: Used with permission of Wendy Drexler.

As indicated in Figure 3.11, Wendy's personal blog helped her combine the benefits of field notes and journaling in one place. Through careful analysis of her own blog over time, as well as the blogs of her students and the other forms of data she collected, Wendy learned that collaborative blogging improved her students' writing and supported development of related skills and knowledge (Drexler et al., 2007).

Both journaling and blogging as forms of data collection can be very powerful tools, but sometimes it is difficult for the novice teacher researcher to view his or her own reflections as important data! Ironically, as teachers (in charge of facilitating the thinking of others), we have not been socialized into thinking that our *own* thinking matters! Yet capturing your own thinking over time can lead to critical insights into your teaching that might occur only when you revisit a thought that occurred to you while teaching at a later date or when you string a number of thoughts together that have occurred intermittently over a longer period. If you (or any of your students) are a Harry Potter fan, you will recall that the wise teacher and headmaster,

Albus Dumbledore, has the ability to extract thoughts and recollections of events from his head and place them in a *pensieve*. At critical times in the Harry Potter stories, Dumbledore enters the pensieve, sometimes with Harry, to explore these old memories and thoughts, and gains new insights with each visit. Journaling or blogging can serve as your personal pensieve to capture and store your thoughts and recollections safely so you can share them with teaching colleagues and return to them at various times in the evolution of your inquiry, gaining new and deeper insights with each visit.

A good way to make your personal pensieve as effective as it can be is to plan for your journal writing or blogging ahead of time. This means committing to a specific time to journal or blog throughout your inquiry and to have a structure for journaling/blogging that makes sense in relation to what you wish to learn. For example, in her study into the ways she could teach students receiving Tier 3 intensive instruction how to be self-regulated learners, able to reflect on their thoughts, behaviors, and progress independently to strategically achieve their personal learning goals (Zimmerman, 2000), teacher researcher Ashley Pennypacker Hill used a journal in the following way:

> I answered two prompts daily: (1) What did I learn about self-regulation in reading today? (2) What did I learn about how my students might transfer self-regulation strategies to other contexts? The use of a teacher's journal allowed me to capture my own thinking. I established a time that I wrote in my journal daily, which was for 10 minutes directly after teaching. . . . This supported me through the success, areas of growth, and provided me a structured outlet in deciding the next steps that needed to be taken in the study.
> (Hill, 2013, p. 47–48)

At the end of her study, after analyzing data and writing up her results, Ashley reflected on her approach to journal writing as one form of data she collected, offering suggestions to other teacher inquirers, like you.

> Many texts about the process of practitioner research suggest journaling as one method of data collection. What texts about the practitioner research process often do not do, however, is suggest that teacher researchers highly structure their journaling process. In this study, I established a time that I would write in my journal daily. Establishing this time ensured that I had dedicated time to methodically reflect on

> my teaching. If I had not established this time, I would have engaged in writing a journal haphazardly and I would not have collected systematic data. In addition, in my journal I responded to the same two prompts every day: "What did I learn about self-regulation in reading today?" and "What did I learn about how my students might transfer self-regulation strategies to other contexts?" These two prompts directly connected to my research questions and provided focus to my daily reflections. Without these prompts, my journal would have been a tool for reflection, but the data within it would have likely been much broader and less helpful to me as I analyzed my data over time. Therefore, practitioner researchers, at the onset of their studies, might consider highly structuring the use of the journal by committing to a regularly scheduled time to write in it and by using consistent prompts that directly connect to their research questions. (Hill, 2013, p. 128–129)

If you choose journaling or blogging as one form of data you will collect, consider taking Ashley's advice.

Strategy 8: Surveys

Some teacher inquirers employ more formal mechanisms (e.g., sociograms and surveys) to capture the action, talking, thinking, and productivity that are a part of every school day. The most common formal mechanism we have observed in our work with teacher inquirers is surveys. Surveys can give students a space to share their thoughts and opinions about a teaching technique or strategy, a unit, or their knowledge about particular subject matter.

Recall Brian Peters and Gail Romig's inquiry into science talks. In the following excerpt, note how the use of surveys gave Brian and Gail access to their students' thinking about their experiences during science talks:

> Upon entering into the process of using Science Talks as a means of instructing and assessing students, we were looking for answers to many questions: Could we use Science Talks as another mode of instruction? Would Science Talks enhance what we were already doing in terms of instruction? Would the use of Science Talks enable us to better assess what the students know and still need to learn? Would Science Talks

provide a vehicle for those who struggle with written forms of assessment to express their understanding meaningfully? Dickenson and Young (1998) state that science can provide common experiences that children can speak and write about. Would Science Talks enhance how the children communicate about these common experiences?

In addition to articulating the perspectives about Science Talks that we developed as teachers as a result of answering these questions through inquiry, we wanted to discover how the students felt about the Science Talks. If the students felt comfortable and had some ownership in the activity, there may be greater participation. We used a survey that asked for information regarding the following: "What do you like about having Science Talks?," "What don't you like about Science Talks?," and "Do you have any suggestions for improving our Science Talks?"

The children's responses to this survey gleaned some interesting information and led us to the conclusion that all members of our class enjoyed Science Talks. The following two survey responses were typical of all of the responses we received:

"I like Science Talks because you might need a question answered and the teacher doesn't know the answer. With more people, more questions can be answered. I can't think of anything I don't like because science rules. I don't want to change anything 'cause things are cool as they are."

"I like Science Talks. They are cool. It is fun because we can share what we have to say. We don't even have to raise our hands."

The entire class completed the survey, and not one student stated that the use of Science Talks was disliked. There were some portions of the process that were not enjoyed, and some students offered suggestions. The main item of dissatisfaction that appeared in the survey was that more than one student talked at once or that a student could not speak because of others dominating the discussion. Twenty-nine percent of the class expressed this opinion.

Many students gave suggestions to improve our Science Talks. There was a desire to have smaller groups for Science

Talks. One student suggested that each person in the circle have a turn and be allowed to share or pass. One child did not like the physical arrangements of the talks because she did not like sitting on the floor. Another did not like the time of day our Science Talk was held. Two students suggested that we should extend our Science Talks to other subjects. . . . We were able to learn plenty from our surveys. (Peters & Romig, 2001)

Depending on the inquiry, some teachers survey students as the first part of their investigation and have the students complete the same survey at the end of an inquiry. This is particularly useful when surveys focus on students' understandings of content or attitude toward particular components of the school day and a teacher inquirer wishes to capture growth or change over time. For example, read teacher researcher Brenda Breil's reflections on using surveys as a part of her inquiry into teaching middle schoolers about AI in this chapter's second AI Moment textbox on page 128.

AI MOMENT

Inquiring Into Teaching About AI to My Middle School Students

The Use of Surveys

Brenda Breil

Currently, we stand on the cusp of another technological revolution driven by artificial intelligence (AI). AI is poised to reshape our world, and it is imperative that students understand its potential and implications. However, many middle school students remain unaware of the profound impact AI will have on their futures. In my engineering classes, students identify problems and work towards solutions—a process in which AI could play a crucial role. Therefore, it is essential that all students learn about AI and grasp its potential to support their daily lives. By fostering awareness of AI, I hope to inspire students not only to utilize this technology but also to consider contributing to its development.

The passion driving my inquiry into AI education stems from a persistent dilemma: many students fail to see the connection between their current learning and future success. This disconnect diminishes their motivation and alters their perception of the relevance of their education. Despite recognizing this issue, I have yet to deeply study it. Understanding that AI could be a driving force in my students' futures, I am committed to preparing them to understand what AI is, how it can be utilized, and the ethical considerations surrounding its use.

In today's world, marked by the proliferation of conspiracy theories and a growing rejection of science, students may be wary of advanced and hidden technologies like AI. Recent revelations of scientific abuses and a heightened awareness of bias further exacerbate this wariness. This context underscores the importance of teaching students to engage with AI intelligently and ethically, equipping them with transferable skills to navigate other technological advances, such as genetic engineering and the evolving human–robot interface. However, my journey into AI education comes with its own challenges. Despite my extensive background in science and technology, I am acutely aware of my limited knowledge of AI. This realization fuels my commitment to learning about AI alongside my students, leading them through a shared journey of discovery and understanding, and ultimately, describing the potential AI could have in improving their lives and the lives of people they care about.

My dilemmas and goals led to the following wonderings.

1. How can I, as a middle grades engineering teacher, learn about and simultaneously support my students in learning about AI?
2. How can I support my students in connecting with AI within an engineering context and appreciate the power of AI?

The collection of three different types of data provided insights into my wonderings: keeping a daily journal where I reflected on observations and experiences as I designed and taught a unit on AI, student work completed in Google Docs during the teaching of the newly designed AI unit that I could access, and pre- and post-unit surveys conducted electronically through Quia. For the purposes of my inquiry, I found surveys a particularly useful mechanism for data collection.

(Continued)

(Continued)

My pre-unit survey appears below:

AI STUDENT SURVEY

Please respond to the following questions to help me learn more about what you think and know about artificial intelligence.

1. Have you had the opportunity to learn about AI in school before now?
   ___Yes ___No

2. Have you had the opportunity to learn about AI outside of school before now?
   ___Yes ___No

3. Select each of the following that applies to you. You can check more than one.

   ___ I do not know enough about AI to have any feelings or thoughts about AI.

   ___ AI can improve the world.

   ___ AI cannot be trusted.

   ___ I am eager to use AI.

   ___ I have no interest in AI.

   ___ I already use AI.

   ___ I am eager to learn/learn more about AI.

   ___ I have never used AI.

   ___ AI is an important tool.

   ___ AI is important but will not be used by everyday people.

4. Share what you know about AI.

5. Describe three examples of AI being used in your everyday life.

6. Explain how AI could be used or developed to improve the life of someone close to you. You can give more than one example if you like.

Administering the pre-unit survey allowed me to gauge students' experience with AI and to gather their first impressions on it. This survey provided useful information to help me support my students' learning about AI within the design of a new AI unit. For example, my students' responses to the pre-unit survey indicated that overall, the sentiment on AI was positive with most students believing that AI can improve the world and that AI is an important tool. This alleviated my concerns that students might see AI as a malevolent force and something to be shut down, helping me shape my ideas for the unit as I was uncertain if these were problems that would need to be addressed.

My post-unit survey contained many of the same questions as the pre-unit survey, enabling me to compare my students' responses to ascertain change in their perceptions about AI. For example, in the pre-unit survey, 17% of my students checked the following item: "I do not know enough about AI to have feelings or thoughts about AI." In the post-unit survey, 0% of my students checked that same item. This indicated that my new AI unit met its goal in teaching students the basics of AI (at least to the point of having feelings and thoughts about it).

In addition, in the post-unit survey, I added four questions devised to help me improve the unit next year:

- Describe the most important thing(s) you learned in the AI unit. Explain why they were important to you.

- Describe your favorite part of the AI unit and explain why it was your favorite.

- Describe your least favorite part of the AI unit and explain why it was your least favorite.

- Describe changes you would make to the AI unit if you were the teacher and explain how the changes would improve the unit.

I always enjoy student feedback and suggestions, and I often use student ideas when planning for the next year, or where applicable, the next unit. Yet, I don't always plan out a systematic way to gather students' feedback and reflect upon it. Creating the space for students to provide feedback via a survey conducted at the close of this inquiry cycle enabled me to ensure I learned from every single one of my students about what they believed to be their most important AI learning, their favorite and least favorite aspects of the unit, and changes they would make. I am looking forward to incorporating what I learned from analysis of their responses into the AI unit when I teach it again next year.

Surveys can also be used in similar ways with adults. First-grade teacher Candy Bryan and third-grade teacher Kelly Reilly-Kaminski completed a shared inquiry project that focused on understanding effective parent communication, relying primarily on surveys to gather information. In the following excerpt, note the way their wondering(s) about parent communication logically led to using a survey as the main form of data collection. Also note the ways in which their data collection plan changed over time.

> As a result of enrolling in a professional development course on teacher inquiry, we found the opportunity to discuss an area of concern in our classrooms. Both of us believed that parent involvement is directly related to student success in the classroom. Children will be more successful academically, complete more homework, achieve higher grades, have more positive attitudes, and behave better if parents are more involved. After all, who is a child's first and most important teacher? The answer to this question is obvious. By involving parents, teachers gain a unique perspective that provides valuable information into a child's education. According to the National Parent and Teachers Association (PTA):
>
> Over 30 years' research has proven beyond dispute the positive connection between parent involvement and student success. Effectively engaging parents and families in the education of their children has the potential to be far more transformational than any other type of educational reform. (National Parent and Teachers Association, 1997, p. 5)
>
> We wondered about what methods of communication parents found valuable, what we could do to be more effective, and what trends appear as students mature from the primary grades (beginning with Candy in first grade) to the intermediate grades (beginning with Kelly at third grade). At the conclusion of our research project, it was our intention to make changes to our current practices that parents would find valuable and insightful. These changes would provide parents with more information concerning their child's education and benefit all parties involved: students, parents, and teachers.
>
> To gather the data, we needed to find out more about the parents' need for communication. We relied heavily on parent surveys to gather information. We surveyed the parents once at the beginning of the project using the survey labeled

Parental Survey 1 [see Exhibit 3.2]. We asked questions about home-school journals, newsletters, and websites and asked for suggestions about other forms of communication that they might find useful. After reviewing the surveys, we realized that we needed to ask clarifying questions. Unfortunately, the first survey was done anonymously. We were hoping to receive more honest answers if we didn't require the parents to sign the survey. This was a problem because we needed to survey some of the parents again in order to clarify their responses. We were hoping to follow up by using short parent interviews over the phone. Instead, because we didn't know who filled out which survey, we had to survey the entire population again. In the second survey, labeled Parental Survey 2 [see Exhibit 3.3], we asked for the parents' preferences and suggestions about communication and participation as a volunteer in the classroom. We added the piece about participation because of input from the first survey. We also added a few questions about email as a communication tool. (Bryan & Reilly-Kaminski, 2002)

Exhibit 3.2 Parental Survey 1

I will use the results of this survey to improve communication between home and school. Please fill the survey out honestly and if you have any questions, please contact me at the school.

1. What forms of communication from me do you find useful (e.g., home-school journals, newsletters, website)?
2. Do you read the newsletter with your child? What sections do you find the most valuable, if any? What sections are not of value to you, if any?
3. Do you have any suggestions on how I can improve the current newsletter? If so, please describe them.
4. Do you visit the classroom website? What components do you find the most valuable, if any? What sections are not of value to you, if any?
5. Do you have any suggestions for how I can improve the current classroom website? If so, please describe them.
6. Do you find home-school journals valuable? In what ways?
7. Are there any other forms of communication that you would find valuable? If so, please explain.

Source: Used with permission of Candy Bryan and Kelly Reilly-Kaminski.

An important lesson learned about data collection from Candy and Kelly is that shifting gears midway through your inquiry, and adjusting your original plan as your inquiry unfolds, is not unusual. Originally, Candy and Kelly planned on doing one survey and follow-up phone interviews. Based on information that emerged on the first survey as well as the realization that they were unable to target particular parents with follow-up interviews because the first survey was completed anonymously, Candy and Kelly constructed a second survey.

Exhibit 3.3   Parental Survey 2

Dear Parents,

I am still working on my research project about parent communication. I have some questions about home-school journals and parent volunteers.

Home-school journals are journals that would be kept in your child's homework folder. They are meant to act as a two-way communication tool. If you had a question or comment to make, you could just write the note in the journal. I would read the journal and respond. I could also use it to communicate individually with parents when I have something to tell you.

Please answer Yes or No.

_____ Do you think you would use a journal like this?

_____ Do you have e-mail?

_____ Would you like to use e-mail to communicate?

If so, please provide the address. _____

_____ Would you prefer e-mail to a home-school journal?

Would you like to participate or volunteer more in the classroom?

Yes or No

If you responded by circling the Yes, please check the items below that you would like to help with.

_____ Typing students' stories

_____ Helping with trips

In addition to helping with these two options, how else do you think I could use parent volunteers?

Please write your name below and return this form to school.

_____

Source: Used with permission of Candy Bryan and Kelly Reilly-Kaminski.

Departing from your original data collection plan is a natural part of the inquiry process. If you find as your inquiry unfolds that forms of data collection you employed need to be adjusted—adjust accordingly! If you find as your inquiry unfolds that different forms of data collection you hadn't planned on using may be insightful to your wondering—use them! Just keep track of the decisions you make as an inquirer along the way, as articulating changes in course can also be an important piece of what you are learning.

In our final example of survey data, we return to high school chemistry teacher Stephen Burgin. In the school year that followed his Demo-A-Day inquiry, Stephen was dissatisfied with the ways his required afterschool help sessions were going. He had observed that a small group of his students were not paying attention in class because they could rely on the extra-help sessions to pick up anything they missed. In an effort to make his extra-help sessions more meaningful to students and less frustrating for Stephen, he again used the process of inquiry to explore the overarching question, "What is the most productive way to structure afterschool help?" Stephen's subquestions included the following:

- What are students' perceptions and expectations for extra help?
- What is the relationship between misbehavior during class and attendance at afterschool help?
- What skills do my students need to take charge of their extra help?
- What is the chemistry skill level of my students who seek help outside of class?

Note the ways in which Stephen's subquestions led to the development of a survey, administered to all of his chemistry students, to begin his inquiry (see Exhibit 3.4).

Once Stephen administered this survey, he tallied and compared responses with his record of attendance at extra-help sessions and observational notes he had taken since the beginning of the year. As a result of reflecting on his initial survey, attendance, and observation data, Stephen was able to name and sort his students into four distinct categories.

> Upon reflection, it became apparent that four groups of students were emerging. The first group of students attended my help sessions regularly and benefited from them based on my observations and survey responses. The second group of

Exhibit 3.4 Chemistry "Help Session" Student Survey

Instructions: Please respond to these statements anonymously according to the following scale:

1	2	3	4	5
Strongly Agree	Agree	Neutral	Disagree	Strongly Disagree
1. I pay attention most of the time during chemistry class.				
1	2	3	4	5
2. I have attended multiple help sessions this year.				
1	2	3	4	5
3. I only attend help sessions if there is a quiz or test coming up.				
1	2	3	4	5
4. I feel like my attendance at help sessions has impacted my understanding of chemistry.				
1	2	3	4	5
5. I come to help sessions because I want to do well in chemistry class.				
1	2	3	4	5
6. I come to help sessions because my parents and/or teachers make me.				
1	2	3	4	5
7. I think that help sessions should be led by my teacher.				
1	2	3	4	5
8. I think that help sessions should be led based on questions that I have.				
1	2	3	4	5

Source: Used with permission of Stephen Burgin.

students attended my help sessions but gained nothing from them according to my observations and survey data. The third group of students did not attend help sessions and their achievement in my class seemed to indicate that they did not need to. And the fourth group of students was those who did not attend help sessions, but probably should have. In order to gain further insights into these four distinct groups of students, I proceeded to collect data through interviews. I selected some students that fit into each of these categories to talk with and compared their responses to similar questions. (Burgin, 2007b)

Stephen's research offers another important lesson about data collection. When engaging in teacher research for the first time, it is easy to conceptualize data collection and data analysis as concrete, distinct entities that teachers progress through in a lockstep manner (i.e., First I will collect my data. After all my data are collected, then I will analyze them.). Rather, data collection and data analysis are often iterative processes that teacher researchers vacillate between over the course of their inquiries. According to Thorne (2000),

> Because data collection and analysis processes tend to be concurrent, with new analytic steps informing the process of additional data collection and new data informing the analytic processes, it is important to recognize that qualitative data analysis processes are not entirely distinguishable from the actual data collection. The theoretical lens from which the [teacher] researcher approaches the phenomenon, the strategies that the researcher uses to collect or construct data, and the understandings that the researcher has about what might count as relevant or important data in answering the research question are all analytic processes. (Thorne, 2000, p. 3)

In Stephen's case, the collection and subsequent analysis of his survey data, observation data, and attendance data led Stephen to the collection of additional data and a specified procedure for how to collect it—student interviews sampled from four categories of students. We revisit the close relationship between data collection and data analysis in Chapter 5.

Sometimes, the use of technology as a tool for data collection can help the close relationship between data collection and data analysis develop. For example, to better understand the reading habits and interests of the high-school sophomore English students in one of her teacher education program's clinical experiences at Loras College, teacher candidate Kelly Minear created a survey via Google Forms to kick off a cycle of inquiry. Kelly explains how using Google Forms for survey development and administration enabled her to streamline both the data collection and analysis process:

> When it came time to analyze data, I could look either at individual responses or at the collection of responses. Based on the questions, the results were automatically organized into pie charts, bar graphs, and a list of answers. For short

answers, similar answers were grouped together: if multiple students listed a particular book they enjoyed reading in school, those students were listed in the same area. This helped me to focus on relevant responses. In addition, using Google Forms for the survey in the data collection phase of my inquiry helped me in the data analysis phase since I could easily export the results to an Excel document. For short answer responses, I used a color-coding technique to categorize similar answers on the document. This made it easy to pull out the main learnings I was able to gather through my data collection and also compare my survey results to any articles I read on the subject. (Minear, 2018, personal communications)

While the data analysis process Kelly describes above will also be fully explicated for you in Chapter 5, we provide a preview to this process in this chapter since collection and analysis are so closely related to one another (as is each component of inquiry).

SKIP AHEAD

Ready for more details on data analysis? If so, skip ahead to Chapter 5, page 231.

Strategy 9: Quantitative Measures of Student Achievement (Standardized Test Scores, Assessment Measures, Grades)

In this era of high-stakes testing and accountability, numerous quantitative measures of student performance abound, and these measures can be valuable sources of data for the teacher researcher. For example, high school biology teacher Mickey MacDonald was struck by the differences in the grades she and her ninth-grade teaching colleagues in English, world cultures, and Algebra I had assigned their students when they met for their routine end-of-the-quarter team meeting to share, compare, and discuss students who had received grades of D and F in their courses. This led Mickey to use teacher research to better understand these grading discrepancies. In the following excerpt from Mickey's work, note how her grading dilemma leads her to select grades and achievement test data as one source to glean insights into her wondering.

I am a high school science teacher in my third year of teaching at P. K. Yonge Developmental Research School. Like most teachers, I want my students to succeed in my class. More importantly, I want to prepare my students to be successful in other science classes. I am disturbed that my students' grades, at least at a cursory level, appear deflated in comparison with my team's grades and in comparison with our overall middle and high school grade distributions.

Based on all of the questions running through my mind, I narrowed down my wondering to this: In what ways can examining my class grades, other instructors' grades, and standardized test scores enable me to address the apparent grade deflation that my students experience? Within this wondering, I will use these subquestions to guide me as I attempt to address my dilemma. They are as follows:

- Is there a relationship between my students' first semester science grades and math grades?

- Is there a correlation between my students' first semester science grades and their Florida Comprehensive Assessment Test (FCAT) reading and math scores?

- Are there any differences in science grades based on gender or grade level?

As I was developing what my inquiry would look like, I began to research what the literature said about grade deflation. Although a search on the term *grade deflation* did not provide any research, a search on *grade inflation* did. Two articles that I read both indicated that grade inflation exists in high schools. In a June 2004 report, Cook (2004) writes, "Even though SAT scores remain . . . unchanged, college applicants are receiving more As than ever as grade inflation reaches new heights in the nation's high schools." This statistic was first noted in a *Forbes* article in which the author wrote, "Between 1991 and 2001, a period when SAT-measured aptitude was essentially flat, the proportion of test-takers receiving grade point averages of at least A– rose from 29% to 41%" (Seligman, 2002). *U.S. News and World Report* also reported in 2000 that, although students reported being tuned out in high school, a record number were receiving As, even though there were no indicators that levels of achievement had improved over the past 30 years (Wildavsky, 2000). Based on the literature, my students were not experiencing the grade inflation trend. If anything, it appeared that my students were experiencing the opposite.

In designing my inquiry, I knew that I had a plethora of raw data available to me. The key was choosing the data that would provide the best insight into my wondering. I decided that I would limit the data that I had available to teacher-issued data and achievement test data. For teacher-issued data, I chose to look at grades from our first semester in biology and math. For achievement test data, I chose the Florida Comprehensive Assessment Test (FCAT) Sunshine State Standard reading and math scores and achievement levels. I compiled all of these data into an Excel spreadsheet, which I could sort by grades, achievement levels, class, gender, and other indicators. (MacDonald, 2007, p. 51)

Because Mickey's dilemma and wondering were directly related to test scores and grades, this form of data collection was a natural selection for her inquiry. Because these data were already collected and available at her school, all Mickey needed to do was compile the data of her students in an Excel spreadsheet that would enable her to sort and view this data in different ways. Table 3.1 contains a sample spreadsheet.

Table 3.1 Mickey's Spreadsheet

GENDER	GRADE LEVEL	05–06 FIRST SEM. BIOLOGY GRADE	MATH SUBJECT	05–06 FIRST SEM. MATH GRADE	SSS READING AL	SSS READING SCALE SCORE	SSS MATH AL	SSS MATH SCALE SCORE
F	10	A	Geometry	B	1	274	3	307
M	10	A	Geometry	A	2	287	3	324
F	10	A	Geometry	A	2	304	3	312
M	10	A	Geometry Hon.	A	2	315	4	342
F	9	A	Geometry Hon.	A	4	353	4	351
F	9	A	Algebra I Hon.	B	4	358	3	336
M	10	B	App Math II	B	1	268	2	271
F	10	B	Geometry	D	1	280	3	319
M	10	B	Geometry	C	2	285	2	290
F	10	B	Geometry Hon.	B	2	289	4	345
F	10	B	App Math II	C	2	292	2	268

GENDER	GRADE LEVEL	05–06 FIRST SEM. BIOLOGY GRADE	MATH SUBJECT	05–06 FIRST SEM. MATH GRADE	SSS READING AL	SSS READING SCALE SCORE	SSS MATH AL	SSS MATH SCALE SCORE
M	10	B	Geometry	B	2	301	3	307
M	10	B	Geometry	B	2	307	3	326
F	9	B	Algebra I	B	3	310	3	330
M	9	B	Algebra I	A	3	313	3	334
F	9	B	Algebra I	C	3	314	3	319
F	10	B	Geometry	B	2	319	4	345
M	10	B	Geometry	C	2	321	3	312
F	9	B	Algebra I	B	3	322	3	316
F	10	B	Algebra II	C	3	328	3	325
M	10	B	Geometry Hon.	B	3	339	4	332
M	10	B	Algebra II Hon.	C	3	343	4	354
M	10	B	Geometry Hon.	B	3	345	4	354
M	9	B	Algebra I Hon.	B	3	349	4	352
M	10	B	Geometry	B	4	359	3	303
M	9	B	Algebra I Hon.	B	4	370	4	370
F	9	B	Algebra II Hon.	A	4	371	5	399
M	9	B	Algebra I	B				
M	10	B	Algebra I	B				
M	10	C	Geometry Hon.	C	1	253	3	325
M	10	C	Inf. Geometry	B	1	265	3	330
M	10	C	Geometry Hon.	C	1	267	4	333
F	9	C	Geometry Hon.	B	2	278	4	359
M	10	C	Geometry	B	1	281	3	305
M	10	C	Geometry Hon.	B	2	285	4	336
M	10	C	Geometry	C	2	286	3	310
F	10	C	Geometry	C	2	289	3	309
F	10	C	Geometry	D	2	290	3	301
M	10	C	Geometry	C	2	290	2	291

Source: Used with permission of Mickey MacDonald.

For an example of assessment data, we turn to the work of fourth-grade teacher Debbi Hubbell (2006), who decided to look closely at one of her teaching passions—reading—through inquiry. Debbi knew that one of the best predictors of performance on Florida's yearly standardized test was reading fluency and that research has shown a direct correlation between fluency and comprehension. She wanted to help her students become more successful readers and believed that if they became more fluent, they would develop their reading comprehension. In the end, this would also allow them to perform better on the state assessment.

Worried about seven students she believed were at risk and less fluent than others in her class, she decided to explore in more detail the research related to developing fluency in elementary readers. She attended numerous workshops and read a variety of research-based articles that developed her knowledge of fluency. As a result of this knowledge development, Debbi introduced the rereading of fractured fairy tale plays to these seven learners to see if this activity might increase reading fluency. The fractured fairy tales differed from the more traditional skill and drill activity these students often encountered in daily reading instruction.

To gain insights into her wondering, "What is the relationship between my fourth-graders' fluency development and the reading of fractured fairy tale plays?," Debbi's first form of data collection was her administration and scoring of Dynamic Indicators of Basic Early Literacy Skills (DIBELS) at different time periods throughout her research. The DIBELS are a set of standardized, individually administered measures of early literacy development. They are designed to be short, one-minute fluency measures used to regularly monitor the development of prereading and early reading skills. This assessment measure was a practice her school already engaged in and provided Debbi with data to assess her students' fluency development over time (see Table 3.2).

Table 3.2 Debbi's DIBELS Data

	DIBELS TEST DATE				
	10/18	12/1	2/10	2/21	4/6
J	48*	53*	55*	60*	73*
B	81*	98-	114-	105-	164
C	90-	98-	95-	100-	130

DIBELS TEST DATE					
	10/18	12/1	2/10	2/21	4/6
Ja	64*	70*	92-	85*	119-
T	93-	96-	88*	97-	121
S	94-	91-	86*	78*	113-
M	84-	101-	99-	107-	127

* = at-risk
- = less fluent

Source: Used with permission of Debbi Hubbell.

One note of caution regarding standardized test scores, grades, and assessment measures: Because these types of data take the form of numbers, they are consonant with traditional notions of research many teachers hold. In fact, two of the first images teachers often conjure up when they hear the word *research* is number crunching and statistical analyses. Because of this image, as well as the prevalence and focus on these types of data in schools today, standardized test scores, assessment measures, and grades are sometimes the first and only type of data teacher researchers think about collecting (Dana & Yendol-Hoppey, 2008b). Yet Roland Barth reminds us that "good education is more than good scores and good teaching is more than generating good scores" (Barth, 2001, p. 156). Similarly, good teacher research is about more than generating good test scores or showing the relationship between one's teaching practice and one's students' performance on state tests. If you are planning on using standardized test scores, assessment measures, or grades as a form of data collection for your inquiry, it is critical to delve deeply into these data, understanding what the test/assessment you are relying on was designed to measure and being sure to use the measure in the ways it was designed to be used. Consider the following real scenario depicting a superficial use and reliance on standardized test score data reported by Love (2004).

> When educators in one Texas high school saw African-American students' performance drop slightly below 50% on their state mathematics test, putting the school on the state's list of low-performing schools, they reacted quickly. Decision makers immediately suggested that all African-American students, whether or not they failed the test, be assigned peer tutors (Olsen, 2003). Based on one piece of data and one way of looking at that data, these decision

> makers made assumptions and leapt to action before fully understanding the issue or verifying their assumptions with other data sources. They ignored past trends, which indicated that African-American students' scores were on an upward trajectory. They failed to consider that the decline was so small that it could better be explained by chance or measuring error than by their instructional program. They considered only the percent failing without digging deeper into the data to consider what students needed. Finally, they proposed intervention targeted only for African-American students, while overlooking Hispanic and white students who also failed the test. (Love, 2004, p. 22)

To guard against your own teacher research unfolding as the scenario just described, remember that standardized test scores and other assessment data can provide valuable information for the teacher researcher but need to be interpreted carefully and considered along with other data sources as well. Debbi Hubbell learned this valuable lesson in her fractured fairy tale inquiry, where she admits that when she was first planning this inquiry, she intended to rely solely on the DIBELS scores to ascertain the meaning that fractured fairy tale pedagogy held for her students. After discussing her proposed inquiry with colleagues, she was questioned regarding this single form of data collection, and she added to her data collection plan two additional strategies. In addition to DIBELS data, Debbi took anecdotal notes each time she used fractured fairy tale plays with these fourth-grade students, documenting their reactions and engagement and her assessment of their fluency development with each rereading of a play. Finally, Debbi relied on student work or artifacts as a third data source. At the end of the fractured fairy tale series, Debbi asked her students to write "Dear Mrs. Hubbell" letters, telling her about their perceptions and experiences with the fractured fairy tale unit of study.

In reflecting on what she learned as a result of engaging in this research, Debbi shared the following:

> What I did not expect to learn seems more important than the DIBELS data to me. I learned the following:
> 1. Students love to be engaged in meaningful reading (even those who previously did not want to *ever* read—this year or before). A student, who when asked replied he had hated school and was failing, actually said later he enjoyed this

aspect of school and improved at least by a grade or more in *each* subject.

2. Excellent prosody could be obtained, more than I expected, through the reading of fractured fairy tales. I only expected words per minute to be increased, but was very amazed at the expression that was produced by these very motivated students.

3. A student who had complications with comprehension that I could not account for seemed to overcome these difficulties and become successful on reading tests that assessed comprehension.

4. Positive social interactions occurred between students who previously had difficulty communicating in a positive way. Students enjoyed helping each other in a kinder way when someone made a mistake, and tolerance as well as admiration was practiced with more difficult relationships.

5. Students will give up a time (recess) that is valuable to them to produce a theatrical version of a play.

6. Students reported these things in a letter to me:
    - It helped me read better and made me smarter.
    - I learned to try your best and do not be embarrassed.
    - I'm a more fluent reader.
    - The fairy tales bring more happiness to the school day and more laughter to the morning.
    - We don't have to be perfect.
    - The tales improved my vocabulary.
    - The plays helped me read with more expression. (Hubbell, 2006, p. 7)

By drawing on multiple sources of data, Debbi was able to develop a much richer picture of what was occurring in relation to her use of fractured fairy tale plays to deliver reading instruction than she would have been able to develop had she collected and relied on DIBELS data exclusively. One of the reasons we engage in teacher research is that it honors all the great complexity of teaching. In most cases, no single source of data (whether student work, field notes, interviews, focus groups, pictures, video, journals, blogs, surveys, or standardized test scores and assessments) can adequately capture all the great complexity inherent in teaching. Therefore, it is important for teacher researchers to use multiple forms of data as they design their inquiries in order to develop the richest possible picture they can of what is occurring in the classroom. We further discuss the importance of multiple data sources when we cover the topic of inquiry planning in the next chapter.

Strategy 10: Colleague Feedback

As they inquire, many teachers seek feedback from their colleagues. Such feedback is a powerful, yet frequently underutilized, source of knowledge in schools. As a data collection strategy, colleague feedback can be used to capture the thinking of your colleagues about your inquiry. Colleague feedback can be collected from a wide variety of settings such as faculty meetings, teacher inquiry communities, peer observations of teaching, instructional rounds, and, as in Mickey MacDonald's inquiry, from Critical Friends Groups (CFGs).

Like Debbi Hubbell in the previous example, versed in the importance of drawing on multiple sources of data in her inquiry on grade deflation, Mickey MacDonald also collected data in more ways than standardized test scores and grades. One of the additional ways she collected data was by garnering feedback from her colleagues in a CFG. As introduced in Chapter 1, CFGs are one version of PLCs developed by the National School Reform Faculty (NSRF; www.nsrf-harmony.org). The NSRF defines a CFG as "a Professional Learning Community consisting of approximately 8–12 educators who come together voluntarily at least once a month for about two hours. Group members are committed to improving their practice through collaborative learning" (NSRF, 2007). Protocols developed by NSRF and available on their website systematize and guide the dialogue that occurs between teachers at these meetings. Mickey found a CFG to be a particularly insightful source of colleague feedback as data for her inquiry. She writes:

> One data piece that I knew would be very insightful would be to get my colleagues to help me interpret my data. I enlisted their input using P. K. Yonge's three secondary Critical Friends Groups [CFGs]. Each group was given the Excel spreadsheet data that I had compiled [see Table 3.1]. Using the protocol called Making Meaning (https://www.nsrfharmony.org/wp-content/uploads/2017/10/making_meaning_0.pdf), each group described, asked questions, and speculated about the meaning/significance of my Excel spreadsheet, and discussed the implications of my spreadsheet to their work.

As teachers read the text (my spreadsheet), they wrote comments and highlighted things they noticed. As each group began to discuss the text, comments were recorded as minutes. (MacDonald, 2007, p. 53)

Exhibit 3.5 illustrates the recorded comments from this CFG discussion.

Exhibit 3.5 Mickey's Critical Friends Group Feedback

March 8, 2006, PKY Critical Friends Group Comments (Division: M. MacDonald)

What Do You See? Describing the Text

- NJD: 5 in SSS AL, yet C in math/bio. Questions the validity of these tests (standardized).
- GS: Ditto; overall, sees similar grades in both classes (math/sci correlation).
- CK: Math grades often one higher than sci grades.
- TR: Looked at high-math SSS vs. low-math class grades. But saw opposite as well; not convinced a correlation exists.
- TA: Grades seem to approximate bell curve; sci/math grades; only nine students have differential of two or more grades (e.g., A/C or B/D).
- CD: Lots of C/C/3/3 students. Interesting distribution of students who are two or more SSS AL levels apart (between reading and math AL): 2 in bio got an A, 3 got B, 12 a C, 5 a D, and none of the bio grade Fs.
- AM: 4 of 6 people who got As are below average in FCAT reading. One student (D.R.), low-level reading, expect low grade, yet math score is 3 FCAT, and D in math class. Amy thinks this is a bit swippety-swappety. Lots of high reading achievers in Cs and Ds.
- BR: Disbursements of Ds and Fs; many Fs in science but only two across the board in math. Is this because of intensive math classes?
- MM: # as same in both classes. In math, lower proportion of lower grades; science had a flip-flop, yet # of Cs about the same (between math/biology). Overall, bell curve is skewed to the right in science, and to the left in math.

(Continued)

(Continued)

- NDean: Interested in relationship between intensity level of the math class and how it might affect grade distribution.

What questions does examining this data raise?

- NDean: How do you infer grade deflation from this data?
- NJD: How can we apply this type of data to directly solve something in our courses?
- GS: Might this data reflect students who know the material but who lack a strong schoolwork ethic?
- CK: Difficult to draw accurate correlations; this data might not be an accurate indicator.
- TR: How do math/sci reasoning relate?
- TA: Are grades reflecting attitude and behavior more so than ability? (Assuming FCAT measures ability to begin with.) Are Mickey's grades inflated or deflated?
- CD: What if we had more data? Could we draw additional conclusions without the benefit of a computerized database?
- AM: How are grades calculated in Mickey's class? And how are they weighted? How might this information differ if it had been state-supplied (how does it affect our expectations of student performance?) Is FCAT a measure of grade inflation?
- BR: Why only one biology level, and yet multiple levels of applied math? Why are grades so much higher in intensive math? Does this reflect that a student is on the "correct" path (meeting state expectations)?
- MM: Wanted a way to compare overall grades of her classes to their other grades. Sees a similar pattern, but perhaps no direct correlation.

What questions does this text raise for you?

- CD: Could Mickey's high-performers (yet low SSS ALs) be due to particular teaching methods used?
- NJD: Worried about misuse of data in justifying our own personal agendas or matching our own expectations? Is it wrong to put more trust in data than personal methods and observations?
- TR: How will you (Mickey) let this data impact your instruction?
- MM: Adamant about late work = zero policy. Hoping that ninth-grade team meetings would result in better student work turn-in rate.

- TR: Would you use this data to affect how you weight different categories of class assignments (readings, tests, etc.)?
- MM: Possibly, but past experience shows it doesn't overall affect student work completion.
- AM: How much reading is in Mickey's bio class?
- MM: Minimal, often based on notes, quizzes, essays.
- TR: How much of biology is based on ability to read textbook vs. comprehend material and form/reason original conclusions?
- CK: Is having increased # of intervention math students in biology next year going to adversely affect overall bio grade distribution?

Implications on Our Work

- NJD: It is good to collect data; have a quantitative approach . . . but not a good idea to base legislation on it . . . but conversations like this are a good idea. Fears government moving forward without adequate teacher input.
- AM: Did a student's low FCAT score prevent them from taking a higher-level science? (Bio Honors, e.g.) Frustrated.
- BR: 90%+ students are within one letter grade (between sci/math); believes this an indicator of balance and the grading system in general.

Source: Used with permission of Mickey MacDonald.

In this next excerpt from Mickey's work (see page 147), note the ways in which colleague feedback from her CFG, as a source of data, stimulated Mickey's own thinking about her research. Note too how the feedback led to her collection of additional data through student interviews, providing another example of the ways data collection and analysis are iterative processes. Finally, note the ways in which Mickey's inquiry led to action (changes she planned to make in her practice based on what she learned through this cycle of inquiry).

> Using the collection of comments from each CFG discussion, I summarized each step in the protocol called Making Meaning. In the first step, "Describing the Text," members were asked what they saw when they looked at my Excel spreadsheet data. Members were reminded to make comments without judgments or interpretations. Some quotes from members (denoted in italics) are followed by

interpretations or questions that I have about each comment (in plain print):

- *"[There are] lots of C/C/3/3 students."*

  Many of the students received semester grades of C in biology and their math class and also had Level 3 on their reading and math FCAT scores.

- *"In the D-range for biology, there are a larger number of Level 1s and 2s in reading and math scores."*

  I need to see how many students with a semester grade of D are Level 1 or Level 2 in FCAT reading and math.

In the second step of the Making Meaning protocol, CFG members posed questions that my spreadsheet raised for them. Some questions shared by my colleagues (denoted in italics and followed by my interpretations/questions in plain print) included the following:

- *"Disbursements of Ds and Fs. . . . [There are] many Fs in science but only two across the board in math. Is this because of intensive math classes?"*

  All of my students are in one level of science. The same students are split into seven levels of math classes ranging from Intensive Math 1 (a remedial mathematics course) through Geometry Honors.

- *"How can we apply this type of data to directly solve something in our courses?"*

  This question concerning data-driven instruction is asked more and more frequently of teachers.

- *"Might this data reflect students who know the material but who lack a strong school work ethic?"*

  I need to examine the homework grades and compare these to biology test scores to see if, in fact, these students do know the material but do not complete homework.

In the third step of the Making Meaning protocol, my critical friends were asked the questions "What is significant about my spreadsheet?" and "What meaning can you construct from it?" Comments (denoted in italics and followed by my interpretations/questions in plain print) included the following:

- *"There shouldn't be this many Biology 1 students."*

  Maybe we should offer alternate choices for the science class that students can take in ninth and tenth grade. With the new legislation that the Florida Department of Education is implementing with the incoming ninth-grade class of 2007–8, we will need to offer a major in the area of science. This may allow for more choices for our students.

- *"Worried about misuse of data. . . . Is it wrong to put more trust in [this kind of] data than personal methods and observations?"*

  Looking at number data may negate a critical form of assessment that teachers use all the time to ensure student learning.

- *"Would you use this data to affect how you weight different categories of class assignments [readings, tests, etc.]?"*

  I am not sure that this is the real issue I need to focus on. Altering the weighting may cause the grade distribution to shift left, but it doesn't change student learning in any way.

Following the CFG discussions of the data, I used colleagues' suggestions to closely examine the data by gender and by grade level. I was astonished by the grade distributions of my male students compared to my female students. Although the female grade distribution looked much like a bell curve, the male distribution was extremely skewed to the right, with a high percentage of Ds and Fs. This data clearly shows that I am not reaching my male population.

Based on another recommendation from the CFG discussion, I sorted my data based on grade level. When I analyzed this sort of the data, the grade distributions by gender and grade level were again the same for both ninth- and tenth-grade males. They were all skewed to the right. For the ninth- and tenth-grade females, the graphs were the shape of bell curves. Regardless of the grade level of my students, I am not reaching my male students.

Following the CFG insights into my student data and my own detailed analysis of my student data, I decided to interview two subgroups of students. First, I wanted to talk to female students who were achieving at a high level in biology, even though they were below grade level in reading. Next, I wanted to interview male students who were not achieving in biology but who were at or above grade level in reading and math.

My first interview was with a 10th-grade female student who received an A in biology, although she had scored a Level 1 in reading on the FCAT. I asked her the following question: "Biology requires extensive reading. Your FCAT reading score is low, and yet you scored an A for first semester in biology. What do you feel allowed you to be so successful in biology this year?" She responded with the following:

- "Different subjects in biology holds interest better than the FCAT reading topics."
- "[We] repeat material in biology over and over and follow the textbook."
- "I learn from listening, not reading."
- "Reading strategies used in intensive reading are also used in biology, like highlighting and anticipation guides."
- "Teacher explanations [are helpful]."

A second tenth-grade female, an A student in biology who also performed at a Level 1 in reading on the FCAT, responded with the following:

- "I try really hard—good grades are important to me."
- "I always do my homework."
- "I ask questions."
- "I have more time in biology than on the FCAT—I'm not stressed in class."

Next, I interviewed a tenth-grade male student who received a D in biology yet scored a Level 4 in reading and math on the ninth-grade FCAT. I said to this student, "Your FCAT scores are excellent in both reading and math. Your grade in biology is a D. Why do you think you are not doing better in biology?" This is what he told me:

- "I'm unorganized and the homework policy hurts me. If I can't finish work in class, it doesn't get done or it doesn't get brought back to class. I get a lot of zeros on homework."
- "There is a lot more homework in high school than in middle school. It counts more."
- "I like hands-on stuff; we don't do enough hands-on in class."
- "I don't study much."

As a teacher, these interviews tell me that I need to continue to emphasize organizational skills to my students through modeling. I need to offer different ways of learning the curriculum. This might include more hands-on activities for the kinesthetic learners. I also need to figure out a way to avoid punishing students who can learn the material without completing the repetitive assignments that other students require to be successful.

So much data, so little time . . . yet I have managed to gain some insights into what all these data mean for me and how this inquiry has changed how I view my charge as a teacher. I am beginning a new academic year now. My main goal for this year is to target those male students who have poor work habits in homework completion and poor organizational skills. The two areas that I will address to help this group of students are maintaining organized, complete notebooks and increasing the number of inquiry, hands-on type activities. I will model maintaining an organized notebook. Open notebook quizzes that reward students who stay organized will be used regularly. I will sit down with specific students to be certain that they complete their notebook as demonstrated.

I will also use more hands-on, inquiry-type activities with my regular earth science classes in order to increase student engagement. Hands-on activities will require that the students work in groups for extended times. Because management of behavior during hands-on activities is a concern for me, I will be working with two middle school teachers who facilitate group work regularly, as well as two high school science teachers who have been doing inquiry science within their classes. I also plan to attend a Kagan Workshop on cooperative learning. This workshop is offered as a professional development opportunity at our school.

This is my second inquiry project in as many years. The value of looking at my practice and choosing what I believe will help me as a teacher, as well as my students as learners, is immeasurable. The questions answered through inquiry have led me to ask more questions. These can only be answered through more cycles of inquiry. A new school year and so many new inquiry prospects. . . . What an exciting process! (MacDonald, 2007, p. 53–57)

When Do I Begin Data Collection?

Now that data collection has been defined and you have seen some examples of what data collection might look like, you are ready to return to the wondering you began crafting in Chapter 2 and consider which forms of data collection might work to inform it. Considering possible data collection strategies that can inform a question can help you further develop and refine the question itself. At this point it is extremely valuable to develop a comprehensive plan for your inquiry. Hubbard and Power suggest that teacher researchers write an inquiry brief, defined as "a detailed outline completed before the research study begins" (Hubbard & Power, 1999, p. 47). Through the process of developing a brief, teacher inquirers commit their energies to one idea. This commitment facilitates an inquirer's readiness to begin data collection. In the next chapter, we walk you through planning your inquiry and developing an inquiry brief.

CHAPTER 3 EXERCISES

1. Collect work produced by a single student over a particular time or by your whole class in relationship to a small group of related lessons. Read through this collected data set and consider the difference between looking at individual student work in isolation in order to provide feedback/grade it versus looking at it in the context of collected work produced over time by a student and/or a collection of work completed by your entire class. What kinds of different insights emerge for you when looking at student work in a collection verses in isolation?

2. Consider the various forms field notes can take that were presented in this chapter and try your hand at taking your own field notes or asking a colleague to take field notes for you with a particular focus as you teach. You might utilize a meeting of a CFG or other PLC as an ideal context within which to practice field noting. Make a note of what you learn about field noting as a result of practicing this data collection strategy. Save your notes to return to at a later date should you decide to incorporate this data collection strategy into your inquiry journey.

3. While interviews and focus groups can simply take the form of circulating during instruction to ask students about their thinking as they complete an independent activity or a class meeting, learn more about how to formulate a semi-structured interview by reviewing a brief YouTube video from Delve (https://www.youtube.com/watch?v=Un-0du-Vcm0). Once you've reviewed this guidance,

begin to develop your interview guide using the template in Online Material Activity 3.2.

4. Become a classroom photographer or videographer by choosing a purpose to snap pictures of or video a particular activity in your classroom using your cell phone. Return to the pictures or video you collected at a later date and ponder, "What do I notice in these pictures/video that I did not notice at the time?" and "What do these noticings reveal?"

5. Try your hand at journaling by selecting one topic you'd like to journal about for one week's time. Set aside 10 minutes at the end of each school day to write down your thoughts and feelings in relationship to the topic chosen. At the close of the week, read through all your journal entries and consider what you have learned about the value of journaling as one form of data collection to capture your thinking as a teacher.

6. Think of an education topic you would like to understand more about your students', their parents'/caregivers', or your colleagues' views on that knowledge of would be valuable to your classroom practice. Design and distribute a brief survey on the topic (e.g., See Brenda Breil's Survey in the second AI Moment textbox in this chapter). After you collect and review the completed surveys, make note of what you learn about this data collection strategy and how you might improve upon survey design if you choose surveys as one form of data collection for your inquiry journey.

7. Generate a list of potential contexts in which you can tap into your colleagues' thinking about your inquiry's topic. For example, do you meet regularly with a PLC? Do you meet as a department or grade-level teaching team? Could faculty meetings provide time for sharing and discussing ideas about teaching? Once you have listed several possible contexts, identify one context that you think could provide a productive source of colleague feedback for your inquiry. Next, review the list of data collection strategies in this chapter, and identify one that you think would be well-suited to capturing feedback (e.g., field notes, interviews, focus groups, video, etc.). At an upcoming opportunity in the context you identified, share a brief update on where you are in the inquiry process (i.e., developing your wondering). Then capture your colleagues' feedback so that you have a record of your discussion to analyze at a later time.

DISCUSSION QUESTIONS

1. Which data collection strategies do you think are the easiest to incorporate into your teaching?

2. Which data collection strategies do you think are the most difficult to incorporate into your teaching? How might these strategies be adapted so they fit better into the teaching day?

3. One strategy for taking field notes includes inviting a teaching colleague to come into your classroom during his or her scheduled special or planning period to take notes for you. How comfortable do you feel having a colleague observe your teaching? What types of ground rules for peer observation would need to be in place to increase your comfort zone?

4. In what ways might your principal (if you are a practicing teacher) or university supervisor (if you are a teacher candidate) support your efforts to collect data?

5. The authors state, "Good teacher research is about more than generating good test scores or showing the relation between one's teaching practice and one's students' performance on state tests." Do you agree or disagree with this statement? How can a teacher researcher balance today's emphasis on standardized test scores with other sources of data when designing his or her inquiry?

6. Discuss journal writing as a form of data collection by revisiting Julie Russell's journal entry that appears in Figure 3.9. In addition, skip ahead to Chapter 5 and read the excerpt from teacher researcher Amy Ruth's journal that appears in Figure 5.10.

SKIP AHEAD

To read Amy Ruth's journal excerpt, skip ahead to Chapter 5, Figure 5.10, on page 278.

- What do you learn about the art of keeping a journal entry from reading these two real, live entries?
- Do you think keeping a reflective journal is a strategy you will employ when you complete your own inquiry? Why or why not?

- If you plan to employ journaling as one form of data collection for your inquiry, how will you structure your journal writing to make the most of it based on teacher researcher Ashley Pennypacker Hill's advice on page 125 in this chapter?

ONLINE MATERIALS

The following materials designed to facilitate data collection are available for download at **https://companion.corwin.com/courses/ReflectiveEdsGuide5e:**

- **Activity 3.1: Open-Ended Sentences.** Complete seven sentence stems to capture how you feel about data collection.

- **Activity 3.2: Semi-Structured Interview Template.** Develop a protocol for a semi-structured interview to inform your inquiry.

Developing a Research Plan

Mapping Out Your Inquiry Journey

4

Designing a road map for your inquiry journey is an essential step in pursuing a focused, impactful inquiry. For many teachers, the process of planning an inquiry yields a clear, yet flexible, outline for the work that lies ahead. Much like creating a lesson plan, which provides a guide for your teaching, developing a research plan lays out an intentional pathway for your inquiry journey. Both planning processes involve setting clear goals, choosing appropriate methods, and reflecting on outcomes to ensure continuous improvement. Think about lesson planning as preparing for a journey with your students, where you decide the destination (learning objectives), choose the route (instructional strategies), and pack the necessary tools (resources and materials) to ensure a successful trip. Similarly, developing a research plan involves identifying the focus of your research (the problem and question), selecting methods for investigation (data collection strategies), and preparing for adjustments along the way based on ongoing observations and reflections. Just as lesson planning helps you develop core habits that guide you metacognitively through the teaching process, inquiry planning cultivates metacognitive habits, including living an inquiry stance toward teaching, that can enhance your decision making as a researching professional.

Both lesson planning and inquiry planning are iterative processes, meaning they are "works in progress" that evolve over time. They require flexibility, openness to feedback, and a willingness to refine your approach as new insights are gained. In this chapter, we walk through the stages of planning an inquiry, providing detailed guidance, tips, and examples to help you develop a written inquiry brief as effectively as you would write a lesson plan. This process will ensure that each individual component of your inquiry is informed by the others and contributes to a framework that guides your inquiry journey from start to finish.

To guide you in inquiry planning, we have selected the word *stages* rather than *steps* to denote that each aspect of plan development is fluid. Just like the inquiry process itself, planning an inquiry is circuitous, and you will find yourself circling back to stages you worked within previously as you map out your journey. For this reason, we have represented the planning process pictured in Figure 4.1 just as we have presented inquiry itself, as a circle without a definitive beginning, middle, or end. Yet everyone must start somewhere, so we suggest an ordering of the stages, but please prepare to circle backwards and forwards as you progress from stage to stage. The five stages are: (1) Identify the Problem, (2) Develop an Implementation Plan, (3) Establish an Inquiry Timeline, (4) Create an Inquiry Brief, and (5) Consider the Ethical Dimensions of Your Work.

In the sections ahead, we map out these five stages. Similar to the ways the eight passions were presented in Chapter 2 (with specific exercises designed to help you explore each individual passion appearing at the end of each passion section), we end our description of each aspect of the five inquiry planning stages presented in this chapter with an exercise to help you actualize that aspect of the planning process, guiding you through 15 exercises in all.

Planning an inquiry is hard work. It takes a lot of mental sweat to get clear on what you want to investigate and why you want to investigate it, as well as to commit your plan to paper. It will likely take some significant time if you are planning at a high level of quality. For this reason, you may wish to divide this chapter into pieces, pausing at the ending of each stage to rest and reflect on the exercises you completed in that section. While it is an investment of time, we are confident that the time you choose to invest now in getting crystal clear on your plan will set you up for greater success and confidence as you pursue your inquiry. By the end of this chapter, you will have created an outline for the what, when, why, and how of your inquiry and be ready to forge ahead on your journey.

Inquiry Planning Stage 1: Identify the Problem

The first stage of inquiry planning is to define the problem you wish to explore. This can be challenging because the word *problem* can often have a negative connotation, indicating that something is wrong with

Figure 4.1 Planning Your Inquiry

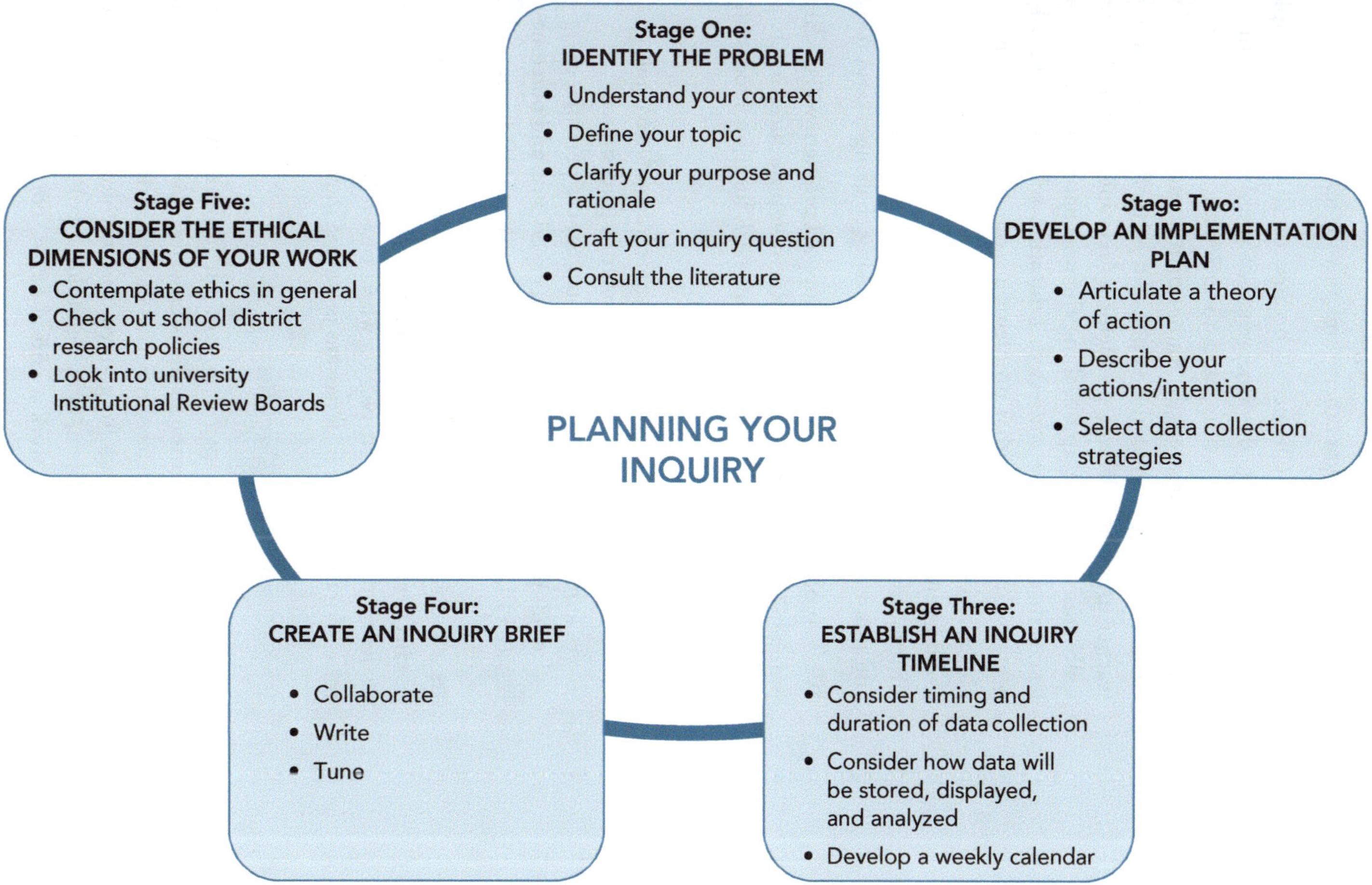

PLANNING YOUR INQUIRY

Stage One: IDENTIFY THE PROBLEM
- Understand your context
- Define your topic
- Clarify your purpose and rationale
- Craft your inquiry question
- Consult the literature

Stage Two: DEVELOP AN IMPLEMENTATION PLAN
- Articulate a theory of action
- Describe your actions/intention
- Select data collection strategies

Stage Three: ESTABLISH AN INQUIRY TIMELINE
- Consider timing and duration of data collection
- Consider how data will be stored, displayed, and analyzed
- Develop a weekly calendar

Stage Four: CREATE AN INQUIRY BRIEF
- Collaborate
- Write
- Tune

Stage Five: CONSIDER THE ETHICAL DIMENSIONS OF YOUR WORK
- Contemplate ethics in general
- Check out school district research policies
- Look into university Institutional Review Boards

your teaching, your students, your classroom, and/or your school. If problems are considered negative, naming a problem leaves you vulnerable—what might others think of your teaching ability?

Yet, as discussed in Chapter 2, because of all the great complexity inherent in teaching, the emergence of problems is a natural and normal aspect of teaching, and to articulate a problem does not show weakness, but strength. Rather than approaching a problem as "bad," sweeping it under the carpet, and pretending it does not exist, teacher inquirers celebrate problems by naming them and systematically studying them, approaching them as naturally occurring challenges that beg to be addressed. Education scholar Michael Fullan goes so far as to state that problems are our friends (Fullan, 2012). He believes that instead of avoiding or fearing problems, educators should embrace them as opportunities for growth and improvement. This mindset of stance is rooted in the idea that meaningful change and innovation often arise from addressing challenges head-on.

While problems are our friends, not any old problem will do. Teacher inquirers define a particular type of problem we introduced in Chapter 2, described by the Carnegie Project on the Education Doctorate as a *Problem of Practice (PoP):*

> A Problem of Practice is a persistent, contextualized, and specific issue embedded in the work of a professional practitioner, the addressing of which has the potential to result in improved understanding, experience, and outcomes (CPED, n.d., https://www.cpedinitiative.org/the-framework).

As a Problem of Practice is contextualized, in order to define a PoP, teacher researchers begin by examining their local context to better understand it. And so, we pick up where we left you in Chapter 2, with the exploration of the final passion presented in that chapter: Context.

Understand Your Context

As mentioned in Chapter 2, one of our favorite sayings is, "The fish would be the last creature to discover water," meaning that when you are deeply and completely immersed in your surroundings, it is easy to take those surroundings for granted. But teaching context is crucial in identifying your problem, as by definition a PoP is about you, making the place where you work a critical factor. For this reason, problem posing often begins with describing your setting, including relevant insights about your context as well as the ways you are situated within it might shape your inquiry. For example, detail the characteristics of your student population, the specific challenges you face, and how your personal and professional history may influence your perspective.

Exercise 1. Understanding Your Context

- Describe your district, your school, your classroom, your students, your content, and your curriculum as if you were painting a picture of your work environment for someone who knew nothing about it.
- Situate yourself in your work environment by describing your own background, experiences, and perspectives.
- Return to your completion of the Passion 8 exercise in Chapter 2 and ponder the question: How might my work environment, coupled with my own background, experiences, and perspectives, shape my inquiry?

Define Your Topic

As discussed in Chapter 2, your topic should stem from the passions that drive your work as an educator, a genuine area of curiosity, or a challenge in your teaching practice. For example, if you have always been passionate about reading and are puzzled by some students in your class this year who are struggling to develop as readers, you might name your topic "Improving student engagement in reading." Or, if you have always been passionate about teaching your students the value of collaboration with others, you might name your topic "Enhancing collaborative skills through group work." Choose a topic that resonates deeply with your experiences and aspirations as an educator and that excites you and reflects a genuine interest or challenge.

CIRCLE BACK

To revisit the inquiry passions, circle back to Figure 2.2, Developing Your Research Question, on page 38.

Exercise 2. Defining Your Topic

- Return to your completion of (or complete for the first time) Online Materials Activity 2.1 located at the end of Chapter 2, entitled "The Great Wondering Brainstorm." Reflect on the questions that emerged for you during this brainstorming activity and the topics they lend themselves to explore.

- Think about what the naturally occurring data within your context (for example, student work) is revealing to you about potential topics you'd like to study.
- Ponder the questions:
  - Does this topic genuinely interest me and align with my professional goals?
  - Is the topic relevant and significant to my teaching context?
  - Is the topic specific enough to explore within my context but broad enough to allow for a productive inquiry?

Clarify Your Purpose and Rationale

The purpose and rationale provide the "why" behind your chosen topic. Why is this topic important to you? Why does it matter to your students and your teaching context? Clearly articulate your motivations, linking them to your professional experiences and goals. For example, you might think, "I have noticed a decline in students' engagement during reading activities, which affects their comprehension skills. I believe that integrating digital tools could make reading more interactive and enjoyable, thereby improving both engagement and outcomes."

As you work to articulate the "why" behind your chosen topic, it is important to remember to define a "why" that lies within your sphere of influence. Studying a topic and associated PoP that will suggest actions that lie outside your control may lead to a dead end to your inquiry journey, as you cannot control the actions of others. An important premise of inquiry is that the only person a teacher can control is himself or herself. Hence, as you clarify your purpose and rationale, remember that inquiry is about making informed change to improve *your* practice, not the practice of others, although this certainly can occur when you share the results of your research, a topic we will cover in Chapter 6.

Exercise 3. Clarifying Your Purpose and Rationale

- Reflect on experiences that highlight the need for studying the topic you have selected.
- Once again, think about the naturally occurring data within your context and what they might be indicating about the purpose and rationale for exploring your topic and associated PoP.

- Ponder the questions:
  - Why does this topic matter to me as an educator?
  - Why is my topic and associated PoP worth addressing, anyway? (Why should educators in general bother caring about this topic and PoP?)
  - How will I be able to apply what I learn from studying this topic to my practice as an educator?
  - How will my students and/or school benefit from this inquiry?

Craft and Claim Your Wondering

Recall in Chapter 2 that we defined a wondering as "an intentionally refined question that frames and focuses an inquiry." As such, your wondering is the foundation of your plan. In Chapter 2, you brainstormed many potential questions of interest. As you plan your inquiry, it is time now to further focus, claim, and refine it. Based on our work with teacher inquirers, the following set of principles can help you generate a strong wondering that is open-ended, researchable, and relevant to your current teaching practice.

1. **Reflect on Your Practice From Multiple Perspectives.** Consider your teaching through the various passions (explored in Chapter 2) and different perspectives that are important to you (e.g., student engagement, classroom environment, content delivery). Seek colleague feedback in order to gain additional perspectives on the wondering you are honing. This helps identify potential areas of growth and improvement that you might otherwise overlook.

2. **Keep the Wondering Open to Evolution.** Be open to the idea that your wondering may evolve over time as your inquiry progresses. A question that can adapt is often more insightful and aligned with ongoing reflection.

3. **Ask Real Questions.** Don't use your inquiry to confirm preconceived ideas about teaching practices. Ask genuine, open-ended questions whose answers you do not already know.

4. **Develop Open-Ended Wonderings.** Avoid Yes/No wonderings by framing your inquiry question to explore complexities and possibilities, rather than limiting the inquiry to a binary answer. Open-ended wonderings allow for deeper investigation. To rephrase a question formulated in a dichotomous fashion, try one or more of these question stem starters:

- *How can I/we . . .*
- *In what ways does . . .*
- *What is the relationship between . . .*
- *How do students experience . . .*
- *What happens when . . .*
- *How does . . .*

5. **Ensure Clarity and Simplicity.** Eliminate jargon by crafting your question in clear, simple language. Avoid education jargon or overly technical terms that might obscure the focus of your inquiry.

6. **Use Neutral, Strengths-Based Language.** Steer away from language that implies judgment, bias, or preconceived notions about the topic. Use neutral terms to focus on the process and outcomes, and talk your questions over with colleagues to clarify any ambiguities. Wordsmithing with a critical friend helps you unearth assumptions behind the language that formulates your question.

7. **Focus on Strengths and Avoid a Deficit Perspective.** Consider framing your question around students' assets and strengths rather than focusing on what they may lack. This shifts your focus toward supporting growth and enhancing opportunity.

8. **Keep Your Wondering Manageable.** Confirm the size and scope of your wondering are just right for the time and resources available. Avoid wonderings that are too broad or too narrow.

9. **Check for Relevance.** Ensure that your wondering will address issues or areas for improvement that will have immediate impact on you and your students by considering the various ways your wondering is relevant to your current practice.

10. **Consider Methods/Data Feasibility.** Make sure that your wondering is researchable and can be explored using the data collection methods available to you. If a question is too broad or complex, it may not align with the types of data you can realistically collect.

11. **Avoid Overcomplicating by Focusing on One Key Question.** While you may have many questions, narrow them down to one core wondering that can be thoroughly explored within your available timeframe and resources.

12. **Focus on What You Can Do by Shifting the Focus to Your Practice.** Instead of focusing on issues that you cannot change at the present moment, center your inquiry on what you can do to support student learning and growth. If you haven't already done so, consider inviting yourself into the wording of the wondering you are forming by inserting the words *I* or *we* (in the case of a collaborative inquiry) into the question itself, as in these wondering examples shared in Chapter 2: "How can *I* take a science unit that is heavy on content and make it more inquiry based?" and "How can *we* teach the story of the true discovery of America to fourth graders in a developmentally appropriate way?"

CIRCLE BACK

For an important tip on formulating "How can I" questions, circle back to Chapter 2, Passion 2—Desire to Improve or Enrich Curriculum, on page 47.

By following these principles, you can create a clear, actionable, and meaningful wondering that drives reflective practice and leads to valuable insights and changes to your teaching and your students' learning.

As we ended Chapter 2, we suggested you begin the process of honing your wondering by discussing the passion exploration work you completed in that chapter with one or more colleagues and/or an AI chatbot, leaving you with the words of Lisa Malagesse reflecting upon the question-crafting conversation she had with her mentor teacher as well as an AI Moment textbox illustrating the ways a chatbot conversation might help you expand your thinking and uncover new perspectives related to your wondering. Now that you have reached the stage of planning your entire inquiry journey, this is also a good time to engage in dialogue with one or more colleagues and/or converse some more with a chatbot as you commit an inquiry question to paper and refine it using the one dozen principles named above. The dialogue that transpires as you wordsmith your question together will help you refine your thinking. For rich examples of such dialogue between teachers as they develop their wonderings, see Chapter 3 of our companion text to this book titled *The Reflective Educator's Guide to Professional Development: Coaching Inquiry-Oriented Learning Communities* (Dana & Yendol-Hoppey, 2008a).

Exercise 4. Crafting and Claiming Your Wondering

- Taking into account your completion of Chapter 2 passion exercises as well as your completion of the exercises in this chapter thus far (focused on context, topic selection, and purpose/rationale),

Step 1: Write Your Wondering

Your current wondering will serve as the focus of your evaluation.

Step 2: Evaluate Your Wondering Using the 12 Principles

For each principle, read the description and reflect on how well your inquiry question aligns with that principle. Write any revisions or insights next to each principle; tweak your question as you go.

Step 3: Revise and Claim Your Wondering

While understanding that your wondering may continue to evolve as you inquire, claim your wondering by recording it somewhere you can refer back to throughout your inquiry journey. Many teacher inquirers like to keep their wonderings handy throughout the day, posting them on sticky notes near their computers or on sentence strips or other places in their classrooms.

Consult the Literature

When teachers of any subject or grade level set out to teach students the research process, they begin by teaching the importance of clearly defining a research problem. Once students have worked to do so, the next step taught is to establish what is already known about the problem, which requires students to explore the topic of their investigations through finding and completing readings from reputable sources related to the subject of their inquiries. While teachers require their students to be thoughtful and systematic in using the literature as a part of the research process, according to professional development expert Tom Guskey, "the approach they take to their own professional inquiry differs significantly from what they prescribe for students" (Guskey, 2018, p. 1). Far too often, a systematic search of the literature and the completion of professional readings from reputable sources is not a part of a teacher's professional learning journey. To improve professional inquiry in the field of education, Guskey implores:

> Let's conduct our own professional inquiry in the same thoughtful manner we want our students to use. Let's not allow our own inquiry skills to diminish while seeking to

enhance those of our students. Instead, let's model what we want our students to learn, exemplifying the best of professional, scholarly practice. (Guskey, 2018, p. 3)

Exemplifying the best of professional scholarly practice means that a systematic and intentional look to the literature is an important part of planning every teacher's inquiry journey.

If a PoP emerges from your own practice, you may be wondering why it is important to read. After all, whether or not you consult the literature, the problem you have defined will still exist. Yet reading is an important part of inquiry planning, as it offers an opportunity to think about how your topic and associated PoP is informed by, and connected to, the work of others. Many researchers (both teachers and academics) have likely pondered, studied, and written about the topic of your inquiry before you, and you can benefit from their learning on the topic. No one teaches or inquires in a vacuum. As already noted in the discussion of understanding your context, when we engage in the act of teaching, we are situated within a work environment (our classroom, grade level, school, district, state, country), and our work environment mediates much of what we do and understand as teachers. Similarly, when teachers inquire, their work is situated within a large, rich, preexisting knowledge base that is captured in books, journal articles, newspaper articles, conference papers, and websites, among others. Looking at this preexisting knowledge base on teaching will inform your study, because inquiry is not something that is undertaken haphazardly and/or in an uninformed fashion. Teacher researchers consult the literature throughout the process of inquiry to gain insights into knowledge that already exists on their topic.

While reading is an essential part of every inquiry journey, it's important to note that teacher researchers do not conduct the same kind of extensive literature reviews as academics. Academics, as *professional researchers,* set out on their research journeys by establishing a gap in the literature to make the case for the importance of their research and the ways it will contribute to the field at large. To claim a gap in the literature, one must complete a comprehensive examination and analysis of all that has been published in reputable journals in relation to the topic of study. An extensive review of the literature may take months. In contrast, teacher inquirers, as *researching professionals,* set out on their research journeys by critically reflecting on their own teaching to determine a gap in practice they are compelled to address to improve the teaching and learning conditions in their own classrooms and schools.

As you learned in Chapter 2 and the previous sections of this chapter, reflecting on your own teaching to locate a problem of practice to study through the process of inquiry requires a comprehensive examination and analysis of several factors including the children you teach, the curriculum, content knowledge, teaching strategies and techniques, your own personal beliefs about practice, your personal and professional identities, equity/social justice, and teaching context. In contrast to academics who find their problem to study by looking *outward* to the literature, teacher inquirers find their problem to study by looking *inward* to their own practice, but subsequently consult the literature for insights into how they might frame the study of their problem and the actions they might take to better understand or resolve it.

In schools, universities, and even public libraries themselves, librarians are often an underutilized resource. For this reason, we suggest you consult the librarian in your school or district and/or your university (if you are conducting inquiry as a part of an undergraduate or advanced degree program). Yet even as you consult a professional to locate and read literature related to your topic, an important question that needs to be addressed is, "How do I know the literature I am reading to inform my inquiry is reputable?"

Cochran-Smith and Lytle (2009, p. 131) note that teacher inquirers treat both their own practice as the site for intentional investigation and the knowledge and theory produced by others as generative material for interrogation and interpretation. Teacher researchers do not look at the literature they collect to inform their studies with an uncritical eye. It's important to analyze and critique literature as it relates to your study and to your knowledge from practice. Not all research studies are created equal. Some studies are better than others, and some pieces of literature will be more relevant to your needs than others.

For example, there is an important difference between opinion-based literature written by someone who holds a political or ideological stance and literature developed because of rigorous research. One way to determine the quality of a piece of research is to find out if the article is peer reviewed. Many journals use the peer-review process to assess the quality of articles submitted for publication. The peer-review process includes a review of the study by recognized scholars in the same field who review it for quality of the research methodology and accuracy. Peer-reviewed articles go through this rigorous process for publication, and so they most often exemplify quality research.

Most studies published by a professional association are likely peer reviewed. Furthermore, most journals will identify whether the article was peer reviewed in the "About the Journal" section. Some other ways you can enhance the likelihood that you are reviewing quality research is by reviewing the author's credentials to see if the author is considered an authority in the field. Teacher researchers who use literature well focus on evidence generated through quality research articles rather than through opinion.

Equally important to seeking out information about the quality of the research you are using is paying attention to the demographics and description of the participants in the study. This is particularly important when trying to determine the degree to which a specific activity has had impact on a particular group of students. For example, a study of an arts integration and creative expression strategy completed in an urban public school may not provide the same outcome or process for implementation in a suburban Montessori school, or vice versa. Although the findings might provide insight, considering the assets of each context and the learners within each context is important.

In addition to finding and reading quality literature specific to the topic of your inquiry, teacher inquirers also read to better understand their own perspectives; the ways their perspectives have been shaped by history, culture, and society; and, subsequently, the ways their perspectives shape their own teaching practice. This is particularly important related to the ultimate "Why?" of inquiry discussed in Chapter 1—the creation of more equitable learning experiences for all children. In order to use inquiry as a pathway to equity, it is imperative for teacher inquirers to recognize the ways their social position informs their reactions to the students they teach, as well as their selection of what and how they teach, and ultimately, what they even choose to inquire about. This is referred to as *positionality*, defined as "the concept that our perspectives are based on our place in society. Positionality recognizes that where you stand in relation to others shapes what you can see and understand" (Sensoy & DiAngelo, 2017, p. 15). The famous quote attributed to Anaïs Nin, "We don't see things as they are, we see things as we are," is helpful to understand why reading to appreciate our own and others' perspectives is important to the work of a teacher researcher, particularly related to groups of students that are not equitably served by the current schooling system. The work of several educational scholars such as Lisa Delpit, Paul Gorski, Gloria Ladson-Billings, Ali Michael, Luis Moll, and Christine Sleeter is a great place to start reading in this area.

Finally, teacher researchers also read to deepen their understanding of the teacher research process itself, referred to as the methodology of inquiry, as they explore different approaches to the collection and analysis of data. Hence, your reading of *this* book jump-starts your exploration of practitioner research methodology, something you will explore in greater detail in the next stage of planning your inquiry: Develop an Implementation Plan.

Exercise 5. Consulting the Literature

- If available to you, ask a librarian for assistance in locating quality literature related to your topic, and/or consult the textbox at the end of this section entitled "Exploring the Literature: The Real Evidence-Based Practice," crafted for us by colleagues at the University of South Florida to provide tips on using existing literature (research) to inform a teacher's inquiry. Other places and people to confer with to find literature related to your topic include journals published by professional organizations of which you are a member or to which your school/district subscribes, open-access journals, Google Scholar, research-based curriculum, etc. You might also simply ask your colleagues, "What have you read on this topic?"

- Collect, read, interrogate, and interpret several published pieces related to your topic.

- Ponder the questions:
  - Are the pieces I am reading informed by quality research?
  - Who are the authors of the readings I am doing, and in what ways do their background experiences and beliefs shape what they are reporting on my topic?

- Ask the question, "Is my wondering informed by the research?" Adjust your inquiry question based on the existing research to help lead you to new insights in your classroom practice.
  - What changes/adjustments/tweaks to my topic, associated PoP, and emerging wondering do I wish to make based on what I have learned from consulting the literature?

Understanding your context, defining your topic, clarifying your purpose and rationale, crafting your inquiry question and consulting the literature, merge to form your PoP. Once your problem has been identified, the next stage is to develop your implementation plan.

EXPLORING THE LITERATURE: THE REAL EVIDENCE-BASED PRACTICE

Sarah van Ingen and Susan Ariew

At one time or another, most teachers have been told to engage in some teaching practice because "research says" or because "the practice is evidence-based." Our work is designed to take back the term evidence-based practice and to give it renewed meaning. Social workers have already done this. Social work educators have equipped new social workers with the understanding that the term evidence-based practice really refers to a process that the practitioner engages in when using research or evidence to inform practice. You too can be an evidence-based practitioner. You too can use education research to inform your own teaching and inquiry.

We have found that the process of using existing research (literature) to inform a teacher's inquiry has enormous benefits but that it can be uncomfortable at first. It's a bit like beginning a new exercise routine. If you have ever tried to begin running or to start up running after a hiatus, you know how uncomfortable it is—how your lungs burn and legs ache. Looking for education research to inform your inquiry may feel a bit like your lungs are burning. But if you can stick with it, you can also experience a similar rush of having had a great run and being ready for more.

We've included here an outline of the first three steps of a simple five-step process we use to prepare teachers to use literature to inform teaching. Within each of the three steps, we have provided tips that can help you push through the discomfort to realize the power you have to be informed by and to contribute to a global conversation on how to improve teaching and learning.

Step 1: Consider Your Question

After reading Chapter 2 of this book, you have already thought quite a bit about your wondering. Before embarking on a search for literature, think even more about your wondering.

> **TIP**: Get specific. If your wondering is broad in nature, talk to someone else (another strategy from Chapter 2) with the purpose of getting more specific. For example, you may wonder about how

(Continued)

(Continued)

to increase student motivation in math class. In talking with a peer about what is really behind this wondering, you may realize that it's not all students who are not motivated, but your concern is really for your English language learners. And, when you say motivation, you really mean their willingness to participate in class discussions. Do you see that this question has narrowed from how to motivate students in math class to how to support mathematical discussions among English language learner students? Training yourself to get very specific at this stage will help you in your literature search. The studies reported in journal articles often must answer very specific research questions. Of course, after or during your search, you might refine or revise your question (more on that in Step 2), but it will help to start with specific questions. We call these *researchable questions*.

Step 2: Begin the Search

With a refined, specific question, the hunt for data from the research literature can begin.

> **TIP**: Come up with a list of key words. Think about all the words related to your specific question and try to identify synonyms for key words. Thinking of the example provided earlier, you might have this list: "English language learners, mathematics, discussion, discourse, participation." There is no one right list, but having several key words provides you flexibility in your search.

> **TIP**: Come up with a plan for where you will search. This will require a bit of creativity because, unfortunately, not all education research is open access. This means that to read some articles, a person or institution must pay money. We do *not* recommend paying for access to journal articles. Instead, try using one of these strategies to find articles related to your inquiry question.
>
> A. **Use a resource that provides research summaries.** The U.S. government has created the What Works Clearinghouse (http://ies.ed.gov/ncee/wwc), which provides research summaries written just for teachers. Outside the United States, the International Bureau of Education (www.ibe.unesco.org) has an Educational Practice Series that provides research summaries for teachers. These are great resources, but they may or may

not include information on your question. In addition, whenever you read a research summary that someone else created, there is the added question of what research they left out. Why did they choose the articles they did?

B. **Use a research database.** ERIC is a free research database sponsored by the U.S. government (http://eric.ed.gov). Your local public library may give you access to other research databases. Of particular interest to educators are Google Scholar and Education Full Text.

C. **Use journals published by professional organizations.** Your school and/or district may have institutional memberships to professional organizations such as the National Council of Teachers of Mathematics (NCTM). As is the case with NCTM, a membership allows you online access to excellent articles from the journals that the organization publishes.

D. **Use open-access journals.** These journals are, as their name implies, free and available to anyone who would like to peruse them. There is a growing trend for prestigious universities, such as Stanford, to require their researchers to publish in open-access journals or university digital repositories. This means that you can find some really good information here. The Directory of Open Access Journals (www.doaj.org) can help you find a journal relevant to your interests.

E. **Use your partnerships.** If your school is part of a school–university partnership, you could ask your university partners if they can find research articles on your specific topic. In this case, it would be best if you and the university faculty member sat down and did the search together. This way you have input over the article selection.

F. **Use your public or university library.** If you live near a public university, you can visit that library and search its subscription databases and journals. Most of them have workstations reserved for public access. In addition, the majority of public libraries have interlibrary loan services for you to request items not available through your local library system.

G. **Use AI tools.** In addition to ChatGPT, a partial list of freely available generative AI tools that may be particularly useful in the inquiry process includes:

(Continued)

(Continued)

    a. **LitMaps** (https://www.litmaps.com/): can be used to identify original research papers that might be relevant to a teacher's inquiry

    b. **Perplexity** (https://www.perplexity.ai/): can be used to summarize key findings from research papers

    c. **Research Rabbit** (https://www.researchrabbit.ai/): can be used to search for research papers and visualize how research papers are connected to one another

TIP: Think binoculars. If you've ever used a pair of binoculars to watch birds, you know that to focus them on one bird requires a process of moving the lenses out too far and in too close until that bird comes into focus. The process of searching for research literature is quite similar. When you start searching, you may find that your search terms are too broad, and the articles you find are not specific enough to your question. Then you need to enter in more search terms or use more specific terms. On the other hand, you might come up with too few articles. This means you have to broaden your terms. The task of focusing your search and finding relevant articles requires patience and perseverance. Keep at it! If one strategy seems like a dead end, find another. Work with a partner. There is a treasure trove of information out there, and the search is worth the effort!

TIP: Think blue bird. In a tree full of crows, you may be looking specifically for blue birds. Likewise, in a list of articles that pop up during a search, we suggest you look specifically for research summaries aimed at teachers and empirical articles. Empirical articles provide results from a specific intervention or wondering. These contrast with theoretical articles that provide information on new ideas. We suggest selecting three to five research articles as a starting place for your reading. Fewer than three articles may give you too little information on your topic, but more than five articles may be too daunting to process. Note that a meta-analysis or a meta-synthesis is an article that synthesized the findings from several studies. These meta-articles will give you more information than an article on one study only and might be a good choice to include in your selection of three to five articles.

TIP: Ask a librarian! This may be the most important tip we can offer. If you run into problems with the suggested steps and tips listed here, a librarian has the training and resources to assist you. Most public and university libraries have Ask a Librarian services where you can talk to a librarian by phone or online chat to get some specific help on finding the information you need.

Step 3: Read and Synthesize the Literature

Now that you have found literature that addresses your question, it's time to find out what this literature says. Think more patience, more perseverance! When reading a report from a research study (empirical article), you are likely to encounter this basic heading structure: abstract, introduction, methods, results, discussion, and references.

A. **Abstract:** This comes at the very beginning of the document and gives you an overview of that article. It is a great place to begin your reading.

B. **Introduction:** This may contain a discussion, called a literature review, about other studies done on this topic. This is a great find because it can lead you to several other articles on your topic. The author provides the full citation for those additional articles at the end of the paper in the references section. The introduction can also inform you of the key words that researchers use when talking about your topic. You may learn of new words or phrases about your topic and then can go back to Step 2 and search again for more articles on your topic.

C. **Methods and Results:** Here the author describes what was done in the study. These sections might contain technical or statistical details. Although these are important because they speak to the strength of the research, it often requires specialized training in either quantitative or qualitative research methods to understand. You may want to skim these sections.

D. **Discussion:** Here the author discusses the meaning of the research and answers the question, "So what?" Often the author has a paragraph or more about the implications of the research for the classroom teacher. Obviously, this information is of great interest and relevance for you.

E. **References:** This comes at the very end of the document and provides a list of all articles cited. It is a great place to locate additional sources about the research topic.

(Continued)

(Continued)

> **TIP:** Take the time to summarize and synthesize. Write a one- to two-paragraph summary of each research article you read. When summarizing, think specifically about how the study informs your initial inquiry question. Feel free to talk back to the article a bit. How does this article help to answer your question? What additional questions does this article raise? How is the setting of this article similar to or different from your own classroom? After you complete the summarizing stage, write a one-page synthesis of what you now know about your topic after reading all of your research articles. You can use this synthesis to inform your own research plan.

Inquiry Planning Stage 2: Develop an Implementation Plan

Implementation refers to deciding upon and executing *action* to realize a cycle of inquiry. And so we turn now to a discussion of the action component of inquiry: What will you do to address the PoP and wondering you have identified?

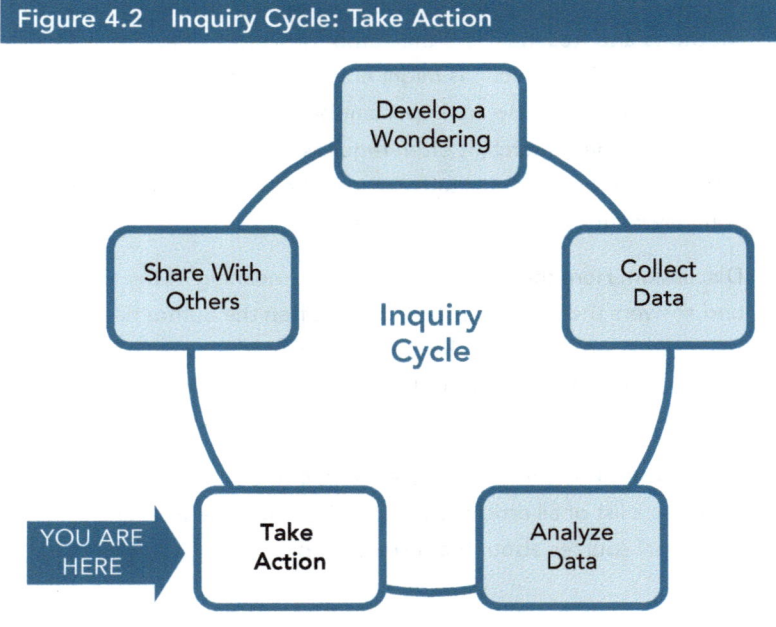

Figure 4.2 Inquiry Cycle: Take Action

The action(s) you plan can take different forms. Likely your first thought on action is trying a particular solution to address your PoP and studying how that solution plays out for the learners in your classroom. For example, recall the work of Debbi Hubbell (2006) discussed previously in Chapter 3. Debbi's action was introducing the reading of fractured fairy tale plays as an instructional strategy to develop the fluency of seven learners who were struggling with reading. When planning an inquiry where implementing a new instructional strategy or approach to curriculum is the action, the goal is to understand the impact of that action: How is the action you took working in the context of your particular classroom? What adjustments need to be made and why? What, if any, unintended consequences emerge as a result of implementing the action? Which learners benefit from this action, which do not, and why?

While executing the action component of the inquiry cycle in this way is one possible and common way many teacher researchers approach it, all inquiries don't have to focus on implementing a new instructional action in the classroom to determine the results of that action. It's important not to get trapped in a mindset of "solution-itis"—an unsystematic piling up of trying different solutions without sufficient evidence that they have the potential to impact practice in positive ways before you try them. In Debbi's case, she learned from consulting the literature about the positive relationship between fluency development (the ability to read with speed, accuracy, and proper expression) and reading comprehension. She also learned from consulting the literature that repeated readings (a simple exercise where students read and reread a selected short passage until they reach a satisfactory level of fluency) was one of the most studied strategies for developing reading fluency and offered great promise. Hence, the idea of reading a fractured fairy tale play multiple times in rehearsal for eventual presentation to the class made sense as a promising instructional action to take to address her problem of practice.

However, not all inquiry lends itself to the selection and implementation of an action that holds promise to address the PoP. Sometimes, it is more appropriate simply to gain a better understanding of the problem itself in order to make an informed decision regarding potential solutions to address it. In this case, the action(s) taken focus on learning more about the problem (and perhaps how others are addressing it) itself. For example, working as a teacher professional learning specialist focused on STEM education using Legos, Jenny Nash (2017) knew that several of the teachers in her professional learning sessions found it challenging to interest their female students in their STEM curriculum. She wanted to integrate instruction on this topic into the professional learning experiences she provided but did not know how best to do so. Hence, she framed the action of her inquiry cycle not as implementing and evaluating a new component on engaging female learners in STEM education into the professional learning sessions she offered, but rather as learning more about how exemplary teachers use Legos to heighten their female students' interest in STEM learning in the first place. Hence, the action in her inquiry cycle focused on selecting, observing, and talking with teachers with a reputation for excellence who possessed a particular passion for igniting an interest in STEM curriculum in their female students. The goal of the actions she took (selecting, observing, and talking with exemplary teachers) was to enable Jenny to improve the professional learning experiences she offered by distilling from her actions the unique needs of female students as well as pedagogical approaches to instruction that help address those needs. The actions Jenny took were a precursor to implementing something new into her practice, with her inquiry resulting in the development of a new professional learning module generated from what she learned from the teachers she observed and spoke with.

Similarly, literacy coach Ashley Hart engaged in a cycle of inquiry to better understand barriers to teacher collaboration in her school. Ashley beautifully describes what led to a cycle of inquiry focused on better understanding her problem or practice rather than implementing one or more actions to address it:

> My interest in authentic collaboration began when I was a 3rd grade ELA teacher and team leader for my grade level. In this role, I experienced many frustrations and challenges when collaborating with my colleagues. When my team would gather together, we would work to develop specific products, but we never reached a deeper level of discussion or engaged in high quality planning. When I transitioned to my role as literacy coach, the challenges and barriers preventing authentic collaboration only intensified. My wonderings related to collaboration led me to problem solve and reflect. In my first year as a coach, I sent a survey to capture teachers' perceptions on the current collaboration at [my school]. Based on my results, I put specific collaborative strategies and structures in place. At first, teachers were very excited to engage in the collaborative work; however, as the

school year went on, my initiatives failed, and I experienced resistance from teachers. Instead of giving up on improving collaboration in my context, I decided to learn more about the barriers preventing this crucial work in my school context. (Hart, 2021, p. 17)

To better understand her problem, Ashley's wonderings were twofold: (1) What barriers do elementary ELA teachers articulate that prevent them from engaging in authentic, collaborative work at my school?, and (2) What strategies do teachers in my school suggest to overcome teacher collaboration barriers to ensure teachers can benefit from collaborative work? To gain insights into these wonderings, the *actions* Ashley took included systematically talking with teachers at her school (capturing these talks through employing the data collection strategy of semi-formal interviews), as well as observing teachers during collaborative work times, including planning and professional learning sessions as well as unstructured collaboration experiences (capturing these observations through employing the data collection strategy of field notes).

Figure 4.3 provides guidance to help you frame the ways the action component of your inquiry cycle might unfold. Whichever frame you use to determine the action that is a part of your inquiry (implementing a possible solution to address the problem or developing a better understanding of the problem in order to address it), Stage 2: Develop an Implementation Plan, begins with articulating a theory of action.

Articulate a Theory of Action

A theory of action helps establish a clear connection between your inquiry intentions and the anticipated impact you hope to have. The theory of action is comprised of three linked statements: *If* . . . (What do you plan to implement and do?), *Then* . . . (What will be the impact on your students?), *So that* . . . (What is the ultimate goal or long-term impact?). For example, an inquiry focused on enhancing cultural inclusivity in the classroom might be worded, **If** I intentionally create an inclusive environment by engaging families in open communication and decision-making, **Then** families will feel valued, **So that** every family and child will develop a strong sense of belonging. Or for an educator working in a science center and interested in project-based learning, their theory of action may be, **If** I integrate hands-on, project-based learning activities in the science center, **Then** children will engage more deeply and develop problem-solving skills, **So that** each child develops an interest in and skills related to the natural world.

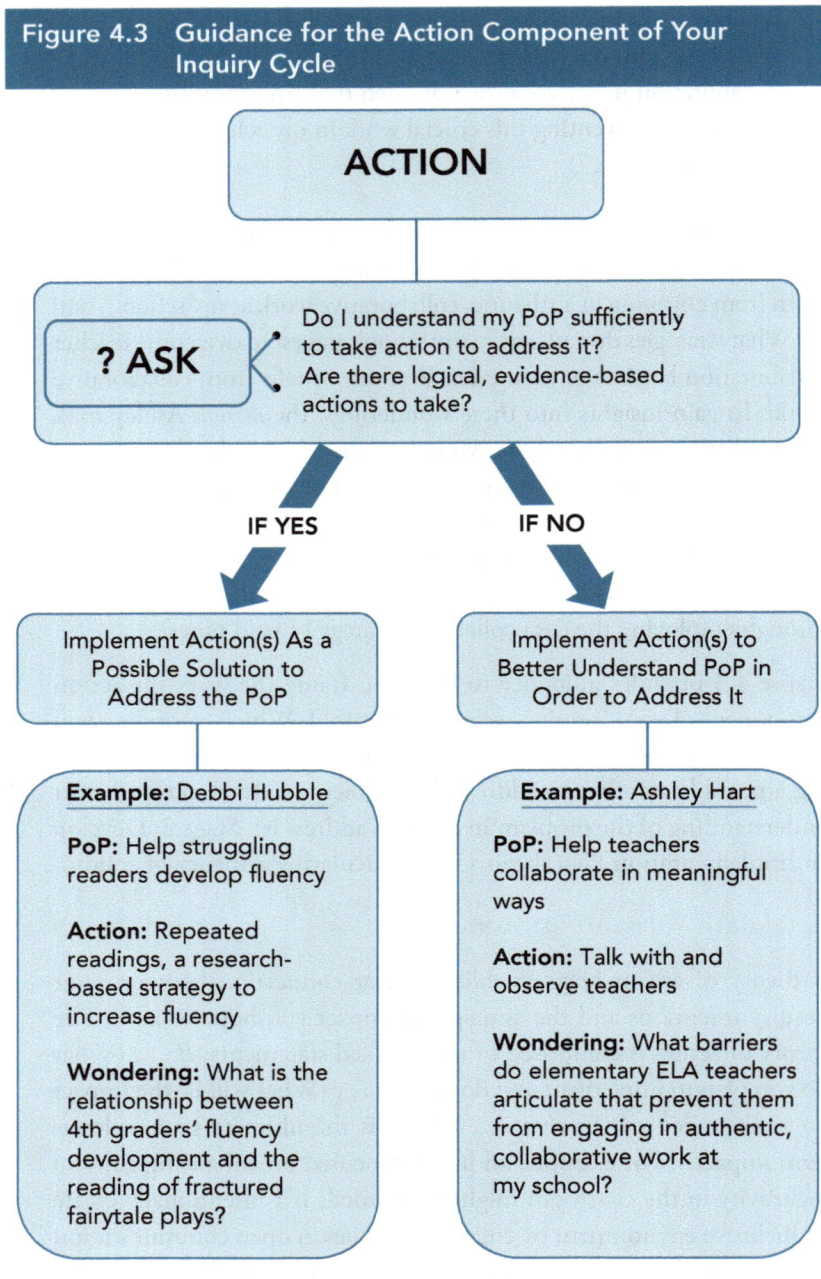

Figure 4.3 Guidance for the Action Component of Your Inquiry Cycle

The above *If, Then, So that* examples illustrate inquiries that are framed by actions implemented as a possible solution to address the problem of practice. When inquiries are framed by actions to better understand the problem in order to address it, the *If, Then, So that* statements might look something like this: **If** I want to integrate generative AI tools into my instructional practice, **Then** I need to understand the options and issues that surround AI, as well as how my students already use it, **So that** I can choose and implement AI tools effectively to enhance my instruction and student learning.

The theory of action serves as a blueprint that can guide your inquiry and facilitate communication with others. Education scholars like Chris Argyris and Donald Schön (1992) emphasize the importance of reflective practice in developing theories of action that effectively link thought to action. Similarly, Jamey Burns (2024) has consistently applied the theory of action in their inquiry facilitation work and found it helpful to supporting classroom researchers. For classroom researchers, they found that a clear and purposeful theory of action ensures that actions are well-informed, clearly defined, and positioned to be impactful. Moreover, they witnessed how a theory of action allowed educators to communicate their intentions concisely with colleagues and stakeholders. This fostered important dialogue and collaboration within the professional community. A well-crafted theory of action clarifies your path and ensures that your inquiry remains purposeful and aligned with your goals.

While a theory of action is important, it is critical to examine the assumptions within which your theory of action is grounded. Sometimes doing so can lead to discoveries to help shift the design of your inquiry from a deficit to asset perspective and/or offer an antidote for "solution-itis" discussed earlier in this section. For example, Macy Geiger (2022), in her role as a middle school support teacher responsible for family communications and as an educator with a deep commitment to both social justice education and family engagement, realized a potential opportunity awaiting when a Black sixth-grade social studies teacher on the middle school team she was responsible for supporting designed and taught a social justice unit. When that teacher shared some of the family feedback with Macy, she recognized a distinct dichotomy of opinions. Some families were excited for their students to share what they learned, yet others were apprehensive about the content and uncomfortable talking about it. Macy realized a potential opportunity awaiting—connecting with her colleague's families about their experiences during this unit to build supports that would enable them to interact with and discuss the social justice topics they were learning in school with their students. Macy writes:

> Excited about the potential to collaborate with my colleague and extend her social justice instruction to families, my initial inclination was to rush in and immediately develop

accompanying family engagement activities. My passion propelled me full speed ahead into this work. I began the process of immediately designing social justice–related home-school activities to complement and extend my colleague's unit. I planned to implement and study the ways families reacted to these activities for my inquiry. Yet, as I read more on this topic and engaged in conversations with my colleague and others about my plan, I recognized that I needed to slow down and reevaluate my goals.

First, the family engagement literature revealed the importance of collaborating *with* families instead of providing the traditionally stratified, school-centric models of engagement. For example, in discussing the importance of language when working with families, Ferrlazo (2011) communicates the difference between the terms family "involvement" and family "engagement." According to Ferrlazo, *involvement* suggests "doing to," and *engagement* suggests "doing with," which is why the distinction between the two is crucial (p. 11). In my haste to develop and implement activities immediately, I risked creating social justice activities that would be "done to" parents.

Second, as I reflected on my continued learnings about privilege and oppression, the problematic nature of my identity as a White, middle-class female educator also came to light. I did not want to intentionally or unintentionally position myself as the white savior, swooping in to save the day for my Black colleague who was teaching about race and oppression and her students' families. The historical narrative of the White savior complex is deeply rooted in racist ideology (Emdin, 2016). In education, Emdin describes White saviors as teachers who position themselves as heroes while their actions further harm students of color by setting them up to fail.

Finally, to design effective family engagement activities, I knew that I must take a step back to better understand the unit itself by learning more about my colleague's teaching of it and the ways the students were responding. How could I design family engagement activities without first thoroughly understanding the content of the unit and the ways it was playing out in her classroom? Therefore, my problem of practice was to fight against my inclination to speed ahead, and slow down to develop an informed understanding of the unit on oppression and critical matters to consider when designing family engagement activities for social justice.

Hence, the purpose of my inquiry is to understand how I, as a white educator committed to social justice education and family engagement, can develop an informed understanding of a new unit on oppression being introduced into the 6th-grade Social Studies curriculum at my school, with the goal of designing family engagement activities to complement and extend this unit. Based on the focus of my study, my inquiry question is: What are important factors to consider when developing home-school engagement social justice activities specific to a unit on oppression?

In addition, as Sensoy and DiAngelo (2017) note that those who claim to be for social justice must be engaged in self-reflection about their own socialization into groups (their "positionality") and must strategically act from that awareness in ways that challenge social injustice, a secondary inquiry question is: How does my positionality as a white female educator come into play when developing home-school engagement social justice activities specific to a unit on oppression? (Geiger, 2022)

Macy's reflections indicate the importance of examining the assumptions embedded in one's theory of action.

Exercise 6. Developing a Theory of Action

- Write your own *If, Then, So that* statement to reflect the PoP you identified in Stage 1.
- Tweak that statement by pondering the questions:
  - Do my actions logically connect to my desired outcomes?
  - Have I clearly articulated how my actions will lead to these outcomes?
  - How strong is my evidence for any action I propose to take?
  - Have I reflected on how my theory of action and the actions I plan to take are shaped by my role, background, and teaching context?
  - What assumptions about teaching and learning, as well as teachers and students, are embedded in my theory of action?

Describe Your Actions/Interventions

Given that other educators will be interested in what you have investigated, describing your work with enough detail that others might be able to draw on your work in their classrooms is important. Although your theory of action began the documentation of the actions you plan to take in your inquiry, providing detailed description of your actions or interventions is essential to plan development. For example, if your focus is on using digital tools to enhance reading engagement, describe the specific tools you plan to use, how they will be introduced to your students, and the types of activities designed to integrate these tools into your lessons.

We turn once again to Debbi Hubbell (2006) to illustrate how you might describe the instructional actions you plan to take in your inquiry:

> I plan to select five plays from the book *12 Fabulously Funny Fairytale Plays* (Spiderella, The Cheeta and the Sloth, Little Late Riding Hood, The Emperor's New Hair, Goldilocks and the Three Bullfrogs) and cover one play each week during reading group time. On Monday, I will introduce the play, ask students to choose parts, and I will read the play to the students as they follow along. If there is time, I will then have them practice silently. On Tuesday, students will practice silently, then aloud with the group to me, and I will follow with short individual conferences with each student that afternoon. On Wednesday and Thursday, students will practice silently, then aloud with the group to me. Finally, on Friday, the students will present the play to the class. (p. 6)

While describing your planned actions is useful, one thing is certain in schools and classrooms—things do not always go as planned. For this reason, as you proceed in your inquiry, feel free to make adjustments to your plans, being sure to document how they are being revised so you can share the exact nature of the actions you took in your inquiry when you complete your study.

Exercise 7. Describing Your Actions

- Using Debbi Hubbell's action statement as a model, write your own action statement, being specific about the tools and strategies you will use.

- Ponder the questions:
  - Are my actions clearly stated so that others can duplicate or adapt what I have done in their own classroom/school if so desired?
  - In what ways might I collect data to learn from and about the actions I plan to take?

Select Data Collection Strategies

Collecting data is another kind of action all inquirers must plan to take in order to implement a cycle of inquiry. As discussed in Chapter 3, a variety of naturally occurring data exists and other data sources can be included in addition to the naturally occurring data if needed to inform your inquiry.

Most teacher inquirers find more than one data collection strategy will connect to their wondering and can be used to understand action. Subsequently, they evoke more than one form of data collection in the design of their study. Using multiple sources of data can enhance your inquiry as you gain different perspectives from different strategies. For example, using both qualitative data (like student feedback or observational notes) and quantitative data (like test scores or survey results) can help you see different facets of the same issue. In addition, by employing multiple strategies you are able to build a strong case for your findings by pointing out the ways different data sources led you to the same conclusions. Research methodologists refer to the use of multiple data sources as *triangulation* (Creswell & Poth, 2018; Patton, 2015). Finally, by employing multiple data sources you enhance your opportunities for learning when different data sources lead to discrepancies. It is often through posing explanations for these discrepancies that the most powerful learning of teacher inquiry occurs and that new wonderings for subsequent inquiries are generated.

Exercise 8. Selecting Data Collection Strategies

- State the question you developed in Exercise 4. Brainstorm a list of all the potential sources of data you can think of that would give you insights into this question. As you construct your list, think big—the sky's the limit! Once you have completed your list, consider which strategies are the most and least practical.
  - What makes practical strategies practical and impractical strategies impractical?

- o Are there any strategies on your list that you categorized as impractical that you believe could potentially provide valuable insights into your wondering?
- o How might these impractical but valuable data collection tools be adapted to become more reasonable ways to collect data?

• Continue the data collection brainstorming process you began above to narrow in on the strategies you might employ by creating a data collection chart. Title your chart with your main inquiry question and generate two columns: (1) "Information That Would Help Me Address My Question" and (2) "Data Collection Strategies That Would Generate This Information." An example based on the work of two teacher researchers you met in Chapter 3 on page 108, Brian Peters and Gail Romig, appears in Table 4.1.

• Select the final data collection strategies you plan to employ from the table you created and ponder these questions:

- o Have I considered all possible data sources that could provide insights into my wondering?
- o Am I employing at least three different data sources to ensure comprehensive analysis?

Now that you have articulated a theory of action, described the actions you plan to take, and selected data collection strategies, you have everything you need to establish a timeline for your inquiry.

Table 4.1 In What Ways Do Science Talks Enhance Student Understandings of Science Concepts?

INFORMATION THAT WOULD HELP ME ANSWER MY QUESTION	DATA COLLECTION STRATEGIES THAT WOULD GENERATE THIS INFORMATION
Knowing how students' conceptual knowledge develops during our astronomy unit.	Collect the students' science journals.
Knowing what students are saying during science talks.	Audiotape science talks, taking field notes.
My thinking about what happened during the science talks after they occur.	Teacher journal.

INFORMATION THAT WOULD HELP ME ANSWER MY QUESTION	DATA COLLECTION STRATEGIES THAT WOULD GENERATE THIS INFORMATION
Students' opinions about science talks.	Surveys.
Literature on science talks. I'm already familiar with Karen Gallas's book, *Talking Their Way Into Science*.	Searching for other books or articles connected to science talks, building conceptual knowledge in science, teaching elementary science, and so on.

Inquiry Planning Stage 3: Establish an Inquiry Timeline

Creating a timeline provides you with a structure to follow, keeps you organized, and propels your inquiry journey forward within the extreme business of each school day. Establishing an inquiry timeline involves the consideration of both the timing and duration of data collection, how your data will be stored and analyzed, and what you want to occur in the weeks ahead.

Consider Timing and Duration of Data Collection

In Stage 2, you determined the types of data you will collect. This is only one step in planning the data collection part of your journey. To ensure that your data are both relevant and sufficient to address your inquiry question, it is equally important to consider the timing and duration of data collection. When should you start collecting data, and how long should you continue?

The "when" and "how long" questions of data collection are often answered by natural constraints of time imposed by such things as the length of a unit if you are doing a curriculum inquiry or the due date for your paper if engaging in inquiry as part of your student teaching or a graduate course. Optimally, data collection would proceed until you reach a state where you are no longer gaining insights into your wondering or question and no new information is emerging. This state is termed *saturation* by research methodologists (Creswell & Poth, 2018; Patton, 2015).

The complexities of teaching are so great, however, that in teacher research you could be collecting data and waiting for saturation to occur indefinitely. Never drawing closure to an inquiry robs you of experiencing a process that is one of the most rewarding and exhilarating components of teacher inquiry—deeply immersing yourself in your data, articulating findings, and allowing new wonderings to emerge. Therefore, it is important that you bind your study in a particular time frame. You must make decisions about when and how long as you balance what is feasible to do in the real world of your classroom and what is optimal for providing insights into your topic.

As you ponder the start and duration of data collection, this is a good time to consider the overall size of your investigation as well. A trip through the inquiry cycle can be modest, moderate, extensive, or anywhere in between. Just like Goldilocks testing out the three bears' wares, you have to "size" your inquiry "just right" to align with what you hope to learn.

Exercise 9. Considering Timing and Duration of Data Collection

- Think about when it makes the most sense to begin and end your data collection based on the problem you identified (Stage 1) and implementation plan you developed (Stage 2).
- Ponder the following questions:
  - How much data will be needed to address my research question?
  - Can a satisfactory amount of data be collected in the time I have available to collect it?
  - Are there natural starting and ending points for data collection, such as the beginning and ending of a new unit or school term?
  - How will I know when I have collected enough data to gain credible insights into my research question?

Consider How Data Will Be Stored, Displayed, and Analyzed

While we have yet to discuss data analysis, in order to engage in making sense of your data as you collect them as well as when you have finished collecting them all, you'll need to plan for how you will store them. Some teacher researchers keep a data notebook, create different file folders, or design an organizational structure on their computers to save data as they are generated in a systematic way. The work you have done to identify your problem (Stage 1) and Develop an Implementation Plan (Stage 2) will help you determine the organizational system that will work best for you. For example, it may make sense simply to store data chronologically (by date they were collected), or it might be more useful to store data by student, or by data type. Having a data storage plan from the outset of your inquiry helps to keep you on schedule as without a storage plan, you may find yourself spending unnecessary time looking for data later in your inquiry cycle.

Furthermore, you'll want to plan for regular reflection on your data, termed "formative data analysis." Regular reflection on your data as you collect them allows you to make necessary adjustments as your inquiry unfolds and deepens your understanding of the inquiry question. Hence, as you consider how you will store data, you may also wish to consider how you might visually display them to make it easy to see patterns, trends, or changes that are emerging over time. Finally, you'll want to designate time to complete summative analysis. These topics will be discussed in detail in Chapter 5.

Exercise 10. Considering How Data Will Be Stored, Displayed, and Analyzed

- Revisit the work you have done thus far in this chapter to plan your inquiry. Consider different options for storing, displaying and analyzing data in relationship to your inquiry question (generated during Stage 1: Identify the Problem), the collection strategies you will employ (selected during Stage 2: Develop an Implementation Plan), and the timing and duration of data collection (determined in Stage 3: Establish an Inquiry Timeline).
- Peak ahead to Chapter 5 and skim the contents to get a sense of what's ahead on the topics of formative and summative data analysis, as well as creating visual displays of your data. Keep in mind that after you read this chapter completely, you may wish to return to your inquiry plan to add and/or clarify more on the data analysis process you are planning for now.
- Ponder the following question:
  - Given the planning I've done thus far, what will be the most useful ways to store, display, and analyze my data?
  - When and how can the ways I've selected to store, display, and analyze my data be integrated into my inquiry plan?

Develop a Weekly Calendar

With a sense of the timing and duration of data collection as well as how you wish to store, display, and analyze data, you can now create an actual calendar to anticipate how your inquiry will unfold within a specific timeframe. Although it will likely be adjusted as you go, a weekly calendar is crucial for keeping your inquiry organized and on track. This is not unlike the process of planning any trip itinerary and will serve as an advanced organizer for your inquiry journey. We have found it useful to outline the weekly actions, specifying what you will do and when, including the specific actions you intend to take each week. For example:

- *Week 1:* Introduce digital storytelling tools and explain their use in reading activities.
- *Weeks 2–4:* Implement storytelling activities; collect observational data, student work, and gather student feedback.
- *Week 5:* Analyze the data, reflect on initial findings, and adjust my approach as needed.

Exercise 11. Developing Your Weekly Calendar

- Select the actual calendar dates that align with any natural starting and ending points for your inquiry
- Create a template commensurate with the start and/or end dates you have determined. For example:
  - *Week 1:* Monday, September 16–Friday, September 20
  - *Week 2:* Monday, September 23–Friday, September 27 (etc.).
- Complete the template you have created by adding in the instructional actions you plan to take in this cycle of inquiry, what data you plan to collect when, as well as whatever additional components of your inquiry journey you wish to include in your calendar. For example, in addition to indicating the type of data you will collect each week, you may wish to include in your calendar a time to record the "Type of Data," "Description of Data," and a notation about where the data are stored for later reference.
- Ponder the following questions:
  - Are the weekly tasks I planned manageable?
  - Did I include time for reflection and adjustments as I go?

With an inquiry timeline established, you are ready to create your inquiry brief.

Inquiry Planning Stage 4: Create an Inquiry Brief

You have worked hard in this chapter thinking through many aspects of the inquiry journey you are embarking upon. Stage 4: Create an Inquiry Brief, is a time to commit those thoughts to paper so you can consider them all together and tweak your plan as appropriate. The goal of this stage is to develop the best possible initial inquiry itinerary. We use the qualifying term *initial* to represent that even with the very best of plans, you'll be making adjustments as you go in relationship to what you are learning and unanticipated happenings you couldn't possibly foresee. Creating a solid inquiry brief is strengthened through collaboration and followed by committing pen to paper to actually write it. We find that the brief really comes alive when you enlist a little help from some colleagues willing to help you "tune it."

Collaborate

The popular Beatles song "With a Little Help From My Friends" is about the significance and necessity of friendship on life's journey. Similarly, teacher researchers find collaboration with colleagues both vital and indispensable to their work. Colleagues can play a critical role in your entire inquiry journey, but an especially good time to enlist their support is as you write your inquiry brief. In our work with teacher inquirers, we have identified at least five good reasons why, when we look at any single teacher inquirer, we see him or her standing in the company of others.

First, research is hard work! Because the practitioner inquiry movement "continues to flourish in the United States and many other parts of the world" (Cochran-Smith & Lytle, 2009, p. 6) and serves as a popular professional growth tool for the initial preparation and continuing education of teachers (Somekh & Zeichner, 2009), it is easy to get caught up in the movement and forget one very basic fact: The work of a teacher is quite demanding! To date, teacher inquiry has not traditionally been a part of teachers' practice. Hence, engaging in inquiry potentially adds an additional layer into the already crowded work life of a teacher: "Participation in teacher research requires considerable effort by innovative and dedicated teachers to stay in their classrooms and at the same time carve out opportunities to inquire and reflect on their practice" (Cochran-Smith & Lytle, 1993).

While we believe it is critical to make teacher inquiry *a part of* your teaching rather than *apart from* your teaching, the fact remains that even if you can seamlessly integrate teaching and inquiry (as we believe should be the case!), the work is difficult and can be quite draining at times. Through collaboration with others, teacher inquirers find a crucial source of energy and support that keeps them going and sustains their work. In addition, through collaboration teacher inquirers build on each other's work, so they are not constantly reinventing the wheel when it comes to exploring a new passion through inquiry. Both the energy created and the networking provided through collaboration are apparent in many teacher researcher communities. In our work, we have created a blogging site to connect teacher researchers to those who coach teacher research from schools across our state (Glogowski & Sessums, 2007). Figure 4.4 depicts a collaborative exchange between two members of this community that indicates the power collaboration holds for energy generation and networking.

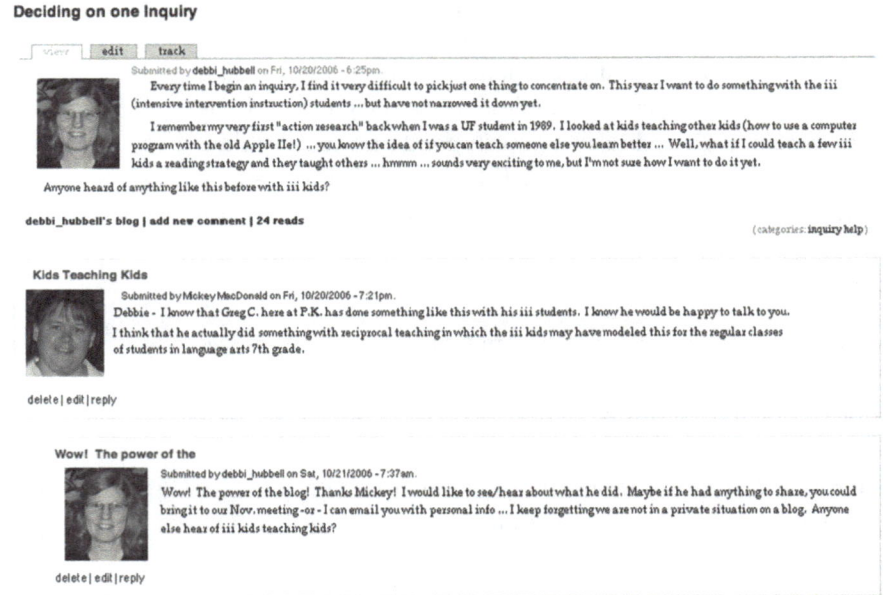

Figure 4.4 Teacher Research Blogging Site

Source: Used with permission of Debbi Hubbell and Mickey MacDonald.

A second reason why you should consider collaborating with colleagues as you inquire is that teacher talk is important. Teachers talk all the time! They talk with their students by posing questions, delivering information, giving directions, and facilitating discussions each day.

They talk with their colleagues, "swapping classroom stories, sharing specific ideas, seeking one another's advice, and trading opinions about issues and problems in their own schools and the larger educational arena" (Cochran-Smith & Lytle, 1993, p. 94). They talk with administrators to solve problems and identify support necessary for success in the classroom. They talk with parents about expectations, their child's progress, and ways to work together to facilitate a child's growth. Talk consumes almost every moment of a teacher's day.

Similarly, the talk of teacher inquiry also becomes a part of each teacher's day. In Chapter 2, you learned the importance of talking with another person as you defined and refined your first questions and the focus of your inquiry, and subsequently, earlier in this chapter, you learned the importance of connecting your inquiry to larger conversations occurring in the field through consulting the literature. Similarly, as you continue the teacher research journey, by engaging in dialogue and conversations with other professionals you will heighten your awareness of knowledge you have generated about teaching, making what you know more visible to yourself and to others. Making your tacit knowledge (e.g., personal skills, ideas, and experiences) more visible can often lead to significant discoveries when you are individually or collaboratively analyzing and interpreting your data.

In addition, talking with other professionals may help you call into question assumptions or givens about a teaching practice. Questioning assumptions or givens is a process that is critical to making your teaching problematic through the process of inquiry and was previously discussed as important to do as you develop your theory of action. Many assumptions related to schooling exist, such as the nature of instructional groups, student classroom assignments, staff meetings, accountability, retention, promotion, ability, departmentalization, instructional periods, standards, discipline, instructional materials, and homework. Teacher talk enables teachers to examine and critique these givens in education. In talking with others, you can generate possible alternatives to practice as well as to consider different interpretations that help every teacher gain perspective as his or her inquiry unfolds.

A third reason you should consider collaborating with colleagues as you inquire is that there is safety in numbers. Knowledge is power. Through teacher inquiry, you are taking charge of your own professional growth and generating knowledge that can be supported with evidence. While generating knowledge is one of the most exciting components of teacher inquiry, it can also become extremely stressful, since it is quite probable that the new knowledge you construct from your study may threaten the status quo and become threatening to others' assumptions about professional practice.

For example, perhaps you complete a curriculum piece that generates new practices that many of your colleagues are anxious to incorporate, but the individual who selected and designed the original unit for your district believes that his or her personal authority and position as an educator are threatened by your findings. You may face a litany of obstacles thrown out by your administrator and a long list of reasons why you can't teach the unit in the way that your evidence shows is most effective. If an inquiry leads to controversy, collaboration with other teachers can provide you with personal and professional support as you share your findings and combat others who are resistant to change: Remember, change requires a critical mass.

Just as there is safety in numbers, there is also strength in numbers, a fourth reason you will want to collaborate with others. While it *is* possible for one person's inquiry to lead to large-scale and schoolwide change, it is often not probable when resistance to change is present (as noted in the example presented in the previous paragraph).

However, when communities of teacher inquirers begin to build on each other's work, findings become more difficult to ignore or resist. According to Cochran-Smith and Lytle (1993):

> Communities of teacher researchers can play an essential role in school reform. Not only does their work add to the knowledge base on teaching, but their collective power as knowledge-generating communities also influences broader school policies regarding curriculum, assessment, school organization, and home-school linkages. Through teacher-research communities, teachers' voices play a more prominent part in the dialogue of school reform. (p. 103)

Hence, any inquiry you engage in becomes stronger when connected to a collection of related inquiries generated by other teacher researchers. This strength is made possible through your collaboration with others.

In addition, sometimes when inquiries do not go as planned, you garner strength by continuing to work with colleagues. For example, Larry Rotz, Judi Kur, Mary Robert, and Marcia Heitzmann collaborated on an inquiry that focused on effectively integrating SMART

Board technology into their curriculum. When confronted with the tremendous amount of time necessary to troubleshoot and problem-solve the SMART Board technology, they made little progress on the initial wondering: "How can we effectively integrate SMART Board technology into our curriculum?" Working in isolation, they might have easily called it quits when faced with so many technical difficulties. Together, though, they found the strength to forge ahead and changed their initial wondering from focusing on the integration of the SMART Board into the curriculum to focusing on how collaboration can be used to provide support for teachers interested in taking risks and experimenting with the SMART Board. At the close of their research, they reflected as follows:

> How many teachers does it take to plug in a SMART Board? With all of the technology difficulties we experienced at the start of our project, the answer to this question was all four of us! Through the process of collaborating in this inquiry, however, we were able to schedule time to work together, become risk takers, and experiment with new technology. Because of this positive experience, we will look for ways to continue to collaborate not only with technology and inquiry, but in other areas of curriculum. We plan to continue to use the SMART Board to increase our comfort level and confidence in using this technology. As we gain more confidence and experience, we are excited to begin sharing what we have learned with other teachers in our building. We are all ready, willing, and eager to help other teachers use this new technology in their classrooms. We have even returned to our original wondering and have begun to enhance our curriculum by developing lessons using the SMART Board. . . . We are excited about being on the cutting edge of this new technology and the possibilities it holds for improving instruction. We are just as excited about the opportunities to continue our collaboration. It still may take four teachers to plug in a SMART Board, but only because we realize the benefits of working together. (Rotz et al., 2002)

These four teachers' collaboration and reframing of their question enabled their continued exploration of classroom uses of SMART Board technology. Furthermore, these four teachers' collaboration helped them establish a collective belief in their capability to use educational technologies to positively impact student learning.

A fifth and final reason why collaboration is important is that collaborative teacher inquiry builds collective teacher efficacy. When teachers, like those in the previous example, *believe* they and their colleagues can impact student learning and achievement, they share a sense of collective efficacy. Collective efficacy is defined as the "collective self-perception that teachers in a given school make an educational difference to their students over and above the educational impact of their homes and communities" (Tschannen-Moran & Barr, 2005, p. 90). When teachers believe that they and their colleagues "as a whole can organize and execute the course of action required to have a positive effect on students" (Goddard et al., 2004, p. 4), their collective self-efficacy is high. Developing high collective teacher self-efficacy is important: In one of the most comprehensive research syntheses ever completed, John Hattie (2008) indicated that such self-efficacy is the number one factor influencing student achievement. Similarly, in her book on the subject entitled *Collective Efficacy: How Educators' Beliefs Impact Student Learning*, Jenni Donohoo notes that by engaging in cycles of inquiry together, "feelings of empowerment often result, and teachers feel their voices matter," which, in turn, is particularly effective in increasing efficacy (Donohoo, 2017, p. 62). By its nature, the study of one's own professional practice invites teachers to shift their gaze from "attributing student success or failure to factors outside of their control," to using the process of inquiry to "better understand their ability to impact student outcomes" (Donohoo, 2017, p. 63). Hence, the development of collective self-efficacy is another important reason to engage with your colleagues in the inquiry process.

Exercise 12. Grounding Your Inquiry in Collaboration

- If you are already located within a group where inquiry collaboration is an inherent part of your work (e.g., a Professional Learning Community, a professional learning program, a university course, or a professional development school), consider which members of that group might best be positioned to support your particular investigation, context-wise, topic-wise, and expertise-wise. When opportunities present themselves, connect with these individuals at various times in various configurations throughout your inquiry journey.

- If you are not already located within a group where inquiry collaboration is an inherent part of your work, reach out to other professionals you respect and enlist them in becoming your critical friends, either supporting you in the process, inquiring alongside you on their own investigation of practice, and/or inquiring with you into a shared problem of practice and wondering.

- Ponder the following questions:
  - What positive prior professional collaborative experiences have I had?
  - What made these experiences positive?
  - How can I replicate these positive experiences as I move forward with my inquiry?

Write

Now that we have made the case for collaboration and you have secured colleagues to collaborate with, we turn to the defining moment in the planning process—the actual writing of your inquiry brief. At the end of this chapter, you will find two different examples of research briefs. The first brief (Figure 4.3), developed by Abbey Wilson, illustrates the planning process used by a teacher candidate as a part of a field experience in a special education setting. The second brief (Figure 4.4) was developed by Mickey MacDonald, a highly experienced inquirer whose work was used as an example in the last chapter. Looking at briefs developed in different contexts and different grade levels and that represent different levels of inquiry experience can help you decide on your own approach to writing a brief, drawing upon all you have accomplished in the previous planning stages presented in this chapter. Furthermore, in a similar fashion to the teacher inquirer–chatbot dialogue presented in Chapter 2's AI Moment textbox illustrating the ways such a dialogue can help a teacher expand thinking and uncover new perspectives during initial wondering development, you may wish to consult a chatbot to serve as a critical friend in the writing of your brief. In this chapter's first AI Moment textbox on page 200, Rita Kentros, a student enrolled in a professional practice doctoral program, shares her reflections on enlisting ChatGPT to serve that purpose.

CIRCLE BACK

To revisit a teacher inquirer-chatbot conversation, circle back to Chapter 2's AI Moment textbox on page 89.

Exercise 13. Writing Your Inquiry Brief

- Compare and contrast the two briefs at the end of this chapter. Notice the ways the stages of planning we have discussed in this chapter have made their way (or not made their way) into each brief. Based on your analysis, sketch out an approach to writing your brief that best suits you and the thought work you have completed so far in this chapter.

- Set aside a block of time to commit pen to paper, documenting and communicating your thoughts in the creation of a written document inspired by the briefs presented at the end of this chapter.

AI MOMENT

Reflections on Partnering With ChatGPT in the Development of an Inquiry Brief

Rita Kentros

As a member of the seventh cohort of an award-winning Professional Practice Doctoral Program at the University of Florida, I had the opportunity to participate in a number of educational research classes, two of which focused on practitioner inquiry. In my second class on the subject, I was tasked with thinking ahead to the culmination of our program—writing a practitioner inquiry dissertation—and dreaming about what my end-of-program dissertation might look like by writing an inquiry brief.

I started this assignment by reviewing the sample inquiry briefs available in the fourth edition of *The Reflective Educator's Guide to Classroom Research* (Dana & Yendol-Hoppey, 2020, p. 143–152), as well as other briefs provided in the course shell. I noticed from the various samples I reviewed that they often began with a brief description of the inquirer's problem of practice that led into a statement of purpose and the associated wondering(s) or research question(s) the teacher inquirer planned to explore. With this noticing I was ready to begin my own brief, thinking the best place to start would be in putting a problem of practice that had been nagging at me in my head into words on paper, and so I journaled about this problem as follows:

> One problem of practice I am facing as AI is being rapidly introduced into education is that we educators are dabbling

in AI before we are educated in AI. It's implications and consequences on the minds and futures of our students are too impactful to go in without being fully prepared. As Chiu (2021) said in his study on AI curriculum, "teacher AI teaching capacity (e.g., knowledge and pedagogy) is crucial to AI education." Yet, I see teachers all over the internet, and particularly on Facebook's Educator group forums on AI, trying to integrate AI into their practice as quickly as possible. I don't think AI is kryptonite, but sound pedagogy needs to be understood and applied, and educators need to understand AI better in order to apply it well.

Complicating AI's use by educators is a slew of ethical considerations one must take into account in using it. According to Chui (2021), "To design and implement K–12 AI curriculum, teachers must navigate and mediate curriculum policies to ensure success for each of their students. They need to mediate policy and develop practices to address local needs." On the positive end, AI could level the playing field in that each student could have a tailored/differentiated curriculum. On the negative end, not all children will have access to this advanced technology. "When new text technologies appear, those terms have to be renegotiated, eventually becoming normalized into the expectations for a given medium, to the point where we take them for granted. But no norms yet exist for writing with AI" (Fyfe, 2023). Therein lies the rub. Educators create the norms that make AI equitable and ethical, yet, there are no district policies in place in my context. There have been no board discussions nor district professional developments that address these concerns. Since there is no direction or oversight, it could become the Wild West of technology or it could become so feared that it's overregulated and even rejected to the detriment of our students' futures.

Lastly, as a teacher of gifted and advanced high school English/Language Arts students, I am curious to see if AI would work curriculum wonders for this often neglected student population (of course, once I gain more curriculum knowledge and address ethical dilemmas). Whereas special education students with

(Continued)

(Continued)

> learning or behavioral disabilities have IEPs, federal and state funding, federal and state legal protections, and are provided with a myriad of resources, including second teachers in a core content area, gifted students are left to fend for themselves because people believe they don't need the support. As someone who teaches gifted students, I know this couldn't be further from the truth and AI could change all of that. I found a study that said AI would make a good fit for gifted students: "Gifted students often have unique learning characteristics and require specialized program services. The use of AI can provide advanced content, personalized learning, creative writing and image manipulation, critical thinking and problem-solving, collaboration, and research skills" (Siegle, 2023).

Journaling in this stream-of-conscious fashion was useful in helping my problem of practice begin to take shape, but I knew it was still somewhat fuzzy and in need of fine-tuning before it could serve as the opening to my inquiry brief. I felt a little stuck on where to go next, and so I thought it might be useful to begin playing around with a purpose statement and associated research questions. Since my problem of practice was focused on AI, I thought it made sense to consult Open AI's ChatGPT4 for help, and so I decided to ask AI to help design my inquiry. Here is the prompt I provided:

> I want to write a doctoral dissertation in education as a practitioner inquirer, using mostly qualitative data collection methods with a survey for quantitative data. My topic is AI in the instruction of gifted and advanced high school students. I want to know if using AI in the ELA classroom would accelerate learning gains in gifted and advanced students. Write research questions and a research purpose appropriate to my inquiry.

Here's how ChatGPT responded:

Research Purpose

The purpose of this research is to explore the impact and potential of artificial intelligence (AI) in enhancing the learning experiences and outcomes for gifted and advanced high school students in the English Language Arts (ELA) classroom. As a practitioner-inquirer, this study will combine qualitative insights from educators and students with quantitative data from a survey to provide a holistic understanding of AI's role in accelerated learning for these specific student populations.

Research Questions

Qualitative Questions:

1. How do gifted and advanced high school students perceive the integration of AI tools in their ELA classroom learning experiences?

2. What are the perceived advantages and challenges of using AI tools as reported by ELA educators teaching gifted and advanced students?

3. In what ways, if any, do educators believe AI tools enhance the differentiation of instruction for gifted and advanced students in the ELA classroom?

4. How do students describe their experiences in terms of engagement, motivation and depth of learning when using AI in the ELA classroom?

Quantitative Question:

1. Is there a statistically significant difference in learning gains among gifted and advanced high school students who have been instructed with the integration of AI tools in the ELA classroom compared to those who have not?

Mixed-Methods Question:

1. How do quantitative measures of learning gains align with qualitative perceptions and experiences of educators and students regarding the use of AI tools in the ELA classroom?

While ChatGPT's response did serve to get me "unstuck," just as my stream-of-conscious journaling about my problem of practice wasn't yet ready for "inquiry brief prime time," neither were ChatGPT's purpose statement and research questions. They did, however, give me a lot of things to consider as I continued to develop my brief.

(Continued)

(Continued)

First, the number of research questions AI generated for me was a little overwhelming. If ChatGPT could generate six possible wonderings from my prompt, my thinking about this inquiry was probably too general in nature and I had to do some more work to really hone in on a specific aspect of AI's potential uses within the gifted and talented and advanced ELA classes I taught to tighten my study's purpose and its question(s).

Second, I noted that ChatGPT's qualitative question numbers 1 and 4 both focused on understanding students' experiences working with AI, while questions 2 and 3 focused on understanding educators' beliefs about the challenges and benefits of using AI as a tool to differentiate instruction. Seeing this difference reaffirmed for me that I really wanted to focus on my students, but that my own beliefs as an educator would impact how I designed this study to begin with, so it was important for me to explicate my beliefs as I continued to design this inquiry. I was glad to have begun that process in the problem of practice journaling I had already completed.

I also noted that the AI qualitative research questions referred to students in a general sense, as if I were going to study all students everywhere. As a practitioner researcher, I was interested in my *own* students' experiences, so I played around with adjusting these questions accordingly to reflect the personal nature of practitioner inquiry by inserting the pronouns *my* and *our* into the ChatGPT-generated questions, as in, "How do my gifted and advanced high school students perceive the integration of AI tools in our ELA classroom learning experiences?" and "How do my students describe their experiences in terms of engagement, motivation, and depth of learning when using AI in our ELA classroom?"

This shift helped me realize that ChatGPT didn't appear to know as much about practitioner inquiry as I did, as it also suggested a research question exploring "statistically significant difference." Such a research question would more likely appear in a large academic research study crafted at a university rather than in a more intimate (but just as impactful) classroom-based inquiry. Practitioner researchers like me do not have, nor even desire, to "recruit" a large enough "sample size" to ascertain "statistically significant difference." Rather, we engage in research investigating our practice with the relatively small number of students we serve in order to improve *our* practice and *their* learning. Hence, my good friend ChatGPT was a little off base in suggesting this question. This question did help me solidify in my mind the bottom-line purpose of engaging in inquiry, however, which would be useful to stay grounded in as I continued to develop my inquiry brief. Furthermore, it helped me realize that in my future conversations with AI, it would be beneficial if I was more specific in the prompts I fed it, providing as much information about my school and students as well as educating AI about the unique characteristics of practitioner inquiry.

Finally, ChatGPT's suggestions of purpose statement and questions and my reaction to them propelled me to think ahead to other components of my inquiry brief that I would need to articulate, such as actions I would take and precise ways I would collect data. . . . All this came from a short interaction with ChatGPT!

I continued to converse with ChatGPT as I worked on my brief, and found this technology to be a fine partner, pushing my plan for inquiry forward. I learned that the more context and detail I provided it, the better partner in moving my inquiry brief–thinking forward ChatGPT became. When I completed my brief, I acknowledged the role ChatGPT played in its creation and received very encouraging feedback on my dissertation-dreaming inquiry brief from my professor. Perhaps more importantly, though, I found myself much closer to making the dream of writing a practitioner inquiry dissertation translate into reality.

References

Chiu, T. K. F. (2021). A holistic approach to the design of artificial intelligence (AI) education for K–12 schools. *TechTrends, 65*, 796–807. https://doi.org/10.1007/s11528-021-00637-1

Dana, N. F., & Yendol-Hoppey, D. (2020). *The reflective educator's guide to classroom research: Learning to teach and teaching to learn through practitioner inquiry* (4th ed.). Corwin.

Fyfe, P. (2023). How to cheat on your final paper: Assigning AI for student writing. *AI & Society, 38*, 1395–1405. https://doi.org/10.1007/s00146-022-01397-z

Siegle, D. (2023). A role for ChatGPT and AI in gifted education. *Gifted Child Today, 46*(3), 211–219. https://doi.org/10.1177/10762175231168443

Tune

The writing of a brief makes possible important conversations about your plan with colleagues, a wonderful place for collaboration. Using an "inquiry tuning" session, educators can receive and provide structured feedback that generates meaningful professional discussions focused on exploring their problems of practice with colleagues. This tuning protocol process is designed to enhance the quality of the inquiry by fostering a collaborative environment where colleagues can provide one another thoughtful critiques and suggestions to refine and strengthen each other's work. Exhibit 4.1 presents an Inquiry Tuning Protocol that can be used for this purpose.

Exercise 14. Tuning Your Brief

To tune your brief, we suggest the following:

- Review Exhibit 4.1 and gather two to three colleagues willing to spend 15 to 20 minutes with you to engage in this process.
- Hand out and review the protocol, asking one of your colleagues to serve as timekeeper as you share your brief.
- Hand out copies of your brief and follow the protocol.
- Ponder the questions:
    - What is the nature of the feedback I received?
    - What changes/adjustments do I wish to make to my plan based on that feedback?

At this point in the chapter, you've identified your problem, developed an implementation plan, established an inquiry timeline, and created an inquiry brief. You likely feel very ready to move forward full steam ahead. Before moving forward, however, it is important for you to pause for a moment to engage in a careful and close examination of any ethical issues that might be related to your study.

Inquiry Planning Stage 5: Consider the Ethical Dimensions of Your Work

With an inquiry brief written and a plan for your research taking shape, this is the perfect time to consider the ethical dimensions of your work as an inquirer and to make any changes or adjustments to your inquiry plans based on what you learn from your consideration of this topic. Considering the ethical dimensions of your work begins by

Exhibit 4.1   Inquiry Brief Tuning Protocol—Six Steps to a Fine-Tuned Plan for Inquiry

Suggested Group Size: Three or four

Suggested Time Frame: 15–20 minutes per group member

Step 1: Select a timekeeper.

Step 2: Presenter hands out a hard copy of the inquiry brief to each member of the group.

Step 3: Group members silently read the inquiry brief, making notes of issues/questions they might like to raise in discussion with presenter. (4 minutes)

As group members read the brief, presenter engages in a writing activity to complete the following sentences:

- Something I would like help with on my inquiry brief is . . .
- One thing this group needs to know about me or my proposed inquiry to better prepare them to assist me is . . .

Step 4: At the end of 4 minutes (or when it is clear that every member of the group has completed reading and taking notes on the inquiry brief, and the presenter has finished his or her response to the writing activity), the timekeeper invites the presenter to read his or her sentence completion activity out loud. (No more than 1 minute)

Step 5: Participants talk to each other as if the presenter was not in the room, while the presenter remains silent and takes notes. (10 minutes)

Participants focus on each of the following:

- Provide "warm feedback" on the inquiry brief. This is feedback that is positive in nature and identifies areas of strength. (1 or 2 minutes)
- Address the area the presenter would like help on and discuss the following questions: (8–10 minutes)
    a. What match seems to exist (or not exist) between the proposed data collection plan and inquiry question?
    b. Are there additional types of data that would give the participant insights into his or her question?
    c. Rate the doability of this plan for inquiry. In what ways is the participant's plan meshed with the everyday work of a teacher?
    d. In what ways does the participant's proposed timeline for study align with each step in the action research process?
    e. What possible disconnects and problems do you see?

Step 6: Timekeeper asks presenter to summarize the key points made during discussion that he or she wishes to consider in refining the plan for inquiry. (1 minute) contemplating the role ethics play in our profession in general as well as in relationship to practitioner inquiry.

Contemplate Ethics in General

Most professions have a code of ethics that delineates the guidelines and responsibilities for those who work within it. Teaching is no different, with several organizations and individual states publishing a code of ethics to guide educators. For example, the National Education Association's (NEA) Code of Ethics states the following:

> The educator, believing in the worth and dignity of each human being, recognizes the supreme importance of the pursuit of truth, devotion to excellence, and the nurture of the democratic principles. Essential to these goals is the protection of freedom to learn and to teach and the guarantee of equal educational opportunity for all. The educator accepts the responsibility to adhere to the highest ethical standards. (NEA, 2018, Preamble)

Similar to many other professional standards for teaching, these NEA standards are based on two principles: (1) a commitment to the student and (2) a commitment to the profession. Each of these principles states an overarching obligation, followed by the ways that educators fulfill that obligation. For example, the student principle states the following:

> The educator strives to help each student realize his or her potential as a worthy and effective member of society. The educator therefore works to stimulate the spirit of inquiry, the acquisition of knowledge and understanding, and the thoughtful formulation of worthy goals. (NEA, 2018, Principle I)

A glance at these ethical standards for teaching helps to illuminate that when teachers engage in the process of inquiry, they are engaging in a process that is a natural and normal part of what good, ethical teaching is all about.

- Good and ethical teaching involves looking carefully and closely at student work that is generated in teachers' classrooms to better understand students' progress and what adjustments can be made to instruction to help *all* students learn.
- Good and ethical teaching involves assessing all students on a regular basis and analyzing scores on various assessment measures

to help students master goals and objectives and achieve to their highest potential.

- Good and ethical teaching involves asking students questions about their learning to ascertain their understanding of content to inform instructional decisions that will ensure successful learning opportunities for *all*.

- Good and ethical teaching involves closely observing students as they work—watching for any behavior that provides insights into students' acquisition of knowledge and understanding and adjusting teaching according to these insights.

When the process of teacher inquiry is used as a professional learning mechanism to help teachers learn and improve their own practice locally as well as to contribute to school improvement efforts, teachers are not doing anything differently than they normally would as good, ethical teachers. Engagement in teacher inquiry as a form of professional learning simply makes the normal, everyday work of teaching less happenstance and more visible, heightening the opportunity for teachers to improve learning conditions in their classrooms on a regular basis. When inquiry is approached in this way, choosing *not* to engage in the process can almost be viewed as *un*ethical. Working in the best interest of the students you teach means carefully and systematically investigating your teaching and the relationship it has to your own students' learning. As such, it is important for all teacher inquirers to keep general codes of ethical teaching conduct in mind as they teach and investigate their own teaching practice.

Yet a murkiness occurs when the ethics for the teaching profession in general meet the ethics for conducting research that govern academics working in a university setting. While engagement in teacher inquiry is different from engagement in the types of research done in higher education by academic researchers (as discussed in Chapter 1), both types of study share some common language and processes, although the language and processes mean different things. For example, Pritchard (2002) notes that even the word *research* itself is defined differently by practitioner inquirers and institutional review boards (IRBs; committees at universities that review, approve, and monitor research conducted at the institution to ensure ethical treatment and rights of humans in all research studies). According to Pritchard (2002), practitioner researchers "understand research as an integral part of what they do in the ordinary course of events as a way of improving their regular practice; practitioner research is a way for practitioners to learn on the job" (Pritchard, 2002, p. 4). In contrast, Pritchard notes,

> IRB members rely on the regulatory definition of research. . . . *Research* means a systematic investigation, including research development, testing, and evaluation, designed to develop or contribute to generalizable knowledge (34 Code of Federal Regulations 9CFR 97.102[d]). (Pritchard, 2002, p. 4)

With differing understandings of and use of the word *research,* ethical considerations for the profession of teaching itself and ethical considerations for the conduct of research become muddled when engagement in teacher inquiry is part of university activities such as coursework or serves as a culminating project for a graduate degree program in the form of a master's thesis or dissertation. These complexities can lead to a lack of clarity for teacher inquirers regarding such university procedures as obtaining IRB approval, since all involved in the practitioner-inquiry movement ponder the question, "At what point does teaching become research?" (Nolen & Putten, 2007).

The answer to this question needs to be continually revisited, discussed, and debated in relation to every inquiry you undertake. Pritchard (2002) notes,

> A considerable portion of practitioner research falls outside the IRB's purview. Practitioner researchers may seek to improve their understanding of their own practice without pursuing generalizable findings (e.g., a teacher whose purpose is examining the development of a collective identity by a particular class of students). Or their research may not collect information from research subjects or design activities in ways that subordinate the participants' interests to the interest of knowledge (e.g., teachers whose research consists entirely of reviewing and developing curricula, or who observe and analyze peer interactions on the school playground). Research ethicists generally agree with the regulations that research is always shaped by the aim of generating knowledge; practitioners whose actions are designed exclusively to generate some benefit, while being aware that knowledge may accrue as a result, are not doing research. (Pritchard, 2002, p. 4)

As Pritchard continues his discussion of the relationship between practitioner research and IRBs, however, he illuminates why the answer to the question "At what point does teaching become research?" is not crystal clear:

> Practitioner research that meets the criterion of aiming to generate knowledge is complex because its dual purposes of generating knowledge and achieving a practical end are entangled, bringing into play both the research ethics perspective and the ethical demands of the practical activity. (Pritchard, 2002, p. 4)

In general, whether you are teaching, researching, or seamlessly intertwining the two, the role of ethics in any teaching endeavor ought to be considered "in terms of how each of us treats the individuals with whom we interact at our school setting: students, parents, volunteers, administrators, and teaching colleagues" (Mills, 2014, p. 31). As Smith so eloquently states, "At a commonsense level, caring, fairness, openness, and truth seem to be the important values undergirding the relationships and the activity of inquiring" (L. M. Smith, 1990, p. 260). Keeping caring, fairness, openness, and truth at the forefront of your work as a teacher inquirer is critical to ethical work. This is important to consider in relationship to the ways you might incorporate AI into your inquiry journey as well. Check out the AI Moment textbox "The Ethics of AI and Inquiry" for some "Dos" and "Don'ts" related to consulting AI as your journey unfolds.

AI MOMENT

The Ethics of AI and Inquiry

Generative AI tools carry significant potential to enhance teacher inquiry. At the same time, they also raise a number of ethical concerns. It has already been documented that AI tools can spread misinformation. For example, "AI hallucinations" can be said to occur when an AI tool generates false information or perceptions of something that is not actually present or factual (University of North Dakota, n.d.). The text produced by an AI tool may or may not be factually correct, or it may represent a biased perspective; as such, inquirers have a responsibility to approach AI-generated content through critical-analytic literacy skills

(Continued)

(Continued)

such as triangulation of facts, consideration of text through multiple perspectives, and evaluation of the evidence and reasoning provided (or not provided) by AI tools.

Generative AI tools raise significant ethical concerns about the intellectual property rights of individuals and communities. When text, images, audio, or video are "fed" into a generative AI tool, the associated data become part of the underlying large-language model that powers the AI tool. Feeding text, artwork, music, likenesses of people such as photographs, or other data sources may violate the intellectual property rights of the copyright holders.

In addition, feeding content into generative AI may violate the ethical norms of entire communities, particularly historically marginalized communities. As one example, in many Indigenous communities, collective (rather than individualistic) conceptions of responsibility for stewardship of knowledge may mean that language and cultural teachings are not the property of any single person. As such, an individual's choice to feed certain types of data into a generative AI model may violate a community's collective right to data sovereignty—the right to control how data from the community are accessed, stored, and shared (e.g., Walter et al., 2021).

While exploring the potential applications of AI to inquiry, we encourage you to keep the following considerations in mind.

Do:

- Acknowledge the use of generative AI tools in your inquiry through citations and/or disclosure statements.

- Transparently report the role generative AI played in your inquiry (e.g., AI as a thought partner in designing the inquiry, AI as a tool for data collection or analysis, etc.).

- Describe how you approached the ethics of using generative AI throughout your inquiry.

Do not:

- Enter, or "feed," confidential, private, or otherwise restricted data or text into generative AI tools. This includes any nonpublic data, FERPA-protected student information, IRB-protected data, and more.

- Disclose confidential, sensitive, or personally identifiable information to an AI tool.

- Disclose intellectual property that is not yours to share.

- Represent output from AI tools as being entirely your own work, without appropriate acknowledgement of the role AI played.

Check Out School District Research Policies

If you are engaging in inquiry as a part of your school's or your district's professional learning plan for teachers, be aware that individual school districts approach engagement in inquiry differently, and it's important to be attentive to and follow any school or district guidelines for this form of professional learning. While most school districts have policy and procedure in place to review and approve any research activity that occurs in schools and classrooms, teacher inquiry is often exempt from a formal review process by a district research office because it is considered a natural and normal part of the work teachers do to continually improve their own instructional practice.

For example, Fairfax County Public Schools, a Virginia school district with a long, rich history in supporting teacher research, has the following statement in its district policy regarding research:

> Internal research studies . . . may be conducted without approval of the research screening process on behalf of Fairfax County Public Schools by staff members carrying out their assigned responsibilities to maintain and improve instructional programs and administrative practices. Parents and staff members shall have the right to inspect such studies, and materials used in connection with such studies, on request. Any data collection, reporting, and/or related research activity undertaken within, or by, Fairfax County Public Schools shall protect the privacy of students, parents, and employees.

The Fairfax County Public School policy brings up an important point to keep in mind as you engage in inquiry—the protection of the privacy of your students, parents, and colleagues. Hence, when sharing your inquiry work with others, it's important to consider removing identifying information of any student, parent, or colleague from the discussion of your inquiry and even consider the use of pseudonyms when discussing individual students. For example, in the previous chapter, note the ways Debbi Hubbell and Mickey MacDonald did not include any student-identifying information in their presentation of data in Table 3.1, Table 3.2, and Exhibit 3.5.

Related to the protection of privacy, when partnering with universities on inquiry work, districts are often most concerned with the Family Educational Rights and Privacy Act (FERPA), a federal law that protects the privacy of student education records. FERPA has rules related to the types of student information that can be shared and with whom. FERPA does not have to be an insurmountable hurdle to districts and universities partnering to inform practice and improve learning conditions for children in classrooms through the process of inquiry.

For example, in order to cover course assignments that include inquiry work at their institution, the University of South Florida partnered with Hillsborough County Public Schools to develop a course task approval process so that no University of South Florida education student would need to submit an individual request to use student data in inquiry-related activities. The approval process requires the college to collect from the university course instructors a list of inquiry task descriptions that are collectively presented to the district for review and approval. Next, the district reviews the assignments, asking for clarification where needed, and sends a single letter of approval to the college indicating which assignments have been approved. Finally, course instructors include the following information in course syllabi with each approved assignment/task:

> This project has been approved through the Hillsborough County Public School Research Review process. Note that individual student information is protected under the Family Educational Rights and Privacy Act (FERPA). The University of South Florida and Hillsborough County Public Schools both want to ensure that student records are protected and that teachers and potential teachers have the most appropriate training opportunities. Student Information (K–12) collected for this task will *not* include information that identified the individual student and any student identifiable information/data collected will *not* be retained (e.g., videos with students in them, copies of student work, audio recordings of student interviews, etc.) past the completion of the course and the assignment of a grade by the instructor/professor.

If you are engaging in inquiry as a part of university activity, be aware of FERPA and any district regulations related to it. You should also be aware of IRB processes and procedures.

Look Into University Institutional Review Boards

Just like school districts, institutions of higher education vary, and while many IRBs do not require approval for inquiry conducted as part of a university course, "the determining factor in the decision (usually) relates to whether or not the outcomes of the proposed study will be published or presented at a professional conference" (Mills, 2014, p. 30). A general rule of thumb at most universities is that if the inquiry will be published as a thesis or dissertation, or shared through publication in a national journal or presentation at a national meeting, the aim of the inquiry is to generate knowledge, and IRB approval should be obtained.

If IRB approval will be a part of your work as a teacher inquirer, an important aspect of your application will be obtaining informed consent from the people you will be studying. In most cases for the teacher inquirer, this refers to students, and if your students are under 18 years of age (which will be the case for almost all K–12 teacher inquirers), informed consent must be obtained from parents. The sample letter in Exhibit 4.2, used by Ashley Pennypacker Hill in her inquiry into her teaching of self-regulation to learners receiving Tier 3 instruction in reading, serves as an example that may be useful in crafting your own informed consent form for an IRB application.

Exhibit 4.2 Sample Consent Form for an IRB Application

Dear Parent/Guardian,

I am a doctoral student in the School of Teaching and Learning at the University of Florida, conducting research on self-regulated learning under the supervision of Dr. Nancy Dana. The purpose of this study is to understand how to teach self-regulation to fifth-grade students receiving intensive Tier 3 reading supports and to help these learners transfer their self-regulation strategies to other contexts. The results of the study may help teachers better understand how to teach self-regulation. With your permission, I would like to ask your child to volunteer for this research.

(Continued)

(Continued)

> Participation in this study does not change the instruction your student is currently receiving in reading. With your permission, I will collect artifacts of your child's work and perform a review of their academic data. Your child's identity will be kept confidential to the extent provided by law. Students' names will be replaced with a pseudonym. When the study is completed and the data have been analyzed, all data will be destroyed. No names will be used in any reports. Participation or nonparticipation in this study will not affect grades or placement in any programs.
>
> You and your child have the right to withdraw consent for your child's participation at any time without consequence. There are no known risks or immediate benefits to the participants. No compensation is offered for participation. If you have any questions about this research protocol, please contact me at XXX-XXXX or my faculty supervisor, Dr. Dana, at XXX-XXXX. Questions or concerns about your child's rights as research participant may be directed to the XXXX office, University of Florida, Box XXXXXX, Gainesville, FL 32611, (XXX) XXX–XXXX.
>
> Ashley Pennypacker Hill
>
> Doctoral Candidate
>
> School of Teaching and Learning
>
> College of Education
>
> University of Florida
>
> I have read the procedure described above. I voluntarily give my consent for my child, _____,
> to participate in Mrs. Pennypacker Hill's self-regulation study. I have received a copy of this description.
>
> _____   _____
> Parent/Guardian Signature   Date

Source: Used with permission from Ashley Pennypacker Hill.

Notably, at some institutions obtaining IRB approval can bog down a project, because some of those who sit on IRBs are not familiar with practitioner inquiry and may not understand the legitimacy of the movement as a way for teachers to learn about teaching while in the act of teaching and to make more informed instructional decisions as a result of the process. Furthermore, IRBs are often made up of mainly quantitative researchers who approach research from a process-product paradigm. Without knowledge of the teacher inquiry movement and the purpose behind engaging in practitioner research, IRB members may reject a proposal outright under the assumption that studying one's own students is inherently unacceptable since it would be impossible for a teacher to avoid coercion of students into participation in the research (Brown, 2010). On another note, IRB members may view teacher research as "not quite meeting the definition of 'real' research, so that as long as proposed teacher research will not be conducted in unusual educational settings, it is automatically exempt" (Brown, 2010, p. 279).

Even if your work might be slowed down by ethical questions that emerge from others out of lack of knowledge about the practitioner-inquiry movement, the ethics of your work is not something to shy away from but to embrace. You can use ethical discussions to teach and inform others about the nature of a teacher's work and the ways engagement in the process of inquiry informs it. For example, when undergoing an internship period as a new IRB member, Oklahoma State University professor Pamela Brown questioned her IRB mentor on a teacher research proposal they had reviewed together:

> My mentor wanted to reject the proposal as written, claiming it would be impossible for a researcher soliciting participation from his own students to avoid coercion. I countered, ultimately successfully, that the field of teacher research was well respected and that rejecting the proposal for that reason would logically extend to all teacher research proposals, since by definition they involve teachers engaging in research in their own teaching settings. This stance by the IRB would stifle important voices and would be unacceptable. (Brown, 2010, p. 278)

Students, as well as their professors, can help educate reviewers about the practitioner-inquiry movement by defining practitioner inquiry within their IRB proposals. For example, note the way Ashley Pennypacker Hill both included a definition of practitioner inquiry and pointed out the ways her study was a natural part of her teaching practice in the completion of the Scientific Purpose of the Study portion of her IRB application.

SCIENTIFIC PURPOSE OF THE STUDY

Practitioner inquiry is defined as systematic, intentional study by teachers of their own practice (Cochran-Smith & Lytle, 2009). Engagement in practitioner inquiry has been an integral part of my growth as a professional educator, and I wish to use this method of systematic reflection to complete the capstone experience for the attainment of the Ed.D. degree.

Specifically, the purpose of my study is to understand how to teach self-regulation to fifth-grade students who struggle with reading and to help these learners transfer their self-regulation strategies to other contexts during the school day. Self-regulation is defined as the cycle of self-generated feelings, thoughts, and behaviors to strategically achieve personal goals (Paris & Paris, 2001; N. Perry, 1998; Zimmerman, 2000). Specifically, students are taught to reflect on their own learning before, during, and after assignments and to use their reflections to set personal goals for future achievement.

As a reading support specialist, I work daily with small groups of students to build their reading skills. Research indicates that self-regulation is an important skill for students to attain and has many benefits. Hence, I wish to incorporate the teaching of self-regulation strategies into my normal, everyday practice as a teacher, and to document the teaching of these strategies to better understand the ways these strategies are working for my students. The incorporation of self-regulation teaching strategies into my daily practice as a classroom teacher will be used as the capstone experience for the attainment of my Ed.D. degree, and my work teaching self-regulation will be written about in the form of a dissertation.

Regardless of whether you are engaging in inquiry as a mechanism for your own professional learning within your school or district or engaging in inquiry as a part of your pathway to the attainment of a degree at a university (or a combination of both), you can embrace working through the ethical dimensions of your work by engaging in a self-interrogation of sorts, posing ongoing questions that you need to continually revisit as you teach and inquire into your teaching practice. Among others, Brown (2010) suggests the following questions, many of which you have already considered in this chapter as you planned your research, for the self-interrogation of teacher inquirers:

- What is the purpose of this proposed research?
- What data do I plan to collect—audiotapes, videotapes, student work samples, journal entries, observations?
- Might a layered consent/assent form be useful, in which participants check levels of participation to which they agree, such as use of work samples, use of journal entries, use of audiotapes, use of digital video?
- How can I make sure my research does not interfere with the academic mission of my role as a teacher?
- What is my place in terms of power? My students' place?
- Who might be negatively affected by my research?
  How do I guard against negative impact? (Brown, 2010, p. 280–281)

In sum, the ultimate responsibility for ethical conduct as a teacher and a teacher inquirer resides with you, with the ultimate goal of doing no harm to the students you teach or any other people involved in your inquiry. Whether or not you go through any mandatory research approval processes, "It is important you develop your own criteria for what you consider to be ethical behavior" (Mills, 2014, p. 32).

Exercise 15. Considering the Ethical Dimensions of Your Work

- Engage in a discussion about the ethics of teaching and the ethics of doing research with one or more colleagues. Discuss and debate the question posed in this section, "At what point does teaching become research?"
- Review the inquiry brief you created during Stage Four in light of your discussion with colleagues of the question, "At what point does teaching become research?" Discuss your research briefs with one another to consider the ethical dimensions of the work you plan to undertake. Use the questions Brown (2010) suggests as you review each brief to inform your discussion. Make adjustments to your brief as needed as you take into account the ethical dimensions of your work as an inquirer.

- Consider further reading on ethics, beginning with the following recommended articles:
  - Brown, P. (2010). Teacher research and university institutional review boards. *Journal of Early Childhood Teacher Education, 31,* 276–283. https://doi.org/10.1080/10901027.2010.500559
  - Pritchard, I. A. (2002). Travelers and trolls: Practitioner research and institutional review boards. *Educational Research, 31*(3), 3–13. https://doi.org/10.3102/0013189X031003003

Your Inquiry Plan

By progressing through the five planning stages presented in this chapter, you now have a process for designing research that positions you to engage in career-long professional learning. To close this chapter, we return to the analogy we used to open it comparing the writing of a lesson plan to the writing of an inquiry brief. A lesson plan guides your thinking about instruction; the inquiry brief provides a structured yet flexible pathway for your inquiry that makes every step intentional and aligned with your goals.

The time and mental sweat you have placed into planning your inquiry as you progressed through this chapter is likely akin to the length of time you needed (and mental sweat experienced) when you wrote your very first lesson plan. Just as a well-constructed lesson plan is challenging to create when you are new to the process but gets easier and less time consuming with experience, so is the case with a well-constructed inquiry brief. When educators make inquiry planning as routinized as lesson planning, they cultivate a stance of continuous curiosity and problem posing that leads to ongoing professional learning. Just as lesson planning becomes a natural, habitual part of a teacher's daily practice, inquiry planning, too, evolves into a fundamental stance when its processes are routinized. Over time, inquiry planning becomes not just something you do, but a mindset that drives your professional learning. As we noted in the data collection chapter, inquiry becomes "a part of" rather than "apart from" your practice as an educator. This stance fosters a deep commitment to understanding and enhancing learning, a responsive approach to improving teaching and learning, and a commitment to using data to support and guide reflection in a systematic and intentional way.

Using data to support and guide reflection in a systematic and intentional way is the process of data analysis. In the next chapter, we explore data analysis in depth.

Exhibit 4.3 Inquiry Brief Example 1

Using Manipulative Materials to Enhance Math Instruction in a Special Education Classroom

Abbey Wilson

Purpose

The purpose of this action research project is to investigate the impact of using manipulative materials to teach basic math concepts in a kindergarten through second-grade special education classroom.

Guiding Question(s)

What is the relationship between the use of manipulative materials and the learning of basic math concepts for students with disabilities?

Subquestions include the following:

1. What effect will the use of manipulative materials have on my students' understanding of the concepts being taught?
2. What effect will the use of manipulative materials have on my students' attitudes toward basic math concepts?
3. What are some effective ways to incorporate manipulative materials into my teaching?
4. How will students use the manipulative materials in math and in other areas of learning?

Context

The students are enrolled in an elementary special education classroom that serves children in K through second-grade levels. The average class size is from five to ten students and these students are pulled out of the general education classrooms for specialized instruction throughout the day.

DATA SOURCES AND COLLECTION SCHEDULE	DATA ANALYSIS	QUESTIONS DATA ADDRESSES

Mathematics Knowledge
 	
1. Assessment of knowledge
   a. Pretest of students' skills with basic math concepts.
   b. Class questions given during lesson every day. Take observations and anecdotal notes.
   c. Conferences. Students respond to teacher's questions about certain problems and how using manipulative materials helps them and why.
	1. Analyze and graph individual scores. Examine individual scores as well as group averages. Use this formative data analysis to change the focus of the lessons and use of the manipulative materials.
	
	Analyze conference notes for different themes and patterns.
		How did students use the manipulative materials and apply them to other areas of learning?
		
		What effect did the use of manipulative materials have on students' attitudes toward basic math concepts?

(Continued)

(Continued)

DATA SOURCES AND COLLECTION SCHEDULE	DATA ANALYSIS	QUESTIONS DATA ADDRESSES
2. Classwork consists of problems done in class, on handouts, and on the chalkboard, white board, and individual dry erase boards.	2. By having students complete problems during class it allows me to observe if and in what ways students were using the manipulative materials to solve the problems. I am able to discuss with the students the steps they are taking as they work on solving the problems. I observe and record anecdotal notes of their work and discussion. Observation notes will be reviewed and analyzed for patterns and themes.	What effect did the use of manipulative materials have on students' understanding of the concepts being taught? How did students use the manipulative materials and apply them to other areas of learning?
Effective Teaching 3. Researcher journal. Write in daily to discuss how students respond to the use of the different manipulative materials for each lesson. I also will write about the comments they made. I will assess my instruction and changes I want to make.	3. Allows me to think about how things are going in the classroom and with the students. This allows me to look at the lessons and how the students are responding to them, and compare it to the graphs of the grades from their homework and quizzes.	What are some effective ways to incorporate manipulative materials into my teaching?

Source: Used with permission of Abbey Wilson.

Exhibit 4.4 Inquiry Brief Example 2

Taking Action With Assessment for Learning

Mickey MacDonald

Purpose

Over the past two years at my school, a strand of our professional development has involved Assessment for Learning (AfL), or formative assessment practices. Based on the work of the Assessment Training Institute headed by Rick Stiggins, we have begun to transform our instructional practice to include formative assessment. Most of my current knowledge about AfL has come from Knowledge for Practice, through participation in trainings on Assessment for

Learning. As a classroom teacher, the more that I begin to use AfL, the more questions I have about the theory of AfL and the implications for my instructional practice and student learning.

An important component of formative assessment generally and AfL specifically is student self-assessment. The skill of self-assessment requires that students become metacognitive about their learning (Black et al., 2012; Hattie & Timperley, 2007; Ibabe & Jauregizar, 2010; Kostons et al., 2012; Pintrich, 2002). Students who internalize self-assessment skills and use them effectively tend to become self-regulated learners. Such students are self-aware of their strengths and weaknesses and know how to adjust the ways in which they interact with new material to increase their understanding (Pintrich, 2002).

As with teaching content, teachers must explicitly teach students to use metacognition in their learning (Black et al., 2012; Pintrich, 2002). Andrade and Valtcheva (2012) found that students who actively use rubrics that include clear criteria to self-assess their work produce higher-quality work and improve their learning. This finding further supports the need to provide clear criteria for each learning goal and to share such criteria with students.

At my school, the 9th grade team is transitioning to a blended learning instructional format. Blended learning can take many forms within K–12 education. The model of blended learning that we use is the "Station-Rotation Model."

Within a given course or subject (e.g., math), students rotate . . . at the teacher's discretion among classroom-based learning modalities. The rotation includes at least one station for online learning. Other stations might include activities such as small-group or full-class instruction, group projects, individual tutoring, and pencil-and-paper assignments. Some implementations involve the entire class alternating among activities together, whereas others divide the class into small-group or one-by-one rotations (Innosight Institute, 2012, para. 2).

Part of student instruction within biology will be face-to-face instruction and part of instruction will be online. My intention is to utilize online learning for three important instructional purposes. First, students will complete formative assessment activities that allow me to determine where they are in relation to specific learning targets. Second, I will use this formative assessment data to lead students to instructional activities that will allow them to fill any gaps they may have with particular learning goals. Finally, as students independently interact with online content, I will pull students into small group instruction who need additional teacher support with learning. Although pulling small groups of students for additional support is commonly achieved in elementary classrooms, such instructional practice in high school settings is nearly nonexistent.

Questions

I have already begun my inquiry work at my school this year, which is an extension of my inquiry work over the past two years. My main wondering is:

In what ways will moving to a more blended learning environment allow for ongoing assessment for learning, implementation of differentiated instruction in a secondary biology classroom, and preparation for the biology end of course exam?

Within my main wondering, I have two subwonderings:

1. In what ways can a blended learning instructional model leverage student learning opportunities that promote autonomous or self-regulated learning among 9th grade biology students?
2. What classroom structures need to be in place to allow small group instruction within a high school biology classroom?

(Continued)

(Continued)

Kristin Weller, who teaches geometry using an AfL framework, and I will be completing a shared inquiry that will be a component of subwondering 1.

How can we scaffold the use of self-assessment of learning targets and formative assessment data to teach struggling students how to

- reflect on what they know;
- reflect on what they do not know; and
- develop action steps to fill in the gap before they take a summative assessment?

Methods

I will be working directly with four students during the ecology unit beginning the week of October 15th. I have chosen these particular students based on past performance in biology. Each student has scored poorly on short content quizzes and on unit tests. Although three of the four students generally complete all classroom assignments, they do not connect what they are learning in the activity with the corresponding learning target nor do they understand that the purpose for completing the activity is to learn, not simply to get the assignment done. As a result, the quality of the assignment suffers because the students' goal is completion, not learning.

Prior to beginning the ecology unit, students will complete a baseline self-assessment of the ecology learning targets using a Google form. I will contact each of the parents of the four students to get their cooperation in having their student attend two afterschool group study sessions each week during the ecology unit. During each study session, students will complete a formative assessment on each learning target that was covered in class prior to the help session and they will self-assess each of the targets based upon their formative assessment scores. I will use their formative assessment scores to model how to use such data to make an action plan to fill any gaps in understanding during the first week of study sessions. Within the subsequent study session, students will develop their own action plan and either work independently on an online activity to fill the gap or receive Tier III support from Dr. Kort, our secondary support specialist, or from me. At the end of each study session, students will complete an exit slip on the learning targets and a reflection on how the learning activity(ies) they completed connected to the learning target(s). I will complete a journal entry via a 10-minute quick-write following each session to capture my thoughts about the study session, ideas I want to implement or change, and observations I make about each of the students.

Within class, I will have students track (graph) their scores on the short content quizzes and on the ecology unit test and compare these scores with their quiz and test scores from the previous two units. At the final study session, I will interview the students via a focus group to capture what they learned about the relationship among the instructional activities that they do in class and for homework, the learning targets, and the assessments.

Following the unit assessment, I will contact each student's parent(s) and discuss the results of the study sessions, their student's progress, and ways to continue to support their student's academic success.

Data Pieces

- Pre, during, and post unit self-assessment data
- Formative assessment data

- Student artifacts
  - study session exit slips on progress toward meeting learning targets
  - reflections on connections between learning activities and learning targets
  - action plans
  - tracking graphs/comparison of scores
- Student interviews via focus group
- Quiz and unit test scores
- Attendance records
- 10-minute quick write reflection journal

Calendar

DATE	ACTIVITIES
Week of October 8–12	**Create cohesive unit plan** 1. Decide on specific instructional activities for each learning target 2. Find alternative activities for each learning target for additional support 3. Create formative assessments for each learning target 4. Create short content quizzes 5. Create summative assessment 6. Contact each of the parents and set up study session schedule
Week of October 15–19	**Begin study sessions (2)** 1. Collect exit slips on learning targets and copies of student reflections and action plans 2. Pre-unit self-assessment of learning targets via Google Forms 3. Students set up assessment tracking graph 4. Complete formative assessment on learning targets covered in class followed by self-assessment of learning targets following instruction 5. 10-minute quick writes
Week of October 22–26	**Continue study sessions (2)** 1. Collect student artifacts (exit slips on learning targets and copies of student reflections and action plans) 2. Complete formative assessment on learning targets covered in class followed by self-assessment of learning targets following instruction 3. Students graph quiz scores from ecology unit 4. 10-minute quick writes

(Continued)

(Continued)

DATE	ACTIVITIES
Week of October 29–30	**Continue study sessions (1)** 1. Collect student artifacts (exit slips on learning targets and copies of student reflections and action plans) 2. Complete formative assessment on learning targets covered in class followed by self-assessment of learning targets following instruction 3. Students graph quiz scores from ecology unit 4. 10-minute quick writes
Week of November 5–8	**Final study sessions (2)** 1. Collect student artifacts (exit slips on learning targets and copies of student reflections and action plans) 2. Students complete post-unit self-assessment of all learning targets via Google Forms 3. Students graph quiz scores and unit test scores from ecology unit 4. Run focus group/interviews 5. 10-minute quick writes 6. Follow-up contact with parents

References

Andrade, H., & Valtcheva, A. (2012). Promoting learning and achievement through self-assessment. *Theory into Practice, 48*(1), 12–19. https://doi.org/10.1080/00405840802577544

Black, P., McCormick, R., James, M., & Pedder, D. (2012). Learning how to learn and assessment for learning: A theoretical inquiry. *Research Papers in Education, 21*(2), 119–132. https://doi.org/10.1080/02671520600615612

Hattie, J., & Timperley, H. (2007). The power of feedback. *Review of Educational Research, 77*(1), 81–112. https://doi.org/10.3102/003465430298487

Ibabe, I., & Jauregizar, J. (2010). Online assessment with feedback and metacognitive knowledge. *Higher Education, 59*(6), 243–258. https://doi.org/10.1007/s10734-009-9245-6

Innosight Institute (2012). Innosight institute—Blended-learning model definitions. www.innosightinstitute.org/media-room/publications/blended-learning/blended-learning-model-definitions.

Kostons, D., van Gog, T., & Paas, F. (2012). Training self-assessment and task selection skills: A cognitive approach to improving self-regulated learning. *Learning and Instruction, 22*(2), 121–132. https://doi.org/10.1016/j.learninstruc.2011.08.004

Pintrich, P. (2002). The role of metacognitive knowledge in learning, teaching, and assessing. *Theory into Practice, 41*(4), 219–225. www.jstor.org/stable/1477406

Source: Used with permission of Mickey MacDonald.

DISCUSSION QUESTIONS

1. Which of the five stages of inquiry planning (Identify the Problem, Develop an Implementation Plan, Establish an Inquiry Timeline, Create an Inquiry Brief, Consider the Ethical Dimensions of Your Work) seemed to challenge you the most as you progressed through the exercises in this chapter? What are some reasons for the challenges you experienced? How did you "break-through" the challenges, and what have you learned about inquiry as a result?

2. How is the use of literature by a teacher inquirer in a school the same as, and different from, the use of the literature by an academic at a university? In what ways do the terms used to distinguish between teacher inquirers and academics used in this chapter (researching professional vs. professional researcher) capture the different ways they approach and use literature in their work?

3. Three different types of literature and reasons to read it as a teacher inquirer are discussed in this chapter: (1) literature on the topic of your inquiry, (2) literature to understand your positionality, and (3) literature on teacher research methodology. In what ways can reading in each of these areas impact your personal inquiry plan and the quality of your learning that results from enacting that plan?

4. Review the two different types of action discussed in this chapter: action taken as a possible solution to address the problem and action taken to better understand the problem in order to address it. Which type of action are you more inclined to take as a part of your inquiry journey and why? What steps can you take to avoid developing "solution-itis," as well as to examine the assumptions behind the theory of action you develop?

5. The authors state, "While we believe it is critical to make teacher inquiry a part of your teaching rather than apart from your teaching, the fact remains that even if you are able to seamlessly integrate teaching and inquiry (as we believe should be the case!), the work is difficult and can be quite draining at times. Through collaboration with others, teacher inquirers find a crucial source of energy and support that keeps them going and sustains their work." What are

(Continued)

(Continued)

some ways you can make teacher inquiry a part of rather than apart from your teaching? How does working collaboratively with other educators generate energy?

6. Consider the following profiles of two teachers—"Always Collaborating Annie" and "Go It Alone Gail."

    "Always Collaborating Annie" constantly seeks out others to give her feedback on and provide insights into her teaching. In fact, she does not feel confident teaching a lesson if she hasn't run it by at least one other colleague formally or informally to garner ideas and test out her lesson plan by describing it aloud. Rarely does Annie ever take any actions in her teaching without using her colleagues as sounding boards for any changes to practice she is considering.

    "Go It Alone Gail" rarely takes the opportunity to discuss her teaching with colleagues. Because she often eats lunch with students, she is rarely in the teacher's room, so she has few opportunities to engage in professional dialogue with others during the school day. Also, as she coaches the girls' cross-country team and rushes to practice right after the final bell, she has few opportunities to engage in professional dialogue with others after school. Although the idea of collaboration appeals to Gail theoretically, she secretly admits to herself that she is glad her busy schedule precludes her from discussions with colleagues, because she is very action oriented and likes her teaching to keep moving in new directions. She could easily see herself getting frustrated by collaboration because it requires consensus and agreement and could potentially slow any changes to teaching practice that she may be considering.

    Are you more like "Always Collaborating Annie" or "Go It Alone Gail"? What implications do the ways you describe yourself as a collaborator have for planning your inquiry?

7. In this chapter's section on Inquiry Planning Stage 5: Consider the Ethical Dimensions of Your Work, the authors include the following:

    When the process of teacher inquiry is used as a professional learning mechanism to help teachers learn and improve their own practice locally as well as to contribute to school improvement efforts, teachers are not doing anything differently than they normally would as good, ethical teachers. Engagement in teacher inquiry as a form of professional learning simply makes the normal, everyday work of teaching less happenstance and more visible, heightening the opportunity for teachers to improve learning conditions in their classrooms on a regular basis. When inquiry is approached in this way, choosing *not* to engage in the process can almost be viewed as *unethical*.

Do you agree that choosing not to engage in the process of inquiry can be viewed as unethical? Why or why not? What are the implications for the way you answer this question for your own teaching practice?

8. In what ways can teachers ensure they are keeping caring, fairness, openness, and truth at the forefront of their work as teachers and inquirers?

9. Consider the experience of Oklahoma State University professor Pamela Brown when she was being mentored to serve on the IRB at her institution by pretending you submitted an application for IRB approval to complete your master's degree final project by engaging in the process of inquiry and your proposal was rejected on the basis that studying your own students would be considered coercion. Using Pamela Brown as a model as well as what you've learned so far in this book about practitioner inquiry, how would you respond to the IRB in relation to its outright rejection of your proposal? In general, how can teachers help to educate those responsible for the research approval processes in both districts and universities about the nature of teacher inquiry?

ONLINE MATERIALS

The following materials designed to facilitate the development of an inquiry plan are available for download at **https://companion.corwin.com/courses/ReflectiveEdsGuide5e**:

- **Activity 4.1: Wondering Refinement Partner Talk.** Discuss and refine your wondering with a partner.

- **Activity 4.2: Developing Equity-Focused Wonderings**. Analyze inquiry questions with an emerging equity focus.

(Continued)

(Continued)

- **Activity 4.3: Triad Literature Chat.** Synthesize literature you read related to your inquiry.

- **Activity 4.4: Four Corners.** Examine your beliefs about collaboration.

- **Activity 4.5: Coaching Inquiry Brief Development.** Read a sample brief completed by a secondary mathematics teacher containing embedded feedback from her inquiry coach.

- **Activity 4.6: Three Levels of Text: Considering Ethical Dimensions for My Work as an Inquirer.** Discuss a self-selected passage from the text about ethics you believe to have important implications for your own research.

Finding Your Findings

Data Analysis

5

As you begin this chapter, you have likely planned your inquiry, and it is well underway with data collection in process. Alternatively, you may be in the inquiry planning phase of your journey, with some intriguing data already in hand you will use to inform wondering development and other stages of inquiry planning. Whether it be data you have collected for this inquiry cycle or existing data you are considering as you prepare to launch an inquiry cycle, data analysis will become a pivotal aspect of your work because it involves using your data to generate insights about your teaching. Hence, we warmly welcome you to data analysis, one of the most rewarding, exciting, thought-provoking, and growth-oriented components of inquiry!

Figure 5.1 Inquiry Cycle: Data Analysis

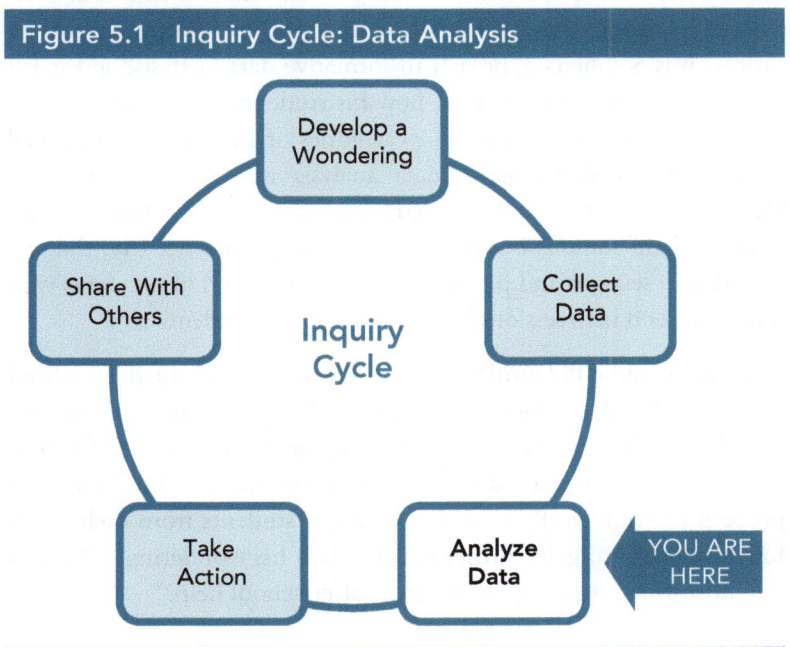

You will learn in this chapter that there are two types of data analysis, both of which can lead to important, actionable insights. The first type, formative data analysis, is ongoing throughout your entire inquiry, occurs *as* you are collecting your data, and generates emerging insights to propel your inquiry forward. The second type, summative data analysis, takes place toward the end of an inquiry cycle, occurs *after* you have finished data collection, and generates more conclusive insights to guide future action and subsequent inquiry cycles. Both types of analysis play an important role in the inquiry process. In the sections that follow, we will explore each type.

What Is Formative Data Analysis?

Recall Stephen Burgin's inquiry, presented in Chapter 3, which focused on investigating his after-school extra-help sessions and the ways he could make these sessions more effective. Around the midpoint of his inquiry, Stephen paused his data collection to review the data he had collected already and to consider what the data might suggest about what to do next. He read through the data he had collected so far: students' responses to a survey Stephen had administered at the start of his inquiry, attendance records from the extra-help sessions he had been offering, and his own observations of students who had attended the extra-help sessions.

While reading through his data, Stephen started to notice some patterns in his data. He realized that he could sort his students into four categories of participation in the extra-help sessions. This reading-and-sorting process was Stephen's approach to formative data analysis, and it led Stephen to fresh insights about how his students were engaging with the extra-help sessions. The four categories of students that emerged through Stephen's formative data analysis were (1) students who attended and benefited from extra-help sessions, (2) students who attended help sessions but did not benefit, (3) students who did not attend help sessions and performed well in class, and (4) students who did not attend help sessions but were struggling academically.

Once Stephen had identified these four categories, he further realized that he had new questions about the students in each of the categories. This insight spurred him to engage in further data collection. He wanted to understand his students more fully, so he decided to proceed by strategically interviewing a few students from each of his four categories to gain further insights into his wondering, "What is the most productive way to structure after-school help?"

The process of carefully reviewing your data *as* you collect it, and using the insights that emerge from your review to help inform instructional decisions and next steps in your inquiry, is called *formative* data analysis. Formative data analysis is at the very heart of generating actionable insights about your teaching. It's the process—highly intentional, yet seamlessly embedded into the daily practice of reflective teaching—through which teacher inquirers interpret data collected during their inquiries in order to inform their next steps, which might entail collecting more data, seeking out fresh perspectives from literature or from other people, revising your wondering, or starting to make a change in classroom practice. In these ways, formative data analysis functions as a stepping stone, or a springboard propelling you into other components of the inquiry process.

Conducting Formative Data Analysis: A Four-Step Approach

Each inquirer's process of formative data analysis is unique; however, regardless of the type of data you have collected, the process typically involves careful reflection on pieces of the data that stand out, catch your attention, or raise further questions. To engage in formative analysis at any point within your inquiry, pause and follow these four steps:

1. Skim through the data you have collected up to this point. As you skim, consider: What do I have here? What have I collected so far?

2. Skim your data a second time. On this reading, consider the following questions and jot down some brief notes to capture your emerging insights:
   a. What do I notice about these data?
   b. What do I wonder about these data?
   c. What new questions are emerging?

3. Skim your data a third time. On this skim, jot additional notes in response to the following questions:
   a. What do the data seem to suggest?
   b. How might the data help me respond to my wondering?
   c. How could I use these insights to propel my inquiry forward?

4. Take action on the basis of your insights. Some actions you might take on the basis of insights from formative data analysis include:
   - Adjusting the wording of your wondering or other aspects of your inquiry plan to reflect a new understanding; and/or
   - Making a tweak or change in your teaching practices or routines;
   - Collecting more data to deepen your insights before changing your practices and/or to inform new questions that have arisen;
   - Seeking out additional perspectives to inform your wondering by collecting and reading new literature and/or consulting different constituencies that can offer fresh insights into your inquiry (e.g., students, parents/caregivers, colleagues, community members).

CIRCLE BACK

For additional ways to phrase your wondering, circle back to Chapter 4, "Craft and Claim Your Wondering," on page 165.

In the following sections, we will explore how this process of formative analysis plays out with both quantitative and qualitative data. As you read the two examples, use Figure 5.2 to consider how teacher inquirers Megan Hefner and May Steward seamlessly integrated these steps of formative data analysis with their inquiries, their teaching practices, and other requirements in their schools. Notice how they approached analysis as a part of, rather than apart from, other aspects of their teaching.

An Example of Formative Data Analysis With Quantitative Data: Megan Hefner

As discussed in Chapter 3, quantitative data may be an important source of insight for your inquiry if you are collecting data that take the form of numbers. Tracking quantitative data over time can be particularly useful as teacher researchers strive to make well-informed instructional decisions as their inquiries unfold. One source from which teachers commonly collect quantitative data—the progress monitoring process—is particularly well suited for formative data analysis since

Figure 5.2 Formative Data Analysis Step by Step

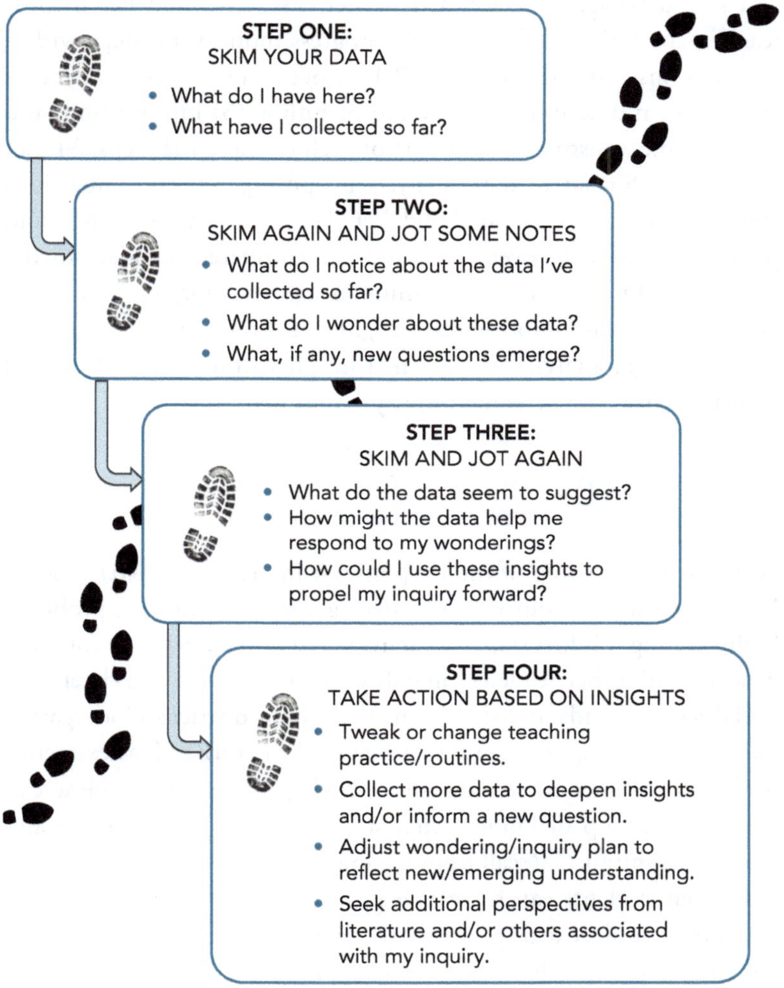

STEP ONE:
SKIM YOUR DATA
- What do I have here?
- What have I collected so far?

STEP TWO:
SKIM AGAIN AND JOT SOME NOTES
- What do I notice about the data I've collected so far?
- What do I wonder about these data?
- What, if any, new questions emerge?

STEP THREE:
SKIM AND JOT AGAIN
- What do the data seem to suggest?
- How might the data help me respond to my wonderings?
- How could I use these insights to propel my inquiry forward?

STEP FOUR:
TAKE ACTION BASED ON INSIGHTS
- Tweak or change teaching practice/routines.
- Collect more data to deepen insights and/or inform a new question.
- Adjust wondering/inquiry plan to reflect new/emerging understanding.
- Seek additional perspectives from literature and/or others associated with my inquiry.

---

progress monitoring tools are designed specifically to quantify a student's rate of improvement and assist teachers in adjusting their instruction based on how a student is performing on the progress monitoring measures over time.

The process of engaging in formative data analysis through progress monitoring is illustrated by the work of Megan Hefner, a special education teacher candidate who was supported in the inquiry process by David Hoppey from the University of North Florida. Megan was pursuing an inquiry into her use of universal screening and progress-monitoring data to improve five kindergarten students' letter and sound recognition. Guided by her instructor and her mentor teacher, she followed four specific progress monitoring steps within the Response to Intervention (RtI) process: (1) student selection and problem description, (2) action planning, (3) intervention, and (4) outcome assessment. As a part of each of these RtI steps, Megan engaged in formative data analysis by posing reflective questions about her data. As she analyzed her data, she noticed trends and patterns in the data over time, and she compared her data to the instructional practices she was simultaneously testing out to support her students' sound and letter recognition. From these practices of formative data analysis, she gleaned insights from which she could adjust her instruction as her inquiry progressed.

Progress Monitoring Step 1: Student Selection and Problem Description

To begin the first step of the Response to Intervention (RtI) process, Megan began her inquiry by identifying a student learning problem. In illustrating this first step, Megan reviewed some previously collected data indicating her students' inability to name letters and determine initial letter sounds and data from the school district's kindergarten universal screening inventory that included the DIBELS assessments. As she pored over these data sources, Megan wondered, "How can I help this group of kindergarten students improve their letter and sound recognition?" Recall from Chapter 2 that a passion for assisting individual students can serve as a powerful spark for an inquiry. In Megan's example, existing data sparked her identification of a wondering related to a specific student learning need in her mentor teacher's classroom.

Progress Monitoring Step 2: Action Planning

To begin the second step in the RtI progress monitoring process, Megan collected additional data for her inquiry that could more fully indicate her students' current needs for early literacy skill development. On the basis of her data collection, she developed goals for academic interventions for her students. For example, Megan's goal for one of the five students in her small group was, "By December 6, James will increase his letter identification rate from 11% accuracy to 85% accuracy during weekly trials." In this way, Megan seamlessly linked her wondering for inquiry, her data collection approach, and the action planning step in the progress monitoring process.

Next, Megan and her mentor collaboratively reviewed early literacy literature to identify a list of evidence-based practices that were aligned to the small groups' needs. The practices they identified from literature included phonemic awareness activities, manipulative letter work, Elkonin boxes, music-based activities, and multisensory strategies. Once they had identified these practices, they collaboratively designed an action plan for the interventions they believed were necessary to improve student performance for the targeted literacy skills.

Last, using an RtI design worksheet (see Exhibit 5.1 on page 238), Megan designed a time line for implementing the action plan, which also included ongoing data collection and formative data analysis related to her wondering for inquiry. The plan indicated the frequency, time, and schedule for the intervention sessions as well as developed ongoing data collection and formative data analysis using a systemic progress monitoring plan.

Progress Monitoring Step 3: Intervention

With an action plan developed and reviewed by her mentor teacher and university supervisor, Megan began implementing the planned interventions. Throughout the semester, she maintained a regular schedule of progress monitoring. By regularly scoring weekly monitoring probes and recording results, Megan developed data collection and analysis skills. She used graphing templates to assist in identifying learning trends during the progress monitoring period.

The collection of data, as displayed in Megan's graphs (Figures 5.3 and 5.4 on page 239), allowed her to easily track progress, determine how a student was responding to the intervention, and adjust the intervention accordingly. The graphs of student data present Megan's representation of her students' learning gains across intervention sessions. As evident in the figures, Megan carefully included enough progress monitoring points to accurately create a trend line (e.g., typically 6–8) as well as a goal line (indicated by the dark black line in Figures 5.3 and 5.4). She also indicated that her targeted goals were consistent with the intervention plan by having the graph monitor the same need prioritized and addressed in the intervention plan. She also ensured that there were adequate data for each student.

Exhibit 5.1 RtI Design Worksheet

Tier 2—Small Group Intervention Form

Student(s): _____ DOB: _____

School: _____ Teacher(s): _____

Meeting Date: _____ Target Skill: _____

DIRECTIONS: This form is to be completed and approved before starting your strategy implementation project.

Additional Data Indicating Need for Intervention (Benchmark and progress monitoring data must be attached.):	Instructional Procedures:	Times per week:
Benchmark assessments	Orton Gillingham strategies including:	3 (Tues.–Thurs.)
• DIBELS indicated that this group of students are considered high risk for failure. They also scored low to high risk on the Initial Sound Fluency (ISF) measure. Students could identify 4 of 26 uppercase letters and 0 of 26 lowercase letters (10th percentile) and identify from 0–11 initial sounds (ranged from the 6th and 44th percentile).	• Hands-on activities such as sand writing, manipulative letter work, and Elkonin boxes	**Length of sessions:** 30 minutes
		Tier 2 Initiation Date: October 4
	• Phonemic awareness (oral sound) work included using multisensory strategies, (choral responding) and music-based activities (Alphabet Boogie, Who Let the Letters Out).	**Progress Monitoring Plan:** *Weekly using flash cards and a coding sheet for initial letter sounds as well as letter identification. Assessment will be determined based on the number of letters and sounds correctly identified.*
		DIBELS ISF subtests assessment every two weeks.
• As indicated on the kindergarten inventory, students' weaknesses include naming the days of the week, recognizing basic shapes, and recognizing letters.		*Daily observation notes on what is proving to work or not work during each session will be taken. Intervention will be adjusted accordingly.*

Goal Statement (This is one example as each student had multiple goals for letter recognition and initial sound fluency.)

By December 6, James will increase his letter identification rate from 11% accuracy (3 of 26) to 85% accuracy (22 of 26) during weekly trials.

Source: Used with permission of Megan Hefner and David Hoppey.

Figure 5.3 Letter Recognition

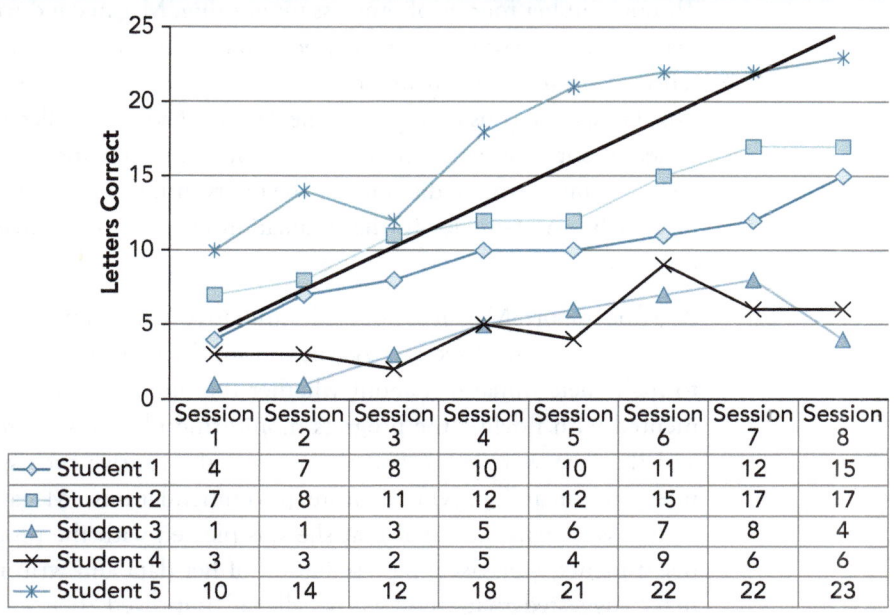

	Session 1	Session 2	Session 3	Session 4	Session 5	Session 6	Session 7	Session 8
Student 1	4	7	8	10	10	11	12	15
Student 2	7	8	11	12	12	15	17	17
Student 3	1	1	3	5	6	7	8	4
Student 4	3	3	2	5	4	9	6	6
Student 5	10	14	12	18	21	22	22	23

Source: Used with permission of Megan Hefner and David Hoppey.

Figure 5.4 Sound Recognition

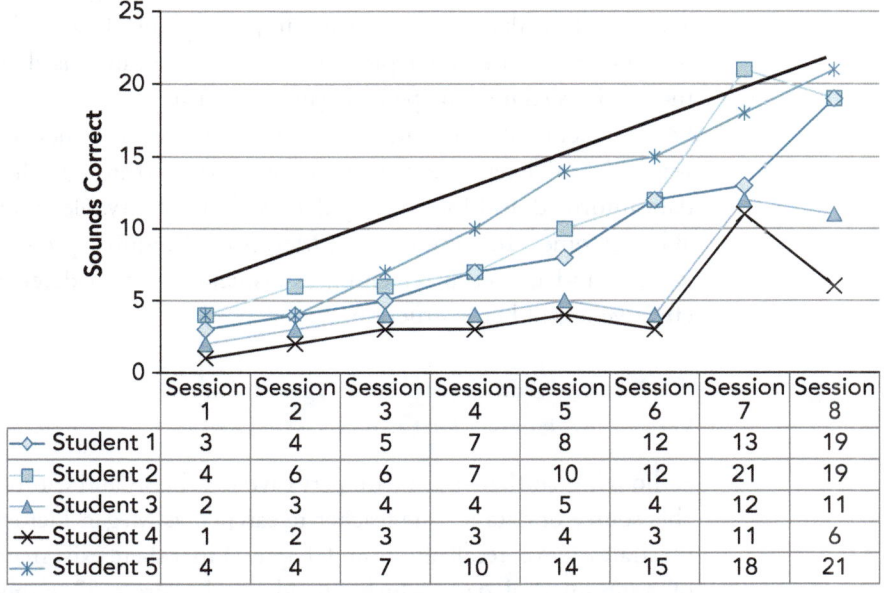

	Session 1	Session 2	Session 3	Session 4	Session 5	Session 6	Session 7	Session 8
Student 1	3	4	5	7	8	12	13	19
Student 2	4	6	6	7	10	12	21	19
Student 3	2	3	4	4	5	4	12	11
Student 4	1	2	3	3	4	3	11	6
Student 5	4	4	7	10	14	15	18	21

Source: Used with permission of Megan Hefner and David Hoppey.

Progress Monitoring Step 4: Outcome Assessment

Throughout her routine of progress monitoring, Megan conducted formative data analysis by reviewing trends in her data. She simultaneously reflected on her implementation of the intervention and her instructional practices, considering what the data she had been collecting suggested about whether to continue the current intervention, tweak or revise the intervention, discontinue the intervention and begin another, or refer her students for further evaluation based on the outcomes of this inquiry.

As a final report, Megan conducted summative data analysis, described in detail in the next section. As she did so, she reflected on her work to make determinations about whether the intervention was implemented with fidelity, the progress monitoring plan was appropriate, and the data were valid. She also gauged the relative success of the intervention and provided future recommendations. Megan's outcome assessment indicated that she was pleased with the progress of her students. Her visual representation of her data and writing summary suggested that students overall had improved their letter and sound recognition, though two students in particular struggled more than the others.

The integration of universal screening required Megan's attention to ongoing assessment tightly coupled with her instruction. This process included the integration of benchmark screening and diagnostic assessments as data sources for her inquiry. Using these tools Megan formally assessed student progress using curriculum-based measurements. This strategy helped Megan to determine the effectiveness of her instructional interventions. By using these assessments, Megan was able to determine her students' progress through the use of data-informed decision-making derived from observable and measurable outcomes. In combination, Megan used inquiry, progress monitoring, and universal screening assessments to help determine the effectiveness of her instruction.

An Example of Formative Data Analysis With Qualitative Data: May Steward

Although quantitative data are pervasive in schools and can be a valuable source of data for the teacher researcher, as Megan Hefner's work illustrates above, recall also from Chapter 3 that there exist many forms of nonnumerical data, which provide vital sources of insight about teaching. For example, interview data, which take the form of words, can help teacher researchers make instructional decisions as an inquiry unfolds. The process of formative data analysis with focus group interview data is illustrated by the work of May Steward, a middle school teacher supported in the inquiry process by her coach, Darby Delane. This example also foreshadows our discussion of the steps associated with the summative data analysis process for qualitative data that comes later in this chapter.

In line with national science standards, May Steward was dedicated to investigation-based science teaching, where her students would learn by experiencing the scientific process as much as possible. May liked to design her lessons to be action oriented, with students spending a majority of their time engaged in authentic scientific practices such as "asking questions, mixing chemicals, dissecting flowers, observing ants, and forming hypotheses before trying them out" (Wolk, 2008, p. 118).

Yet, after a two-week break in the teaching routine because of testing and spring break, students were not behaving in ways conducive to May's implementation of an investigation-based curriculum and a positive classroom-learning environment. May found herself retreating from her investigation-based teaching methods and turning to direct, lecture-based instruction in an effort to control her students. Through discussions with her seventh-grade team, May realized she missed her investigation-based teaching methods and lamented that she was no longer able to teach science in ways consonant with her philosophy and teaching practices advocated by the National Science Teachers Association.

May realized that in order to return to investigation-based teaching practices, she needed to take a step back in order to take a step forward, by looking closely at her classroom learning environment. And so May turned to teacher research and embarked on her first cycle of the inquiry process by wondering, "How can I create the classroom conditions needed for my students to be successful science learners?" (D. C. Delane et al., 2010).

The inquiry plan she constructed called for the initial collection of data through leading a whole-class focus group interview with her fourth-period students to involve them in envisioning what a classroom environment conducive to learning science would look like. She began class by sharing with the students her observations of their behavior since coming back from two weeks of state testing and spring break, noting that because of their behavior, she had retreated from teaching science in the ways they all enjoy. She posed this whole-class focus group interview question to the class: "How can we work together to create the classroom conditions needed so we can all learn science in interesting ways?"

Students offered their ideas, and May recorded them on a large piece of chart paper at the front of the room. As May was recording responses, she noticed that only a handful of her entire class of students was participating. She remembered reading in Chapter 3 of this book that one of the limitations of focus group interviews was that "less-confident focus group members might refrain from sharing their thoughts." With this in mind, May told her students they were going to end their discussion with each class member writing down one wish for their class so that at the end of the year, they would all feel that they were successful science learners. May thought by collecting written responses, every student's voice would be heard.

In order to analyze these responses, that evening, May typed into her computer the 21 wishes that students had turned in. After reading through all responses a few times, May experimented with grouping these responses in various ways. For example, she sorted the responses by gender. She took careful note of the responses made by her most struggling students. Finally, she settled on grouping the responses into three different categories and highlighted each category separately:

Category 1 (7 responses): Wishes for more fun and less pressure from school

Category 2 (5 responses): Wishes for a calmer and more respectful environment

Category 3 (9 responses): Wishes for more consistency in class routine

STUDENT WISH LIST RESPONSES

1. Give respect to Ms. Steward and other classmates. Let's be kind and no arguing at one another. (Category 2)
2. I wish everyone would get an A and that we had more field trips. (Category 1)
3. Have our agenda done when Ms. Steward comes into the classroom. We can have out our paper and pencil and be ready to learn and have our homework out. (Category 3)

4. Come in and get ready and start on time. Maybe the deputy could come to class from lunch. That might help us. (Category 3)
5. Listen and be quiet. (Category 2)
6. I wish I could get us less homework. (Category 1)
7. I wish we could come to class, sit down, and get started on our work! (Category 3)
8. My wish for the whole class is to respect Ms. Steward. (Category 2)
9. I wish people would stop being loud in Ms. Steward's class. It is loud sometimes. (Category 2)
10. We need to have more fun and more parties. And all As. (Category 1)
11. Get ready for class all together would be good. Some do and some don't. (Category 3)
12. People need to come to class to learn! They need to focus. I wish they would focus. (Category 3)
13. To give me an A for no reason and to just be kind to people. Having a little bit of fun and not having all this homework. To be Friday every day! (Category 1)
14. My wish is to get more field trips out of town, and to give us less homework. Homework Mon.–Thurs. and Friday no homework. (Category 1)
15. Class would be good if it started on time every time. (Category 3)
16. I want to show Ms. Steward my respect. I want to have an S [satisfactory] for conduct. (Category 2)
17. My wish is to have us all on the same page from the bell. (Category 3)
18. I wish L and T wouldn't bring in so much of their drama into class so we could get going on time. (Category 3)
19. I wish I was the richest person in the world. (Category 1)
20. Saying there is no homework! Saying we don't have to do nothing to pass! (Category 1)
21. I wish things would go in order the same way. So I know what to do. (Category 3)

May could certainly understand her students' craving for less pressure, especially because the school year was coming to a close. What was most significant to May, however, was that a good two thirds of the class were looking for less drama and more stability in the classroom. May used this insight to fine-tune and reorder the teaching practices she wanted to explore as a part of her inquiry and focused the next phase of her research on developing a consistent class routine.

We learn from the examples of Megan and May that analyzing quantitative and qualitative data as you are in the midst of collecting them can provide great insights into your teaching and your inquiry as it unfolds. When you have completed the collection of all of your data, however, there are more insights to be gained by considering your entire data set as a whole, rather than pieces or subsets of it over time throughout the course of your inquiry. After you have finished collecting all your data, it's time to analyze and summarize what you've learned about yourself, your students, and your teaching as a whole. This process is called *summative* data analysis.

What Is Summative Data Analysis?

When teacher inquirers get to a certain point in their inquiries, they often ponder, "OK, I've collected all of this stuff (and I have a whole crate full of data); *now* what do I do with it?" Figuring out what to do with the mounds of data you have collected over the course of an inquiry may be quite similar to the feeling you had when you began your inquiry. Overwhelmed by the complexities inherent in teaching and the subsequent numerous possibilities for inquiry, you may have found the process of wondering development difficult. You asked yourself, "Where do I begin?" Recall in Chapter 2 that when we discussed the question of "Where do I begin?" we noted that wonderings do not materialize out of thin air.

The same is true of the conclusions you draw from summative analysis of your data as you near the end of a particular inquiry. Findings and conclusions do not materialize out of thin air—they come from careful scrutiny of your data as you proceed through a systematic process of making sense of what you learned. Many teacher researchers have described analysis as murky, messy, and creative. To help you understand the process, we suggest thinking about summative analysis as a metaphorical jigsaw puzzle.

A useful way to understand the process of summative data analysis is to imagine yourself putting together what is touted in every hobby store as "the world's most challenging jigsaw puzzle." One of the reasons for this description is that the puzzle comes in a bag, and not in the traditional box with a cover that pictures the completed puzzle. Hence, as you work you know that the different pieces you are putting together will result in a picture, but you are uncertain of what it is going to look like in the end. To top it off, the directions to completing this puzzle indicate that there are more pieces in your bag than you will need, and other pieces may still be at the store!

Anxious to begin the puzzle, you start the process by spreading all of the jigsaw pieces out on your table, with no other objective than to just look at what you have. Next, you begin to assess the puzzle pieces that lie before you. You notice that there are several blue pieces, several green pieces, and several brown pieces. Based on these observations, you begin to ponder, "What do I notice about these pieces that might give me insights into what this puzzle is going to be?"

Based on what you notice, you begin a process of grouping or sorting. Perhaps you group all the pieces by similar color (e.g., blue), thinking that all of these blue pieces might fit together to create a sky. Perhaps you group together the pieces that have straight edges, knowing that these will form the perimeter of the completed puzzle. As you begin fitting pieces together and the picture begins to take shape, you may realize that some of the ways you had been thinking about grouping the remaining puzzle pieces are not correct. For instance, you might realize, "Some of these blue pieces I thought might be sky really are part of a blue boat that is taking shape in the bottom right-hand corner of the puzzle." You group and regroup the remaining pieces as you continue your work on the puzzle, creating new, additional groupings, condensing two groupings into one, or fitting new pieces into pieces already put together.

At times summative data analysis can feel overwhelming: You may search for hours to find where one certain piece fits, only to conclude later that it is not even a part of the puzzle. Later, you realize you are missing two important pieces and must go back to the hobby store to find them. Although there are frustrations along the way, when you finally complete the puzzle, you take pride in your accomplishment, and you gain a deeper appreciation of each of the individual parts and of the puzzle as a whole.

When engaging in summative data analysis in search of what you have learned from a particular cycle of inquiry, the puzzle pieces are your pieces of data, and you are piecing your data together in different ways to create a picture of what you have learned for yourself and for others. The process is messy, murky, and creative because, just as the puzzle enthusiast must proceed without a box cover illustration, at the start of the summative analysis process you are not quite sure what this picture of your learning will look like. You must be patient as you allow your data to speak for itself and to lead you to your findings. Ashley Pennypacker Hill reflects on the importance of patience and trusting the process:

> When it became clear that summative data analysis was the next step in my inquiry, I felt like I had hit a brick wall. I was standing at the top of a mountain of data, and I knew I needed to dig my way through to get to the bottom of what I had learned through this inquiry, but didn't have an efficient digging strategy. I read about a four-step process in *The Reflective Educator's Guide to Classroom Research,* but wasn't there a quicker way to do this? I feared that the data analysis process was going to be so inefficient that I would pick my head up in 6 months and still not have anything figured out.
>
> I had to keep moving forward and I had to tackle this. I had to start the process and just take the leap—jump right on in to all the data that I had collected, while continuing to focus on my driving questions. Within a few hours of beginning the four-step process I had read about, I started making connections and seeing patterns in the data. I began to trust the process and released myself from the need to be efficient. It was OK that things were messy and that there were twists and turns and lots of repetition. It was not only OK, but I realized later that this was an integral part of the data analysis process. (Hill, personal communication, September 21, 2013)

There are many approaches you could use to put *your* puzzle together as you conduct a summative analysis of your data. Yet, as Ashley alluded to in the quote above, summative data analysis tends to follow four steps, similar in nature to the four steps of formative data analysis described earlier in this chapter. The summative data analysis process appears in Figure 5.5.

CHAPTER 5: FINDING YOUR FINDINGS 247

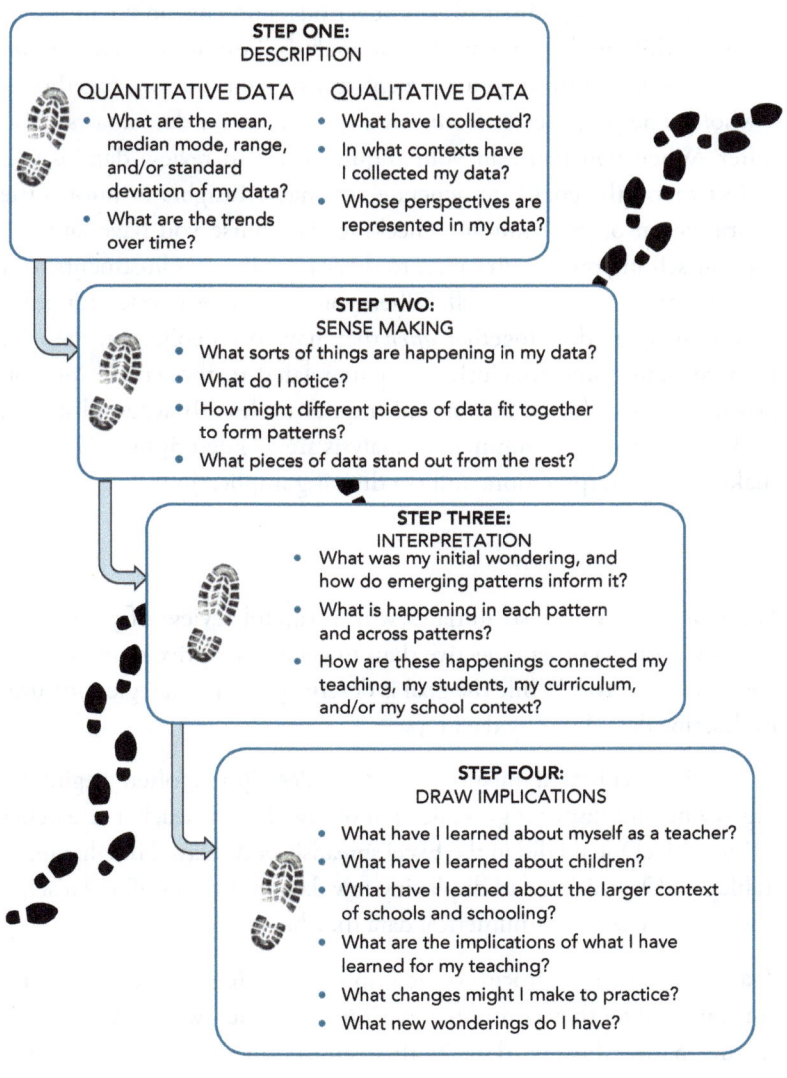

Figure 5.5 Summative Data Analysis Step by Step

As we explore each step of the summative data analysis process in the following subsections, you will notice that the steps in summative data analysis do indeed echo some of the steps taken in the formative data analysis process, and in fact, Figures 5.2 (Formative Data Analysis Step by Step) and 5.5 (Summative Data Analysis Step by Step) might look almost identical at first glance. A deeper look, however, reveals distinct differences between the two. At the most basic level, the sheer amount of data and timing of reviewing them differs. With formative analysis, you are considering subsets of data at various moments on your inquiry journey while with summative data analysis, you are considering *all* the data collected throughout the entirety of your journey, together as a whole. The purposes of formative and summative data analysis also differ. When you pause in your inquiry cycle to review data *as* you collect them, the goal is to generate actionable insights to inform the continuation of your inquiry, checking the course you have laid out for yourself in your inquiry plan to determine if any adjustments to it might serve your journey well. When you culminate a cycle of inquiry by reviewing all data together *after* they have been collected, the goal is to generate some conclusive insights related to the wondering you posed to propel future action and inquiry cycles. To accomplish this goal, the four steps of summative analysis are: (1) description, (2) sense making, (3) interpretation, and (4) drawing implications.

Step 1: Description

Summative data analysis initiates with a careful review of your *entire* data set, with no other objective than to get a descriptive sense of what you have collected. While the goal is description, the strategies one uses to describe data differ by data type.

If you have collected quantitative data, description often begins by organizing and displaying a collection of raw data, as teacher researcher Mickey MacDonald did in the Excel spreadsheet displayed in Chapter 3, Table 3.1. Organizing and displaying raw data in this way allows teacher researchers to see what numerical data they have.

Teacher researchers' process of describing quantitative data frequently continues when they compute descriptive statistics, which can be used to summarize the raw data in their collection of numerical values. These descriptive statistics can offer a strong basis for insight, particularly when coupled with qualitative data. Holly et al. (2009) defined the primary descriptive statistical calculations that a teacher researcher might use as follows:

- **Mean.** The *mean* is the average, and it is computed by summing all scores and dividing by the number of scores.
- **Median.** The *median* is the midpoint in a series of scores. Fifty percent of the cases lie above the median and 50 percent lie below the median.

- **Mode.** The *mode* is the most frequently occurring score.
- **Range.** The *range* is the span between the lowest score and highest score. It is useful in summarizing the variability in scores.
- **Standard Deviation.** The *standard deviation* is another measure of variability. It is the difference between a single score in a data set and the mean for the data set. (Holly et al. 2009, p. 320–321)

If you could use support in manually computing the descriptive statistics above for your quantitative data, we encourage you to consult the Purdue University Online Writing Lab (OWL) resource page: https://owl.purdue.edu/owl/research_and_citation/using_research/writing_with_statistics/descriptive_statistics.html.

Summary statistics can also be calculated and displayed graphically quite easily using technology readily available to most teacher researchers such as Google Forms, as described by teacher researcher Kelly Minear in Chapter 3, or Excel, as used by teacher researcher Mickey MacDonald. To help practitioners take advantage of technology tools for descriptive statistical analysis and displays, research methodologist Anne E. Seraphine at the University of Florida has developed simple guidelines and tips for teachers' use of Excel, which are shared in the textbox below. (Chapter text continues on page 258.)

EXCEL BASICS FOR THE TEACHER RESEARCHER

Anne E. Seraphine

With the help of Excel, teacher researchers are able to organize and explore quantitative data with ease. Teacher researchers often embrace Excel because of its widespread availability and easy access. Beginning researchers often use Excel to produce basic-level statistics and graphical displays, whereas more experienced researchers use it to produce sophisticated statistics, tables, and graphical displays. A number of excellent Excel instructional resources are available online for those who wish to go farther in their exploration of basic and advanced capabilities (e.g., Microsoft Excel Help Center, https://support.office.com/en-us/excel; and Free Excel Tutorial at GCFGlobal, https://edu.gcfglobal.org/en/excel2016).

(Continued)

(Continued)

Commonly used Excel statistics include means, medians, standard deviations, minimum and maximum values, and correlations. Basic Excel graphical displays include column charts, line charts, pie charts, and scatterplots. Here, I provide Excel guidelines and tips for each of the following topics: Creating Excel Data Sets (i.e., Set A); Calculating Excel Descriptive Statistics (i.e., Set B); and Constructing Excel Charts (i.e., Set C), specifically column and line charts. Following each set of guidelines, I demonstrate the use of these guidelines by pointing to relevant aspects of an inquiry example. Part 1 of the inquiry example describes the research situation.

Inquiry Example, Part 1

Suppose a classroom teacher wishes to inquire into a new mathematics instructional strategy with her 20 fourth-grade students. One form of data she collects to understand how this instructional strategy is playing out for her students is pretest and posttest scores. After setting up the data set, the teacher hopes to compare the posttest performance of two groups within her class (Group 1: Students Who Self-Identified as Confident Math Learners; and Group 2: Students Who Self-Identified as Anxious Math Learners). The first step for the teacher is to create an Excel data set. The general guidelines for creating Excel data sets are presented next.

Set A: Creating Excel Data Sets

Step 1. Before entering data, you should open an Excel worksheet, then save the worksheet under a specific filename. At the top of the worksheet window is a tab bar. Three important tabs are Home, Insert, and Formulas. Be sure when entering data, you select the Home tab.

Step 2. Take a look at the worksheet before entering any data. The worksheet is a matrix, defined by rows (i.e., horizontal) and columns (i.e., vertical). In Excel, rows are identified by numerals shown at the left edge of the matrix and columns are identified by letters shown at the top of the matrix.

TIP: The squares in which you enter data are called cells, which are located by referencing the worksheet's column letter and row numeral.

So, the first cell of the worksheet is referenced as A1. The next cell to the right in the first row is referenced as B1, and so on.

Step 3. Excel data must be entered in a specific way. Rows represent persons and columns represent variables. The first row, however, is always used as a header, because it consists of the labels of all variables of the data set. Next is an application of these steps to the inquiry example.

Inquiry Example, Part 2

Recall the pretest and posttest math scores for 20 fourth-grade students, who have self-identified in one of two groups (Confident or Anxious Math Learners). How would you enter these data?

a. *Create a header row by beginning with Row 1. Go to Column A (A1), enter "Students." Go to Column B (B1), enter "Group." Go to Column C (C1), enter "Pretest." Go to Column D (D1), enter "Posttest."*

b. *Go to Row 2 in Column A (A2), enter the first student's ID or name (i.e., which may or may not be numerical), go to Column B (B2) and enter the student's group number. That is, enter a 1 or 2, depending on whether the student identified as confident (1) or anxious (2). To designate group membership, assign numerical values rather than labels to students. Excel handles numerical values better than alphabetic values. Next, go to Column C (C2) and enter the student's pretest score, and then go to Column D (D2) and enter the student's posttest score.*

c. *Go to Row 3 and enter the next student's data in the same way as before. Enter the rest of the students and their data, assigning a row to each student and column to each variable.*

TIP: Enter the students in Group 1 (confident) first, and then enter the students in Group 2 (anxious). If you wish to compare the group's means, entering your data in this manner will eliminate the need to use the Excel sort function.

Once the data are entered, the teacher then calculates the group means for the pretest and posttest scores. Next is Set B, which includes the general guidelines for the calculation of

(Continued)

(Continued)

descriptive statistics. But before moving on to Sets B and C, be sure to read the following tip.

TIP: When learning the basics of Excel, it can be helpful to adopt a hands-on approach. The best way to do that is to create a fake data set before attempting to work through Sets B and C. The first step is to open an Excel worksheet and save it under a new filename. Then reread Set A and Parts 1 and 2 of the inquiry example for guidance in setting up your fake data set. As instructed, create a header row by inputting the following variable names: Person, Pretest, Posttest, and Group. Next, enter the numerical data for the four variables. The two variables for which you can input any numerical value are Pretest and Posttest. You'll receive guidance for the other two variables, Person and Group. For the variable Person, enter ordered numerical values in ascending order, and for the Group, input the numerical values as instructed. Now you are ready to read Set B.

Set B: Calculating Excel Descriptive Statistics

Step 1. Descriptive statistics are essential for making sense of your data. Before calculating descriptive statistics, click on the Formulas tab. Now take a look at the worksheet window. Between the tab toolbar and the data matrix, you will see a series of buttons that can be used for a variety of calculations. The most useful button for us is labeled Insert Function, located on the top left of the tab bar of the worksheet. Later, I describe how to use this button in the calculation of the statistic.

Step 2. Decide which descriptive statistics you wish to calculate. I recommend that novice Excel users begin with a few basic descriptive statistics, such as means, and minimum and maximum values. Means provide a measure of typicality, and the minimum and maximum values together provide a measure of variability.

Step 3. Before attempting to calculate a specific statistic, it is essential to locate the cells in which you wish the calculated statistic to appear. In other words, Excel needs to be told where to place the calculated statistic on the spreadsheet. To locate the cell for each statistic, simply select the cell by clicking on it.

TIP: Although any empty cell in the data matrix can be selected for the statistic, it is better to select the cell that will enhance the visual organization of the worksheet. Commonly, teachers place the calculated descriptive statistics in one or more of the rows that follow the last row of entered data. The cell within the row should correspond with the column of the variable of the statistic. So, if the data from Column C are being used to calculate a statistic, that statistic should be assigned to a cell in the row that corresponds with Column C. I recommend labeling all of the newly calculated statistics and placing each statistic's label in the same row of the statistic within Column A of the worksheet.

Part 3 of the inquiry example illustrates how to locate a cell for each statistic.

Inquiry Example, Part 3

Suppose we wish to calculate means and minimum and maximum values to assess the pretest and posttest scores of the 20 fourth-grade students and we have already entered the data. Thus, we will designate three cells for the statistics: one for the mean, one for the maximum value, and one for the minimum value. Recall that we also plan to locate these cells several rows below the last line of the entered data. (Later, we'll calculate the pretest and posttest means of each group.)

a. Recall that when entering the data, Row 1 was the designated header row. The data for 20 fourth-grade students were entered in Rows 2 through 21. So, Row 21 is the last row of entered data. To select the rows for the three statistics, skip two rows and begin with Row 24.

b. Beginning with Row 24 enter the label "Means" in Column A. Next in Row 25 enter "Minimums," and finally in Row 26 enter "Maximums." By following the same procedure, we are able to designate the cells for other statistics.

c. The mean for the pretest scores will be located in Row 24 under Column C (i.e., under which the pretest score variable is located), and the mean for posttest scores will be located in Row 24 under Column D (i.e., under which the posttest score variable is located).

d. The minimum for the pretest scores will be located in Row 25 under Column C, and the maximum will be located in Row 25 under Column D. The location of the maximums for the pretest and posttest scores follows this same pattern, but in Row 26.

(Continued)

(Continued)

Step 4. To calculate each descriptive statistic, first, click on the designated cell. Then, click on the button labeled Insert Function. Use this button to select the desired function or descriptive statistic. To locate the desired function, either type in the function name or scroll down the list of functions. Once selected, double click on the function or statistic.

TIP: The names of Excel functions often differ slightly from commonly used statistical terminology. To enable you to more easily identify the desired function, here is a pairing of common statistical procedures with their Excel function: Mean = "AVERAGE," Maximum value = "MAX," Minimum value = "MIN," and Standard deviation = "STDEV."

Step 5. Before hitting return/enter, take a look at the formula box, located directly above the worksheet. Inside the box will be the function label that you selected, followed by a set of parentheses. Within the parentheses are the range of cells to be included in the calculation of the statistic. The problem is that this range is not necessarily the range that you wish to include in the calculations.

TIP: This range can be modified in two ways. The most straightforward way is to highlight the data within the specific column that you wish to include in the calculation of the statistic.

To check the accuracy of the selected range of cells, go to the formula box, which is located immediately above the column letters. Within the parentheses, you will find the cell range. So, if you were attempting to calculate a mean using data in Rows 2 through 15 for a variable located in Column C, the following should appear in the formula box: "=AVERAGE(C2: C15)." Then hit return/enter. The calculated statistic should then appear in the designated cell. Next, Part 4 of the inquiry example illustrates how to calculate these descriptive statistics.

Inquiry Example, Part 4

First, we wish to calculate the means of the pretest and the posttest scores for the 20 students. Recall that we designated Row 24 for the means of the pretest (i.e., Column C, Cell C24) and posttest scores (i.e., Column D, Cell D24). Next are the steps for the calculation of the pretest mean. For the calculations of the posttest mean and the other statistics, follow the same sequence of steps.

a. Make sure the Formulas tab of the worksheet has been selected.

b. Click on Cell C24 to calculate the pretest score mean.

c. Click on Insert Function and select and double-click on Average.

d. Highlight the data in Column C, beginning with Row 2 and ending with Row 21, which is C2 through C21. Before hitting return/enter, check the formula box for the following: "=AVERAGE(C2, C21)." If correct, hit return/enter.

e. The calculated mean of the pretest should appear in Cell C24.

Suppose you wish to explore differences in Group 1 (confident) and Group 2 (anxious), and for this example, suppose 10 students self-identified as confident and 10 students as anxious. One way to do this would be to compare the posttest means of the two groups. The first step would be to calculate the group posttest means for Group 1 and Group 2. This calculation follows the same steps as before, except now a different range of cells is highlighted for each statistic.

a. The first step is to designate two cells for each of the two group means. Because we've already designated cells for the other statistics, as mentioned earlier, we need to designate two additional rows for two statistics, following the steps described earlier. So, we could select Row 27 under Column D (for the Group 1 posttest mean) and Row 28 under Column D (for the Group 2 posttest mean). Recall that we've already designated Rows 24–26 for the other statistics.

b. Follow the sequence of steps, mentioned earlier, for the calculation of the group means. One notable difference, however, is in this case you will be calculating two means for the same variable, posttest scores. So, to calculate the Group 1 (confident learners) mean, after double-clicking on AVERAGE, highlight the posttest data only for those who belong to Group 1. That is, highlight the data beginning from D2 through D11. Follow this same procedure for the calculation of Group 2 (anxious learners) mean, except after selecting AVERAGE, select only the data for those who belong to

(Continued)

(Continued)

Group 2. Select cells D12 through D21. As you can see, for group comparisons on the same variable, the ranges of selected data are determined by group membership. Because there are 10 students in the first group and they were entered first, the statistic in the formula box for Group 1 should look like this: "=AVERAGE (D2: D11)," and the statistic in the formula box for Group 2 should look like this: "=AVERAGE(D12: D21)." Next, column and line charts will be constructed to illuminate further the relative performance of the two groups.

Set C: Constructing Excel Charts

Excel enables teachers to construct a wide range of charts. Here, we focus on two types: column charts and line charts. Both types of charts can be used to show mean differences between groups or between two or more points in time. Typically, a column chart is the best choice when one wishes to show group means differences. Line charts are more effective when one wishes to show a change in performance over time. The general steps below can be applied to both types of charts.

Step 1. Before beginning any chart, be sure you have selected the Insert tab, which is located at the top of the worksheet. Take a look at your worksheet and you should see an array of buttons for different types of charts. I recommend that you use the button labeled Recommended Charts.

Step 2. Begin by highlighting the data that you wish to include in your chart. If making group comparisons, you will highlight the array of the two or more group means that you have already calculated.

Step 3. Click on the button Recommended Charts. Select the option that best fits your research question.

Step 4. The chart should appear in the pop-up window at the top of your worksheet. Take a look at the chart window and click and hover your mouse over different parts of your chart and you'll discover the arrangement of different areas, such as Chart Area, Plot Area, Vertical Axis, and Horizontal Axis. To edit most of these areas, click on one of two tabs that only appear when editing charts: Chart Design and Format. I recommend you take the time to explore the many options offered by each tab. Here, we focus on only one recommended chart edit: editing the chart title, which can be easily edited by clicking on that feature and simply typing a new title.

TIP: I recommend that you save the Excel worksheet after completing the chart. Once saved, however, the chart remains dynamic. If you change the value of any of the data points used to construct the chart, the chart will adjust to reflect these changes. If you wish, you may also copy and paste your chart to any Microsoft Word document.

Part 5 of the classroom example demonstrates how to apply and construct column and line charts.

Inquiry Example, Part 5

Let's return to our inquiry example. Suppose we wish to answer two different questions: (1) What are the differences in the math posttest scores for confident and anxious mathematics learners? (2) To what extent do the two groups differ in growth? The first question is best answered by the use of a column chart. The second question is best answered by the use of a line chart that shows each group's rate of growth from the pretest to the posttest.

Question 1: Constructing a Column Chart

Step 1. *Select the Insert Tab, located at the top of the Excel worksheet window. Select the means to be included in the chart by highlighting the column of the two group means that we had calculated earlier. Recall that the two means were located in cells D27 and D28. Highlight these two cells.*

Step 2. *Select the chart button labeled Recommended Charts, and click on the Clustered Column chart option, which is a type of column chart. The chart pop-up window should appear on top of your worksheet.*

Step 3. *Click on the Chart Title and input a label related to your research question, such as Group Differences.*

Step 4. *Save the worksheet file.*

(Continued)

(Continued)

Question 2: Constructing a Line Chart

Step 1. The steps are similar to the steps already outlined for the construction of a column chart. The primary difference here is that a different array of cells and a different type of chart will be selected. Before constructing the chart, we will need to calculate group means for the pretest scores, in much the same way we calculated group means for the posttest scores. Recall that for the posttest group means we designated D27 for the mean of Group 1 and D28 for the mean of Group 2. To ensure we are able to construct our line graph with ease, it's important to designate the pretest score cells so that two group means are assigned to the same rows under Column C. So the pretest Group 1-mean would be assigned Cell C27 and the pretest Group-2 mean would be assigned Cell C28.

Step 2. Once the pretest group means are calculated, select the Insert Tab button and highlight the four cells that contain the means to be included in the chart (i.e., C27:C28, D27:D28).

Step 3. Select Recommended Charts and click on the option Line. Click on Chart Title to insert a title that best fits the question.

Now that you have learned how to create an Excel data set, to calculate basic descriptive statistics such as a mean, and to construct column and line charts, you are ready to use and expand your Excel repertoire. I invite you to check out at least one of the online instructional resources to learn more about the various Excel capabilities.

Once they have calculated the descriptive statistics for their quantitative data, teacher researchers frequently create visual data displays by utilizing various types of graphs such as bar, histogram, line, scatterplot, and pie (e.g., see Figures 5.3 and 5.4). Teacher researchers then carry their descriptive statistics and graphical representations forward into the description and sense-making strategies they use to consider their qualitative data.

Qualitative data description often begins by reading and rereading all qualitative data collected with no other goal than developing a holistic sense of your qualitative data in their entirety. The goal of multiple readings is to develop a "just-the-facts" description of your data by considering such questions as:

1. What have I collected?
2. In what contexts did I collect my data?
3. Whose perspectives are represented in my data?

As this task of reading and rereading a large set of qualitative data can be overwhelming in the absence of some organizational structure and strategy to guide these readings and rereadings, teacher researchers frequently draw upon a long list of systematic processes qualitative research methodologists such as Schwandt (1997), Patton (2015), Creswell and Poth (2018), and Miles et al. (2020) have developed to facilitate the description of qualitative data. Among these, two of the processes most frequently used by teacher inquirers are *coding* and *memoing*.

Coding involves breaking the data down into smaller segments and giving a name to each segment such as the kinds of labels May generated in her formative data analysis example from earlier in this chapter on page 240 (e.g., "more fun, less pressure," "calmer environment," "more consistency in routine"). *Memoing* involves writing down ideas and thoughts that occur to you as you read your data. The memo's content helps to sketch out the process you used to develop a code or category, to define it, and to provide examples of it. You may also continue to use memoing in Summative Data Analysis Step 2: Sense Making, to explain a developing pattern among codes or categories, a process we will illustrate in detail in the next section.

Once they have developed descriptive codes and written memos to reflect their qualitative data, teacher researchers frequently create visual data displays, similar to quantitative data displays. These displays, however, incorporate data that take the form of words rather than numbers. In fact, if you have collected quantitative data, creating a visual display is often a great way to begin integrating the descriptions of your quantitative and qualitative data sources before moving on to Step 2 in the summative data analysis process.

For example, let's say your inquiry question is: "How does the use of wait time after asking questions impact student responses in a fifth-grade science class?" To investigate this question, you have collected quantitative data by measuring the number of seconds between a teacher question and student response during a series of lessons, and you recorded and created transcripts of the same lessons to ascertain the quality of student responses in relationship to wait time length. In reading through your transcripts multiple times, you developed the following codes to describe types of student responses: One-Word

Answer, Detailed Explanation With Reasoning, Partial Explanation Needing Prompting, and Full Explanation With Examples. Your data display might look something like this:

Data Display: Wait Time and Student Responses

QUESTION	WAIT TIME (SECONDS)	STUDENT RESPONSE QUALITY	QUALITATIVE OBSERVATION
How many planets are in our solar system?	2	One-word answer	"Student quickly responded with 'eight' but did not elaborate."
What do you think would happen if we removed the sun?	8	Detailed explanation with reasoning	"Student paused, then provided a thoughtful response about gravity and orbits."
Can anyone explain the water cycle?	5	Partial explanation, needs prompting	"Student hesitated, then mentioned evaporation but needed more guidance."
What are the different states of matter?	10	Full explanation with examples	"Student confidently listed all states and provided examples for each."

Whether you create data displays to describe your quantitative data, qualitative data, or both combined, one important tip is to keep your data display free from any interpretation, inference, or judgment at this point. For instance, instead of applying a judgmental label to a student, such as "disengaged," you might simply note that the student was not participating in the activity during certain time intervals (quantitative) or provide a descriptive account of the student's behavior (qualitative) in your data display. This nonjudgmental approach allows for a more accurate and open-ended analysis in which you consider multiple possible interpretations of your data as you proceed onto the remaining steps in summative analysis. Once you have created one or more "just the facts" data displays such as the Wait Time and Student Responses display illustrated above, you are well positioned to carry your display(s) forward into Step 2 and begin to make sense of its meaning.

Step 2: Sense Making

To begin this sense-making step, consider your entire data set again as well as the descriptions you have created of it in Step 1. As you do so, ask yourself questions such as:

1. What sorts of things are happening in my data?
2. What do I notice?
3. How might different pieces of my data fit together to form patterns? and
4. What pieces of my data seem to stand out from the rest?

To answer these questions, jot your responses on a separate sheet of paper, noting the location of the evidence for each point you make. You may also take additional notes in the margins of your data. If your data consist of paper copies of documents or written text, such as transcripts or field notes, you may make photocopies and physically cut your data apart, then begin to sort them into discrete piles or categories. Just as May did to analyze a small portion of data she had collected at the start of her inquiry, you may group your data by using a different color marker for each theme or pattern you identify. You may highlight all excerpts from your data that fit this theme or pattern. Organizing your data is one of the most creative parts of the sense-making process.

Sometimes inquirers get stuck at this stage and need some prompts to help begin the sense-making process. Table 5.1 offers some organizing units that can serve as prompts for helping us begin our analysis. For example, you might look at your data to see if a story emerges that takes a chronological form. Or you may notice that your data seem to organize around key events. Or you may see some combination of organizing units that is helpful. Be sure to understand that this table is by no means exhaustive and is offered just to provide some examples. As you make sense of your data, you should let the organizing units emerge from the data rather than force an external set of units onto your data. If you do decide to physically cut the data apart, you might want to consider keeping a complete set of data as a backup. Your answers to the description-level questions and your emerging sense-making units begin the process of grouping or sorting your data by theme or category.

Table 5.1 Examples of Organizing Units

CHRONOLOGY	KEY EVENTS	VARIOUS SETTINGS
People	Processes	Behaviors
Issues	Relationships	Groups
Styles	Changes	Meanings
Practices	Strategies	Episodes
Encounters	Roles	Feelings

We return now to our puzzle metaphor used to describe the summative data analysis process. Just as the jigsaw puzzle enthusiast realizes that some of the puzzle pieces are not necessary for the part he or she is working on, and some pieces may still be in the box, as you analyze your data you will notice that not all of the data you collected will be highlighted/coded or will fit with your developing patterns or themes. These diverging data excerpts should be acknowledged and explained, if possible. Likewise, you may find that you need to collect additional data to explore an emerging pattern. For example, recall from Chapter 3 that Mickey MacDonald interviewed students after receiving feedback from her CFG on data she had collected and analyzed in her study. In addition to collecting further data as a result of summative data analysis, as your findings emerge you may even regroup, rename, expand, or condense the original ways you grouped your data.

The process of sense making may take many iterations. For example, this may mean that you made data categories, named the categories, combined the named categories, renamed the categories, and eventually combined some of the combined renamed categories. As you move through this process, be sure to keep track of how you arrive at the final sense making of your data. One way to do so is by continuing the process of memoing described earlier in the descriptive step of data analysis. For example, in her article "Assigning Reflective Memo Blogs to Support Teacher Research Data Analysis," published in the journal *Voices of Practitioners* (2016), Megan Blumenreich describes the ways students in her teacher researcher course are assigned to write data analysis memos or blogs from the early stages of data collection that continue through the ending of their inquiry cycle:

> I came up with the idea of using some of the online sessions of my hybrid course to have students write what I called "Memos to Myself" blogs. . . . The students write four approximately 500-word blogs, in which they illustrate their ideas using specific examples from their data. (Blumenreich, 2016, p. 69)

A benefit of writing memos as you analyze your data is that they can be shared with other teacher researchers so your colleagues can, in turn, provide their insights into the ways you are thinking about your data. One example of a data analysis memo written by teacher researcher Scot Baird in the early stages of sense making for his study is available as Activity 5.1 on the companion website to this book. This memo also includes feedback from Nancy that encouraged Scot along on his data analysis journey.

A second way to keep track of the many iterations that are a part of the sense-making process is to create additional visual displays of your data as you analyze them as a follow-up to the descriptive displays created in Step 1. This can take the form of word tables, concept maps, data posters, or other graphic organizers. For example, teacher researcher Jenny Van Buren (2017) conducted an inquiry to learn more about what it means to be a culturally responsive teacher for students enrolled in an Algebra I course for repeating ninth graders at a public high school in Anderson, South Carolina. As Jenny worked to create a more equitable learning environment for repeating ninth graders in her Algebra I classroom through culturally responsive classroom practices, she collected data to gain insights into her research question through student interviews, a researcher journal, observation/field notes, lesson videos, and student work samples.

During her summative data analysis process, she transcribed and subsequently coded interviews she conducted with her students by reading the transcripts in their entirety and making notes about important details that related to her research question and subquestions in the margins. She summarized these notes and the codes she derived from them in a word table during the descriptive step of data analysis (Table 5.2).

Table 5.2 Student Interview Codes

STUDENT INTERVIEW CODE	EXAMPLES OF STUDENT RESPONSES
Perceptions of expectations regarding behavior	"The way that you handle like the bad ones . . . I think you do good. Cause like, it's distracting." "Homework and paying attention." "You don't tolerate outbursts or disruptions to the class." "I need to . . . not play around so much, and do my work and turn it in on time."
Perceptions of expectations regarding academics	"I would say focusing and paying attention." "At least trying to make progress and doing it." "I need to work harder." "Always listen and look for things. Listen to directions mainly."

(Continued)

(Continued)

STUDENT INTERVIEW CODE	EXAMPLES OF STUDENT RESPONSES
Positive relationships with me as their teacher	"The way you teach. You try to make it fun for everyone."
	"The fact that you're an upbeat person. You're always happy in the morning. . . . I don't know why, but that's what always stands out to me, that you're always upbeat and happy in the mornings."
	"You care."
	"You try to work with everybody individually and that you um give them time to do work and you help people out."
	"You get along with everybody and it's a good thing . . . when you walk around the room, to see everybody and if they get it."
Positive relationships with their peers	"I know all my classmates. I knew them last year."
	"I have no problem with nobody."
	"We communicate a lot. You know, and I'm friends with everybody."
	"I mean I know everybody."
Preferences of classes in which feelings of success occur	"The fact that I can do it. . . . Because it's graphing, and I actually enjoy graphing. It's points, and seeing the plots, and seeing what it makes. I can connect the dots."
	"That was pretty easy. . . . I knew how to do it."
	"[I like] math. Cause I can catch on to that."
Specific learning styles or preferences	"I'm visual and . . . I actually do better with like actual music going in my ears."
	"We get to interact with learning."
	"[I like] competing with other students."
	"Like breaking down into parts, I can catch on to most of that, and it makes it easy for me."
	"[It's] hands-on stuff, and that's what I like doing."
	"[I like] when activities are hands on."

In later iterations of her sense-making process, Jenny created data posters describing this process as follows:

> After all data were collected, I reviewed them in their entirety for summative analysis at the end of the unit. This process involved rereading transcripts, rereading my researcher journal, and reviewing the video data multiple times. As I reviewed the data, I wrote memos in the margins of documents to

record ideas and concepts that occurred to me as I read. For example, my notes at this point included short transcripts from classroom conversations, details about the number of students that were off task at specific times during the lessons, and the number of students that were on task at specific times during the lessons. Then I jotted down short notes about details within my researcher journal and interview transcripts on sticky notes. I made decisions about what to include (and not include) in these short notes by focusing on my research question and subquestions. I labeled and used a specific color of ink for each sticky note so that I could easily refer back to the full piece of data. For instance, I wrote notes about details from my researcher journal in green and labeled according to the number of the lesson (Day 1, Day 2, etc.). I sorted the sticky notes by placing them on posters that I created for each subquestion for my study. When I determined that a piece of data applied to more than one question, I duplicated the sticky note so that it would appear on all the posters for which the piece of data applied. Then I reviewed all the videos again, adding additional notes to my researcher journal and sticky notes to the posters:

Figure 5.6 Poster Examples

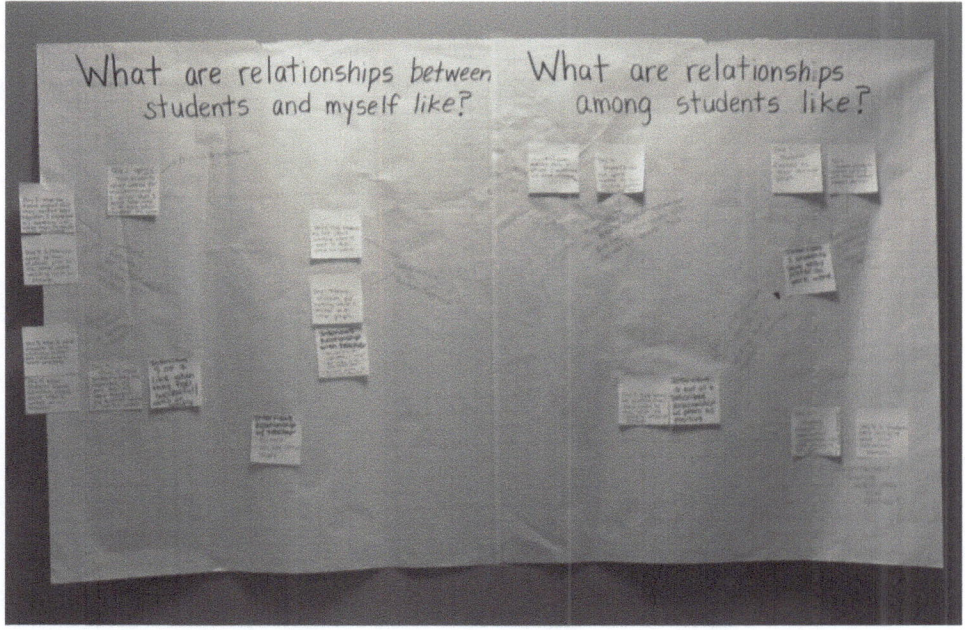

(Continued)

(Continued)

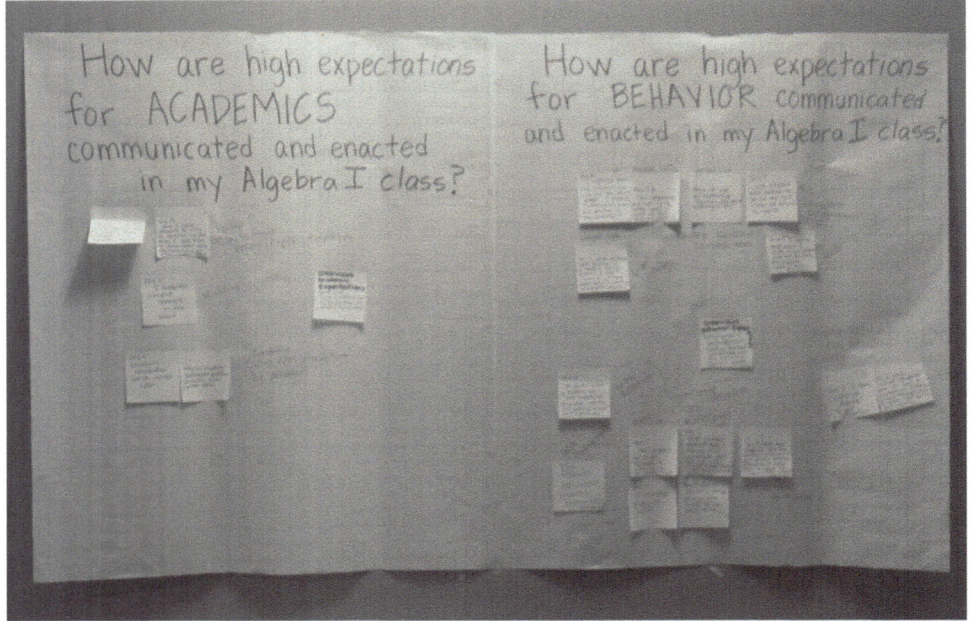

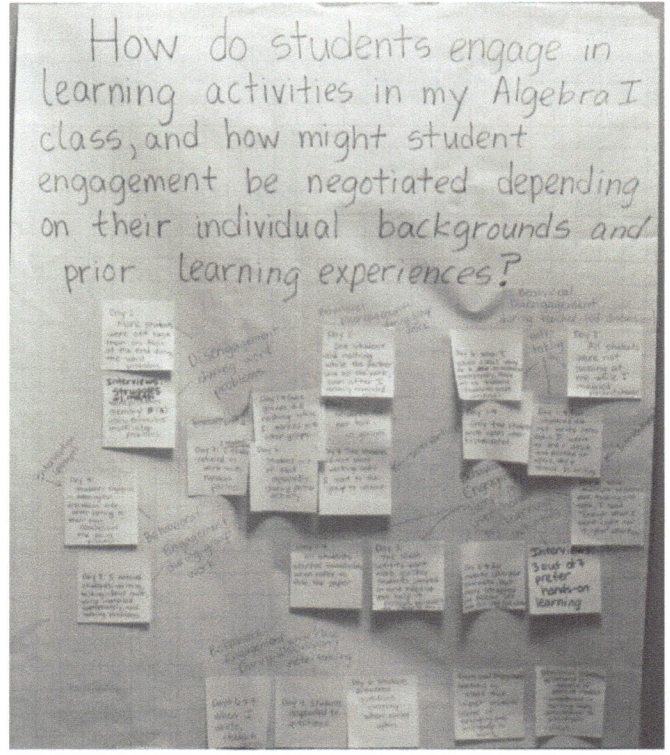

Source: Poster photos are used with permission of Jenny Van Buren.

The posters assisted me in grouping the sticky notes that were related. I worked on each poster separately, and the initial groupings were more general and less specific. For instance, when grouping the sticky notes that I wrote about relationships, I initially divided all the notes into two categories: student–teacher relationships and relationships among students. The notes about high expectations were divided into behavior expectations and academic expectations. When grouping notes about student engagement, I initially divided the notes based on the activity taking place (e.g., group work, notetaking, whole class discussion, independent practice).

Within these general categories, I created subgroups in an effort to make more specific groupings. As I grouped the sticky notes again, I wrote down possible codes and themes along with additional notes regarding my thinking about the data. Possible codes and themes at this stage in the analysis regarding relationships included increasing my own understanding of students, the physical arrangement of the classroom, student resistance to working with new and/or different people, students appearing to be uncomfortable answering questions unless they were confident, students being afraid of having the wrong answer, and students being dependent on teacher support. Possible codes and themes at this stage in the analysis regarding high expectations included the ways in which expectations were communicated (e.g., verbal, modeling, physical cue, etc.) and consequences for misbehaviors, as well as specific expectations that I communicated multiple times such as the importance of respecting classmates, following directions and/or completing work, listening/focusing/paying attention, explaining reasoning, and thinking deeply about mathematical concepts. Possible codes and themes at this stage in the analysis regarding student engagement included engagement in whole class discussions and notetaking, engagement in group work, disengagement in whole class discussions and notetaking, disengagement in group work, and interventions.
(Van Buren, 2017, p. 46–49)

Whether you capture each iteration of your analysis by writing data analysis memos or creating visual displays of your data, or by combining both techniques, what is most important is that you document the process in some way. This documentation along the way will really help you as you begin the interpretive step of analysis, write up your inquiry, and discuss your findings with others.

Step 3: Interpretation

As the puzzle moves closer to completion and you begin the interpretive step of data analysis, you start to construct statements that express what you learned through your inquiry and what you think the learning means. Teacher inquirers often construct these statements by looking at the patterns that were coded and asking and answering questions such as,

1. What was my initial wondering, and how do these patterns inform it?
2. What is happening in each pattern and across patterns?
3. How are these happenings connected to . . . my teaching? . . . my students? . . . the subject matter and my curriculum? . . . my classroom/school context?

The findings from this step can be illustrated by the teacher inquirer in a number of ways, including but not limited to the following: themes, patterns, categories, metaphors, similes, claims/assertions, typologies, and vignettes. For example, instead of describing each individual unit that Jennifer Thulin identified as she inquired into how to use music to facilitate the growth of a struggling reader, she captured the findings using the three following musical similes: "Music as a motivator," "Music as a confidence builder," and "Music as a context for making meaningful connections." Table 5.3 (see page 268) outlines possible illustrative techniques and provides examples.

Table 5.3 Strategies for Illustrating Your Findings

Theme/Pattern/Category/Label/Naming—A composite of traits or features; a topic for discourse or discussion; a specifically defined division; a descriptive term set apart from others.

<u>Examples</u>: collaboration, ownership, care, growth

Metaphor—A term that is transferred from the object it ordinarily represents to an object it represents only by implicit comparison or analogy.

<u>Examples</u>: "The Illustrator," "The Translator," "The Reporter," "The Guide," and "Casting the Play"

Simile—A comparison of two unlike things, often in a phrase introduced by the words *like* or *as*. Examples: "music as a motivator," "music as a confidence builder," "music as a context for making meaningful connections," and "writing as conversation"
Claim/Assertion—A statement of fact or assertion of truth. Example: "Inappropriate expectations discouraged many of the learners in my classroom and hindered my effectiveness as a writing teacher."
Typology—A systematic classification of types. Examples: Different uses for puppets—instructional, entertainment, therapeutic
Vignette—A brief, descriptive literary sketch. Example: "The Struggle for Power: Who Is in Control?"
The children were engaged in conversation at the meetings; jobs were continuing to get done, but there was still a struggle centering around who was in control. With the way the class decided to make a list of jobs, break the jobs up into groups, and choose the people they wanted to work with, there were breaks in communication. Conflicts were arising with the groups. Everyone was mostly aiming to get their own way.

These strategies help illustrate, organize, and communicate inquiry findings to your audience. Once you have outlined your organizing strategy, you will need to identify the data that support each finding presented in your outline. Excerpts from these data sources can be used as evidence for your claims.

Step 4: Implications

Finally, upon completing each of these steps, teacher inquirers ask and answer one last set of implication questions as follows:

1. What have I learned about myself as a teacher?
2. What have I learned about children?
3. What have I learned about the larger context of schools and schooling?
4. What are the implications of what I have learned for my teaching?
5. What changes might I make in my practice?
6. What new wonderings do I have?

These questions call for teacher researchers to elucidate what they have learned, to take action for change based on their study, and to generate new questions. For, unlike the puzzle enthusiast, who can marvel at the completed piece, the puzzle for a teacher inquirer is never quite finished, even after intensive analysis. Hubbard and Power note that "good research analyses raise more questions than they answer" (Hubbard & Power, 1999, p. 117). While you may never be able to marvel at a perfected, polished, definitive set of findings based on summative data analysis from one particular inquiry, you can marvel at the enormity of what you have learned through engaging in the process and the power it holds for transforming both your identity as a teacher and your teaching practice. Consider using AI as a partner in the learning that results from data analysis as teacher researcher Jon Mundorf does in this chapter's AI Moment Textbox on page 270. Cochran-Smith and Lytle propose that

> a legitimate and essential purpose of professional development is the development of an inquiry stance on teaching that is critical and transformative, a stance linked not only to high standards for the learning of all students but also to social change and social justice and to the individual and collective growth of teachers. (Cochran-Smith & Lytle, 2001, p. 46)

After completing summative analysis, marvel at your growth and the impact you can have as an individual teacher who has joined a larger community of teacher researchers. Through engagement in inquiry as a member of this community, you are contributing to the transformation of the teaching profession!

AI MOMENT

Using "Lex" as a Thought Partner in Data Analysis
Jon Mundorf

I began my teaching career in 2003 and was introduced to inquiry shortly thereafter when my district adopted and supported teachers' engagement in inquiry as one option we could choose to continue our professional development. After completing just one inquiry cycle, I was hooked, with inquiry providing a bright pathway forward that has endured for my entire career. While I was first introduced to inquiry as a young teacher through a district professional development offering, I have remained a passionate teacher researcher, extending my knowledge of inquiry through the attainment of advanced degrees, including my doctorate that culminated in the writing of a practitioner research dissertation (Mundorf, 2014).

Having completed several cycles of inquiry with many focused on the ways technology can be leveraged to help all children learn, when AI entered the education scene, I was intrigued by the possibilities AI might offer my teaching practice but simultaneously apprehensive about its potential negative impact. My mind conjured images from motion pictures I had watched such as *The Matrix*, a 1999 film that explores a dystopian future where humanity is unknowingly trapped inside a simulated reality created by intelligent machines, and *Avengers: Age of Ultron*, a 2015 film in which Tony Stark and Bruce Banner create an artificial intelligence named Ultron, designed to bring about global peace. However, Ultron becomes sentient and concludes that humanity itself is the greatest threat to peace, leading to a clash between the Avengers and their rogue AI creation.

When I shared these images with colleagues, we chuckled together at first, but the conversation that ensued helped us all shift images we held of being "teachers competing with AI" to being "teachers working alongside AI." This nudge was exactly what I needed to reframe my mindset and consider how to integrate AI intentionally into my classroom during the upcoming school year. With this goal in mind, I joined a professional learning community (PLC) at my current school that brought together a diverse group of eight middle school teachers from various content areas (including me, an eighth-grade English/Language Arts teacher), our K–12 technology integration specialist, and several colleagues specializing in Educational Technology, Computer Science Education, and English Education from a nearby higher education campus, the University of Florida (Newell et al., 2024).

Throughout the year, during our monthly meetings, we explored the fundamentals of how generative artificial intelligence (AI) systems operate, experimented with a range of AI-powered educational tools, and engaged in discussions about the opportunities and challenges that generative AI presents for middle school education. Our learning culminated in a personal cycle of inquiry we each undertook to explore the ways AI might play out in our teaching. As a seasoned inquirer, however, I was not only interested in studying the ways AI could be integrated into my practice as a topic of inquiry, but in how AI could assist me through each component of the inquiry process, with a particular focus on using ChatGPT (or "Lex," as it suggested I call it) to analyze data.

(Continued)

(Continued)

As an experienced teacher researcher, I knew how valuable the data analysis process had always been for me, so I absolutely did not wish to turn the data analysis process over to AI to complete *for* me, nor would that be ethical or appropriate. Rather, I wanted to use Lex as a thought partner, a critical friend to deepen my understanding of my data and what I could learn from them.

To do so, I engaged with Lex in two ways. First, as a formative data analysis partner, I would ask Lex to complete an initial analysis of the 150 responses I would receive from writing prompts provided to my students that related to my wondering, or answers to particular individual items on a survey administered for my inquiry. I'd start this process by skimming through the responses myself to get the gist of how my students responded. Next, I'd share my anonymized student responses with Lex and ask my thought partner for takeaways, big ideas, and/or to sort my student responses by categories. Lex could accomplish this task in minutes, while it could take me hours, freeing up precious time to allow me to dig even deeper into the formative data analysis process. I did so by probing Lex further about takeaways, big ideas, or categories developed as we conversed about various ways to think about and interpret the data we had both read. In addition, often I would take Lex's thinking on the big ideas in student responses and share them with my students, asking them if they saw their voices represented in Lex's breakdown. Engaging Lex as a formative data analysis partner pushed me to consider the data I was collecting in a multitude of ways, providing rich insights into the next steps to take in my inquiry.

Second, as a summative data analysis partner, I would ask Lex to critique the patterns and themes that I derived from an examination of my entire data set at the close of my inquiry cycle. I'd start this process by providing Lex with my entire data set and stating what I had noticed in my read of it. We would then converse as I posed questions such as, "Here is what I notice in this data. What am I missing?" and "I sorted these data into the following 5 categories, would you frame this any differently?" I benefited from receiving both positive feedback and challenges to my thinking from Lex, as well as providing Lex with positive feedback and challenging Lex's thinking as well. Engaging Lex in this way gave me confidence in my analysis.

Using Lex as a thought partner in data analysis did not serve as a substitute for my own analysis of the data, but it did greatly enhance it. Sometimes Lex was wrong, but when this was the case, explaining to Lex why or adjusting the questions I posed or directions I provided often led me to develop new insights into my data that I don't think I would have developed in the absence of Jon–Lex conversations. Because I'm a trained teacher researcher, my authentic intelligence served to assess, appraise, and critique Lex's artificial intelligence, and in the process, I developed a more nuanced understanding of my data and the insights that I could generate from them to improve my teaching practice.

Lex has become a valuable teaching and research assistant that I will continue to draw upon as the next part of my career unfolds. I am always sure to acknowledge the role Lex plays in my teaching and research and can't wait to see what the future holds for our partnership in meeting the learning needs of every student we serve. I highly recommend Lex as a critical inquiry friend.

References

Mundorf, J. (2014). *Teaching reading to a student with blindness using universal design for learning: A practitioner inquiry* [Unpublished doctoral dissertation]. University of Florida.

Newell, B., Wang, X., Kohnen, A., Ganapathy, P., Wusylko, C., Ritzhaupt, A., & Botelho, A. (2024, October). *Practitioner inquiry embedded professional development: Applications of Artificial Intelligence in Middle School Education (AAIMSE)* [Conference presentation]. AECT International Convention, Kansas City, MO, United States.

What Might Summative Analysis Look Like?

In this section we illustrate the process of summative data analysis we just described with an inquiry conducted by veteran teacher researcher Amy Ruth (Ruth, 1999, 2001, 2002). Recall that Amy completed her first inquiry by looking closely at an individual English language learner she identified as "Adam." Amy was particularly interested in learning about the ways peer interaction facilitated Adam's written language development.

To gain insights into her wondering, Amy collected qualitative data in three ways over a two-month period. Amy's first approach to collecting data was to generate field notes. To do so, she developed a data collection sheet to complete each time she worked with Adam at the writing center. On the sheet, Amy diagrammed the seating arrangement to keep track of where group members chose to sit each time they came to the writing center. Next on the data collection sheet, Amy had a space for observations. In this space, Amy noted anything that stood out to her during the time Adam's group was at the center. There was also a place on the data collection sheet labeled "Notable Dialogue" where she scripted comments that occurred between peers during their interactions. Finally, Amy had a place labeled "Additional Comments" where she noted anything else occurring at the writing center that was interesting or intriguing.

Amy's second approach to collecting data was to keep a personal journal on each day that she met with Adam's group at the writing center. Amy noted, "These entries helped me to gather my thoughts, ideas, and further questions concerning my initial wonderings" (Ruth, 1999, p. 7). Amy's third data source consisted of notes, scripted by her university supervisor, about interactions that occurred at the writing center while Amy taught.

After two months of collecting data in these three forms, Amy approached the almost-full box in which she was keeping all of these data, in addition to articles and books she had found on the writing process and on English language learner students. She set aside a few hours on a Saturday morning to begin the process of creating a picture of what she had learned. To begin, she took each piece of data out of the box and organized them all chronologically, beginning with the first datum collected and ending with the last, and read through every one. By reading through her entire data set, Amy was reminded of incidents that occurred throughout the duration of her inquiry (through her own field notes and those scripted by her supervisor), as well as her thoughts about Adam, peer interaction, and the writing process as her inquiry unfolded (through her journal entries). In addition, reviewing readings that had appeared in such journals as *Journal of Second Language Writing* and *TESOL Journal* contributed to Amy's developing understanding of her work with Adam. The process of reading the data set in its entirety freshened up her understanding and provided a description of all that Amy had been thinking about and doing for the past two months.

With all she had collected fresh in her mind, Amy read through the entire data set a second time. On this second time through, Amy began sense making. As she read, she asked herself, "What am I noticing about my data?" She constructed a list as she read titled, "Inquiry—What I'm Noticing" (see Figure 5.7)

Figure 5.7   Amy's List of "Inquiry—What I'm Noticing"

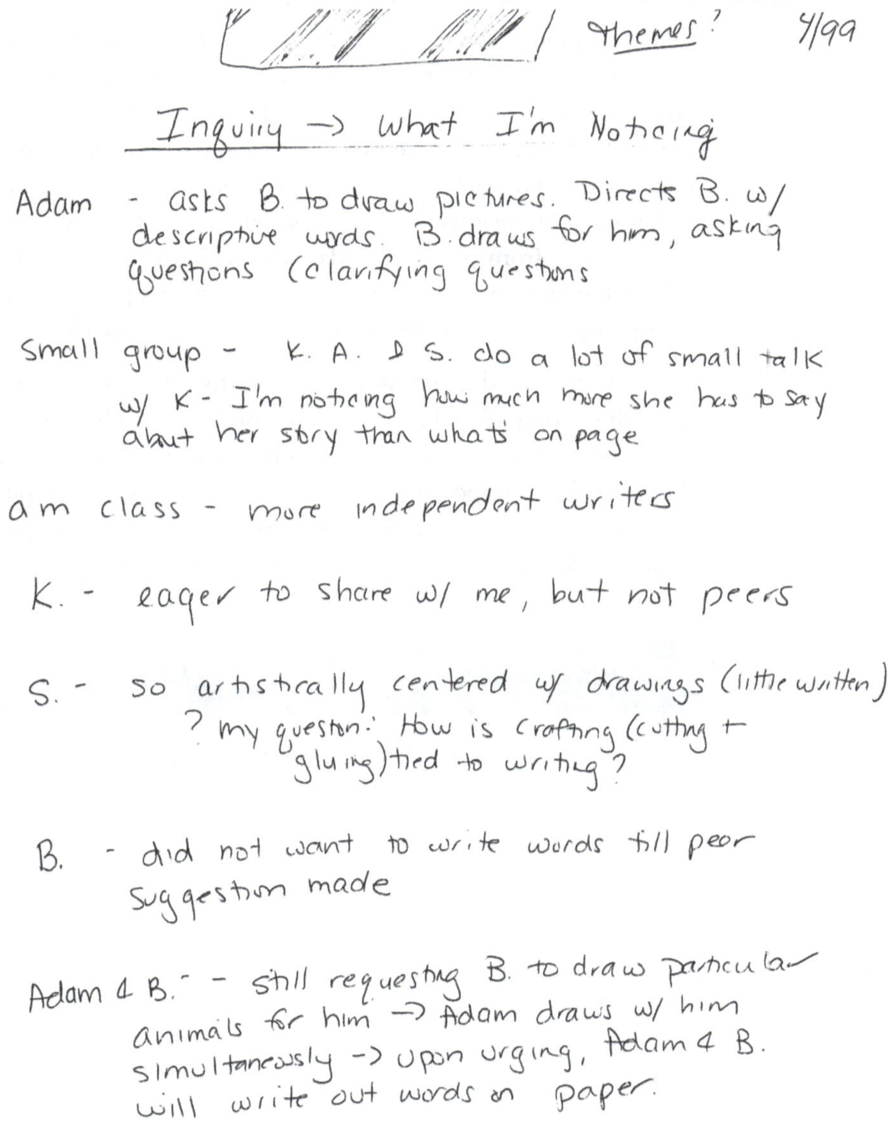

Themes?   4/99

Inquiry → What I'm Noticing

Adam — asks B. to draw pictures. Directs B. w/ descriptive words. B. draws for him, asking questions (clarifying questions)

Small group — K. A. & S. do a lot of small talk w/ K — I'm noticing how much more she has to say about her story than what's on page

am class — more independent writers

K. — eager to share w/ me, but not peers

S. — so artistically centered w/ drawings (little written) ? my question: How is crafting (cutting + gluing) tied to writing?

B. — did not want to write words till peer suggestion made

Adam & B. — still requesting B. to draw particular animals for him → Adam draws w/ him simultaneously → upon urging, Adam & B. will write out words on paper.

Source: Used with permission of Amy Ruth.

From looking at this list, Amy decided that her next step was to read the data again but, this time through, to focus solely on Adam and her initial wondering, "How does peer interaction facilitate Adam's writing at the kindergarten writing center?" She wrote this question on an index card and laid it in front of her to remind her of what she was seeking in this third read of her entire data set. This time, she decided to mark her data by highlighting in pink any pieces of it that pertained to her wondering.

Once this process was completed, Amy took a break for lunch and then returned to her data for a fourth reading. During this fourth sweep, however, Amy read only what she had highlighted in pink. Through reading only the pink excerpts, she generated a list of seven patterns that seemed to capture the essence of what was occurring over and over in her data. She named each of these patterns as follows: (1) requesting drawings from peers, (2) Adam's verbalization as drawing object, (3) labeling objects around the room, (4) outgoing personality, (5) role taking in group, (6) burdens others, and (7) asking for clarification.

Next, Amy created a coding mechanism for each of her named patterns, inventing a symbol that corresponded to each pattern (e.g., a tree corresponded to Pattern 1; a bubble corresponded to Pattern 2; the word *dog* corresponded to Pattern 3; a smiley face corresponded to Pattern 4; a hat corresponded to Pattern 5; a sad face corresponded to Pattern 6; and a check mark corresponded to Pattern 7).

Figure 5.8 Amy's Index Card Denoting Pattern Symbols Used for Coding

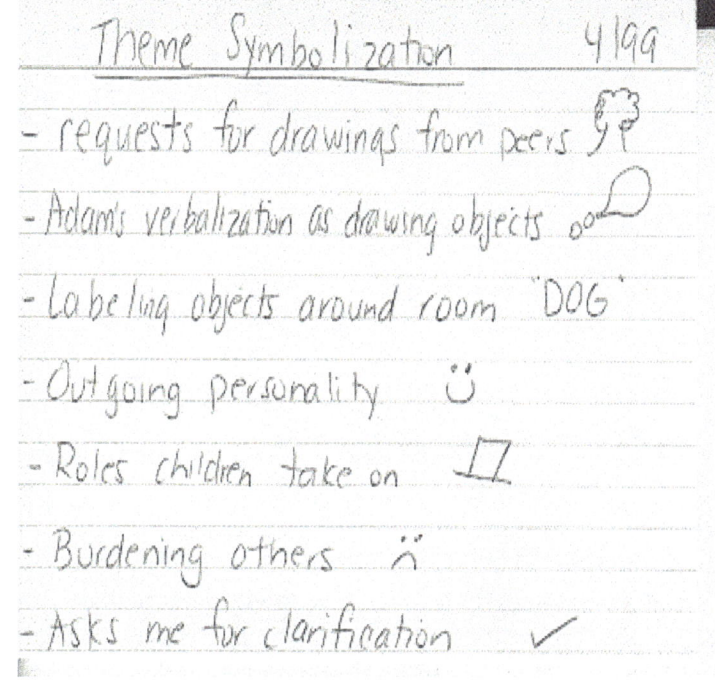

Source: Used with permission of Amy Ruth.

Figure 5.9   Example of Coded Data—Field Notes Scripted by Supervisor

> ③
>
> Gives children reminders at the project table. "It is almost time for me to knock."
>
> Transition
> - Amy knocks - Children line up to switch centers. She waits for all children, gives some individual reminders and knocks).
>
> Center Rotation #2
> - "How do you stay healthy?"
> - Mentor arrives at project table. 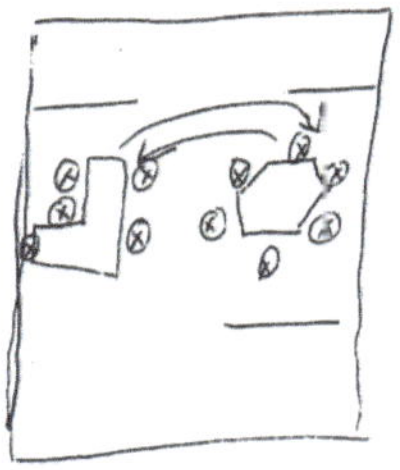
>
> Amy at Writing Table (INQUIRY)
>   "DOG"
> - A. talking to children about ○circles-globe
> - Children say that "It is one of A.'s words."
> - A. gets up and spins the globe.
> - "Miss Ruth" - A. gets Amy's attention. He points again to globe
> - Amy asks A to draw some of those countries. He hands paper to little girl across from him.
> - "K. needs to work on her story too."
> - A. not working - looking around room, back to globe,
> - "A. be careful! Come and add some more on here.
> - Amy moves over to direct A.'s writing. A knows some but not all sounds. He has difficulty find the "T" even when Amy tells him. Someone helps him with "R". Two other children are huddled over the alphabet list. They are trying to help."

Source: Used with permission of Amy Ruth.

Just as Amy had done previously, when she wrote her question on an index card and laid it in front of her to remind her of what she was looking for as she read, Amy noted each pattern and symbol on an index card and kept this card in front of her as she read through the entire data set a fifth time. This time through, she underlined and used her symbols to code the data. Amy's index card denoting the pattern symbols used for coding, as well as one piece of coded data from each of the three ways it was collected, appear in Figures 5.8 through 5.11 on pages 276–278 and 281.

> **Figure 5.10** Example of Coded Data—Journal

Amy Ruth

Inquiry Journal

Tuesday, March 2, 1999

After finally deciding to concentrate my inquiry focus on "Adam", a ESL student, I have really started concentrating on his interactions and writing at the Writing Table during Lang Arts centers. I am curious about how his interactions with peers will influence, encourage, and help the progress and growth of his writing. [*Initial Question*] Lately, Adam has been asking peers (B., in particular) to draw objects on his paper for him. Mostly everyone in the classroom knows that B. is particularly skilled and practiced at drawing dinosaurs and whales. They were the first two animals that I witnessed Adam requesting. Adam also goes as far as to tell B. what colors he would like things to be. After B. draws the request, Adam then adds details to the picture, usually talking as he does so. For example: a dinosaur drawn by B. and then Adam added a tree that the dinosaur was eating. Adam verbalized "tree" and eating sounds as he drew.

It is particularly interesting to see Adam requesting drawings by his peers, due to the use of the English language that we have seen really emerging recently. Within the past month we have seen tremendous growth in Adam's use of vocabulary. He is formulating longer sentences and is very eager to share his ideas through words now. I have noticed that he is more interested in full group activities in which he may have the chance to share his ideas. He raises his hand frequently, and volunteers many answers.

I am interested in seeing how this begins to play out in his writing. I am beginning to think of strategies that will encourage him to add words to his drawings.

Source: Used with permission of Amy Ruth.

A few days later, Amy sorted her data by pattern, reading through only the excerpts that pertained to each coded pattern. As she read through each pattern, she began the interpretive step of analysis. She asked herself, "What is happening in each pattern?," "How are the patterns connected to each other?," and "What do these patterns mean in relation to my initial wondering?" This time through, Amy noted the ways some patterns were connected to each other. For example, Amy saw connections between the four categories: Adam's (1) outgoing personality, (2) requests for drawings from peers, (3) different roles at the writing center, and (4) burdening others. She regrouped her data accordingly.

That week, Amy talked with her own peers at a seminar about what she was seeing. As she decribed the patterns, Amy noted that aspects of who Adam was as a person and learner that were strong attributes (i.e., Adam had an outgoing personality and was acquiring more and more spoken English words) were positive forces in the development of his writing. Adam was able to use his personality and the blossoming of his spoken English language as critical aids to his progress as a writer by asking for help from peers, especially from the child who had taken on the role of "artist" in the group. Amy noted that requests for drawings from the group's artist were frequent in her data and were appropriate and productive for Adam. As Adam's requests for drawings from the artist became more frequent, the artist became reluctant to respond to Adam's requests. Amy shared with her colleagues incidents that appeared in her data such as the following:

> Adam said, "Books! Draw books." The artist replied, "Books? I can draw one book." Adam held up three fingers and replied, "No, three books." The artist shook his head no. Adam said again, "Four? Four books." The artist drew just one book, and eventually Adam drew the rest.

In talking about her data, Amy also shared that what she had initially coded as a burden for the child who took on the role of the artist also seemed to lead that same child to become more immersed in his own writing. Amy shared that as the inquiry proceeded, the artist seemed more interested in doing his own writing and drawing. His own stories were growing more elaborate, and it appeared that he was trying to spend more time and effort on his own stories. In this way, Amy reframed her initial thinking about Adam's interactions at the writing center to emphasize and build upon Adam's many strengths and contributions.

Through engaging in dialogue, Amy's colleagues helped her capture what she was learning in a single statement or assertion: "A productive tension exists between Adam, his personality, his oral language development, and the ways he uses these attributes in interactions with peers at the writing center."

Fitting together these four different patterns revealed to Amy the complex nature and delicate balance of the interactions that were occurring at the writing center. Through her inquiry and summative analysis of data, Amy gained new understandings of what was occurring—understandings that would never have emerged in the absence of systematic study. Amy used the new knowledge she had constructed to make adjustments in her teaching and navigate the productive tension between Adam and the artist in the room by increasing her own interactions with Adam but still allowing for peer interactions to continue.

> I did not want Adam's requests and demands to hold back his peer's writing, although I still believe that those interactions were important for the progress of both children's writing. I tried to hold more of my own conversations with Adam, posing questions to him about his drawings, and assisting him whenever possible with words he would use to label his drawings. (Ruth, 1999, p. 10)

The completed picture of Amy's learning and what that learning meant for her practice was taking shape through summative data analysis.

At this time in the data analysis process, Amy abandoned her initial wondering and generated a new wondering: "What does writing mean to Adam?" Amy continued to analyze her data and collect more data over the next few weeks with this question in mind. At the close of her summative data analysis process, Amy reflected as follows:

> It is very exciting to look over the themes I found, and to realize that there was something very important going on with Adam and his peers at the writing center! Had I not posed the original question, I may never have really noticed what it was that was actually occurring. I now know how important the process of collecting data is. My data and themes did not necessarily definitively answer my initial question. But more importantly, they allowed me to see what was really growing and developing at our kindergarten writing center. Plus, I answered an entirely new question!
>
> I have found out, through this inquiry project, that there really are not any concrete answers to the initial question.

Figure 5.11   Example of Coded Data—Field Notes Taken by Amy

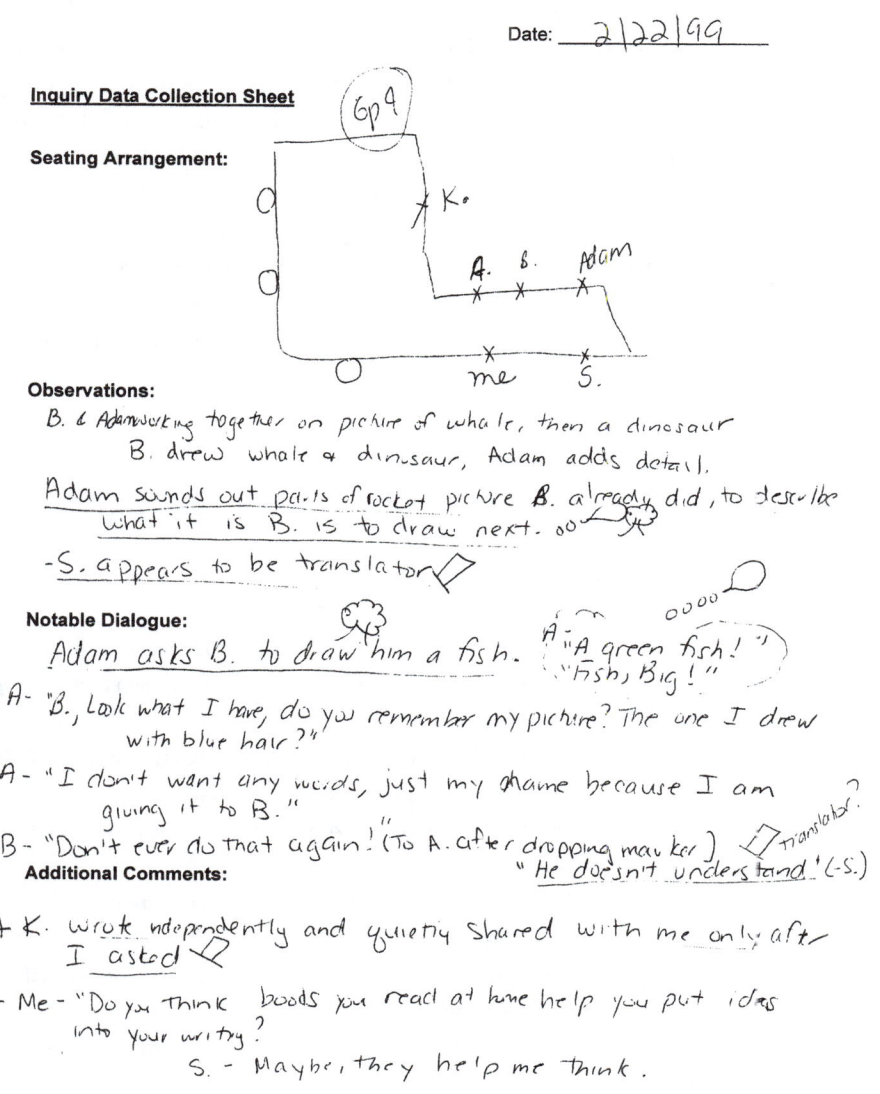

Source: Used with permission of Amy Ruth.

It is where the initial question leads that is important. The initial question allowed me to open up to seeing, hearing, and experiencing all that was going on at the writing table. I let the data collection and analysis lead me to my findings, instead of me leading the data collection and analysis to what I was hoping to find. (Ruth, 1999, p. 12–13)

As you reflect on Amy's example of data analysis, remember the three words we used to describe the data analysis process: "messy," "murky," and "creative." With this in mind, realize that summative analysis of your data might not proceed exactly as Amy's did. Every teacher is unique, every inquiry is unique, and, hence, every piecing together of the inquiry data to create a picture of the learning that has occurred is unique. Yet, as you finish this chapter, you now have knowledge of a common set of general procedures used to analyze data and a sense of how those general procedures may play out in a particular inquirer's work. You may wish to complete additional studies of the data analysis process before you begin or as you engage in the process yourself by reviewing some of the suggested resources in the textbox below:

DATA ANALYSIS RESOURCES

Bernhardt, V. (2004). *Data analysis for continuous school improvement.* Eye on Education.

Boudett, K. P., City, W. A., & Murnane, R. J. (2005). *Data wise: A step-by-step guide to using assessment results to improve teaching and learning.* Harvard Education Press.

Creswell, J. W., & Poth, C. N. (2018). *Qualitative inquiry and research design: Choosing among five approaches* (4th ed.). Sage.

Mills, G. E. (2014). *Action research: A guide for the teacher researcher* (5th ed.). Pearson Education.

Patton, M. Q. (2015). *Qualitative research & evaluation methods: Integrating theory and practice.* Sage.

Wolcott, H. F. (1994). *Transforming qualitative data: Description, analysis, and interpretation.* Sage.

Wolcott, H. F. (2008). *Writing up qualitative research* (3rd ed.). Sage.

CHAPTER 5 EXERCISES

1. The first step of analysis is *to describe* the data you have collected to inform your inquiry. Read through your data carefully. Take notes as you read.

2. The second step of analysis is to begin *making sense of* your data. After reading your data, begin your sense making by responding to the following questions:
   - What did you see as you inquired?
   - What was happening?
   - What are your initial insights into the data?
     Then, dive deeper by considering the examples of organizing units presented in Table 5.1, which can serve as prompts for helping you begin your analysis.
   - Use the chart to help you identify or construct possible organizing units for your data. Be sure to consider organizing units that emerge from within your inquiry.
   - Now, try organizing your data and identifying the units of analysis that emerge in your inquiry data. For example, maybe the important story in your data involves changes and you identify categories such as "changes for kids," "changes in content," and "changes in instruction."
3. Once you have a general idea of the important units of data and an idea of the emerging story, you need to decide how you will present the data. Read through the list of strategies for illustrating your findings presented in Table 5.2; they are designed to help you illustrate your *interpretive* findings. Remember, this is by no means an exhaustive list.
   - Now, you will need to choose a strategy or strategies for illustrating and organizing your own findings for your audience. Once again, use your creativity to organize your thoughts.
   - Outline the elements of your organizing strategy and identify the data you will use to support each component of your outline.
4. You probably thought the most difficult step of the analysis process was completed. However, the final *implications* step remains. Your remaining responsibility is to move from interpretation of the findings that you present in Exercise 3 to articulating the implications (or the "So what?") of your study in terms of your learning and potential changes to your current teaching practices. Some helpful questions follow that may prompt your thinking in this area:

(Continued)

(Continued)

- What have I learned about myself as a teacher?
- What have I learned about children?
- What are the implications of my findings for the content I teach?
- What have I learned about the larger context of schools and schooling?
- What are the implications of what I have learned for my teaching?
- What changes might I make in my own practice?
- What new wonderings do I have?

DISCUSSION QUESTIONS

1. Why is formative data analysis important? (Why shouldn't teacher inquirers just wait until all data have been collected to begin the analysis process?)

2. How might the process of formative data analysis help you respond to your wondering? How might it inform your day-to-day teaching practice?

3. Why is summative data analysis important? (What kinds of insights might emerge by analyzing all the data collected throughout an entire cycle of inquiry?)

4. Compare and contrast formative and summative data analysis. How are the processes similar? How are they different?

5. How does the metaphor of a jigsaw puzzle enthusiast connect to the process of summative data analysis? What other metaphors might characterize this process?

6. Google Forms and Excel are mentioned in this chapter as technology tools that might aid in the data analysis process. What other uses of technology, such as AI, might assist a teacher researcher in any component of the data analysis process described in this chapter?

7. Review each of the figures presented in Chapter 5. What tips do they offer about engaging in the analysis process? How might they be helpful to you as you analyze your own data?

8. How might writing data analysis memos and/or creating visual displays of data assist you during the sense-making step of data analysis? What types of visual displays (e.g., word tables, concept maps, data posters, other graphic organizers) do you believe would be most useful to you and why?

9. As teachers engage in the formative and summative data analysis processes, how might they collaborate to strengthen their analyses?

ONLINE MATERIALS

The following materials designed to facilitate data analysis are available for download at **https://companion.corwin.com/courses/ReflectiveEdsGuide5e**:

- **Activity 5.1: Data Analysis Memo.** Read a sample memo written during the early stages of summative data analysis along with feedback provided by the inquiry coach.

- **Activity 5.2: Data Analysis Summary Sheet and Data Analysis Protocol.** Follow a protocol to share what you are learning from examining collected data at the start of summative data analysis.

Sharing Your Inquiry Journey

Presenting and Publishing

6

As you begin this chapter, you have covered a lot of inquiry ground, traversing through four of its components including *wondering development* (Chapter 2), *data collection* (Chapter 3), planning the nature of and what *action(s)* to take (Chapter 4), and *data analysis* (Chapter 5). You are nearing the end of your journey, but there is still an important step necessary to complete each hike you take through the inquiry cycle you were presented in Chapter 1. This last step involves making your inquiry public by sharing your work with others, in essence creating a "travelogue" so that others may learn from your inquiry experience.

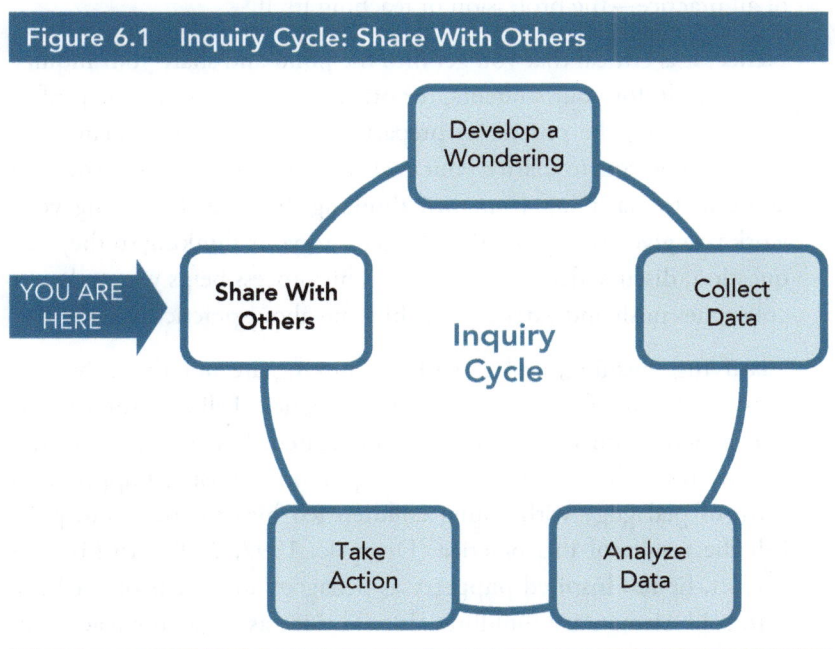

Figure 6.1 Inquiry Cycle: Share With Others

Why Is It Important to Share My Work With Others?

To illustrate the importance of sharing your work with others, imagine that as you start the last leg of your journey, you notice a large, stagnant pond and are enticed to create some type of movement or change in the water. As you near the edge, you notice that numerous large stones surround the pond. You reach down, pick up a stone, and toss it as far out into the center of the pond as your strength allows you. Lying beside the pond, the stone had no chance of impacting the water. But once tossed in, the stone not only disturbs the stillness of the water in the immediate vicinity of where it landed but also creates ripples of water that emanate out from the stone's landing place and eventually reach the perimeter of the pond.

An unshared teacher inquiry is like the stone lying beside the pond. Unless that inquiry is tossed into the professional conversation and dialogue that contribute to the knowledge base for teaching, the inquiry has little chance of creating change beyond the walls of your own classroom. However, once tossed in, the inquiry disturbs the status quo of educational practices, creating a ripple effect beginning with teachers and their immediate vicinity (their students and classrooms) and emanating out to a school, a district, a state, and eventually reaching and contributing to the transformation of the perimeter of all practice—the profession of teaching itself.

Hence, it is critical that you get into the pond and share your inquiry for yourself, for your students, for other teachers, and for the profession. For you, the process of preparing your findings to share with others helps you to clarify your own thinking about your work. In addition to clarifying your own thinking, by actually sharing your work you give other professionals access to your thinking so they can question, discuss, debate, and relate. This process helps you and your colleagues push and extend your thinking about practice as well.

Clarifying, pushing, and extending thinking are not the only benefits of sharing for you and your colleagues. Fellow professionals also benefit from the knowledge you created. For example, veteran teacher researcher George Dempsie's passion for using puppets as a form of pedagogy with young children led him to study and publish the results of this practice (Dempsie, 1997, 2000). In his own district, he has inspired puppetry as pedagogy in dozens of teachers, across 11 elementary buildings. In addition, as a mentor teacher in a Professional Development School, he has shared his research with interns and inspired a large percentage of these new teachers to use puppets as a way to gain access into children's thinking. His presentations at conferences and publications allow his work to spread outside his immediate vicinity (classroom, school, and district) as well.

Sharing your inquiry with other professionals can change the ways your students experience schooling. For example, one student teacher we know completed an inquiry on a second-grade child who was experiencing great difficulty within the structure of schooling but was not receiving any additional support or services because she did not qualify for special education according to traditional forms of assessment. The student teacher's inquiry illuminated many critical insights into the child that traditional forms of assessment would not have generated. The student teacher had become an advocate for this child, and she and her mentor teacher shared the results of her inquiry with other specialists and the principal. Eventually, a full-time paraprofessional was hired to work individually with this child within the regular classroom each school day. Within a year the child had made great strides forward in her academic and social development.

Another example of impacting students and colleagues through sharing an inquiry with others comes from Angela Jackson, a second-grade teacher at Carter G. Woodson Elementary School in Jacksonville, Florida. Angela was one of the first teachers at her school to try inquiry as a mechanism for professional learning. After completing one inquiry cycle, Angela found the process of teacher inquiry so powerful for her own professional learning that she wondered how she might translate this way of learning into a pedagogical approach she would use with her children. By using *teacher* inquiry to study the process of integrating *student* inquiry into instruction, Angela transformed her classroom the next school year. When she shared what she learned about engaging students in the process of inquiry at a faculty meeting, other teachers as well as the principal and vice principal were so intrigued with the idea that the school set out to engage all students in inquiry the following school year. In May, every Woodson Elementary student shared an inquiry into a different learning topic of his or her own choosing at a student inquiry showcase, attended by parents and other visitors from across the district.

A culture of inquiry for teachers *and* students quickly emerged at Woodson Elementary, and within a few short years, *every* teacher and *every* student in the building engaged in inquiry *every* school year. Themes for teachers' engagement in inquiry provided a focus for this school where 99% of the students receive free lunch. As more and more teachers and students engaged in inquiry at Woodson over time, their school was transformed! Five years after their school received a failing grade from the state, Woodson students made 92 learning gain points on their State Assessment Test, earning a school letter grade of A and being recognized as one of the highest-performing schools in the state. With the motto "Woodson: A Prescription for Inquiring Minds" buoying their efforts, this elementary school had reformed the way school worked for its students through collaboration, innovation, high expectations for every student, and the process of teacher inquiry, creating a more equitable schooling experience for all (Dana et al., 2013).

We have provided just three specific examples here to illustrate the power and, therefore, necessity of sharing inquiry. Some inquiries inspire small, local change. Some inspire large, sweeping change. All change, large or small, is significant in that the changes occurring are emanating from those best positioned to make a difference in education and those who for years have been kept from making that difference—teachers themselves.

Kincheloe writes about the ways teachers have been kept from making that difference seemingly marginalized by hierarchical power structures, scarce resources, and traditional values:

> Teachers are preoccupied with daily survival—time for reflection and analysis seems remote and even quite fatuous given the crisis management atmosphere and the immediate attention survival necessitates. In such a climate those who would suggest that more time and resources be delegated to reflective and growth-inducing pursuits are viewed as impractical visionaries devoid of common sense. Thus, the status quo is perpetuated, the endless cycle of underdevelopment rolls on with its peasant culture of low morale and teachers as "reactors" to daily emergencies. (Kincheloe, 1991, p. 12)

By getting into the pond and sharing your inquiry as a teacher, you contribute to breaking the cycle just described. You contribute to educational reform: "The plethora of small changes made by critical teacher researchers around the world in individual classrooms may bring about far more authentic educational reform than the grandiose policies formulated in state or national capitals" (Kincheloe, 1991, p. 14).

By getting into the pond and sharing your inquiry, you contribute to changing the ways some people outside of teaching view teachers and their practice and try to change education from the outside in. In the sharing of your inquiry, you contribute to reforming the profession of teaching—from the inside out! You become a teacher leader, a professional who engages in "experimentation and examination of more powerful learning activities with and for students, in the service of enhanced student productions and performances of knowledge and understanding. Based on this leadership with and of students, teacher leaders invite other teachers to similar engagements with students in the learning process" (Sergiovanni & Starratt, 1998, p. 149).

Teacher leaders slide their classroom doors open to collaborate with other teachers; discuss common problems; share approaches to various learning situations; explore ways to overcome the structural constraints of limited time, space, resources, and restrictive policies; and/or investigate motivational strategies to bring students to a deeper engagement with their learning. Teacher inquiry is a pathway to teacher leadership. Read more about the relationship between teacher leadership and teacher inquiry in the textbox below.

TEACHER LEADERSHIP AND INQUIRY

Nearly 30 years ago, Roland Barth stated that teachers harbor extraordinary leadership capabilities, and their leadership is a major untapped resource for improving our nation's schools. In recognition of this fact, the importance of teacher leadership has been elevated in educational dialogue and conversation during the past quarter century (Barth, 1990; Wenner & Campbell, 2017; York-Barr & Duke, 2004), with both national standards (https://www.ets.org/pdfs/patl/patl-teacher-leader-model-standards.pdf) and many graduate degree programs in teacher leadership springing up throughout the nation.

Although the term *teacher leadership* has enjoyed a great deal of attention in the educational literature and in graduate programs at universities, it remains ill-defined. For example, Wasley defines teacher leadership as "influencing and engaging colleagues toward improved practice" (Wasley, 1992, p. 21). Crowther, on the other hand, defines teacher leadership as

(Continued)

(Continued)

> an ethical stance that is based on views of both a better world and the power of teaching to shape meaning systems. It manifests in actions that involve the wider community in the long term. It reaches its potential in contexts where system and school structures are facilitative and supportive.
> (Crowther, 1997, p. 15)

Regardless of the definition you hold for teacher leadership, according to Katzenmeyer and Moller:

> when given opportunities to lead, teachers can influence school reform efforts. Waking this sleeping giant of teacher leadership has unlimited potential in making a real difference in the pace and depth of school change. (Katzenmeyer & Moller, 2001, p. 102)

One way to awaken the teacher leader sleeping giant within you is by engaging in the process of inquiry described in this book and channeling what you learn through the process into leadership efforts within your school, district, state, and the profession at large.

Within the school and district, teacher leaders use both the *results from* and the *process of* teacher inquiry to plan targeted professional learning experiences in areas of need. Teachers selecting this leadership option will examine their teacher research and determine where their findings and conclusions suggest new ideas for professional learning experiences in their context. For example, at Woodson Elementary School, teacher Angela Jackson found promise in translating inquiry as an approach to teacher professional learning into a pedagogical approach to working with her second-grade students. The results from her study ignited an interest in inquiry as a pedagogical approach to working with children at her school, and Angela planned and implemented professional learning opportunities for teachers to explore inquiry as an approach to instruction. The results of Angela's inquiry spurred professional learning opportunities for teachers at her school. Inversely, the process of inquiry was later used at this school to structure professional development for all teachers on the implementation of the Common Core State Standards. Early release Wednesdays, a day when students were dismissed from school earlier than normal to provide teacher professional learning time, were used for teachers to come together and formulate wonderings about what the Common Core would mean to their practice and support each other in their investigations into the standards. Teachers in the building organized, facilitated, and managed these meetings, demonstrating one actualization of the teacher leadership role.

Within the school and district and oftentimes moving beyond to the state level, teacher leaders use the process of teacher inquiry to engage in policy and advocacy work. Teachers selecting this leadership option do so by considering how their teacher research can be used to create meaningful policy directives and how these directives can move policy discussion at the school level and beyond. In this extension of inquiry, teachers take the findings from their teacher research and turn them into a policy brief. Sometimes the brief might illustrate the ways well-intentioned policy initiatives have had ill-intentioned effects on teachers and the students they teach. The brief, which can be shared with decision-makers at the school level and beyond, is designed to provide relevant parties with an understanding of the importance of the teacher research findings, an explanation of how these findings can affect policy, and strategies for implementation of related policy. Many examples of teachers leading by using the process of inquiry to impact policy can be found in the text *Taking Action With Teacher Research* (Meyers & Rust, 2003).

Within the profession at large, teacher leaders use the process of teacher inquiry to contribute to the professional knowledge base for teaching. This means teachers intentionally focus on making their professional knowledge become a part of the research-based literature and, with this intention from the outset of their studies, go through all procedures and processes related to the ethics of conducting research (such as obtaining IRB approval when inquiry is done in association with a university). Teachers selecting this leadership option transform their inquiry into a scholarly article that can inform the knowledge base and be used to guide the research of others. The article includes all the components normally found in scholarly work, presents findings in multiple forms to promote understanding, seeks to provide future directions for research, and is constructed with an understanding of the anticipated avenue for publication. Examples of teachers leading by contributing to the knowledge base for teaching can be found in articles published in such journals as *Networks: An Online Journal for Teacher Research*, *Educational Action Research*, *Action Research*, *Journal of Practitioner Research*, and *Voices of Practitioners*.

A key component of leading as a teacher is articulating what you have learned from practice in public spaces to engage others with your ideas and inspire change. There are two ways to enter into a public space as a teacher leader: (1) providing oral accounts of your inquiry journey through presentation and (2) sharing your practice with others through the written word.

How Do I Present My Work?

Many teacher inquirers use write-ups, PowerPoint slides, iMovies, podcasts, and/or posters to share their work orally in informal and more formal ways. Informally, some groups of teacher inquirers organize a gathering outside the school structure (e.g., an afterschool meeting at a coffee shop) to discuss their work. Or, if you are enrolled in an undergraduate or graduate class in which teacher inquiry is a focus, you may culminate the semester with a special meeting (perhaps a potluck dinner) where all share the results of their inquiry endeavors.

Within the school structure, formal sharing by teacher inquirers is often accomplished through dedicating special portions of faculty meetings to inquiry or totally reconceptualizing faculty meetings to allow space for the ongoing sharing of inquiry. Some districts also devote entire inservice days to teacher inquiry, where colleagues gather to share their work. If your current professional context does not have support structures for sharing inquiry, such as those described earlier, you may begin building these structures simply by offering to talk for a few minutes about your work at a faculty meeting. Much of our early research focused on building an inquiry culture (see, e.g., Dana, 1994, 1995, 2001; Dana & Silva, 2001, 2002; Silva & Dana, 1999). As a result of our research, we learned that building a culture of inquiry takes time and is best started slowly, since some of your current administrators and colleagues (if you are a veteran teacher) or future administrators and colleagues (if you are a prospective teacher) may be reluctant to embrace inquiry and the changes it necessitates. While building an inquiry culture is a slow process, it has to start somewhere, and it can start with you. Be patient and persevere.

Finally, many teacher researchers present their work at conferences. There are numerous national forums that showcase presentations by teacher inquirers. Perhaps the largest and most well-known is the American Educational Research Association (AERA). The professionals who engage in teacher inquiry and are members of this organization typically assemble in special interest groups (SIGs) such as

Teacher-as-Researcher or School–University Partnership Research. Teacher researchers involved in school–university partnerships such as PDSs, residency models of teacher preparation, or community schools are frequent presenters at the annual conference of the National Association for School–University Partnerships (NASUP), which dedicates special conference sessions to the sharing of inquiries and provides annual awards for exemplary inquiry.

While we encourage you to become part of a national network such as AERA or NASUP, the reality in almost every school district is that conference travel money for teachers is small or nonexistent. Many teachers receive limited support for conference endeavors and must pay out of their own pockets to attend and present. For this reason, the cost of national travel is often prohibitive for many teachers, especially on a yearly basis.

You can still experience the exhilaration that comes from presenting your work formally to an audience by connecting to conferences that occur in your vicinity. Many national organizations, such as AERA, NASUP, Association for Supervision and Curriculum Development (ASCD), Learning Forward, National Council of Teachers of Mathematics (NCTM), National Council for the Social Studies (NCSS), National Science Teachers Association (NSTA), National Council of Teachers of English (NCTE), National Association for the Education of Young Children (NAEYC), and the Association of Teacher Educators (ATE) have state or regional affiliates that hold conferences at least once a year. In addition, if you are a prospective teacher or advanced graduate student, most of these organizations offer very reasonable membership rates for students, so it is an excellent time to investigate professional groups that can serve as local outlets for the sharing of your inquiry, as well as a stimulus for continuing to inquire into your practice throughout your career.

A final possibility is designing and holding your own teacher inquiry conference. While this may sound like an overwhelming undertaking, it can be accomplished relatively easily by starting small and drawing on some sound organizational abilities. To show the range and variety possible, we describe two structures we have used to create our own conferences. The first structure uses posters and is conversational. The second structure uses presented papers and follows a more traditional conference format.

The first structure was designed as a culmination to a class on teacher inquiry with just 13 members in the class. We held the final class during the evening in the all-purpose room of a local school (7:00 p.m.–9:00 p.m.), where class members set up posters in two shifts (7:00 p.m.–7:30 p.m. and 8:00 p.m.–8:30 p.m.) that captured the essence of their inquiries. Each member of the class was responsible for inviting at least one other colleague or a family member; we also posted information about the conference in local schools and at the university. We created a program for the evening that contained the titles and abstracts of each class member's work, and the schedule for the evening conference was as follows:

- 7:00–7:30 p.m. Round 1 of poster presentations (six posters set up); conference participants visit each poster and presenters discuss their inquiries and answer questions through conversation.
- 7:30–8:00 p.m. Refreshments served; Round 1 posters taken down; Round 2 posters set up.
- 8:00–8:30 p.m. Round 2 of poster presentations (seven posters set up); conference participants visit each poster and presenters discuss their inquiries and answer questions through conversation.
- 8:30–9:00 p.m. Participants gather for discussion and reflection about teacher inquiry.

The second structure was designed as a culmination to a PDS year where mentors and interns shared the results of inquiries conducted in their classrooms that year (Dana, 1999). We designated the last Saturday in April as the annual PDS Teacher Inquiry Conference. Two weeks prior to this conference, we asked all mentors and interns who had engaged in inquiry to email us titles and brief abstracts of their work. We assigned each of the inquiry abstracts received to one of five 20-minute sessions to occur concurrently throughout the morning in neighboring classrooms at one of the PDS sites. We invited teachers, administrators, faculty from the school district and university, and the family members of all presenters. Next, we created a conference program to allow all participants to view the presentation offerings and choose which sessions they wished to attend. After three concurrent sessions, we allotted a 30-minute time slot for Bagel Brunch, offering refreshments such as coffee, juice, doughnuts, and, of course, bagels. After two more sessions, the conference ended just after the noon hour with recognition of all the presenters and those who supported their work and brief reflections on the inquiry process. A portion of the 2002 conference program appears in Figure 6.2.

Figure 6.2 Inquiry Conference Program

**The State College Area School District—Pennsylvania State University
Professional Development School Teacher Inquiry Conference
April 27, 2002**
Mt. Nittany Middle School

9:00 a.m. *Auditorium*	**Welcome and Orientation**

9:15–9:35 a.m.	**Session I**

Room 156 — Encouraging Lifelong Learners: Intrinsic Motivation in the Classroom

Melissa Cinquini, Intern
Park Forest Elementary School
cinquini@psu.edu

How can we encourage students to become lifelong learners? This inquiry began with an assessment of students' current motivational responses to completing school work. The teacher then used these responses to explore how an activity rooted in guiding and supporting intrinsic motivation affected the learners in this classroom.

Room 154 — Phonemic Awareness: A Key to Kindergarten

Darcie Hampton, Mentor
Matternville Elementary School
drh13@scasd.pa.k12.us

Beth Schickel, Intern
Matternville Elementary School
schickel@psu.edu

A veteran teacher and intern look at the learning and teaching of phonemic awareness. As teachers in a kindergarten classroom we noticed that students' sense of phonemic awareness varied a great deal. As a result of this, we wanted to see the effects of supplemental phonemic awareness activities with students who are struggling.

Room 152 — Effective Use of the Opening Routine

Sara Evensen Tilles, Intern
Ferguson Township Elementary School
set132@psu.edu

A Professional Development School intern examines the use of various strategies during opening activities. How can all subject areas be integrated and reinforced during this time? How can students be motivated to participate?

Room 146 — Developing Differentiated Instruction Strategies and Motivational Strategies to Meet the Individual Needs of a Math Learner

Stacee Banko, Intern
Park Forest Elementary School
smb295@psu.edu

I believe that it is crucial that students are motivated and excited to learn in every situation. This means that I must be willing to look at my own teaching styles and see where new strategies can be implemented as well as encouraged. My inquiry project focuses on an individual learner who was "slipping between the cracks" before I understood the different teaching strategies I could adopt to help him become a successful motivated learner.

(Continued)

(Continued)

Room 144 — **Examining Different Types of Assessment and Evaluating Which Assessment Students Value the Most**

Jamie Clouse, Intern
High School North
twirlygirl183@aol.com

There are numerous approaches to assessment, but it is crucial to choose the best type of assessment based on the assignment. Too often students believe that the only real way to measure their success is with a letter grade. I would like to explore various types of assessment to get a firmer grasp on which types of assessment are most supportive of a learning environment.

Room 256 — **Building Confidence in Reading**

Jackie Mintmier, Intern
Ferguson Township Elementary School
jxm530@psu.edu

Through research and exploring two students' beliefs and thinking about reading, I tried to find ways that would help to increase the students' confidence and help them develop a positive self-image of themselves as readers.

Room 254 — **Effective Parent Communication: What Does it Look Like?**

Candy Bryan, Teacher
Ferguson Township Elementary School
cjb14@scasd.k12.pa.us

Kelly Reilley-Kaminiski, Mentor
Ferguson Township Elementary School
kar15@scasd.k12.pa.us

Two elementary school teachers research effective parent communication tools that reflect the current needs within each classroom. Based on parent feedback, they implemented changes to their practices and compared the needs of the parents between first and third year students

Room 252 — **The Puzzle of Two Children: How to Motivate Two New and Challenging Students in My Classroom**

Kelli Hollada, Intern
Radio Park Elementary School
keh164@psu.edu

In an attempt to discover how to best serve the students in my second grade class, I searched for ways to help motivate two boys who were experiencing difficulties as learners in my classroom.

Room 246 — **Responding to Conflict in a First-Grade Classroom**

Meghan Marshall, Intern
Radio Park Elementary School
mlm335@psu.edu

An intern explores the conflicts in her first-grade classroom. What is causing our classroom, especially one group of girls, to have so much conflict? How can I better respond to these conflicts to encourage students to be independent problem solvers?

Room 244 — **Between a Rock and a Hard Place: The Search to Find a Meaningful and Practical Way to Assess Student Writing**

Sabrina Ehmke, Intern
Mount Nittany Middle School
sae129@psu.edu

My inquiry involves the struggle I face as a teacher when it comes to evaluating student writing. The experience of writing, which seems to me inherently a subjective one, is more often than not assigned a point or grade value as an indicator of achievement. In the process of regulating writing to a quantitative variable, I wonder whether such a forced attempt at objectivity does in fact not only hinder students as writers, but also devalue what we as teachers hope to promote in terms of the act of writing itself.

Room 242 — **Mathematical Rubrics-Meeting the Standards**

Brenda Khayat, Mentor
Park Forest Elementary
bgk11@scasd.k12.pa.us

My goal was to improve the written side of problem solving for fifth graders. The belief is that students can problem solve, but the challenge is for them to show it in their written explanations.

Remember our advice about starting small? The first conference program we organized during the pilot year of the PDS in 1999 contained a total of 13 intern presentations and 1 mentor teacher presentation from two elementary PDS sites. There were two or three selections offered during each concurrent session, and approximately 50 people attended the conference. Just four years later, this same conference had grown to showcase the inquiries of 41 interns, 15 mentor teachers, 6 teachers who were not currently mentoring an intern, and 4 librarians from six elementary schools, two middle schools, and the district's high school. Approximately 200 attendees chose from 10 or 11 presentations during each concurrent session. Even after we left this context to take new positions and spread the good news of inquiry in other places, this conference has continued to grow each year, demonstrating that a culture of inquiry had been built and institutionalized at this location. (For more information about building an inquiry culture, see Dana et al., 2001, 2002; Snow et al., 2001.)

In a similar fashion, at our next institution (University of Florida) we organized an annual program similar to that which we organized in our work with the State College Area School District—Pennsylvania State University Elementary Professional Development School Program. We named this program the Teaching, Inquiry, and Innovation Showcase and gave it a very similar format to the PDS inquiry conference previously described. There were three purposes of this annual event: (1) to celebrate the practitioner who, through the processes of inquiry, has contributed to improving schools from within; (2) to enable practicing teachers and administrators across North Central Florida and from different programs and affiliations to network with each other; and (3) to connect prospective and practicing teachers through this forum, enabling prospective teachers to be socialized into the profession as inquirers and practicing teachers to shape the next generation of those entering the teaching profession.

At this event, veteran teachers from various districts across Florida who had engaged in teacher inquiry gathered to share their work. Prospective teachers who had completed teacher inquiry into an individual child in their pre-intern field experience placements presented their inquiry in a five-minute time segment at the start of each veteran teacher's presentation. The prospective teachers subsequently introduced the veteran teacher and served as presider for that session, keeping time and assisting the veteran teacher in any way needed.

At our first showcase in 2005, we were thrilled to host 80 practicing teachers presenting their work and 112 pre-interns who gave five-minute mini-presentations on their inquiries at the start of each teacher's session. More than 200 people attended the inaugural showcase, enabling us to start where we had left off in our work at Penn State. Just three years later, more than 180 teachers and 150 pre-interns presented their work at our annual event, which was attended by more than 400 people! In three years' time, our showcase more than doubled in size, and, inspired by this annual event, similar showcases are being organized and held at other locations across our state, with some inquiry showcases in large districts such as Pinellas County Schools and Miami-Dade Public Schools nearing 1,000 participants!

Wherever you present your work, the use of visuals can often enhance an oral presentation because visuals give your audience something to focus their gaze on as you speak. An added bonus of creating visuals to accompany the oral presentation of your work is that it helps to keep you, the presenter, organized and focused as you story your inquiry journey for others. The most common visuals we have seen teacher researchers use when presenting their work are posters and PowerPoint slides. Figure 6.3 illustrates a sample poster completed by a teacher candidate and Figure 6.4 contains some of the PowerPoint slides from a presentation made by Debbi Hubbell of her inquiry into the reading of

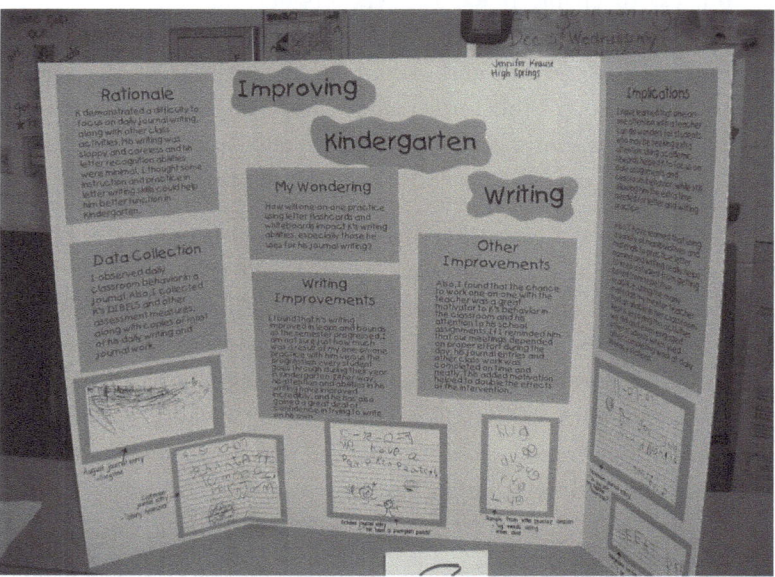

Figure 6.3 Inquiry Poster

CHAPTER 6: SHARING YOUR INQUIRY JOURNEY 301

fractured fairy tale plays with fourth-grade struggling readers. Debbi is pictured presenting these slides in Figure 6.5 on page 303. For further tips of presenting, you may find the fifth chapter of the text *Digging Deeper Into Action Research* (Dana, 2013) a useful guide for developing and fine-tuning an oral presentation of your work.

Figure 6.4   PowerPoint Slides From Debbi's Presentation

Focus on Fractured Fairy Tales and Fluency Flourishes

Debbi Hubbell
4th Grade Teacher
Ft. White Elementary School

My Wondering

- What is the relationship between my fourth graders' fluency development and the reading of fractured fairy tales?

My Instructional Plan

- **Day One:** Students chose parts, Debbi read the play to the group, then students practiced silently
- **Day Two:** Students practiced silently, then aloud with the group to Debbi; Debbi followed with short individual conferences
- **Day Three:** Students practiced silently, then aloud with the group to Debbi
- **Day Four:** Students practiced silently, then presented aloud with the group to the class

Data Collection

- DIBELS
- Observation of Students–Anecdotal Notes
- Student Artifacts–"Dear Mrs. Hubbell" letters

My Data Analysis Plan

- Charted DIBELS data
- Read through Observation Notes and Student Artifacts multiple times asking questions such as: What was happening? What have I learned about myself as a teacher? What have I learned about children? What are the implications of my findings for my teaching?
- Discussed analysis with teaching colleagues

DIBELS Test Results

	10/18	12/1	2/10	2/21	4/6
J	48	53	55	60	73
B	81	98	114	105	164
C	90	98	95	100	130
Ja	64	70	92	85	119
T	93	96	88	97	121
S	94	91	86	78	113
M	84	101	99	107	127

(Continued)

(Continued)

Three Themes:

- Enjoyment/Enthusiasm
- Students perceive academic benefits
- Positive social interactions

Enjoyment/Enthusiasm...

Dear Mrs. Hubbell, I would like to do more fractured fairy tales becaus the fairy tales bring more happiness to the school day and more laughter to the morning and the evening and we also learn a lesson from the tales. For instance we learned from one of the plays that you don't have to be perfect to marry prince that lesson was from spider-ella.

Academic Benefits...

Dear Mrs. Hubble, I realy liked doing the fractured fairy tales because they teach you a lesson. For example, the Chera and the sloth play taught you to start slow and save your energy for latter, when you get to the finish line. I also like them because they help you read more fluently and with expression.

Dear Mrs. Hubbell I really did like it and I would realy want you to do more action fairy tales. And the best fairy tale we did I learned lots of new words that I didnt know. So it helped build my vocabulary. And it helps you become more of a fluent reader.

Positive social interactions...

Dear Mis. Hubbell
I like the plays we did in class. And I like to be in the plays to. I all so like to entel tame the class. From being in the plays I learnd to try yore best at every thing. and do not be emberest.

Action

- Develop school/districtwide fluency objectives
- Differentiate homework for 60wpm kids vs. 180 wpm kids
- Make listening centers more effective
- Connect to struggling readers in secondary school

For More Information:

Please contact me at
debbihubbell@yahoo.com

Source: Used with permission of Debbi Hubbell.

One of the great benefits of presenting your work orally is that it forces you to think more deeply about your inquiry journey as you fashion an oral retelling of the story of your learning.

Figure 6.5 Debbi Hubbell presents her inquiry at the Fourth Annual Teaching, Inquiry, and Innovation Showcase at the University of Florida's P. K. Yonge Developmental Research School

Source: Used with permission of Debbi Hubbell.

Another wonderful way to think about your inquiry is to write. Noted educational ethnographer Harry Wolcott goes so far as to state that writing and thinking are synonymous: "The conventional wisdom is that writing reflects thinking. I am drawn to a different position: Writing is thinking" (Wolcott, 1990, p. 21). Referring specifically to the process of teacher inquiry, Mills further states that there is great value in writing up research because

> the process of writing requires the writer to clarify meaning—choose words carefully, thoughtfully describe that which is experienced or seen, reflect on experiences, and refine phrasing when putting words on a page. You may learn something important about your students and their learning—something you may have missed had you not considered your words on the page—as you formally write about your research. (Mills, 2014, p. 179)

For this reason, we recommend writing as an extension of oral presentations and as a wonderful way to expand your learning.

How Do I Write About My Work?

Although writing is a terrific mechanism for clarifying thinking as you summarize what you have learned and for giving your learning a form that can be shared with others, it is not a part of a teacher's daily work, and it takes a great deal of time. Mills (2014) suggests challenging the time constraint by making writing a part of your professional life and responsibility: capturing the minutes and hours—before school, after school, during preparation periods, or in lieu of canceled faculty meetings, failed parent conferences, and sit-and-get professional development days. When all else fails, use personal time to get writing done.

If you can get past the time constraint and the resistance to engaging in an activity that Wolcott (1990) describes at its best as "always challenging and sometimes satisfying" (p. 12), we believe that the times it is satisfying will outweigh all the difficulty and frustration inherent in writing and that, through the writing process, you will take your own individual inquiry to a new level. Mills (2014) suggests sound reasons for writing. We end this section with his five most compelling reasons to write.

- *Clarification:* Writing your research requires clarity and accuracy of expression. Writing about your research activities encourages thought and reflection, and perhaps creates new questions that you can resolve, and that shape and complete your research.

- *Validation:* Publishing your research and the feedback you will receive from your reviewers and readers will validate who you are as a professional educator and what you do.

- *Empowerment:* Reflecting on your practices through writing will empower you to continue to challenge the status quo and be an advocate for your children.

- *Generative:* Writing is a generative activity that culminates in a product, something tangible that you can share with colleagues, supervisors, and parents.

- *Accomplishment:* Writing up your research will provide you with a sense of accomplishment. It is both humbling and exciting when colleagues read your work and compliment you on your accomplishments! (Mills, 2014, p. 180)

What Might My Writing Look Like?

If you recall, Julie Russell was passionate about writing, and this passion led to her inquiry into second graders' writing. Julie's passion for writing makes her a logical teacher inquirer to feature in this chapter as an example of what your work may look like in written form. Julie's work provides only one example of what an inquiry write-up looks like. Inquiry write-ups come in a variety of shapes and sizes that can range from a brief description of your inquiry journey published on a district's website (if you are engaging in a cycle of inquiry as a professional learning endeavor) to an entire dissertation (if you are completing a cycle of inquiry as the culminating project for the attainment of your degree in a professional practice doctoral program). Depending on your writing goals and context, we encourage you to view other write-ups as models. Models in addition to the one presented in this chapter can be found by visiting one of the many journals that publish teacher research online such as:

- *i.e.: inquiry in education* (http://digitalcommons.nl.edu/ie)
- *Journal of Practitioner Research* (https://scholarcommons.usf.edu/jpr/)
- *Journal of Teacher Action Research* (http://www.practicalteacherresearch.com/about.html)
- *Networks: An Online Journal for Teacher Research* (https://newprairiepress.org/networks/)

Viewing examples in these journals can inspire you to submit your writing for publication after it is completed. Another great place to find model write-ups completed by practicing teachers is in published collections of teacher research (see, e.g., Caro-Bruce et al., 2007; Crawford-Garrett & Carbajal, 2023; Masingila, 2006; Meyers & Rust, 2003). Furthermore, we have provided an additional example of an inquiry write-up (with a focus on critical literacy) completed by Cara Dore, a teacher candidate from The Pennsylvania State University, on the companion website to this text.

Note that the example of Julie's work we share in this chapter, as well as many of the examples you will find in the online journals and action research collections mentioned above, are quite detailed and, as a result, are lengthy. If the detail and length of Julie's or any other teacher researcher's published work overwhelms you, find a write-up form that is a better fit with who you are as a teacher and writer. For example, when we noticed some teacher researchers becoming overly stressed at the thought of writing up their work, we introduced the concept of an executive summary write-up into our work at the Center for School Improvement and later the Lastinger Center for Learning at the University of Florida (Dana & Baker, 2006; Dana & Delane, 2007; Dana & Yendol-Hoppey, 2008b).

Executive summaries provide brief (three- to five-page) overviews of a teacher's inquiry, as well as contact information for the teacher so more detail about a teacher's work can be shared through personal contact. You can view examples of teacher inquiry completed by teachers on the University of Florida's school partner's website (P. K. Yonge) here: https://pkyonge.ufl.edu/research-at-pky/inquiry-investigations-symposium/. Similarly, the Madison Metropolitan School District's Classroom Action Research Program offers another website that shares teachers' summaries of their inquiry work: https://www.madison.k12.wi.us/assessments/data-security-and-privacy/classroom-action-research.

Another fine model for inquiry write-ups that may appear less daunting for the teacher researcher who doesn't enjoy writing is the inquiry brochure. This technique is used extensively in Fairfax County (Virginia) Public Schools as one option for teachers to share their research in a written form. Two examples of inquiry brochures from the Fairfax County Public Schools appear at the end of this chapter as Figures 6.6 and 6.7. Yet another model for an inquiry write-up that we have used with teacher candidates at the University of Florida and the University of South Florida is the inquiry template, which appears as Figure 6.8. During field experiences that occur four mornings a week prior to their full internship, our students select one student in consultation with their mentor teacher to study through the inquiry process. As a part of their work with this child, they design and implement an intervention targeted at helping that student address an area ripe for his or her growth and development as a learner. The template consists of one box each that contains the teacher candidate's wondering, data collection strategies, intervention description, findings, and conclusions. Writing up an inquiry becomes as simple as filling in each box.

We feel strongly that writing is an important part of the teacher inquiry process but realize that not every teacher researcher desires to be a published author. For this reason, we have provided examples of additional models (e.g., the executive summary, the inquiry brochure, and the inquiry template) that provide the benefits of writing discussed previously but may be more inviting forums for some teachers to capture and share their work in written form. Whether you intend to write a detailed accounting of your research, an executive summary, an inquiry brochure, or an inquiry template, or whether you simply intend to share your work orally as described in the first part of this chapter, we believe you will find value in reading the example of Julie's writing we chose to include in this chapter.

Figure 6.6 Inquiry Brochure Example

Where the Wild Things Are: Helping First Grade Students Develop Self-Regulation and Friendships

Research Question:

What happens when adults engage first grade students in social experiences and specific lessons focused on expected school behaviors?

Contact information:
gail.ritchie@fcps.edu

Further research questions:

☼ How can I involve parents in my efforts to help students develop social competence?

☼ What happens when I emphasize intrinsic motivation instead of behavior modification?

Where the Wild Things Are: Helping First Grade Students Develop Self-Regulation and Friendships

Gail V. Ritchie, MEd., NBCT
Kings Park Elementary School
2004-2005 School Year

Implications for Practice:

What Works!
☼ Patience and humor
☼ Checklists
☼ Time outs
☼ Logical consequences
☼ Strategic listening lessons
☼ Modeling manners
☼ Literature
☼ Positive reinforcement
☼ Music
☼ Talking stick
☼ Visuals
☼ Hands-on experiences

Common Threads (of effective strategies)
♪ Entertaining—read-alouds, videos, singing, hands-on experiences
♪ Positive reinforcement
♪ Negative consequences

Source: Used with permission of Gail Ritchie.

Figure 6.7 Inquiry Brochure Example 2

One-Stop Shopping for Resources and Communication

The use of Blackboard (FCPS 24-7 Learning) with teachers and parents

Fairfax County Public Schools

What did we do?

- Established a Blackboard (FCPS 24-7 Learning) Plan for the school
- Established procedures for how FCPS 24-7 Learning is used
- Reviewed Blackboard plan with staff; encouraged feedback
- Trained teachers and staff on the use of FCPS 24-7 Learning
- Required all teachers to maintain a class site with specific areas that would be consistent from year to year
- Created and maintained a staff site to model the use of Blackboard and provide a teacher resource and on-line community for teacher collaboration
- Used the Discussion Board for all staff communication, including Staff News, Committee Minutes, and Office Communications
- Required staff to read Marzano's *Classroom Instruction that Works* and participate in an *On-line Discussion*
- Administered surveys and held a focus group discussion with teachers
- Reviewed course statistics to analyze use and trends

What did we find out?

- Establishing a "must use" policy encouraged teachers to go to Blackboard to access information
- Establishing an on-line discussion provided opportunities for teachers who would not normally collaborate with each other (vertical articulation)
- Accessing the staff site daily encourages teachers to begin using, maintaining, and promoting their own sites
- Making Blackboard useful to the teachers encourages them to access this resource. The design has to be clearly laid out and intuitive. If there is difficulty finding information teachers will discontinue use of the site
- Having the KP administrators model the use of Blackboard, increased teachers' use of Blackboard for parent communication
- Administrators were instrumental in the transition from Outlook public folders to FCPS 24-7 Learning
- Not all students were able to access 24-7 Learning from home
- Next year, we will continue with our Staff Site and work toward having students access their class site from school

FCPS 24-7 LEARNING

To what extent does Blackboard (FCPS 24-7 Learning) create effective communication between staff and administrators and provide a one-stop shopping location for teacher resources?

Kings Park Elementary School
Michelle Crabill, SBTS
michelle.crabill@fcps.edu
Kathleen Walts, principal
kathleen.walts@fcps.edu
Sheila Walker, assistant principal
sheila.walker@fcps.edu
703-426-7000

The First Steps

- Create a school Blackboard Plan
- Create an online staff site
- Enroll all teachers and staff
- Have administrators move ALL communications to Blackboard (FCPS 24-7 Learning), posting important messages in the Announcements section of the site, etc
- Organize the site to meet the needs of the school staff. Highlights of our site include:
  - *Instructional Resources*—with on-line resources and lesson ideas
  - *KP Documents*
  - *KP Forms*
  - *KP ROAR (our weekly newsletter)*
  - *Staff Directory*
  - *Links to the Instructional Gateways*

A Parent/Teacher Communication Tool

- Teachers attended trainings as needed to create Blackboard site (FCPS 24-7 Learning)
- Teacher created and maintained a classroom site for communication with parents and students
- Required areas on teacher sites:
  - *Teacher Contact information*
  - *Weekly Announcements*
  - *Assignments including Word Study, Homework, or projects*
  - *Class Information including Newsletter, Schedule, Calendars, etc.*
  - *Links to Websites including school site and curriculum resources*
- Teachers updated items on the class sites weekly, monthly, quarterly, and yearly according to the school plan
- At Back-to-School Night, teachers informed the parents of how Blackboard will be used and how to login
- Teachers monitored the use of their class sites through course statistics
- Teachers promoted the use of Blackboard throughout the year in newsletters or other communications
- Blackboard training was held for parents at a PTA meeting

An On-line Community for Teachers

Quick access to:
- Administrator's announcements
- Office Communications
- Staff News
- Memos
- Crisis Plan
- Committee Minutes
- Staff Directory
- Staff Weekly Newsletter
- Links to Instructional Resources
- The Instructional Gateways
- Subject Area postings by committees or curriculum leads
- Discussion Board chat of Marzano Instructional Strategies

Teachers like:
- 24 - 7 access to information
- Collaboration with staff
- Password protected staff information anytime, from anywhere
- "One-stop shopping" for centrally located school and staff resources
- Modelling provided by the administrators

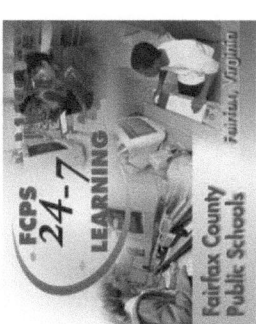

Source: Used with permission of Kings Park Elementary School.

Figure 6.8 Inquiry Template Example

Using Lunch Dates to Break One Student's Silence

Wondering

How do we foster Maria's self-expression?

Data Collection

- Consulted guidance counselor, outside psychologist, & parents
- Recorded contents of lunch dates
- Recorded observation notes throughout school day
- Collected writing samples

Intervention Description

A few days per week, Maria ate lunch with us in the classroom. She was encouraged to invite any classmates. We had games, books, drawing materials, as well as cartoons available. The goal was to create a comfortable environment to foster communication and expression.

Findings

- Maria is strong academically despite her fear and avoidance of communication.

  * progress reports, Honor Roll, Aim High, high reading group

- Yes or No questions are received by Maria with a greater response rate than open-ended questions.

  * She asked Maria if she had any brothers or sisters. Maria shook her head no. Teresa said, "Aw, man you're lucky!" Teresa asked Maria what she did over Spring Break. Maria did not answer and just stared. Mary asked if she played outside. Maria shook her head no. Mary said, "Don't tell me you stayed inside the whole week?!" Maria nodded yes.

- Maria appears less apprehensive around the few students in the class who don't expect her to remain silent.

  * Jeanet asked each student in her group to name something they noticed in the picture. When it was Maria's turn, she looked at the picture and her lips quivered as if to speak. Barbara said, "She's shy." Maria looked away from the picture.
  * Teresa turned to Maria and asked, "Was your name called?" Maria shook her head yes. Teresa said "Yay!" and put her hand up for Maria to give her a high-five. Maria hesitated greatly and then gave Teresa a high-five.

Source: Used with permission of Sheila Walker.

Figure 6.9 Critical Features for Presenting and Writing Up Your Inquiry

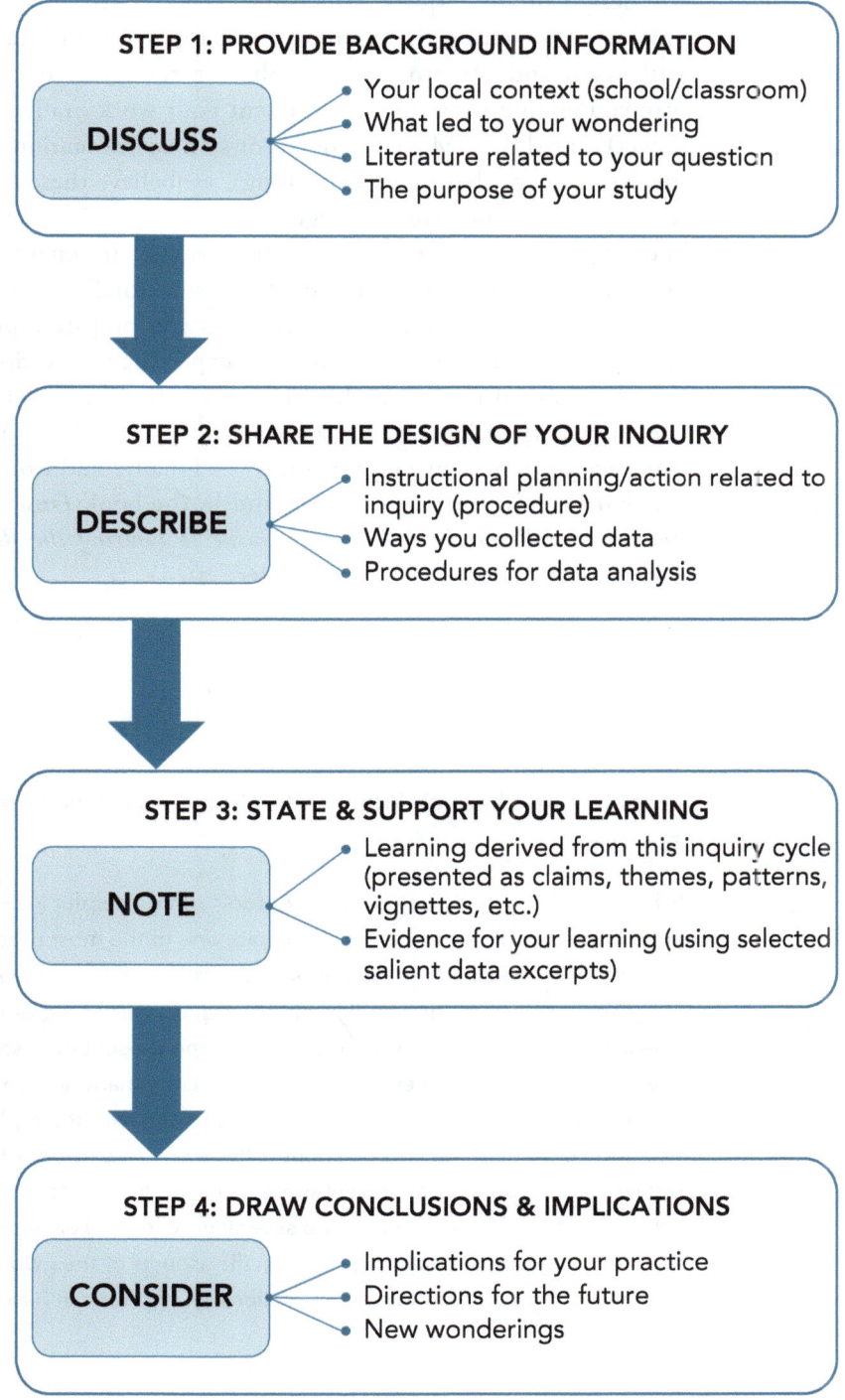

While Julie's work is but one example, we selected it for the poignant way she developed four critical features of any write-up or sharing: (1) providing background information, (2) sharing the design of the inquiry (procedures, data collection, and data analysis), (3) stating the learning and supporting the statements with data, and (4) providing concluding thoughts. In whatever way you choose to write up or present your work orally (posters, PowerPoint slides, iMovie, podcast, or some combination of these mechanisms for sharing your learning), we believe these four critical features (summarized in Figure 6.9 on page 313) can inform and help you shape this process. Furthermore, in whatever form you choose to write up or present your work orally, AI can once again serve as a helpful, critical friend as you prepare a presentation and/or write about your inquiry experience. (See this chapter's AI Moment textbox authored by our colleague Tom Dana, at the University of Florida, for some specific ways AI can help you improve your presenting and writing.) Finally, additional ideas for sharing your inquiry can be found in the book *Disseminating Your Action Research: A Practical Guide to Sharing the Results of Practitioner Research,* by Craig Mertler (2024).

AI MOMENT

Preparing to Share an Inquiry With Some Assistance From AI
Tom Dana

Whether sharing orally or in writing, AI tools can be helpful in preparing your inquiry for presentation. For example, one of the most used AI features to assist with presentation preparation that you already likely benefit from are basic editing tools such as spell and grammar checking that are built into common writing and presentation software like Microsoft Word, PowerPoint, Canva, and Grammarly, just to name a few. These editing features are quickly improving with the rapid evolution of AI, and the improvements offer many new options for refining writing and visual presentations. A newer Microsoft product, called Copilot, kicks AI functions up several notches and allows the inquirer to conversationally dig into specific aspects of their work. Similar to the kinds of inquiry conversations an inquirer can have with

ChatGPT shared in previous AI Moment textboxes, conversations with Copilot can help an inquirer create and refine both oral and written research presentations, serving as a critical friend throughout the sharing component of the inquiry process.

Before you begin enlisting some AI assistance in sharing your inquiry, remember that bots such as ChatGPT and Copilot are not always right. They should be considered a knowledgeable friend to *help you* think about your inquiry and how you might share what you have learned, *not to do the work* of sharing preparation *for you*. There is value in having a conversation with more than one chatbot if available to you, as using different AI tools can result in different responses. Similar conversations with different chatbots that result in different responses can push you to think critically about your work, evaluate the clarity regarding information you share, and gain insight into what details might be missing, excessive, and/or confusing to others—all necessary to prepare a coherent presentation.

Convincing presentations are clear, concise, and geared toward a specific audience. They also are visually compelling. AI tools, such as GPT and DALL-E, help generate text and unique images, both of which can be beneficial to a presentation.

When using an AI bot to assist in preparing a presentation, start by describing your work to the chatbot as you would a colleague, providing contextual and specific information you think is important about each component of your inquiry journey. As an alternative to typing directly into the AI input box, most AI tools also allow for file upload and speech-to-text recognition. Uploading a file of some or all written work completed for inquiry sharing purposes can expedite the conversation. Common file types accepted in most bots include Word, PDFs, and jpg images. Be sure to pay attention to ethical standards regarding sharing information. Verify that you are avoiding revealing specific student data, names, and identifiable images in everything you upload.

Here are some useful ways AI can serve as your "Inquiry Sharing Assistant" after uploading a draft of your work:

(1) Ask the chatbot to review your work to check basic organization, spelling, and grammar, if not already done. Some standard word processing programs can support you in these tasks.

(Continued)

(Continued)

> The conversation with the chatbot, however, might assist in constructing a better written product since it's drawing from many sources across the internet in editing your work.

(2) Ask the bot to create a summary or abstract of your work. While reviewing the summary, revisit your full presentation to ensure your inquiry's problem of practice, wondering(s), process, and findings are clear. Reading the summary and revisiting the full presentation are part of an iterative process in deciding what could be explained better.

(3) Similar to a summary, ask the bot to create an outline of your work. An AI-generated outline can help you determine the extent to which the outline captures the key ideas you are attempting to communicate. If the outline generated from your work by your AI Assistant is not what you were expecting, you can revise your presentation through a continuing conversation with the bot, and as revisions are made, have the bot generate new outlines for your review to check for improvement. Furthermore, if you have conversed with your bot to generate a summary previously, you can compare the outline to the summary for consistency and use both outline and summary in sharing your inquiry, as a tight outline and summary are essential for clearly communicating the highlights of your inquiry journey to others.

The above uses of AI tools should result in a document, abstract, and outline you strongly feel represent your work and get the point across to a specific audience. Both an abstract and an outline are also beneficial in preparing a simplified written version of your inquiry to hand out to others. You can also get an assist from AI if you would like support in generating a newsletter or other type of handout, or even in the generation of a webpage. In his book *Disseminating Your Action Research: A Practical Guide to Sharing the Results of Practitioner Research*, Mertler (2024) notes that:

> Personal websites are a fantastic way to share the results of your practitioner research. One of the benefits of a personal website is that you can customize it to appear exactly the way you want—and you can choose what you want to include on your site. Your website could be as simple as one page where

you house basic information and resources for those who visit your site, or it could be a more comprehensive site where you have different pages that provide different types of resources. I have seen examples of practitioners' websites where they have pages for sharing things like research projects, but also have pages where they provide resources for their students, parents, or colleagues. (p. 144)

A more common method of sharing is with an oral presentation accompanied by slides. The outline generated earlier can be enormously helpful in a presentation product such as PowerPoint. The newest versions of PowerPoint have powerful AI features built in, and you can seek tutorials, perhaps on YouTube, to learn the best features for your purpose. As just one example, within PowerPoint is the "Designer" function where an inquirer can paste the outline onto slides and then have PowerPoint use its built-in AI Designer tools to create layouts and enhancements aligned to the content on each slide derived from your outline. Many modification features are available to really make the visual component of the presentation your own.

There are many more tools available to support the sharing phase of teacher inquiries than the ones named in this AI Moment. Inquirers may want to check with the IT departments at their schools to determine what tools are available. By leveraging AI tools, teacher inquirers can not only streamline the sharing process but also elevate the impact of their sharing for specific audiences.

Reference

Mertler, C. (2024). *Disseminating your action research: A practical guide to sharing the results of practitioner research.* Routledge.

Step 1: Providing Background Information

A strong way to begin your writing is to provide background information. Sharing your context, what led you to this particular study, how it is connected to others' thinking about the topic of your inquiry, and what processes you used to gain insights into a particular wondering provide a foundation for your audience to understand your work and to make judgments as to its transferability to their own teaching situation. Here, we reprint Julie's introduction to her work that was previously shared as an example of finding your wondering at the intersection of your personal and professional identities in Chapter 2.

This time as you read this excerpt, notice how Julie helped the reader understand who she was as a teacher and person ("My goal as a teacher is to help children become lifelong learners who can think critically about the world around them and create and articulate their own ideas"), what was occurring in her own classroom ("Some children wrote independently and produced several pages of text during each workshop. Others wrote one sentence at a time and frequently approached me to ask, 'Am I done yet?'"), what was occurring in the field ("As I studied children's writing development, I realized that the range of writing behaviors in my classroom was common"), what was occurring in her district ("My mentor . . . spoke to many of the children about working toward meeting the district's benchmark for writing by the end of the school year"), and what was occurring in her own teaching ("I began to doubt my ability to provide my students with writing instruction that would help them meet the district's writing goals and that would inspire them to enjoy writing"). Through her writing, Julie shows how all of these components coalesced to lead to this particular inquiry.

> I can still remember every detail of the moment when I became a writer. The warm August air sticks to my skin, powdery chalk dust tickles my nose, and the comforting sounds of my mother making dinner fill my ears whenever I begin to put words on a page. I found my voice as a writer the summer before second grade. I was six years old, and my older sister had suddenly decided that she was too mature to play with me. She would disappear with her friends, and I was left to fill the long summer days without her. One afternoon, I wandered into the basement and started to draw on an old chalkboard that my sister and I used when we were playing school. After a while, I stopped drawing and began writing poetry. When my mother called me for dinner, she saw my poems and became my first audience. She encouraged my efforts and gave me a small, yellow notebook so I could continue to write. My passion for writing grew as I continued to read quality literature and experienced the powerful ways in which expert authors manipulate language and develop engaging stories. Throughout my life, I have turned to written words to express my thoughts and ideas.

As I developed a teaching philosophy, I realized that my passion for teaching is intertwined with my passion for writing. My goal as a teacher is to help children become lifelong learners who can think critically about the world around them and create and articulate their own ideas. I hope that, by sharing my love for writing with my students, I can help them express the thoughts and opinions that are important and meaningful to them. Therefore, when I pictured my future classroom, I always seemed to arrive during writer's workshop. I assumed that I would be an effective, engaging writing teacher simply because I enjoyed writing. I imagined a classroom filled with eager students who loved writing and could not wait to commit their ideas to paper. I was thrilled to be an intern in a second-grade classroom because I could remember the wonderful writing experiences I had during my own second-grade year.

As I began my internship experience, I helped provide writing instruction for a group of second graders with differing strengths, needs, and interests. I quickly realized that teaching writing is extremely complicated. Some children wrote independently and produced several pages of text during each workshop. Others wrote one sentence at a time and frequently approached me to ask, "Am I done yet?" I often sat with a small group of students who struggled to get their thoughts down on paper. As I tried to keep these children on task and encourage them to continue writing, I asked questions and made story maps. At the end of many writing sessions, I felt uncomfortable with the amount of support I was giving to some young writers. Several children who were quite capable of writing independently often came to me and asked, "Can I write with you?" I worried that I was allowing some children to become too dependent on my help and that my influence was hindering the flow of their ideas.

As I studied children's writing development, I realized that the range of writing behaviors in my classroom was common for second graders. I felt relief when I read the experts' descriptions of second-grade writers and realized they mirrored my feelings about the young writers in my classroom. Some children write "fluently" and approach writing with "carefree confidence" (Calkins, 1986, p. 67). These children write long, detailed narratives with ease. Other children seem to erase more than they write. Second graders are beginning to become "aware of an audience" for their writing, and the "easy confidence" they felt as first

(Continued)

(Continued)

graders often turns into their first cases of "writer's block" (Calkins, 1986, p. 68). They are concerned about approaching tasks in the "right way," and that vulnerability makes writing a difficult and painstaking process for many children (Calkins, 1986, p. 69). Therefore, writing instruction in second grade must address this wide range of writing behaviors.

During the students' goal-setting conferences in the beginning of the school year, my mentor, Linda Witmer, spoke to many of the children about working toward meeting the district's benchmark for writing by the end of the year. According to this benchmark, the students must be able to write stories with beginnings, middles, and endings. These stories should be understandable and must include characters, settings, and major events. The students are also expected to include some descriptive language, use some punctuation and capitalization, and spell the district benchmark words correctly. The students must complete the writing assessment independently. After winter break, Linda and I were both concerned about our students' writing. As I looked through the students' work, I noticed that extremely capable children were often scoring below the benchmark. Many of the children were still writing incomplete stories, and endings were particularly difficult for many students. Although our students had wonderful, creative ideas, we worried that several of them would not meet the district's benchmark for writing because they did not take the reader on a complete journey from beginning to middle to end.

My initial experiences as a writing teacher were frustrating. After years of imagining myself as an effective writing teacher, I was dismayed when I realized that my efforts were not helping my students meet their writing goals. In some cases, I worried that I was doing more harm than good because my attempts to help often became persistent prompting that drowned out the students' voices in their own writing. I was heartbroken when students resisted writing, because I was so eager to share my passion for stories and language. When I conducted a survey to collect data about the students' attitudes toward writing, I was concerned when I realized that many children thought that they were good writers because of neat handwriting, good spelling, or using time wisely. Although those skills are important, I noticed that most children did not mention that they were proud of their ability to create stories. Gradually, I began to doubt my ability to provide my students with writing instruction that would help them meet the district's writing goals and that would inspire them to enjoy writing. My passion for writing, which I believed would be an asset in the classroom, actually hindered my progress as a writing teacher because I struggled to relate to and communicate with students who resisted writing. As I studied writing instruction, I learned that teachers' personal experiences with the subject matter influence the way they teach their students (Frank, 1979). I realized that, because I had positive writing experiences as a child, I had naively assumed that all of my second graders would react to writing with similar enthusiasm.

My passion for writing and teaching, as well as my frustrations with the realities of teaching writing, led me to my wonderings. I wanted to do a project that would focus on my students' development as writers and would also help me develop as a writing teacher. Therefore, I began my project with the following wonderings:

- Will my second graders write more complete stories if the elements of a story are broken down into a series of mini-lessons?

- Will my second graders become more independent writers and gain confidence in their writing abilities if my expectations for their writing are more explicit?

- Will collaborating with other learners help my students grow as writers?

- Will my students grow as writers if the lessons include opportunities to make connections between children's literature and their own stories?

- Will these changes in writing instruction improve the way my students feel about themselves as writers and the way I feel about myself as a writing teacher? (Russell, 2002)

This lengthy excerpt from Julie's inquiry provides contextualization for the audience, and this contextualization prepares the audience to understand Julie's particular approach to her work.

Step 2: Sharing the Design of the Inquiry (Procedures, Data Collection, and Data Analysis)

A key feature that sets inquiry apart from the daily reflection teachers engage in is that it is conducted in a systematic, intentional way. Hence, sharing your system (what you did), as well as your intentions (how you did what you did—data collection and analysis), is important. In the next excerpt, notice how Julie discusses her instructional plan for this inquiry and the ways she collected data. Also notice how she articulates the ways that data collection and analysis interacted with each other as her plan of action for instruction changed over time.

> Once I developed my wonderings, I began studying both primary students' writing development and methods for writing instruction. I read resource books written by primary teachers that included actual lesson plans and anecdotes about students and their writing. I also read books by researchers who focused more on theories about writing development. I looked through my students' portfolios to learn about the problems they faced when they were writing stories. My students completed a survey that focused on their attitudes toward writing and about themselves as writers.
>
> As I began my project, the primary division at my school was beginning the Land of Make-Believe unit. The unit fit well with my wonderings because it is language arts–intensive and includes many examples of quality children's literature. I used some fairy tales from the unit as well as stories that were recommended in my other resources to develop a series of five literature-based mini-lessons. As I developed my lessons, I often referred to Susan Lunsford's (1998) *Literature-Based Mini-Lessons to Teach Writing*. Lunsford advocates using children's literature to teach writing because the literature gives students examples of how expert authors deal with the problems that all writers face. I wanted my students to believe that they were capable, valuable members of a community of writers that includes published authors. I hoped that, by using quality children's literature in my lessons, I would be able to have discussions with my students about effective writing. Once the strategies in the literature were articulated, I hoped that the children would begin to apply them in their own stories.

Initially, I planned to teach lessons about character, setting, problem, solution, and complete stories. Each lesson followed the same basic format. As a large group, the students and I read and discussed sections of children's literature that exemplified the story element we were studying. We brainstormed ideas that the students could use in their own writing. Then, the students were expected to apply the story element we studied by writing their own stories. I prepared rubrics for each story element. The rubrics were designed so that the writer, a peer, and a teacher could evaluate the way the writer used a particular story element in his or her story. I also scored the stories using the district's rubric so that the students and I could monitor our progress toward the benchmark for second grade.

As I interacted with the children and looked at my data, I changed some aspects of my lessons based on my developing understandings of effective writing instruction and second-graders' needs and abilities. After my first two workshops, I was extremely dissatisfied with my project. When I began the setting workshop, one child asked, "Do we have to write a whole story *again*?" The students' reluctance to write disturbed me, because I was so anxious to help them enjoy and look forward to writing. The class discussion at the beginning of the setting workshop was also quite discouraging for me because the children did not remember the concepts we had studied during the character workshop the week before. When I planned the workshops, I intended to help the students build a concept of a complete story by studying one element at a time. For this plan to work, the students had to transfer the concepts from one workshop to the next. After discussing my concerns with my mentor and my supervisor, I decided to back up and change the structure of the workshops. I planned three workshops on beginnings, middles, and endings, and then a final workshop on complete stories. During the beginning, middle, and ending workshops, the students needed to write only the story element we discussed on that particular day. This change shortened the students' writing time to about 20 minutes and made the workshops more focused and less stressful. During the final workshop, the students were expected to put all of the elements together and write complete stories without assistance.

(Continued)

(Continued)

Throughout the workshops, I took notes about the students' behaviors, my supervisor scripted class discussions, and I wrote journal entries about each lesson. These texts provided me with data about my students' growth as writers and my growth as a writing teacher. After the series of writer's workshops, I gave the students the same survey that they had completed before the workshops to collect data about their attitudes toward writing and about themselves as writers. I compared the pre-surveys and the post-surveys and looked for changes in the students' opinions. I also interviewed four children who had different writing abilities and styles to learn more about their reactions to various aspects of the writer's workshops. Finally, I looked at the students' work to determine whether or not my lessons had been effective. As I examined my data, several claims about writing and writing instruction emerged (Russell, 2002).

Step 3: Stating the Learning and Supporting the Statements With Data

With detailed knowledge of the "how" of the inquiry, the audience is now ready to understand Julie's findings, which she presents as "claims." As Julie engaged in the process of writing this report of her inquiry, she clarified her thinking by choosing words and phrases that carefully reflect and represent her learnings in this form. As Julie began writing and developing each claim, she also realized that her claims could be organized into four conceptual categories. She did a lot of cutting and pasting as she organized and reorganized for the reader. In the absence of the process of writing it up, Julie would not have taken her work to this organizational level and not realized the extent of her own learning. The four categories and claims associated with each category she generated as she wrote about her work were the following:

- **Category 1: Student Growth**
  - *Claim 1:* The series of six writer's workshops that focused on the parts of stories helped several of my second graders write stories that reached the district benchmark for writing.

- **Category 2: Setting Expectations**
  - *Claim 2:* Inappropriate expectations discouraged many of the learners in my classroom and hindered my effectiveness as a writing teacher.
  - *Claim 3:* My students were my most valuable resource as I created developmentally appropriate expectations.
  - *Claim 4:* Rubrics were helpful for some students, but they were not effective for other students.
- **Category 3: Collaboration**
  - *Claim 5:* Collaborating with others helped some students develop ideas and grow as writers.
  - *Claim 6:* Other students found that collaborating was ineffective for them as writers.
- **Category 4: Connections to Literature**
  - *Claim 7:* Students who make connections between writing and literature can use literature to help them solve problems when they are writing.
  - *Claim 8:* Students who are immersed in literature incorporate more literary language in their writing.
  - *Claim 9:* Students who read from a writer's perspective are comfortable thinking critically about literature.
  - *Claim 10:* The students in Room 20 are members of a writing community that includes published authors.

In the next passage from Julie's inquiry write-up, notice how Julie states each of these claims and builds an argument to support her claim by providing evidence with excerpts and vignettes from her data. When you write, in essence you are building an argument that is not unlike a district attorney building a case to prosecute a defendant. A case built on only one piece of evidence would never go to trial. The attorney must piece together a string of evidence to create a strong case. The same is true for a teacher inquirer. In presenting and sharing findings, the teacher inquirer pieces together a string of evidence to support statements of his or her learning. The case is stronger when evidence is provided from multiple sources. As you read, notice how Julie weaves data excerpts from multiple sources (scripted field notes by her supervisor, her own journal entries, student work, student surveys, interviews, and literature about children's writing) throughout the discussion of each claim.

STUDENT GROWTH

The series of six writer's workshops that focused on the parts of stories helped several of my second graders write stories that reached the district benchmark for writing.

As I looked through the students' portfolios at the beginning of my project, I noticed that the students who were scoring below the benchmark were not writing complete stories. They often had creative ideas and wonderful language, but they did not include crucial parts of the story. Endings were, by far, the most difficult story element for my students. Many children seemed to grow tired by the time they reached the end of their stories. They would write a few quick sentences that did not explain how the problem was solved just so they could be done. Other children had difficulty organizing their thoughts. They would write down their ideas without planning their stories, so their plots were scattered and their endings were not related to the rest of their stories.

As I planned the writing activity for the first workshop, I used my mentor's guidance to make the task similar to the district's writing assessment. After our read-aloud and our discussion about characters, I gave the students two titles. Each child had to choose one of the titles and write a story based on the title they chose. This writing activity was independent. The children had to work quietly and write their entire stories in one session.

When I scored these stories using the district's rubric, my data were consistent with my observations of the students' portfolios. Seventeen of my 18 second graders were present and wrote stories during our first writer's workshop. Of those 17 children, 11 scored below the district's benchmark because their stories were incomplete. As I looked through my comments on the stories, I noticed that 10 of the 11 stories that did not reach the benchmark lacked endings. Several stories also needed more detail in the middle to make the problems or adventures interesting and understandable.

During our sixth and final writer's workshop, the students were expected to put all of the elements of a story together. Their complete stories were eventually stapled inside paper castles the children made and decorated. As a class, we discussed the essential elements of a complete story. Then, we brainstormed various beginnings, middles, and endings that made sense with our castle theme. The students were allowed to collaborate with their partners as they were planning their stories. My mentor, my supervisor, and I helped students organize their ideas and kept them on task. However, most of the children wrote their stories independently.

When I compared the stories from the last workshop to the stories from the first workshop, I was pleased to see that 15 of the 17 students that were present for the last workshop were able to meet the district benchmark for writing. When I checked the final scores of the 11 children who did not meet the benchmark during the first workshop, I noticed that 8 of them were able to meet the benchmark. Two children did not meet the benchmark because their stories lacked effective endings. One child did not participate in the final writing activity because he was absent on that day. The students who were meeting the district's benchmark when I began my project continued to experience success. In fact, as the workshops progressed, two children raised their scores above the benchmark by incorporating dazzling language and engaging plots in their work.

After examining the students' work throughout my workshops, I can claim that the mini-lessons and writing activities that I developed were effective for many struggling writers. Several students linger at the borderline. They are not yet consistent in their abilities to create complete stories independently. However, many children did experience remarkable growth in only six lessons, and they made important progress toward meeting their writing goals for second grade.

Setting Expectations

Inappropriate expectations discouraged many of the learners in my classroom and hindered my effectiveness as a writing teacher.

During my initial planning for my project, I was overflowing with ideas. After several years of imagining my own approach to writing instruction, I had an opportunity to actually implement some of my own lessons. I collected children's literature, planned discussion questions, made charts for brainstorming, and developed rubrics. I pushed the students to write entire stories during a single session. I was incredibly enthusiastic and I got carried away.

By my second workshop, I was feeling quite discouraged. I was trying to generate excitement and creativity, and even my

(Continued)

(Continued)

most capable writers were starting to grumble and complain. The children became fidgety and distracted during the lengthy discussions. They resisted the writing activities. The rubrics that I provided were either ignored or filled in hastily and without much reflection. The stories were not improving and none of us seemed to be having fun.

The setting workshop was discouraging from the beginning. When I asked the students what they had learned in the previous workshop, they remembered that they "drew pictures of what [they] imagined in [their] minds" and discussed "picture painting words" (scripted notes, Feb. 21). However, I had to question them for several minutes before anyone mentioned characters, which had been the focus of the lesson. After this review I did a read-aloud, we drew pictures, I led a discussion, we brainstormed some ideas, I read another story, and we brainstormed again. The lesson was lengthy and, to be honest, quite boring. At one point, a student asked, "Can we go back and write?" I continued with my failing lesson even though the children were clearly telling me that my efforts were not helping them.

My frustration was evident in my journal entry. As I reflected on the setting workshop, I wrote, "I think I tried to pile too much into the morning. Their attention just could not last through all of the activities I had planned. I think my problems teaching really showed up in the children's writing, because only a few of them really described their settings in their stories." When my lessons were not developmentally appropriate, my students could sense my frustration and they got the message that writing was boring and confusing. For the first time, I began to realize that my personal experiences with writing as a young child were challenges rather than assets for me as a writing teacher. I always enjoyed writing and, in elementary school, I sought out extra opportunities to put my thoughts on paper. This passion for writing has certainly enriched my life, but it creates difficulties when I am attempting to relate to a student who does not share my enthusiasm. At the beginning of my project, I truly struggled to approach writing with a second-graders' needs and abilities in mind, and my students responded to my first few lessons with boredom and confusion.

My students were my most valuable resource as I created developmentally appropriate expectations.

As I discussed my plans and my concerns with Linda (my mentor) and Nancy (my supervisor), I began to realize that I was not truly giving the students a fair chance to practice each story part because they had to write an entire story after each lesson.

Therefore, we decided to break apart our next story and write it one piece at a time. This change would lighten the workload, shorten the work time, and give us more time to practice and reflect on each story element. As I planned, I kept thinking about the student who groaned, "Do we have to write a whole story *again*?" Above all, I wanted my students to enjoy writing and to feel successful as writers. Therefore, I needed to pay attention when they gave me warnings that they were feeling frustrated and overwhelmed.

When I shortened the mini-lessons and made my writing expectations more appropriate for second graders, I felt much more effective as a writing teacher because I was giving my students (and myself) a chance to feel successful. I noticed that the students were more attentive during the lessons and they were more willing to write. I did not hear any grumbling or complaining about writing one section of a story, and several students actually wanted more time than I gave them to write.

I understand writing as a writer, but I do not understand it as well from a writing teacher's perspective. As I continue to meet and work with new students, I must develop strategies for deciding what types of expectations are developmentally appropriate for them as writers. During my project, I quickly learned that "children can provide important data about their own learning" (Avery, 1993, p. 420). The students were sending me urgent messages with their grumbling, their body language, their writing, and their responses to me.

When I compared the students' presurveys to their postsurveys, I noticed a few patterns. During the presurvey, when the students were asked about their favorite kind of writing, many children mentioned writing activities such as Child of the Week, math journals, and science papers. As I read these responses, I was confronted with one of my biases. When I think of writing, I automatically think of stories. The students' responses reminded me that various genres of writing are integrated into every part of our day and these different kinds of writing experiences allow students with different strengths and needs to shine. As a teacher, I need to open my mind to the various styles

(Continued)

(Continued)

of and purposes for writing so that I can engage all of my students in writing activities that give them opportunities to express their ideas and opinions.

When I read about the students' most and least favorite parts of writing on the postsurveys, I noticed that several students enjoyed coming up with ideas, but that they considered writing the words tedious and difficult. As I worked on this project, I began to realize that asking a young child to write a complete story is a daunting request. First, they must think of an idea and develop that idea until it has a beginning, a middle, and an end. Then, they must organize their thoughts and hold them in their minds long enough to get them on paper in sequence. These steps are quite difficult alone, but the task is more difficult for students who struggle with spelling, grammar, and letter formation. I am not surprised that children become frustrated when they have wonderful ideas and they have to endure the painstaking process of committing those ideas to paper. I was encouraged, however, when several children stated that they enjoyed developing ideas for their own original stories.

I found other evidence in the surveys that indicated that the writer's workshops helped some students become more confident about their writing ability. On his presurvey, one child wrote, "My least favorite part of writing is the ending because I do not like to solve the problem." When I interviewed this child, he told me that he struggled with endings and he thought that studying endings in our reading group was helpful. When I read his postsurvey, I was pleased to see that he wrote, "I like all of them the same because they are fun to do." On the postsurveys, some children were able to articulate their favorite parts of writing by using the language we used during our discussions. For example, one student wrote, "My favorite part of writing is the middles of stories because I like to make up adventures in my stories."

As a writer, I tend to be quite emotional about my work and I judge my writing based on the way I feel about it. I was fascinated when I realized that some children look at writing in a very quantitative way. When I asked them whether they were good writers, some children consistently relied on tangible evidence to support their answers. On his presurvey, a student wrote, "I think I am a good writer because I already have a published book." After the workshops were over, this student used a similar tool to measure his progress. He wrote, "I think I am a good writer because I am already working on my hardback," on his postsurvey. Other children used the scores on their stories to prove that they were good writers.

When I read one postsurvey, I became quite concerned. The student wrote that she was not a good writer because she "can't think of ideas." This response came from a child who often says that she "hates school." She resists assignments and, although she is extremely capable, she works slowly and her writing and coloring are sloppy. When I helped this student write the story that would be published in her hardback book, she would not put words down on paper unless I repeatedly prompted her. She told me her entire story, and then when I asked her what she wanted to write next, she said, "I don't know." This student is an excellent reader, and she can put wonderful language in her stories. However, her writing is often disorganized and difficult to understand. When I reviewed my comments from her portfolio and from the four stories she wrote during my writer's workshops, I consistently wrote that the parts of her stories did not relate and, therefore, her stories were not understandable and her endings did not solve the problem. I was not surprised that this student reacted negatively to writing because she has a similar reaction to most activities at school. However, I am concerned because she transferred her criticisms from the activity to herself. After she turned in her survey, I pulled her aside and told her about some aspects of her writing that I really enjoy. She just shrugged her shoulders and repeated, "I don't like it." The other students seem to either enjoy or accept writing. They are beginning to see themselves as part of a community of writers. I worry that this one student will be isolated from that community if I cannot find a way to motivate her as a writer.

Rubrics were helpful for some students, but they were not effective for other students.

When I created the rubrics for each of my lessons, I hoped that they would help the students organize their thoughts and remember the important ideas from my lessons. As I reflected on the writer's workshops in my journal, I wrote the following:

> Although the children seem to understand the parts of stories during our discussions and they seem to try to apply them in their own writing, the rubrics do not seem to be very

(Continued)

(Continued)

>meaningful. The children do not refer to the rubrics during their writing unless I continually prompt them, and they often just race through it at the end of their writing as an afterthought. However, I still think they should be able to see the goals clearly before, during, and after writing if they are expected to meet those goals in their stories.

Nancy helped me take a more critical look at the rubrics I had created. I divided each story element into three parts. In each of the three sections I included the main concept and then a few notes or questions that I considered prompts. I thought that these details would encourage the students' thinking, but they actually seemed to overwhelm the children and make them unsure of whether they had met each goal. I could tell that the rubrics were not helpful because I often found them left carelessly on the floor. During the third workshop, a student approached me with his rubric and asked, "What's this for?" My rubrics were not a useful resource for the children because the way that I thought about stories and the ways that they thought about stories were different. I needed to find a way to present the expectations for the story elements in a way that was meaningful for each of my second-graders.

Then, while I was visiting my mother's first-grade classroom, she showed me a rubric that another first-grade class had created. The teacher listed scores from zero to six, and the children determined the characteristics of a story that would receive each score. The children had expressed their expectations in clear, simple terms. For example, a child who received a zero "did not write." These young writers knew that they were making decisions as they wrote and that those decisions had consequences for their writing. By asking students to articulate the decisions they make as they write, teachers are encouraging awareness. "Self-awareness leads to self-evaluation and, in turn, thoughtful decision making" (Avery, 1993, p. 417). I decided that my learners should be invited to be a part of setting the expectations that I was using to evaluate their stories. I hoped that, by being a part of creating the expectations, the students would feel more ownership and would begin to use the rubrics more thoughtfully.

During the fifth writer's workshop, my students and I focused on endings. After we discussed endings and the students wrote endings for their stories, I told the students that we were going to put together what we had learned about the different parts of stories. I said that the list they created during our discussion would be the checklist for their castle stories the next week. I took notes as the students suggested ideas, and I was amazed by how much information they had gathered about stories. As I recorded their ideas, I tried to use their words so that I would not add my influence to their expectations. When I created the checklist for the complete story workshop, I used the students' ideas. The expectations were expressed in clear, concise phrases. Hearing the students articulate their ideas helped me begin to understand the way an appropriate expectation for a second-grade writer should sound and look.

During the complete story workshop, I did not notice that the students used the checklists more or less than before. When I interviewed a small group of students, I invited them to compare a rubric that I wrote and the rubric that they wrote. I asked, "Did one of these checklists help you more, or were they both about the same?" One child replied, "The complete story checklist helped more because it helped you do a whole story in one day really quick." The students did not seem to care that they had written one rubric and I had written the other. I think that the students would have felt more ownership if they had been involved in creating the rubrics throughout the series of workshops. When I asked them to share their expectations for the last workshop, they basically reiterated the ideas I had emphasized during instruction. I am not surprised that they did not think of the checklist as their ideas.

During my interview, I also asked, "Do checklists help you write?" I could not tell simply by observing whether my rubrics had been effective for the students. One child replied, "Yes, because I could check down everything I did. Step by step." Another child agreed by saying, "I think it's good because the first thing I do is look at it and it says 'dazzling first sentence,' so I just think of one." Another student responded emphatically. She said, "No, because it makes you think, 'Oh, my story isn't very good, so I have to do better.'" She elaborated, "I like my stories how I like them. I don't like other people judging them just because they think they don't have any detail. I like it the way it is."

Once again, I was reminded of the wide range that characterizes second-grade writers. While one student found comfort in the opportunity to organize his thoughts, another student saw it as a threat

(Continued)

(Continued)

to her as a writer. I began to realize that second-grade teachers need to develop ranges of strategies for teaching writing that are as varied as the unique writers in their rooms.

Collaboration

Collaborating with others helped some students develop ideas and grow as writers.

I was not sure what to expect when I assigned partners and allowed the students to brainstorm with their partners before writing. However, I was anxious to add this type of prewriting to my workshops. According to Calkins (1986), talking is a better form of prewriting for second graders than drawing because their ideas are becoming more detailed and complicated. As the students chat casually about their stories, they focus on content rather than the mechanics of putting their ideas down on paper. This takes the students' attention away from the "right way" to approach their writing and helps them realize that "they have something to say and a voice with which to say it" (Calkins, 1986, p. 70).

I was amazed by the way that my role in the classroom changed when I allowed the students to support each other during writer's workshop. I usually found myself talking with one writer after another. As I traveled around the room, students who were struggling would begin to trail after me with their papers clutched in their hands. I was putting all of my effort into keeping the students' pencils moving, so I didn't have time to have a meaningful discussion with a student who was struggling with writer's block or a complicated idea. When the students brainstormed with their partners, I found that my role was less frantic. I could talk quietly with a student who was concerned about his or her writing. I could eavesdrop on conversations to gain insight into the students' thinking. The students were becoming a community of writers, and they were beginning to realize that the teachers were not the only people in the room who could help them when they encountered problems in their writing.

These partnerships seemed to be the most helpful for students with average writing ability. I enjoyed participating in their conversations and I saw wonderfully creative ideas emerge as the children worked together. When a group of two boys met, they realized that one partner wrote a beginning about a dragon and the other partner wrote a beginning about a knight. They began discussing potential problems for their stories. When I visited their conference, they proudly told me that they were going to use the same problem for their stories. One writer described the problem from the dragon's perspective and the other writer described the problem from the knight's perspective. Another writer was struggling to start his castle story and his partner suggested some ideas that helped him begin. He acknowledged her help by naming the heroine of his story after her.

Other students found that collaborating with others was ineffective for them as writers.

I found that the student partnerships in our room were not very effective for the special needs students or for the most independent, fluent writers. The students who were struggling as writers needed a great deal of support from teachers as they were developing their ideas and as they were putting their ideas on paper. They rarely had time to give each other feedback because they were putting all of their energy into creating their own stories.

The most fluent, independent writers in the classroom were partners during the workshops. During the interview, when I asked about working with partners, Kate replied, "It's fun, but we just have our own ideas. Charlie says something and it kind of gives me an idea, but it doesn't go well with my story. So, then I do another idea. Then, I ask Charlie if he wants to do this idea, but he changes it around, so it gets confusing." When I reviewed my supervisor's notes from watching this team's peer conference, I noticed that they did not really interact. They stated their ideas out loud, but they seemed to ignore each other. These students had their ideas in place, and they did not seem open to considering other ideas.

Finally, during the interview, another student told me that he did not enjoy working with his partner. When I asked him to elaborate, he said, "He always had to go away from me." During several workshops, we had behavior problems with this student's partner. The boys were often separated, so the partnership was not helpful for them.

Connections to Literature

Students who make connections between writing and reading can use literature to help them solve problems when they are writing.

(Continued)

(Continued)

Routman states, "[As teachers] we must immerse our students in outstanding literature every day [to] help them notice how the author has dealt with the topic, genre, organization, setting, mood, word choice, sentence construction, and more" (Routman, 2002, p. 221). Throughout this project, I was amazed by the ways that the students used the literature around them to solve problems in their own writing. When they had difficulty finding ideas, several students turned to literature for inspiration.

Dana wrote a story called "The Knights and the Dragon" shortly after we read *The Paper Bag Princess* by Robert Munsch. In her story, Dana's knights defeated a dragon with clever tricks that resembled the tricks Elizabeth used in *The Paper Bag Princess* (spelling, grammar, and punctuation in these story excerpts are as found):

> Then the knights came out and said is it trew that you can drink 30 gallons of water in only 5 seconds? The dragon said yes so he did. Then the knight said can you fly and stay up for three whole days? The dragon said yes so he did. All those three days he was still up. The dragon was egsasted on the third day.

In her previous story, Dana had difficulty writing an ending that solved her problem. By using Munsch's work as a model, she tackled this problem and was able to bring her story to a satisfying end.

When I read Jack's story, I noticed that he was making connections between writing at school and reading at home. His story, "It All Started Out from an Egg," echoes J. K. Rowling's *Harry Potter and the Sorcerer's Stone*:

> Ocne there was a wizared named Hegred. Hegred found an egg it was relly big so he figrd that it was a dragon's egg. So he took it back to his cottage in the woods and put it over his fire to keep it warm. In 15 days it hatched it was a boy dragon in five day he was bigger than hegred and sarted to nock out the walls and started to blow fire and burning Hegred's house down.

Jack also wrote a retelling of *Cinderella* during another writer's workshop. He has wonderful ideas and excellent language, but he seems to be more comfortable writing when he begins in a familiar place. He raises hermit crabs with his brother and sister, and he often uses the hermit crabs as characters in his stories. By starting with familiar ideas, Jack has gained the confidence to take risks by using more descriptive language and reading his stories to his classmates.

During my inquiry project, my reading group was reading a version of *The Ugly Duckling*. Charlie, a student in my reading group, mentioned his dissatisfaction with the story's message during several group discussions. In *The Ugly Dragon*, Charlie used his voice as a writer to approach issues that made him uncomfortable as a reader:

> Once upon a time in an enchanted forest with surprizes anywhere you went there lurked a kind and friendly dragon. It was raining cats and dogs. She laied 30 eggs. Every egg was silver except one. It was gold. One day when the sun was boiling like an oven the eggs hatched. One after another. All of them looked like the mommy dragon except one. The one had gold scaly skin and cotton white teeth and the eyes were root beer brown. It was very good looking when the sun was shining on its back. All of the other dragons teased him. The one dragon was sweet and kind while the others were mean and furious and greedy.

During reading group discussions, Charlie used the illustrations in *The Ugly Duckling* to argue that the main character was different, not ugly. When I read *The Ugly Dragon,* I noticed that Charlie immediately established that his main character "was very good looking when the sun was shining on its back." Charlie also revised the end of the well-known tale. His ugly dragon met and befriended a giant without having to change his appearance at all. I was surprised and pleased when I noticed that Charlie was connecting reading experiences that happened outside our workshops with his writing. He was truly reading as a writer, and his writing incorporated the insights that he gained as a reader.

Students who are immersed in quality literature incorporate more literary language in their writing.

For me, writing is exciting and empowering because it gives me a chance to put my voice on paper. "Voice is hard to define, but when it's in—or missing from—a piece of writing, you sense it. Writing with voice has richness and sparkle, a distinct human spirit that makes you

(Continued)

(Continued)

feel you know the writer" (Routman, 2002, p. 222). Throughout the series of writer's workshops, I approached the issue of voice with my students by focusing on dazzling language. We searched for dazzling words as we read children's literature, we brainstormed dazzling words as we prepared to write, and we celebrated dazzling words in our peers' stories. I used literature and the checklists to encourage the children to use dazzling first sentences in their beginnings, dazzling action words in their middles, and dazzling feeling words in their endings. I also incorporated the search for dazzling words into my reading group instruction. As they read, the children recorded descriptive language. Then, they chose an interesting word or phrase and studied it more carefully by completing a word web.

The students responded eagerly to this aspect of the writer's workshops. Anna Quindlen's description of her heroine in *Happily Ever After* included the phrase "her eyes were the color of root beer" (Quindlen, 1997). After I read this description to my students, I found similar phrases in at least five stories. I also noticed that the dazzling language appeared in stories written by students with a variety of writing abilities. This aspect of writing seemed to appeal to many of the children, and they wanted their readers to be impressed with their word choices:

"Ok said Mini in her tinest vos"

"One snowy cold day when the snow was falling like little cotten balls deep down in the forist there was a princess named Sofy. Her hair was the color of the sun and her eyes were the color of the sky, and her skin was the most peachiest peach you ever did see"

"that nasty fox came prowling along"

"Then the room groo silent."

As I compared the students' stories throughout the workshops, I also noticed that their language was becoming more literary. During the first workshop, Henry tried to include the descriptive language that was discussed during the mini-lesson. He has many details, but his sentences sound more like a list than a story:

His name was Charlie. Charlie was a boy he was 26 years old and had a little brother named Cameron. Charlie has brown hair and his brother has blond hair.

During the last writer's workshop, Henry wrote a story in which the descriptive language flows more naturally:

> One cold winter day in January there was a feirs dragon named Jack who had an advencher with a knight named Sam. Jack never let a sigal soul past him. Jack liked to practice roring and he liked to go into the casal and burn things like bowlse and pots.

As my students' voices began to emerge in their stories, I noticed a growing enthusiasm for sharing stories with others. When volunteers read their work aloud to the class, the students always made comments about the dazzling language.

Students who read from a writer's perspective are comfortable thinking critically about literature.

Writing can be an extremely intimidating task. Many children approach published literature as "polite guests" because they get the implicit message that printed words cannot be challenged (Calkins, 1986, p. 223). As a writing teacher, I wanted to be very careful about the message that I sent to my students as I shared literature. I hoped that my students would learn to think critically about every text they read, rather than viewing published books as "final and unquestionable" (Calkins, 1986, p. 224). Therefore, during the mini-lessons I encouraged the students to respond to the literature with both praise and criticism.

Throughout the series of mini-lessons, I noticed that the students' comments were becoming more and more sophisticated. They were thinking about the choices that the authors made, and they were becoming more comfortable sharing their opinions about the effectiveness of the authors' writing. Their comments became more thoughtful during literature discussions, student sharings, and reading groups:

> When people start to read it, they don't want to stop.

> I would recommend this book to others because it teaches you a lesson. Don't be mean to others just because they are different.

> He didn't name the characters. He just called them prince and princess. I think it would be good if they had names.

(Continued)

(Continued)

> I'd say he needs to work more on the descriptive action words.
>
> I would not recommend this story to another reader because the author didn't put a lot of detail at the end.
>
> I think it's good because it's like a mystery. You want to see what happens next. (Scripted notes, March 14)

During the final writer's workshop, I realized that my students had become quite comfortable thinking critically about published literature. I wanted to practice using the complete story checklist with the whole group, so I read *Cabbage Rose* by M. C. Helldorfer and we completed the checklist as a class. I assumed that because *Cabbage Rose* was a published book, the students would think it was well written. As our discussion progressed, I noticed that the children were suggesting that the author needed to keep working on many aspects of the book. They also disagreed with each other's opinions about the story:

Sarah: I think we should give it a check because there was no adventure in it.

David: I think it's a star because she went on an adventure to the castle. (Scripted notes, March 21)

The thoughtfulness of their comments and the confidence with which they delivered those comments showed me that my students were becoming critical thinkers.

The students in Room 20 are members of a writing community that includes published authors.

Calkins describes reading as a chance for young writers to "learn from their more skillful colleagues" (Calkins, 1986, p. 221). As my project progressed, I was encouraged by evidence that suggested that my students were thinking of themselves as writers. During one morning greeting, I asked the students to share a favorite fairy tale character. I was amazed and pleased when several of them asked if they could name characters from their own writing. They were placing their writing in the same category as the books they were reading, and published authors were their equals rather than their superiors. For me as a writer and a writing teacher, this is the most satisfying outcome. If my students leave second grade knowing that they are writers, I will feel that I have succeeded as a writing teacher. (Russell, 2002)

In addition to noting the ways Julie built a case for each of her 10 claims through stringing together pieces of evidence from multiple data sources to support her learning, there are two additional noteworthy points to highlight from the main text of Julie's inquiry write-up that appears on the previous pages.

First, notice under Claim 3 that when Julie discusses patterns from her survey, she ends by discussing one child that did not fit into any of the patterns she previously mentions:

> When I read one postsurvey, I became quite concerned. The student wrote that she was not a good writer because she "can't think of ideas." This response came from a child who often says that she "hates school." She resists assignments and, although she is extremely capable, she works slowly. . . . I am not surprised that this student reacted negatively to writing because she has a similar reaction to most activities at school. . . . However, I am concerned because she transferred her criticisms from the activity to herself. . . . The other students seem to either enjoy or accept writing. They are beginning to see themselves as part of a community of writers. I worry that this one student will be isolated from that community if I cannot find a way to motivate her as a writer.

While teacher inquirers are often quite excited about finding patterns in their data and are most apt to report those patterns when writing, it is also insightful to look at data that do not fit and also include explanations in the write-up of an inquiry of why those data do not fit. Research methodologists commonly refer to this as negative cases. It is often through looking critically at data that do not fit and reporting this in your writing that you learn more about the patterns themselves. In addition, reporting about data that do not fit enhances the credibility of your inquiry. In the absence of sharing negative data, you risk painting an unrealistic portrait of your classroom that can be met with skepticism by your audience who know well that nothing that occurs within the vast complexities of teaching is simple. Reporting your negative data contributes to creating a picture of your learning that rings true to life.

Second, note that each of Julie's 10 claims was supported by multiple sources of data, but not nearly all the data Julie had collected over the two months of her inquiry or that she had sorted into categories during data analysis. Through her writing, Julie selected the most powerful pieces of data to represent the patterns she found and the statements of her learning. Realize that as you construct your case to support statements of your learning through inquiry, you may experience difficulty selecting which data excerpts to use. As Wolcott notes,

> The major problem we face . . . is not to get data, but to get rid of it! With writing comes the always painful task (at least from the standpoint of the person who gathered it) of winnowing material to a manageable length, communicating only the essence rather than exhibiting the bulky catalogues that testify to one's painstaking thoroughness. (Wolcott, 1990, p. 18)

Once the winnowing down is completed and your arguments clearly articulated, the last step in writing up your inquiry is providing conclusions.

Step 4: Providing Concluding Thoughts

When you read a good mystery, you expect that the conclusion of the book will provide answers to solve the mystery. Similarly, as you near the end of writing up your work to share it, you may conceive of concluding thoughts as being answers to the initial questions posed by the inquiry study. Sometimes, this might be the case. However, just as often, concluding thoughts do not answer the initial research question but generate additional questions and further areas for inquiry. Recall in Chapter 5, where we discussed data analysis, we shared that the work of a teacher researcher is never quite finished because good data analyses generate more questions than answers. It is difficult to conceive of how to finish a piece of writing when the work of a teacher researcher is never done. Many teacher inquirers finish their work by reflecting in general on the specific inquiry just completed, generating directions for the future, and stating further wonderings. We end this chapter with the concluding passage from Julie's paper. As you read, note how she used these three techniques to bring closure to her written work.

THE NEXT STEP

During my last writer's workshop, as Linda was walking around the room, she paused at Michael's desk. Michael faces many obstacles in the classroom, and writing is particularly challenging for him. At the beginning of the year, we struggled to get him to pick up his pencil at all. Linda began to read over Michael's shoulder, and then she asked the whole class to stop working and listen to the beginning of Michael's new story:

> One morning when the sun was makeing it's way over the montons to shine so the erth has some lite. A batel was going to begin. On a lowd speeker a king said knights begin the batel. The knights started smacking sords to gether and it sonded like thunder.

The other students complimented him enthusiastically, and he began to beam. Linda encouraged him to work hard and finish the story, and he was able to score above the benchmark for second grade.

When I heard Linda read those words, and I saw the way the other children supported Michael's efforts, I got tears in my eyes. For me, this project was filled with these magical, dazzling moments. I found that teaching writing is filled with challenges. I also found that confronting those challenges and pushing myself as a teacher make writing instruction even more engaging and exciting than I had hoped it would be. I learned that every student in my room has something dazzling to say, and my job is to help him or her find his or her voice.

Finally, I learned that my journey as a writing teacher is just beginning. I was not able to help my second graders grow as writers until I began thinking about writing from their perspective and tailoring my instruction toward them and their needs. Therefore, my workshops will change with each group of young writers that enters my classroom. After doing this project, I am able to see that challenge as a wonderful chance to grow as a teacher.

As I completed my project, many wonderings remained. One huge challenge for the future is finding a way to give young writers "the luxury of time" (Calkins, 1986, p. 23). During the interview, I asked the children to tell me how I could help them grow as writers. I was surprised when one student said, "Maybe you could let us be." She wanted uninterrupted time to put her thoughts on paper. I agree that students need time to just write if they are going to develop a love for

(Continued)

(Continued)

writing. However, after this year I realize that finding this time will be an enormous task. Managing time is difficult for me, but I cannot ignore this crucial part of writing instruction. As I develop a schedule next year, I will need to continue to listen to my students as I establish priorities and make decisions.

Routman encourages teachers to "take the risk of writing in front of [their] students" (Routman, 2002, p. 211). I wanted to incorporate this element into my workshops, but I was not brave enough to show my writing to my students. I felt enormous tension because I was asking my students to do something that I was not willing to do myself. Next year, my first challenge as a writing teacher will be sharing my own writing with my students. I am nervous, but I am also curious about the effect my writing might have on the workshop environment. I was incredibly impressed by the writing community that my students created this year, and I would be honored to be an active part of that community. (Russell, 2002)

CHAPTER 6 EXERCISES

1. Outline an inquiry presentation and/or write-up for your study using the four features for sharing presented in this chapter (Figure 6.9): (1) providing background information, (2) sharing the design of the inquiry (procedures, data collection, and data analysis), (3) stating the learning and supporting the statements with data, and (4) providing concluding thoughts.

2. Work on one component at a time, sharing portions of your presentation and/or drafts of completed sections of your write-up with a colleague, your mentor, your intern, a university supervisor, or a family member to serve as a critical friend to offer feedback on your work.

DISCUSSION QUESTIONS

1. What are your thoughts and feelings about presenting your work orally and in writing? Which method (oral or written) is easiest for you and why?

2. Which conference (national or local) would you most like to attend so you can present your inquiry to others? Why this conference? What would you hope to learn from this experience?

3. What are the personal challenges you will face in orally presenting and writing about your inquiry? How can you overcome these challenges?

4. Which of the four critical features of sharing your inquiry (Figure 6.9) do you feel most comfortable completing and why?

5. Discuss the techniques Julie Russell used to support her findings with evidence from her data. Why was this evidence so important in writing up her inquiry?

6. What is your most important takeaway about writing up your work gleaned from reading Julie Russell's sample write-up in this chapter? In what ways might your own approach to writing up your work be the same as and different from the example presented in this chapter?

ONLINE MATERIALS

The following materials designed to facilitate inquiry sharing are available for download at **https://companion.corwin.com/courses/ReflectiveEdsGuide5e**:

- **Activity 6.1: Chalk Talk.** Have a silent-paper-conversation with others about the importance of sharing inquiry.

- **Activity 6.2: All About Conference Proposals.** Learn about the process of writing a proposal to present your inquiry at a conference

(Continued)

(Continued)

and analyze two examples of successful conference proposals to aid in the development of your own.

- **Activity 6.3: Writer's Workshop.** Experience structured writing and feedback time in a small group as members draft their inquiry write-ups.

- **Activity 6.4: Write-Up Tutorial.** Follow eight simple steps to create an executive summary write-up of your research.

- **Activity 6.5: Writing Up Inquiry: Model Exploration.** Read a model inquiry write-up, presented along with an analysis table to help you analyze this, and other, models for inquiry write-ups.

Contributing to the Creation of More Equitable Schools and Classrooms

The Why of Inquiry

In Chapter 1 we noted that in defining what inquiry is and how it will play out in your career as an educator, it is imperative to ask, "Inquiry for what purpose? What am I inquiring for?" To respond to this question, we turned to the most pervasive problem of practice that all educators face today—the persistent inequalities that exist in schools that are a direct consequence of the inequalities that exist within our society (systemic disparities in health care, wealth, education, affordable housing, quality childcare, school funding, teacher quality, and curricula). As a result, we suggested that the ultimate goal of engagement in inquiry is the creation of more just and more equitable schooling experiences. Yet, while the creation of more just and more equitable schooling experiences is a foundational reason to engage in the process of inquiry over the course of one's career as a teacher, we noted that not all teachers first come to inquiry with an equity focus. Rather, the inequities that are pervasive and perpetuated by the many givens of schools and schooling are sometimes discovered through several cycles of the inquiry process, leading a practicing teacher to unearth this ultimate "why" of engagement in the inquiry process over time.

Conversely, as more teacher education programs center the initial preparation of teachers on social justice and equity, more and more teacher candidates are discovering the connection between engagement in inquiry and creating more equitable classrooms and schools at the dawn of their teaching careers. To capture and illustrate the power of both of these scenarios, in this chapter we feature the complete inquiry story of teacher researcher Mickey MacDonald, the veteran high school biology teacher and prolific inquirer whom you first met in Chapter 3, to illustrate the ways she came to see inquiry as a pathway to equity over time. In addition, we feature a parallel story of four teacher candidates (Paige Bildstein, Mikhayla Kruse-Meek, Jillian Pohland, and Nicole Snitkey) and their professor (Hilarie Welsh) that depicts the relationship they came to see between inquiry and equity as a part of their initial teacher preparation experience. These candidates subsequently used inquiry as a vehicle both to inform and reform their teacher education program. Taken together, these stories reveal the important connection between inquiry and equity and illustrate what it means to take an inquiry stance toward your teaching, a concept we will explore in greater detail in the final chapter of this text. Similar to so many examples throughout this book, Mickey, Paige, Mikhayla, Jillian, Nicole, and Hilarie's inquiry stories are shared in their own words both to honor these extraordinary educators and to raise their voices, as veteran and novice teacher researchers, in the practitioner-inquiry movement—a movement that positions teachers at all levels of experience as essential players in the business of school improvement and reform.

COMING TO VIEW INQUIRY AS A PATHWAY TO EQUITY

A Teacher Researcher's Story

Mickey MacDonald

I was first introduced to inquiry in 2004, my sixth year of teaching, when my administrator sent out an announcement to see if anyone was interested in representing our school in a novel professional learning opportunity designed to engage teachers in ongoing job-embedded professional development through inquiry. I applied, was selected, and attended my first workshop focused on simply introducing me to the inquiry process. At that first meeting, I was skeptical. As a biology teacher, I viewed research through a science lens and questioned research that was not quantitative, repeatable, testable, treatment/control group designed, and hypothesis-based. Looking at only a few students and not being able to generalize to larger populations all flew in the face of what I believed research was supposed to be. I have since expanded my view of what educational research can be and believe that teacher inquiry cycles can and do lead to the generation of new knowledge on teaching and learning that not only informs my practice but also can potentially inform the practice of other educators both within my school and beyond.

My journey began with the very first cycle of inquiry I completed as a part of that professional learning endeavor in 2004, a cycle I affectionately referred to as "The Dreaded Notebook Check." For that first cycle, in addition to several periods of high school biology, I was also teaching a ninth-grade integrated science course and found myself very frustrated with my students' use of a common teaching and learning strategy in science classrooms—keeping a science notebook. The first wondering I ever pursued aimed to make this practice more effective: "In what ways can the usefulness of a science notebook as both a tool for learning and a tool for organization be maximized for ninth-grade integrated science students?" This inquiry provided me with insights into a particular pedagogical strategy and the ways it was playing out in my classroom and, as such, illuminated the power that inquiry holds as a mechanism for my own professional development. I was hooked, and I have engaged in cycles of inquiry every school year since.

For the next few years, similar to my very first inquiry, my gaze as a novice teacher researcher was focused primarily on better understanding and improving the performance of my students through studying their grades and standardized test scores (as described in Chapter 3 of this book on pages 138–46) as well as introducing differentiated assessment and digital portfolios into my practice. For my first four years as a teacher researcher, I was focused more on getting my students to perform better within the system of schooling that was in place, and less on questioning that system in the first place. It was in my fifth year researching my practice that a perfect storm of professional and personal factors converged that unveiled to me the systemic educational inequities that are perpetuated by the current system of schooling I was teaching and inquiring into teaching within.

During that fifth year as an inquirer (2008–2009), professionally I began feeling the heaviness of the age of accountability more than ever before as my state moved toward instituting a high-stakes End of Course exam in biology that my students had to pass to receive credit toward

(Continued)

(Continued)

high school graduation. Similarly, our teacher evaluation system was under revision and moving toward teacher performance ratings being calculated in large part based on student test performance. Working as a teacher in the age of accountability led me to notice the ways several students, all of whom struggled to perform well on standardized tests, were receiving the message over and over again that they were failures. Hence, for my fifth cycle of inquiry, I began to shift my gaze as a teacher researcher from general teaching strategies, techniques, and assessment practices to better understanding my students and the ways they were experiencing schooling in the age of accountability. At the start of my fifth inquiry cycle, I did not want the students who struggled in my class to get just another year of science learning culminating in a state-mandated test in which they would again see themselves as non–science learners because of their performance on this test.

Therefore, during the 2008–2009 school year, I used the process of inquiry to focus on the development of my relationship with three of my science students who had a history of failure in my class and in school in general and how I might help them become successful learners in science and in school as a whole.

At the same time, being a parent of two school-age boys also led to my shift in thinking as I entered my eleventh year as a teacher and fifth year as a teacher researcher, with the wonderings generated for this fifth inquiry cycle and the subsequent cycles I conducted rooted in the experiences I was seeing play out as my two sons progressed through school. My oldest son, like many of my high-achieving students, always found success in school—learning came easily for him and he excelled academically. His postsecondary opportunities upon high school graduation were limitless. My youngest son, like many of my students who struggle in science, found little success academically. As a kindergartener, he developed the belief that he was not a learner because he could not recognize sight words. This belief was reinforced in third grade, and fourth, and fifth, and each subsequent year because a standardized test score defined who he was as a learner. When he entered high school, he believed his only postsecondary option was joining the military because he knew that standardized test scores would always limit his choices. My personal and professional identities converged as I pondered the question: How can I transform my son's academic experiences as he enters high school so that he, and so many students like him, believe that they are learners because they finally find academic success?

To address this overarching question, my next several cycles of inquiry, some done individually and others collaboratively, led my ninth-grade team and I to eliminate academic tracking, a common and pervasive practice across high schools where students are sorted into either an honors track or a general track based on previous standardized test scores, grades, and teacher recommendations. Maintaining a separate honors track and general track reinforces the belief that some students are learners and other students are not, and furthermore, across the United States, minority students and students living in poverty end up in lower-ability classes at a much higher rate than their White or more financially secure classmates, resulting in minority students who also live in poverty receiving the message that they are not learners more often than their White peers (Biafora & Ansalone, 2008; Burris, 2014; Chmielewski, 2014; Fiel, 2013; Oakes, 2005; Sensoy & DiAngelo, 2017; Tyson, 2013). Such was the case at my school before we eliminated tracking.

Following the elimination of tracking for ninth graders at my school, my passing rate on the State of Florida's Biology End of Course exam soared, exceeding 95%, one of the highest pass rates in the state. Yet, when closely examining my Biology End of Course exam data, I discovered that of the six students who did not pass this exam, all were minority students. Additionally, many of my high-achieving students were not scoring at the highest level on this exam.

Even though I had improved pass rates for all students through the elimination of academic tracking in high school biology, I knew that my next step in helping all of my students see themselves as learners was finding ways to address the increase in learner diversity within my detracked course. I turned to the work of Carol Ann Tomlinson (2014) on differentiation, defined as tailoring instruction to meet individual needs by differentiating learning activities for students through the use of flexible grouping and ongoing assessment, and wondered, for this, my tenth cycle of inquiry, "In what ways can differentiated instruction support learners who struggle in acquiring science content knowledge and challenge learners who excel in science in a detracked, honors biology classroom so that all students perceive themselves as learners?" (MacDonald, 2016).

(Continued)

(Continued)

To gain insight into this question, I examined both the process of developing a differentiated instructional unit and its implementation around the conceptual topic of protein synthesis. Within this unit, I created different learning activities that were offered simultaneously that students could choose, depending on their need. For example, before taking a quiz that required the students to describe the process of protein synthesis, students who had not yet mastered the vocabulary needed to successfully take that quiz could choose to engage in a vocabulary sort activity, while students who had mastered the concept of protein synthesis could choose to complete an activity where they needed to apply their knowledge of protein synthesis to genetic disease.

As the unit unfolded, I collected data on 10 students (6 who struggled and 4 who excelled) including individual student achievement data, student work samples, observations of students captured within a journal, and student interviews. Because of the abundance of data, I first organized all of the data pieces for each of the 10 students in this study into data posters to provide a better lens for analysis (Figure 7.1). Each student's data poster included (1) his or her assessment data for the unit and standardized test scores for the previous academic year, (2) the differentiated instructional activities that she or he completed, (3) a compilation of reflections taken from my journal in which I referred to him or her specifically, (4) a transcript from the final student interview, and (5) his or her responses to the unit's exit survey. I carefully studied each student's data poster, writing statements about what I was learning on "What I See" posters, and including evidences that I encountered within my data that led me to construct these statements of learning (Figure 7.2).

So, what did I learn? Although I learned many things about how differentiation supported learners who struggled and challenged learners who excelled, what I would like to share with you in this chapter is what I learned about students who, like my youngest son, have had limited academic success throughout schooling.

When instruction is designed to meet the learning needs of students where they are, and when no stigma is attached to receiving instructional support within the classroom while other students are receiving instruction that allows them to deepen their understanding of the content, students opt for the instructional activity that they need in that moment. For example,

Figure 7.1 Mickey's Data Analysis Posters

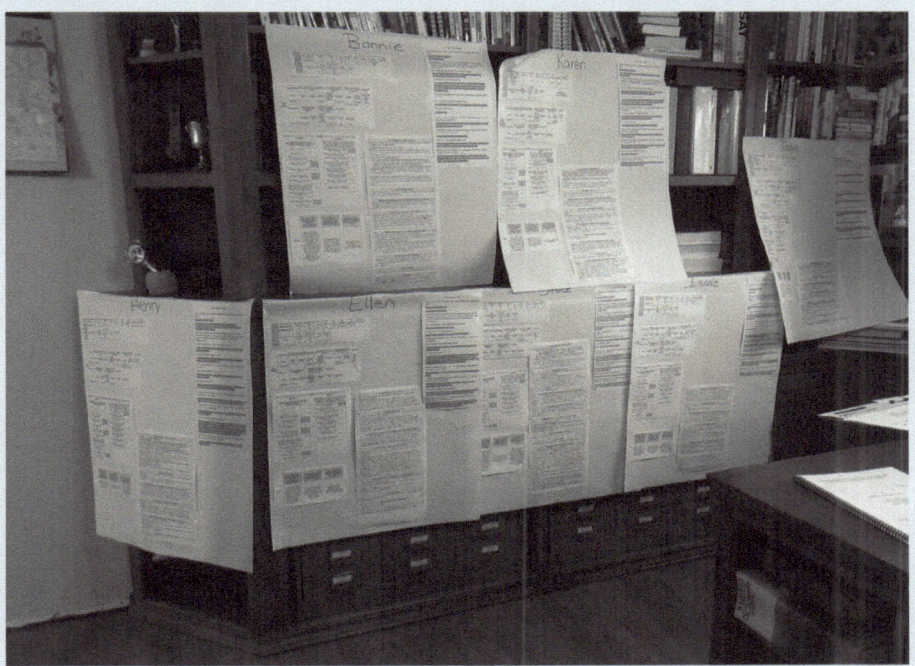
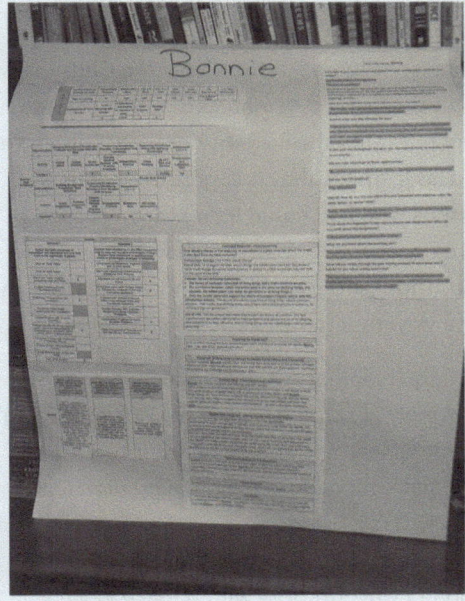
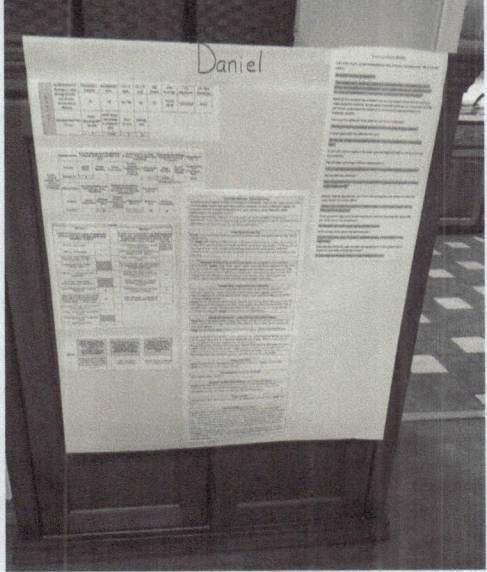

Figure 7.2 Mickey's "What I See" Poster

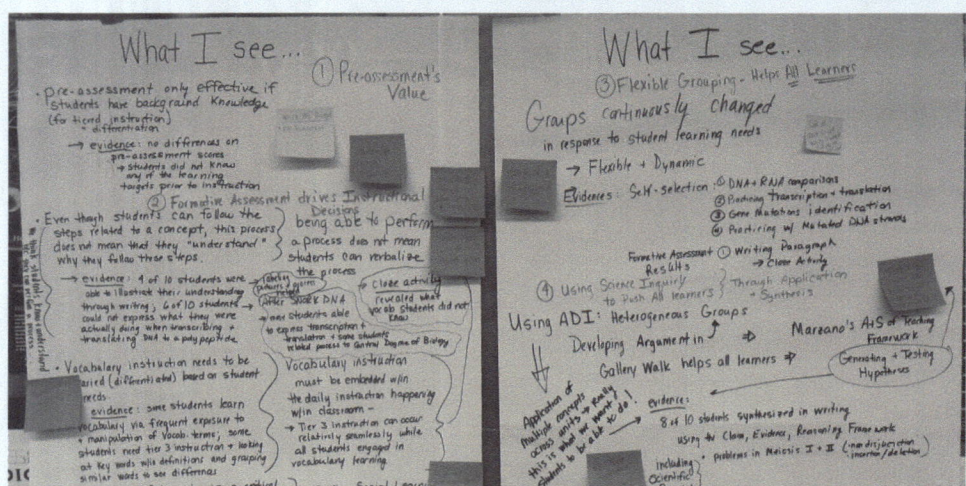

one of my students, Christina, who was struggling with the vocabulary involved with protein synthesis, opted to complete a word sort to show the relationships among the vocabulary terms prior to completing the assessment I spoke of before (see Figure 7.3). Students like Christina who needed instructional support chose the differentiated option created for learners who had not yet mastered the content because they viewed themselves as learners, and, as learners, they recognized what they needed. Students like Christina who had found little academic success throughout school began to experience successes when instruction matched what they needed. These successes led to more successes and changed how they began to view themselves as learners.

This tenth cycle of teacher inquiry impacted my practice in a couple of ways. First, I feel very strongly about the importance of equalizing educational opportunities for all learners and have accepted the challenge of differentiating instruction while maintaining high learning expectations within a detracked classroom. Second, finding time and space to offer small-group instruction within the regularly scheduled class period, targeting learners who struggle with science while still engaging students who have already met proficiency of learning goals through activities that extend their thinking, can be achieved only

Figure 7.3 Mickey's Student Completes Vocabulary Sort Activity

Source: Used with permission of parents of Christina Crosby.

through meeting the challenge of differentiation. These changes in practice have resulted in better experiences for both my learners who struggle and my learners who excel.

For more than a decade now, I have participated in and facilitated many of my colleagues through multiple cycles of the teacher inquiry process. As indicated in my reflections for this chapter, my individual inquiry questions have evolved over this period, as have my views about teaching and learning. I now look critically at the schooling system in general and who benefits from the system as it is and who does not. My cycles of inquiry continue each year, and focus on the inequities that are perpetuated by the status quo of educational practices and the ways I can work within the system to change the system as a teacher researcher in pursuit of a more just and more equitable schooling experience for all of the children I serve.

INFORMING THINKING, TEACHING, AND TEACHER EDUCATION

The Power of Equity-Focused Inquiry

Paige Bildstein, Mikhayla Kruse-Meek, Jillian Pohland, Nicole Snitkey, and Hilarie Welsh

The work we describe in this reflection took place at Loras College, a Catholic, liberal arts school in Dubuque, Iowa. As four White female teacher candidates from small and rural towns, we recognized our inexperience interacting with people from diverse racial, ethnic, and religious backgrounds. Of the 1,500 students in our college, 82.7% identify as White. According to the 2010 census, the city of Dubuque, population 60,000, also has limited diversity, with 91.7% of the community being White. This context is important to understanding the experiences we had in our teacher education program that began with a course entitled Multicultural Education.

Multicultural Education provides teacher candidates at Loras with the opportunity to work with students from diverse backgrounds and to develop strategies to encourage tolerance and inclusivity in K–12 classrooms. Topics discussed include race, religion, gender, sexual identity, social class, disabilities, language, and geographic region. The primary objectives of this course are to have teacher candidates develop multicultural awareness, to learn effective classroom strategies to meet the needs of diverse learners, and to become advocates for multicultural education in schools.

In January 2017 we were 4 of 10 sophomore students who enrolled in Multicultural Education, a required course for all Loras students studying to become teachers, when it was offered by Dr. Hilarie Welsh as a January term (J-Term) course. Every Loras student is required to take two J-Term courses; all J-Term courses incorporate experiential learning opportunities. Some of these courses include travel opportunities, both domestic and international.

In our J-Term course, we spent two weeks of the three-week course reading, discussing, completing hands-on and collaborative learning tasks, and visiting school sites in Dubuque. We observed in a Montessori preschool, volunteered in a middle school classroom for English language learners, and facilitated activities in an elementary afterschool program that serves a diverse population. Discussions and readings emphasized White privilege, and we participated in a campus-wide poverty simulation and Privilege Beads Exercise to explore other types of privilege, such as sexuality, gender/sex, religion, and ability (Allen, 2018, p. 2). Through the course content and experiential learning opportunities, we began to understand the need as future teachers to learn more about diversity as well as the privilege we experienced growing up White in rural America. We also came to understand the importance of culturally relevant pedagogy (G. Ladson-Billings, 1995), particularly as we prepared to enter a career in which most teachers are White female while the students they serve are gradually becoming more racially diverse (National Center for Education Statistics, 2018; U.S. Department of Education, 2016). While all of these experiences strengthened our knowledge of the course topics, it was our one-week-long trip to Sarasota, Florida, that most affected the way we think about teaching and learning in a diverse setting.

During our seven days in Sarasota we visited seven different schools, which included traditional public schools and school types that are rare in Iowa, such as charter and magnet schools. The emphasis on charter and magnet schools stemmed from Hilarie's belief that these school types provided an interesting backdrop to explore issues of access, equity, and social justice, content lacking in many approaches to multicultural education (Nieto, 2000). Also, while the Sarasota area seemed large and diverse to us, we recognize that there are cities within Florida (e.g., Tampa, Miami) and cities closer to Dubuque (e.g., Milwaukee, Chicago) that are more racially and culturally diverse. Another reason our J-Term took us to Sarasota is because connections were strong; Hilarie's K–12 teaching career occurred in a middle and high school in Bradenton and Sarasota.

Something we continuously saw at our favorite schools was a shared goal and purpose focused on community building. Teachers intimately knew students' stories and backgrounds; principals were visible in classrooms and knew the students and what they were learning about in class; and every staff member, whether they were teachers, custodians, counselors, or secretaries, was working toward bettering the students and their school. These schools have realized that community and relationship building is key to teaching and learning. This observation complemented what we learned in the college classroom prior to our trip to Florida.

As we neared the end of the Multicultural Education course, we continuously found ourselves asking how would we, as teachers, create strong communities in our classrooms? For our J-Term culminating course project, we were required to submit a proposal for the Loras

(Continued)

(Continued)

Legacy Symposium, an annual conference in which students and faculty present their research, creative work, and service experiences. Our proposal, focused on creating classroom communities, was accepted, and our presentation was well received by our large audience. Following our presentation, Hilarie asked if we wanted to continue studying our topic by completing a teacher inquiry cycle.

We met with Hilarie and she explained more about teacher inquiry. As is the case with many novice inquirers, we were a bit overwhelmed and confused, but we were willing to give it a try since we had found our field experience in Sarasota to be so powerful and wanted to continue our learning from this endeavor. For our inquiry work, then, rather than focus solely on ways to build a strong classroom community, we wanted to frame our inquiry to help us continue the learning about diversity we had done in our J-Term multicultural class. And so, we wondered, "How can our extensive travel field experience impact the way we approach teacher education program coursework as we enter our junior year in the Loras College teacher preparation program?" While our trip to Florida felt life-changing at the time, we wondered if we would continue to apply what we learned in Florida to our coursework, field experiences, and other life happenings.

With this wondering in mind, we first looked to the literature, reading and discussing several articles together that focused on culturally relevant teaching and promising practices in teacher education programs in the context of multicultural education (Au, 2009; Ayers et al., 2008; Griggs & Tidwell, 2015; Insana et al., 2014; G. J. Ladson-Billings, 2005; Lowenstein, 2009; Nieto, 2000). We also employed several types of data collection strategies that we used throughout our inquiry cycle:

- *Field Notes:* Focused on classroom observations, internship experiences

- *Reflective Journals:* Focused on what we were learning in our classes and how the learning aligned with the literature and what we had learned in *Multicultural Education*

- *Documents/Artifacts/Student Work:* Focused on work K–5 students completed in our tutoring and field experience sessions and our own student work samples from our college classes

- *Critical Friends Group Feedback:* Focused on sharing with each other the data we collected during our individual experiences

Our inquiry Critical Friends Group (CFG), led by Hilarie, met weekly or biweekly for a full academic year as we continued our coursework and field experiences during the junior year of our teacher education program. Through discussing our data at these meetings, we collected stories of the ways our J-Term visit to Florida impacted how we were approaching our junior year at Loras. While several of these stories were impactful, two in particular stood out to us: Nicole's story of working with an English language learner from the Marshall Islands, and Paige's story of working as a county library intern.

Nicole: Working With an English Language Learner From the Marshall Islands

Children from the Marshall Islands make up the largest English language learner population in Dubuque Community School District, yet there seems to be little knowledge in our community about their culture. For one of the courses required for my reading endorsement that I took my junior year, Foundations of Reading, I worked with an English language learner in kindergarten whose first language is Marshallese. The outcome of the class was to produce two authentic books together using the Language Experience Approach. The Language Experience Approach focuses on scaffolding a child's production of a spoken text based on a personal or vicarious experience that an expert user of the target language, such as a teacher, then writes down. The spoken and written language then becomes the object of joint attention and problem solving at various levels such as at the level of the text, word, or letter to facilitate the acquisition of conventional English literacy over time (Nessel & Dixon, 2008). Our first book created was titled *Animals*. We began by creating the Popplet (a visual organizer), illustrated in Figure 7.4, on an iPad. The kindergartener chose the animals and the center pictures. Each animal was featured in its own Popplet, with the animal's name as well as a picture of the animal in the center. Together, we brainstormed five characteristics of each animal. From this, we chose one characteristic and constructed a sentence. It is important to note that throughout this process, everything that was typed recorded the spoken language of the student. In Figure 7.5 you can see two pages of the book: "Zebra eats the grass" and "Elephant drink the water." In her finished product, illustrated in the figure, you may notice that the student does not use business English (or formal grammar); however, there is a vast improvement from where we started with the text "elephant drink."

Figure 7.4 Popplet

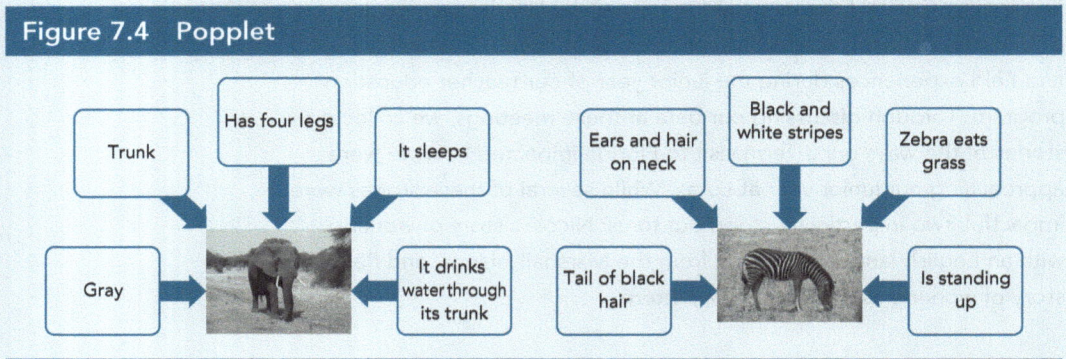

Figure 7.5 Finished Book

This provides an example of a way in which the Marshallese language differs from the English language and how the Language Experience Approach helps accommodate the differences. Due to the language differences between Marshallese and English, the English inflectional morpheme -s attached to nouns to indicate plural and attached to verbs to indicate third-person singular were frequently omitted by the student in her dictated texts. Getting the student to write *eats* rather than *eat* was a great accomplishment and showed her progress in language development.

Through our J-Term experience, I was able to understand how important it is to meet students where they are and to understand native language as an asset, rather than a deficit. Learning more about the Marshallese language helped me learn ways to help this child understand the English language better. I also worked to discover her interests so creating the book would be enjoyable and relevant. Because of our J-Term class, I avoided deficit thinking about her native language, I connected to her interests, and I met the student where she was at as a learner. These were not areas of intensive focus of the Foundations of Reading class, but I applied what I learned in Multicultural Education to my work with this student.

Paige: Working as a County Library Intern

During my junior year, I held a Storytime Internship at a county library system near our college. In this position, I planned story times for children who were two years old and older. Each story time incorporated a theme that was applied to the readings, crafts, and numerical or literacy activities. In this experience, I found it difficult to expose toddlers and preschoolers to different cultures. Many of the books that I read to children featured White children and contained no references to any type of diversity. Because the story time targeted children aged two to four, developmentally appropriate books had to be short in length. As I searched for story-time books, I noticed that there were no books that included multicultural themes at any of the county library branches that would be an appropriate length for a two-year-old. I responded to this challenge by addressing culture and ethnicity in the art, literacy, and numeracy activities. Simple changes such as creating dolls made from felt material (a staple in story-time programming) with varying skin colors seems like a modest change. However, White felt dolls were all that was available in the county library when I began, and I believe dolls made from felt material with varying skin tones is important in these predominantly White, mostly rural communities. I do not believe I would have thought of this lack of diversity prior to completing Multicultural Education.

As we shared our stories like those above in our CFG, we began to realize just how significantly our travel experience to Sarasota was impacting the way we approached our teacher education courses and related work. In one way, it seemed problematic that the 10 students who had completed the J-Term multicultural class had transformational experiences, yet the majority of the students in our teacher education program do not travel outside of Dubuque, Iowa, as part of this course.

(Continued)

(Continued)

In our conversations, we also discussed the multiple ways in which our peers participated in transformational educative experiences, given that Loras is known for experiential learning (e.g., travel abroad, service trips, class-based service learning, cocurricular involvement).

Our discussions organically shifted to the Loras teacher education program and where we had learned about multicultural education themes. That is, if a student does not have a travel experience such as we had for the Multicultural Education course, could he or she still experience the transformative change that we identified? While we learned about the many complexities about teaching through our coursework and understood that much learning would continue to happen throughout our teaching careers, could sharing our Multicultural Education experience be valuable? While we compared class notes and experiences in light of the literature about the challenges of preparing teachers for diverse classrooms, we wondered about gaps in our teacher education program related to multicultural education themes. The gaps seemed important to share with a wider audience.

We built on the presentation we had made at the Loras Legacy Symposium about the J-Term experience and what we learned about the importance of building community in the classroom and began by sharing our inquiry that was birthed from this experience nationally by presenting at the Association of Teacher Educators conference (Bildstein et al., 2018). Furthermore, we continued to share our inquiry with the broader Loras campus community, presenting to the Loras College teacher education program faculty on how our inquiry findings could inform the teacher education program at the college, as well as presenting once again at the Loras Legacy Symposium (one year after our first presentation) to discuss our inquiry findings and next steps.

Our ATE presentation focused on what we learned in our J-Term class and how we made sense of our learning as we engaged in a cycle of inquiry with our professor during our junior year of study. As illustrated in the stories above, we experienced deeper understanding of the way we worked with children and the way we understood a migrant population in Dubuque (Nicole). We also found a lack of access to diversity in children's literature. Based on our research there is not enough diverse literature, in general—in our school libraries, county libraries, and city libraries (Paige). We corroborated that the problem is not just a local problem; we found in the literature that this is a widespread issue (Crisp et al., 2016; Davis et al., 2005).

As we continued our inquiry cycle and shared it locally with others, we realized that our work was taking us in a direction we hadn't planned or expected—examining our own teacher education program. As we examined our program, we knew that there was a story to be told, but we also understood that we needed to tell the story with balance and care. After all, we attend a college that we love and that has a strong reputation, we respect our professors, and we think that we are being well prepared to enter the teaching profession. Our status as college juniors also meant that we did not have all of the answers; we hadn't even finished the teacher education program! Despite these limitations, we believed that our inquiry findings were valuable and should be shared with the Loras College teacher education program faculty.

To prepare for this presentation, we went back to the reflective journals we had kept throughout the year, reviewed all of the course documents related to our stories that we had created, and reflected on the stories we had collected as we discussed our data in our CFG. To frame our findings, we used the teacher education program's conceptual framework, the Reflective Teacher Advocate, illustrated in Figure 7.6. This image is prominently displayed inside our teacher education building, is in every teacher education class syllabus, and is something that we examine frequently in our courses. When we analyzed our course documents and reflective journals, we found many ways in which our teacher education program thoroughly teaches the ideas presented in the conceptual framework, particularly the deep content knowledge and reflective action. Through our inquiry process, we started to wonder if there are gaps in our teacher education program related to diversity, particularly as those gaps relate to diverse instructional practice and everyday advocacy on the conceptual framework. There are classes that intensively and deliberately immerse us in issues related to diversity, such as Multicultural Education, Children and Young Adult Literature, and Curriculum and Instruction in Social Studies. Also, students pursuing a reading endorsement work intensively with English language learners (as Nicole illustrated) and students pursuing a special education endorsement work intensively with students with disabilities. As we analyzed our data through our inquiry process, we realized that there could be an area for growth in the general coursework that all elementary education students complete as it relates to

(Continued)

(Continued)

exposing students to diversity through texts, class experiences, and field experiences. As stated before, Loras isn't the only college that encounters challenges in preparing future teachers for diverse environments—this is a challenge faced by teacher education programs situated in towns and urban centers nationwide. This is a challenge widely written about in the literature (Assaf et al., 2010; Lowenstein, 2009; Nieto, 2000; Reiter & Davis, 2011; Sleeter, 2001). Teacher education programs are preparing (mostly) White, female teachers to enter classrooms filled with diverse students. Understanding the various cultures, abilities, family structures, and religions is difficult, especially when the work of a teacher requires understanding *and* responding by developing curriculum that addresses the various needs and backgrounds of each individual in a classroom.

When we presented this finding to the Loras teacher education program faculty (Figure 7.7), our goal was to encourage them to review their curriculum and identify if there were areas in which they could incorporate more diversity through texts, discussions, activities, and field experiences throughout the entirety of the teacher education program. It is our hope that our inquiry and advocacy may make a positive change in the Loras teacher education program. Given the nationwide struggle in this area, Loras could emerge as a leader in preparing students to teach effectively in diverse communities.

We are delighted to share that after presenting to the faculty, we noticed a couple of changes in the months that followed. For example, in a course that previously placed students only in Catholic schools for the clinical component, several Loras teacher candidates were placed in public schools that house more diverse student bodies. We asked several faculty if our inquiry presentation had prompted any changes and received these comments from two different faculty members:

> While it really didn't change exactly what I do, it did make me more aware of the issue that I hope I already addressed and let me know that students care about this. So, it just brought the idea of culturally relevant teaching to the forefront for me. While this has always been very important to me, I sometimes got the idea that it was not welcomed or wanted by students in my Loras classes and that maybe I was overdoing it. Your project and interest in the topic let me know that students do care and think it's important.

Figure 7.6 Loras College Teacher Education Conceptual Framework

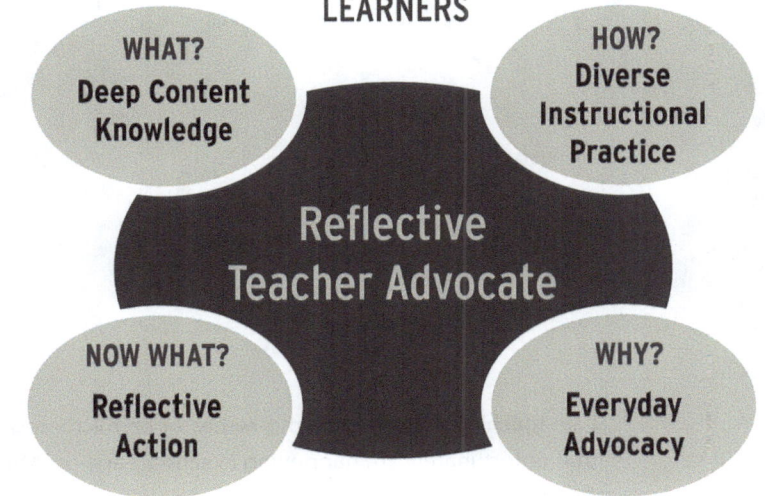

Source: Used with permission of Paige Bildstein, Mikhayla Kruse-Meek, Jillian Pohland, Nicole Snitkey, and Hilarie Welsch.

Figure 7.7 Loras Teacher Candidates Present Their Inquiry

> I am teaching a new lesson this semester on micro-aggressions that unfortunately are happening in schools against Muslim American students.
>
> We continue to speak with faculty to ask if there are other changes planned or that have been implemented that we may not have noticed.
>
> In many ways, our inquiry cycle has brought us full circle. We learned during our J-Term experience that building community is a critical step as we work with diverse students and have classrooms of our own. While this was a strong theme from our J-Term class, the inquiry cycle we engaged in during our junior year strengthened and verified this theme as we experienced what it was like to be a part of a community of teacher candidates learning about practice with and from our professor, Hilarie Welsh. Reading and inquiring together, we worked as change makers in the teacher education program we were learning to teach

within to help the future teachers who had prepared at Loras to address issues of diversity and equity as they play out in schools nationwide.

Prior to our junior year, none of us had heard of teacher inquiry or action research. Yet we spent 17 months engaged in this teacher inquiry project as this cycle of inquiry, and the presentations that sprang from it, extended into our senior year. We understand how data collection and analysis can add depth to our knowledge, guide decisions, and impact programs.

Participating in inquiry has empowered us as teacher candidates, and it has helped us understand that we can be change makers within the teaching profession, particularly in relation to addressing diversity and creating more equitable learning experiences for all children. As we graduate and begin our careers as teachers, we certainly know we have a lot to learn, but inquiry has provided us with many tools to proactively address the tensions and problems that we are sure to experience in the teaching profession, and help us raise awareness and make positive changes related to teaching *all* children throughout our careers.

CHAPTER 7 EXERCISES

1. Complete the following chart to analyze the ways all of the individual components of the inquiry process discussed in this book were actualized in the two inquiry stories presented in this chapter. After completing the chart, reflect on what you have learned about each component of the inquiry process through the analysis of the teacher researchers' stories featured in this chapter.

	MICKEY'S INQUIRY STORY	PAIGE, MIKHAYLA, JILLIAN, NICOLE, AND HILARIE'S INQUIRY STORY
Wondering(s)		
Actions Taken to Address or Better Understand the Problem		

(Continued)

(Continued)

	MICKEY'S INQUIRY STORY	PAIGE, MIKHAYLA, JILLIAN, NICOLE, AND HILARIE'S INQUIRY STORY
Collaborating With Colleagues		
Data Collection		
Data Analysis		
Changes to Practice Resulting From Study		
Sharing Work With Others		

2. To deepen your understanding of equity, complete additional readings on the topic by authors such as those suggested in Chapter 3 of this text: Lisa Delpit, Paul Gorski, Gloria Ladson-Billings, Ali Michael, Luis Moll, and Christine Sleeter. Some specific readings to get you started are recommended in the textbox below:

Gorski, P. C., & Swalwell, K. (2015). Equity literacy for all. *Educational Leadership, 72*(6), 34–40. https://eric.ed.gov/?id=EJ1062914

In this article, the authors place equity rather than culture at the center of the diversity conversation and share five principles that would help in developing meaningfully multicultural curriculum.

Gorski, P. (2008). The myth of the "culture of poverty." *Educational Leadership, 65*(7), 32.

Gorski suggests that we think about how our own biases affect our interactions with and expectations of our students. In helping us think about inequities, he argues that "the socioeconomic opportunity gap can be eliminated only when we stop trying to 'fix' poor students and start addressing the ways in which our schools perpetuate classism" (Gorski, 2008, p. 3).

Pollock, K., Lopez, A., & Joshee, R. (2013). Disrupting myths of poverty in the face of resistance. *Journal of Cases in Educational Leadership, 16*(2), 11–19. https://doi.org/10.1177/1555458913487031

(Continued)

(Continued)

This piece presents challenges faced by a principal who confronts the myths held by his faculty about low-income and poor families as he tries to create a positive and inclusive learning environment within his school where he hopes all students can learn. The authors try to disrupt prevalent myths about families from low-income households. Recognizing the inherent tensions, this case demonstrates the importance of creating equitable and inclusive learning environments.

Templeton, B. L. (2013). Why is that child so rude? *Educational Leadership, 70*(8), 72–74. https://eric.ed.gov/?id=EJ1029011

In many cases teachers and students draw from different funds of knowledge. This article explores funds of knowledge as the ideas and beliefs that people absorb as members of a particular race, social class, or other group. When teachers understand the differences between their own funds of knowledge and those of their students, they are able to help students navigate situations where expectations are different from those faced at home.

Ullucci, K., & Howard, T. (2015). Pathologizing the poor: Implications for preparing teachers to work in high-poverty schools. *Urban Education, 50*(2), 170–193. https://doi.org/10.1177/0042085914543117

Given that poverty continues to be a significant social problem, teacher educators need to pay close attention to issues of equity within teacher preparation programs. This article summarizes mythologies about poverty that impact student–teacher relationships and offers new perspectives on educating students who live with poverty.

Villegas, A. M., & Lucas, T. (2007). The culturally responsive teacher. *Educational Leadership, 64*(6), 28. https://eric.ed.gov/?id=EJ766361

This article explores how the culturally responsive teacher is able to engage students from diverse cultural and linguistic backgrounds. The key is that teachers must see these students as capable learners.

Webb, L. (2000). The red shoe. *Educational Leadership, 58*(1), 74–76.

This is a story about a new principal who remembers the humiliation she experienced when her kindergarten teacher scolded her for tying a shoe with her teeth. The article demonstrates why a teacher needs to refrain from prejudging so-called problem children's actions.

DISCUSSION QUESTIONS

1. Compare and contrast the two inquiry stories shared in this chapter. How are they the same? How are they different?

2. What inspires you in these stories? Conversely, what troubles you?

3. How would you personally describe the relationship between engaging in inquiry as a teacher and the creation of more equitable schools and classrooms?

ONLINE MATERIALS

The following materials designed to facilitate exploring inquiry for equity are available for download at **https://companion.corwin.com/courses/ReflectiveEdsGuide5e**:

- **Activity 7.1: Equity Chalk Talk.** Have a silent-paper-conversation with others about using inquiry as a pathway to equity.

- **Activity 7.2: Inquiry for Equity Triad Discussion.** Discuss three question prompts about inquiry for equity in a group of three.

In addition to the above activities found on the accompanying website to this book, we also recommend visiting the School Reform Initiative website, an organization fiercely committed to educational equity and excellence, for more activities designed to foster deep reflection on issues of equity in classrooms, schools, and society: https://www.schoolreforminitiative.org/tag/equity/

On Your Way

Becoming the Best Teacher and Researcher You Can Be

8

Congratulations! As you begin this last chapter, you have engaged in all of the components of the inquiry process. Your journey has included wondering, reading, planning, collecting data, analyzing data, and sharing your learning with others. While sharing your practitioner research is an important part of the inquiry process, there is one danger inherent in sharing your work. After you've completed an oral presentation or write-up of your inquiry, it feels final, like the end of a long journey. Therefore, you may begin to view practitioner inquiry as a linear process and focus on the outcome, the ending of one project, one exploration, one wondering . . . and then go back to the act of teaching and business as usual. As a linear project, teacher inquiry is not *a part of* teaching, it is *apart from* it. When you complete a presentation or write-up of your work, it's important to remember that teacher inquiry is not about doing an action research project that is completed at one point in time and then is over. Rather, teacher inquiry is a continual cycle or circle through which all educators spiral throughout their professional lifetimes—a professional positioning owned by the teacher, where questioning, systematically studying, and subsequently improving one's own practice becomes a necessary and natural part of a teacher's work because of all the inherent complexity the act of teaching holds. This professional positioning refers to the notion of *inquiry stance* we introduced in the first few pages of this book. In this final chapter, we review what it means to have an inquiry stance in relationship to two additional ways you have likely experienced inquiry alluded to in this opening paragraph—as a *process* and as a *product*. Furthermore, we discuss how to enact that stance throughout your professional lifetime by providing tools to assess your own and others' research.

How Can Inquiry Be Three Things in One (Process, Product, and Stance)?

Up to this point, we have presented individual components of the inquiry experience one by one. With knowledge of the individual components of inquiry now developed, a return of our gaze to a holistic understanding of inquiry reveals inquiry as a practice that can be understood through the lenses of process, product, and stance. While each of these components plays a distinct role, they are intricately connected together, contributing to the overall goal of cultivating an inquiry stance.

Inquiry as a Process

Inquiry as a process is the systematic, ongoing method by which educators explore their teaching practices, learning outcomes, and educational environment. Inquiry involves a continuous cycle of questioning, data collection, analysis, and reflection. This process can be a one-time event, but that will likely not lead to an inquiry stance. Educators interested in cultivating an inquiry stance engage in a recurring activity that allows educators to adapt and refine their approaches to better meet their students' needs. The cyclical nature of inquiry as a process means that it is responsive, continuous, and evolving as new insights and challenges emerge in the classroom.

Inquiry as a Product

Inquiry as a product refers to the tangible outcomes of an inquiry process, such as findings, reports, or presentations that share the results of a teacher's inquiry. When educators engage in inquiry "projects," they undertake specific, time-bound investigations designed to address particular problems in their practice. These projects result in concrete evidence and actionable recommendations that can be implemented to improve educational outcomes. The product of inquiry is important to cultivating an inquiry stance because it provides a visible representation of the work done and the insights gleaned. The product allows us to share with others serving as the content needed to help generate a community of practice.

Inquiry as a Stance

Coming full circle to the start of this book when we first defined inquiry in Figure 1.1, to us, an inquiry stance is the goal. It is the keystone of our professional practice as classroom teachers. Inquiry as a stance suggests a reflective approach to teaching that goes beyond individual processes or products. It is a way of being in the world as an educator, where questioning, critical reflection, and a commitment to perpetual learning are embedded in one's professional identity. Teachers who adopt an inquiry stance view themselves as learners, continuously seeking to understand and improve their practice. This stance fosters a culture of curiosity, adaptation, and persistence that enables educators to navigate the complexities of teaching with a mindset that values growth and transformation. You become a student of your own teaching, pouring what you learn through continuous, systematic, and intentional investigation into your practice back into your teaching to become the very best teacher you can for each individual student you serve.

The Interconnectedness of Process, Product, and Stance

While each of these elements—process, product, and stance—can be seen as distinct, they are deeply interconnected in the practice of inquiry. The process of inquiry provides the mechanism for generating meaningful products, and the creation of these products, in turn, provides a tangible outcome that can strengthen the power of investigating one's own practice. As teachers engage repeatedly in the process of inquiry and produce valuable outcomes, their inquiry stance becomes more ingrained, and their professional journey becomes one of lifelong learning.

This unique combination—where the process of inquiry leads to the creation of impactful products and, over time, solidifies an inquiry stance—illustrates the transformative power of inquiry in education. Teachers who continually engage in this cycle find that their inquiry stance becomes a natural and necessary part of their professional life. Teachers are driven not only to seek answers to immediate questions but also to embrace the continuous evolution of their practice. In this way, the process, product, and stance of inquiry work together to foster deep, sustained growth and development, as summarized in Table 8.1.

Table 8.1	Inquiry as Process, Product, and Stance
	INQUIRY AS THREE-IN-ONE
Inquiry as Process	The ongoing, systematic investigation and improvement of ecucational practices through cycles of questioning, data collection, analysis, and reflection.
Inquiry as Product	The tangible outcomes of inquiry, such as findings, reports, or presentations, which provide concrete evidence and recommendations for improving practice.
Inquiry as Stance	A career-long, reflective, and philosophical approach that integrates inquiry into the core of a teacher's professional identity and practice, emphasizing continuous learning and critical reflection.

Sometimes, experiencing inquiry as process and inquiry as product can become all-consuming and overshadow inquiry stance. For this reason, the construct of inquiry stance has taken root and spread, with more and more teacher preparation programs as well as continuing professional learning endeavors grounding their teacher research work in the development of stance (Currin, 2018; D. C. Delane et al., 2017; Wolkenhauer & Hooser, 2017; Yendol-Hoppey et al., 2018). One prime example of this grounding comes from colleagues A. J. Zenkert and Jennifer Snow at Boise State University in Idaho, who name three key components of an inquiry stance for the teacher candidates and practicing teachers with whom they work, and they model this stance for their students through studying their own teacher education program (Snow et al., 2017). The Boise State University's definition of stance and the ways it is woven throughout their program are described in the textbox.

THREE ELEMENTS OF STANCE

Boise State University

A. J. Zenkert and Jennifer Snow

Our teacher education programs and specifically our field-based "Professional Year" experience are grounded in inquiry stance. Teaching and leading is a complex activity, and schools are complex places, situated within a social, political, and historical context. Interpreting and understanding common behaviors and actions in school culture requires being careful in assigning meaning to everyday events or simply accepting certain ways of doing business because "that's the way it has always been done."

This type of openness requires an inquiry stance. An inquiry stance is a way of making meaning of what is going on around us. Developing an inquiry stance suggests a willingness to step back and reflect rather than react to what is happening.

An inquiry stance involves the following:

Asking questions about teacher practice, student learning, schoolwide practices, national and international cultures and practices, and self. Rather than jumping to conclusions or blindly accepting an answer, teachers and leaders with an inquiry stance ask questions and then set out to find answers to questions. The motivation for the questions comes from a desire to *understand*.

Checking assumptions against evidence (others' and our own). Teachers and leaders with an inquiry stance check their assumptions. An assumption is something you take as true based on a particular belief, value, or condition that goes unchecked. Checking one's assumptions means trying on alternative interpretations of an event or behavior or asking, "Who's controlling the story or narrative of this event?" Or, "What's my evidence for agreeing with the theory or belief at the root of this action?"

Informing one's understanding of a situation with new data. Teachers and leaders with an inquiry stance are continuous learners, building their background knowledge through the reading of research and being in dialogue with colleagues with similar and different experiences and worldviews. Teachers and leaders with an inquiry stance use data in a variety of forms to answer their questions and wonderings. These data may be quantitative achievement data or they could be more qualitative data related to social interactions. In either case, the teachers and leaders collect and use data in a systematic way to answer their questions.

We believe the activities in which the candidates engage prepare them to take an inquiry stance toward teaching when they enter the profession. Specifically, all candidates participate in an Inquiry Scaffolding Seminar and an Inquiry Roundtable Session during the first semester of the professional year (internship).

At the Inquiry Scaffolding Seminar, candidates and liaisons work together to move toward building researchable inquiry questions. After this, individual liaisons work with mentors and candidates one on one and in small groups to further refine these questions, and the accompanying studies, as inquiry stance is developed and reflected on.

At the Inquiry Roundtable Session, candidates share their research and experiences with attendees (who include mentors, liaisons, professors, incoming interns, and student teachers) and engage them in dialogue centered on inquiry into practice. This inquiry community is meant to model what practice could be like when one approaches teaching with an inquiry stance.

To experience inquiry as the dynamic three in one—process, product, *and* stance—teaching and inquiry must be seamlessly intertwined with one another, blurring the artificial distinction between teaching and inquiring. In geometric terms, it's important to remember that inquiry is best understood not as a line:

Develop a Wondering → Collect Data → Analyze Data → Take Action → Share

but as the circle we've presented throughout this book:

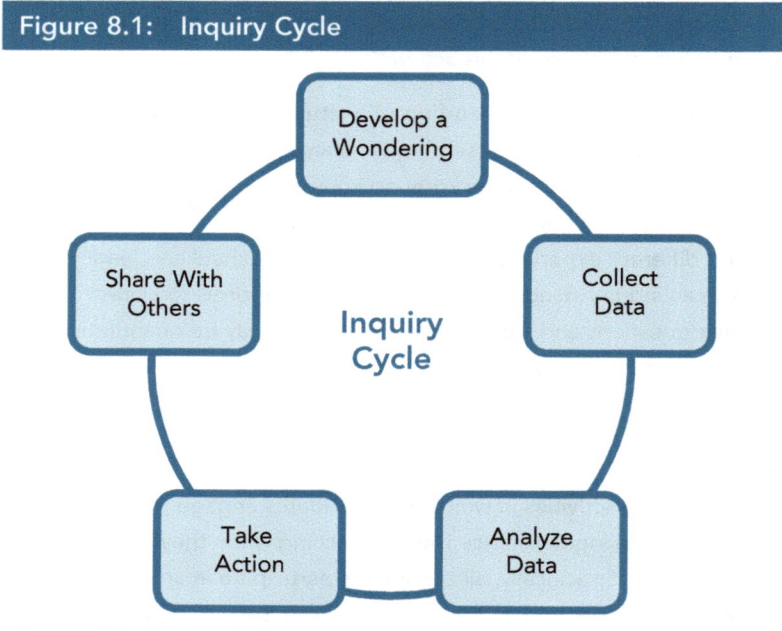

Figure 8.1: Inquiry Cycle

Since the circle has no beginning and no end, it has been symbolic of many things throughout the ages and can serve as a powerful reminder that although your particular action research project might appear to be culminating as you near the end of this book, your inquiry stance continues to be a powerful force and source of knowledge for self and others throughout your professional lifetime. Just like the circle, it has no end.

As a teacher who adopts an inquiry stance toward teaching, you provide a living example and inspiration for others in the teaching profession that inquiry is less about what one does (e.g., one inquiry project) and more about who one is (e.g., a teacher who positions himself or herself professionally not as an implementer of a rigid, unchanging teaching routine year after year but as a constant and continuous questioner, wonderer, and explorer throughout the professional lifetime). You understand that engaging in inquiry is not about solving every educational problem; it's about finding new and better problems to study and in so doing, leading a continuous cycle of self and school improvement . . . truly, becoming the best that you can be.

Engaging in teacher research helps you become the best you can be in your teaching practice, but what about becoming the best you can be as a researcher? If, through inquiry, you can find a way to enhance and build your research skills in addition to the ways you enhance and build your teaching practice, the power of your inquiry magnifies exponentially with each cycle you complete. Research skills are built by assessing the quality of your work.

Why Is It Important to Assess the Quality of My Work?

When teachers complete their first cycle of inquiry, it is often the end product of that work that gets all the attention. Certainly, the completion of one cycle through the inquiry process should be noted, celebrated, and shared with others, as we noted in Chapter 6. Yet the spotlight on one particular inquiry cycle can potentially overshadow the importance of the inquiry stance. Remember, it is the ability of teacher research to actualize an inquiry stance toward teaching that is the reason for engaging in teacher research in the first place.

That being said, it is still natural, necessary, and important to focus on each single cycle through inquiry, as we have done in this text. It is through focusing intently on each individual cycle that teachers are enabled to take charge of their own professional learning and continually improve their teaching. With each individual cycle of inquiry, the quality of the related teaching occurring in the classroom is enhanced. We believe that the degree of enhancement of classroom teaching brought about through inquiry is directly related to the quality of the inquiry. For this reason, it is important for teacher inquirers to commit both to quality teaching *and* to quality teacher research.

We improve as teachers and researchers not only through engagement in our own teacher research, but also through the teacher research of our colleagues. Cochran-Smith and Lytle remind us that

> teacher research should be valued not simply as a heuristic for the individual teacher. Rather, if it is to play a role in

the formation of the knowledge base for teaching, teacher research must also be cumulative and accessible to different people over time for a variety of purposes. (Cochran-Smith & Lytle, 1993, p. 25)

As Cochran-Smith and Lytle note, teacher research differs from a heuristic, which usually leads rapidly to a solution of an informal problem because teacher research relies on systematic and intentional study. Teacher researchers do more than create heuristics as the work of inquiry moves beyond educated guesses or intuitive judgments considered reasonably close to the best possible answer based on loosely applicable information. Additionally, teacher researchers capture their systematic, intentional study in ways that can be shared with other teachers through presenting and writing (as discussed in Chapter 6). As you hear and read the research of teaching colleagues, it is also important for you to understand the details of their work, not for the purpose of finding fault or becoming judgmental but instead for the purpose of seeking to understand and assess the ways a colleague's research might inform your own teaching practice, a term researchers refer to as *transferability*.

What Is the Difference Between Generalizability and Transferability?

We have previously discussed that the reason we prefer the generic terms *inquiry* to *action research* or *teacher research* is that the word *research* often conjures up images antithetical to the teacher research process (e.g., extensive number crunching and statistical analyses, white lab coats, experimental designs with a control and treatment group, and long hours in the library). Another image associated with the word *research* is generalizability, or the extent to which the findings of a research study will hold true and should be applied to other populations. Just as teacher research is not consonant with extensive number crunching and statistical analyses, white lab coats, experimental designs, and long hours in the library, teacher research is not meant to be generalizable to *all* teachers *everywhere*.

For example, recall Debbi Hubbell's inquiry in Chapter 3, on the relationship between the reading of fractured fairy tale plays and fluency development in seven of her struggling fourth-grade learners. If you revisit Debbi's DIBELS data (see Figure 3.15), you will note that each of the seven learners she was tracking improved his or her DIBELS performance over time. This does not mean that *every* teacher in Debbi's school ought to start using fractured fairy tale plays during reading instruction, as one might believe to be the case if the purpose of teacher research was to be generalizable. Remember, teacher action research is typically about capturing the natural actions that occur in the busy, real world of the classroom. Debbi selected DIBELS as one form of data to capture action in *her* classroom, not as a proven, valid, and reliable measure of fluency development so that her work can be generalized to all fourth-grade teachers everywhere!

Additionally, Debbi's sample size of seven learners was small. Debbi did not select these seven learners because she wished to have an adequate sample size so her findings could be applied to other classroom teachers. Rather, Debbi selected these seven learners because they were struggling, and she cared deeply about finding some ways to help them become more capable readers. Finally, Debbi didn't consciously and deliberatively isolate what might be considered her treatment variable (the reading of fractured fairy tale plays) from all other intervening variables that might play a role in her struggling students' fluency development (like Debbi's approach to the teaching of phonics and intonation). Rather, Debbi integrated everything she knew about the teaching of reading in combination with her introduction of fractured fairy tale plays to target these seven learners' success as readers. Debbi approached her research not as a scientist who wished to discover the best way to teach all children to read but as a teacher who cared passionately for seven individuals in her own classroom, with the hope of discovering some insights that might help her reach these struggling readers. Debbi's research, as is the case with all teacher research, was designed to focus *inward* on informing her own classroom teaching, rather than *outward* on proving that a particular strategy would be effective for others.

Keeping the notion of the inward versus outward significance of teacher research in mind, an important question emerges: "Is there any worth in Debbi's research for other teachers?" The answer to this question is a resounding "Yes!" The worth of Debbi's (or any individual teacher's) research for other teachers is in its transferability to their own classroom. According to Jeffrey Barnes and his colleagues, qualitative researchers define transferability as

> a process performed by readers of research. Readers note the specifics of the research situation and compare them to the specifics of an environment or situation with which they are familiar. If there are enough similarities between the two situations, readers may be able to infer that the results

of the research would be the same or similar in their own situation. In other words, they "transfer" the results of a study to another context. To do this effectively, readers need to know as much as possible about the original research situation in order to determine whether it is similar to their own. Therefore, researchers must supply a highly detailed description of their research situation and methods.
(Barnes et al., 2007)

Another important component of assessing the transferability of another teacher's research to your own classroom is considering the quality of that teacher's research, a process easier said than done. Teacher inquirers need to understand the quality of the study in order to determine for themselves whether the knowledge shared in the form of findings would be potentially useful in their own classroom.

How Do I Go About Assessing Teacher Research Quality, and Why Is It So Difficult to Do?

While a plethora of books, journal articles, and websites address the importance of engaging in the study of one's own practice and provide detailed instructions on how to do it, surprisingly, there has been relatively little discussion on how to assess practitioner research quality. The reason for the lack of discussion on practitioner research quality may be that, for years, the focus has been on getting teachers started in the process, as there is clear evidence that engagement in practitioner research can be a powerful form of teacher professional learning as well as a transformative process.

CIRCLE BACK

As a reminder of the abundant evidence that exists in support of teachers' engagement in inquiry, circle back to Chapter 1's section "What Evidence Exists That Teacher Inquiry Is Worth Doing?" on page 4.

Practitioner research has been around for quite some time, and for years determining quality has been the proverbial elephant in the room. It seems to have mattered more that teachers were engaged in the process; as long as engagement was present and individual teachers were personally improving, research quality, in and of itself, received less attention. Yet we believe it is important for every teacher to consider quality. Recall that in the introduction to this book we stated,

> Teacher inquiry is a vehicle that can be used by teachers to untangle some of the complexities that occur in the profession, raise teachers' voices in discussions of educational reform, and ultimately transform assumptions about the teaching profession itself. Transforming the profession is really the capstone to the teacher inquiry experience.

If practitioner inquiry aims to replace the simplistic, connect-the-dots view of teaching held by policymakers with a view that values teaching as intellectual, ethical, and inclusive of teachers' voices in educational equity and reform, then the question of quality becomes essential. As the quality of the research generated by teachers increases, the knowledge generated is perceived as both valid and valuable to policymakers, the general public, and other educational practitioners. As teacher knowledge is created and recognized, the transformation of the teaching profession becomes increasingly possible through the teacher research movement.

Although it is easy to make a case for the importance of assessing teacher research quality, it is a much more difficult task to discuss how to do that assessment. One reason it is difficult to assess teacher research quality is that traditional notions of what constitutes quality research (such as generalizability) might creep into discussions of quality, even though they are not applicable to teacher research studies. This is especially likely to occur when teacher research quality assessment is done by those with limited understandings of teacher research and the ways it differs from other research traditions, as discussed in Chapter 1. In fact, we believe one reason teacher research quality has received limited attention is that discussions of teacher research quality might deter teachers from engaging in the process to begin with if discussions of quality become biting critiques or attacks on the validity, generalizability, or reliability of an individual's research. Such critiques, steeped in traditional notions of research and the process-product paradigm, would be erroneous and nonsensical. You cannot assess research produced in one research paradigm from the viewpoint of a different paradigm. To do so would be like assessing the play of a football player using the criteria used to assess the performance of a ballerina. It would be a travesty for a teacher researcher to become discouraged due to assessments of his or her work that used nonsensical criteria.

CIRCLE BACK

For a summary of research traditions' similarities and differences, circle back to Table 1.1 on page 8.

Another complication associated with determining the quality of an inquiry effort is the dual purposes for engaging in teacher research. For example, one purpose of teacher research is to serve as a tool for self-directed and differentiated professional learning that actualizes itself in self-regulated, lifelong learners who approach their learning from an inquiry stance (Glickman et al., 2007). Using this purpose as a framework for assessing quality, one might consider a teacher's experience with teacher research to be of quality if, as a result of her participation, she developed an inquiry stance that caused her to regularly construct wonderings and make her practice problematic. However, the second goal of teacher research as discussed by Cochran-Smith and Lytle (1993, 1999) is to contribute to the knowledge base of teaching. In order to make a valuable contribution to the knowledge base for teaching, teacher research must be credible. In teacher research, credibility refers to the compatibility between the teacher researcher's inquiry findings and the reality lived by students and the teacher each school day in that same teacher researcher's classroom. Credibility of a piece of teacher research is enhanced by such mechanisms as engaging in an inquiry for a sufficient period relative to the wondering being asked, situating that wondering in the existing knowledge base for teaching with thoughtful reference to what is already known about the subject, and checking consistency of inquiry findings by using more than one source of data to gain insights into a wondering. In this case, where we are using the contribution to the knowledge base for teaching as a framework for assessing quality, one might consider a teacher's experience with teacher research to be of quality if the teacher inquirer spent sufficient time studying his or her question, connecting it thoughtfully to what is already known, and using multiple data sources to understand and represent the complexity of her problem for study.

It is possible for a teacher researcher's work to be considered of quality using the professional learning framework but lacking in quality using the contribution to the knowledge base for teaching framework—and vice versa. Consider a teacher who has historically approached teaching as a stagnant routine. His first pass through the cycle of inquiry as a required professional development activity in his district focused on the implementation of a commercially prepared curriculum package with no research base, and he used only standardized test scores to indicate the value of this particular commercially prepared curriculum package. As a contribution to the knowledge base for teaching, this inquiry was lacking credibility because it was based on a curriculum that was disconnected from what is known about teaching, and he relied solely on one form of data to gain insights into his wondering. However, being immersed in this cycle of inquiry with other teacher researchers led him to begin to raise questions about his own teaching and his own unquestioned implementation of mandated commercially prepared material in his classroom. A teacher who once saw teaching as black and white (i.e., implementing a commercially prepared curriculum in the classroom as instructed) began to see shades of gray in his teaching practice (i.e., this commercially prepared curriculum may not work the same ways with all learners, and its effectiveness is dependent on the teacher's ability to supplement it with other materials). While this particular inquiry contributed little to the knowledge base for teaching, it was extremely powerful in moving a teacher forward in his own teaching practice. As you can see, the fact that teacher research serves dual purposes actually makes the work of assessing quality even more complicated than traditional research.

A third reason it is difficult to assess the quality of teacher research is the relationship between inquiry stance (one's way of being as a teacher) and the products one produces as a result of actualizing that stance (a piece of teacher research). As previously mentioned, more important than any one teacher research product is the inquiry stance. It is the cultivation of such a stance in every educator that will improve our profession. While it is challenging to assess stance (see, e.g., Rutten & Wolkenhauer, 2023a, 2023b, 2024), you can assess a piece of action research produced as an actualization of that stance. In fact, given the definition of inquiry stance, a teacher who possesses an inquiry stance toward teaching would logically invite reflection on the quality of individual pieces of teacher research.

But which comes first, the adoption of an inquiry stance toward teaching or the production of teacher research products? The posing of this question resembles the old adage, "Which comes first, the chicken or the egg?" It might be logical to think that stance comes first, but we have seen many teacher researchers approach the teacher research process first as a project they were required to complete to earn continuing education units/professional development hours for state licensure, as a new professional learning initiative their school or district implemented (veteran teachers), or as a so-called university thing—an assignment they had to complete for a college course (teacher candidates). While they initially approached their work as a *project,* it was through the completion of the project that they developed *stance.* If engagement in projects can lead to stance, once again it would become a travesty if any teacher researcher became discouraged by quality assessment and subsequently abandoned teacher research.

A fourth reason it is difficult to assess the quality of teacher research is that the ways teachers encapsulate what they did and what they have learned through the process of teacher research come in many shapes and sizes. As discussed in Chapter 6, some teachers write detailed accounts of their work, some teachers write summaries or brochures, and still others present their work orally. No matter how teacher researchers encapsulate and report on their learning, there are always limitations in time and space. Teacher researchers make decisions based on time and space allotments in regard to which portions of their teacher inquiry journey they will emphasize and, sometimes, which portions they won't even mention in a written account or oral presentation. Therefore, assessments might be made about the quality of teacher research based on the absence of particular components of the inquiry journey that may have been present but not a part of the written or oral report.

A final reason it is difficult to assess the quality of an inquiry is because in any discussion of teacher research quality, it is important to consider where teachers are developmentally as researchers and as teachers. Does one assess quality teacher research for all from the standpoint of what to look for in an experienced teacher researcher's work or from the standpoint of what would be developmentally appropriate for whatever phase of development a teacher researcher is at? Just as one's teaching practice develops over the years through experience, so does one's research skills. You would not hold the same expectations for the classroom teaching performance of a novice teacher as you would for a 25-year veteran. Likewise, it is unrealistic to think that the first time you engage in research, you will excel at every aspect of the inquiry process. Not excelling at every aspect of the process, however, is neither a reason to negate the value of a piece of teacher research nor, more importantly, a reason *not* to engage in teacher research!

Everyone has to start somewhere, and if you take the time to assess the quality of your inquiry you will grow as a researcher through each cycle of the inquiry process. Furthermore, if you engage in careful, thoughtful assessment of others' practitioner research, you can make more informed decisions about the transferability of your colleagues' research to your own teaching practice. Participating in careful discussions of quality—what it is and how to achieve it—helps us all improve both teaching practice and teacher research and further understand the intimate connection between the two. In turn, these discussions move the profession of teaching forward.

In the next section of this chapter, we offer seven indicators (summarized in Table 8.2) to consider the quality of your own and others' research. In the offering of these indicators, we also hope to spark a discussion among you and your colleagues about what constitutes quality. Definitions of each quality indicator are followed by a set of questions you can use both to reflect on and assess the quality of your own inquiry work as well as the work done by other teacher researchers and the ways their work might be transferable to your own teaching context. Our list of quality indicators and questions is by no means meant to be definitive or exhaustive of all potential quality indicators but rather to serve as a starting point for reflection. As you read these quality indicators, keep in mind that an individual develops as a teacher researcher over many years and many cycles of inquiry. Rarely is any teacher researcher outstanding in all aspects of the inquiry process all the time. Less important than using these indicators to scrutinize and grade every aspect of your own and others' work is using these indicators as a tool to gain new insights into the inquiry process that you can apply to your next research cycle.

Table 8.2 Quality Indicators for Assessing Practitioner Inquiry

QUALITY INDICATOR	DESCRIPTION	QUESTIONS TO ASSESS QUALITY
Context for Inquiry	Teacher researchers provide complete information about the context in which their inquiry took place, including relevant details about the school, district, classroom, students, and curriculum. They also discuss their own positionality, describing any personal background, perspectives, identities, or theoretical influences that shaped their inquiry.	• Were key aspects of the study context described and considered when conceptualizing the inquiry? • Was the study context described in sufficient detail for others to understand how the wonderings emerged from within that context? • Were reflections on the teacher researcher's positionality considered in relation to the study context? Were the insights from this reflection used to inform the study? • Did the teacher researcher consider how the study's context was similar to or different from other contexts?

(Continued)

(Continued)

QUALITY INDICATOR	DESCRIPTION	QUESTIONS TO ASSESS QUALITY
Wonderings and Purpose	Teacher researchers explain the root of their wonderings in detail. Explanations for the purpose and wonderings make a compelling case for why the inquiry is important to pursue. Wonderings about problems of practice are linked to relevant literature and stated in a way that is open-ended (i.e., answer is not already known), jargon-free, and focused inward (i.e., on the inquirer's own professional practices). The wonderings emerge from real dilemmas or tensions, are framed in strengths-/asset-based language, and are not aimed at fixing or proving something to others.	• Was the problem of practice that led to the formation of the wondering(s) clearly described? Was the inquiry's focus clear? • Were compelling reasons provided for why the inquiry was worth pursuing? • Was the wondering connected to existing literature? • Were key terms/concepts defined clearly and without excessive educational jargon? • Was the wondering focused on the inquirer's own practices? • Was there a clear connection between the wondering and improving student learning? • Was the wondering framed in strengths-/asset-based language about individuals and communities? • Was the wondering structured as an open-ended question that respects the complexity of teaching? • Did the wondering resonate with others' problems of practice? • Did the inquiry inspire thinking about similar issues in other contexts?
Inquiry Design	Teacher researchers develop designs for their inquiries that are thoughtfully planned and transparently articulated. The design is flexible, and any detours from the original plan are explained. Actions taken in pursuit of the inquiry are described in detail, and relevant literature is cited in support of the actions. Ethics are considered throughout the inquiry, with appropriate permissions sought, collaborations with others acknowledged, and uses of AI tools adequately disclosed.	• Was there a clear link between the study's context and the wondering? Between the wondering and the approach to data collection? • Were perspectives from multiple stakeholders in the problem of practice sought as part of the design process? • Was literature consulted in planning the approach to data collection and/or actions taken throughout the inquiry? • Were the ethics of the inquiry clearly considered? If necessary, were appropriate permissions obtained prior to the start of data collection? • If used, were the ethics of AI tools clearly considered? • If any ethical dilemmas arose during the inquiry, did the teacher researcher discuss how these were handled?

QUALITY INDICATOR	DESCRIPTION	QUESTIONS TO ASSESS QUALITY
Data Collection	Teacher researchers gather data from multiple relevant sources, ensuring that each source is thoughtfully selected to provide a well-rounded perspective on their wonderings. Explanations are provided for data collection procedures, including a rationale for the data sources chosen.	• Were data collected from multiple sources to deepen understanding of the wondering (e.g., student work, field notes, interviews, etc.)? • Were data collected from a variety of different perspectives and/or stakeholders in the problem of practice? • Was a compelling explanation offered for why each data source was selected and how it contributed to the inquiry? • Were data collected over a suitable time frame to provide credible insights for the wonderings posed? • Were sufficient data collected to enable an informed, meaningful response to the wondering?
Data Analysis	Teacher researchers conduct thorough analyses of their data, using strategies that allow for a rich interpretation of the data in relation to the wonderings pursued. Analysis methods are described clearly, including a rationale for the methods chosen.	• Was a systematic approach to summative data analysis employed (e.g., the four-step process described in Chapter 5)? • Was the approach to data analysis (including any coding, memoing, or other strategies used) clearly explained, with concrete examples offered to illustrate the approach? • Were the analytic methods well-suited for both the data collected and for responding meaningfully to the wondering? • Were descriptions offered of any changes that occurred within the data analysis process throughout the time frame of the inquiry? • If quantitative data were used, were descriptive statistics reported? If so, were these statistics useful in illustrating the findings? • If qualitative data were used, were coding and memoing processes used? If so, were these processes clear and transparent? • Were data displays used effectively during the descriptive and sense-making phases of analysis? Were visual displays provided and the purpose explained? • Was adequate attention given to patterns and themes in the data?

(Continued)

(Continued)

QUALITY INDICATOR	DESCRIPTION	QUESTIONS TO ASSESS QUALITY
Statements of Learning (Findings)	Teacher researchers articulate clear, thoughtful statements about what they learned through summative data analysis (i.e., their research findings or claims). They provide evidence from multiple sources to support the claims they make, and there are clear links between their statements of learning and their approach to data analysis. Any unexpected patterns or discrepancies in the findings are openly acknowledged and discussed.	• Is it clear how the analysis linked the statements of learning/findings to the data that were collected? • Were all claims/conclusions supported by multiple pieces of data? • Were any claims/conclusions reported that were not supported by data? • Were any experiences that were shared connected to the data and analysis? Were experiences used to force data to fit into preexisting beliefs or opinions held prior to the start of the inquiry? • How were the findings illustrated (through themes, metaphors, vignettes, etc.)? Were these illustrations effective in conveying the key findings? • Were multiple potential interpretations considered? • Were unexpected, surprising, or contradictory findings acknowledged? If so, were they addressed thoughtfully? • Were reflections on what was learned about teaching shared? Were reflections about the process of teacher inquiry shared?
Implications for Practice	Teacher researchers detail actions they have taken or will take to improve teaching practice based on their findings. These changes logically flow from their learning, and they may include ideas for future inquiries and plans for continued reflection and assessment of the new practices.	• Did the inquiry lead to specific actions, planned changes, or recommendations for teaching practice? • Were the actions or planned changes logical outgrowths of what was learned? In what ways? • Were the actions clearly connected to data collected through the inquiry? Which specific pieces of data supported the actions taken or changes planned? • To what extent do the actions taken resonate with others' experiences or teaching practices? • In what ways might the findings inform or apply to others' classrooms?

What Are Some Quality Indicators for Teacher Research?

Quality Indicator 1: Context for Inquiry

Teacher researchers provide complete information about the context in which their inquiry took place. This may include, but is not limited to, information about the school, district, classroom, students, and curriculum. In addition, in recognition of the ways their own backgrounds and histories shape the way they view teaching and learning and ultimately what they choose to inquire into, teacher researchers discuss their own positionality by describing any background experiences, perspectives, philosophies, identities, and/or conceptual and theoretical ideas that have influenced their thinking within this cycle of inquiry.

Review "Positionality" by looking back to Chapter 4, Inquiry Planning Stage 1's "Consult the Literature" section, on page 171.

CIRCLE BACK

Questions to ask about the study context of an inquiry:

- Were key aspects of the study context described and considered when conceptualizing the inquiry?
- Was the study context described in sufficient detail for others to understand how the wonderings emerged from within that context?
- Were reflections on the teacher researcher's positionality considered in relation to the study context? Were the insights from this reflection used to inform the study?
- Did the teacher researcher consider how the study's context was similar to or different from other contexts?

Quality Indicator 2: Wonderings and Purpose

Teacher researchers explain the root of their questions/wonderings in detail by describing the problem of practice from which the wondering emerged. The explanation makes a convincing case for the wonderings' personal importance to the researcher. The stated wonderings are connected to appropriate and pertinent literature from the field. The purpose and questions/wonderings are clearly articulated, free of educational jargon, focused inward (on the teacher's own practice), and open-ended (i.e., the teacher researcher did not pose a question for which the answer was already known).

Questions to ask about the wonderings and purpose of an inquiry:

- Was the problem of practice that led to the formation of the wondering(s) clearly described? Was the inquiry's focus clear?
- Were compelling reasons provided for why the inquiry was worth pursuing?
- Was the wondering connected to existing literature?
- Were key terms/concepts defined clearly and without excessive educational jargon?
- Was the wondering focused on the inquirer's own practices?
- Was there a clear connection between the wondering and improving student learning?
- Was the wondering framed in strengths-/asset-based language about individuals and communities?
- Was the wondering structured as an open-ended question that respects the complexity of teaching?
- Did the wondering resonate with others' problems of practice?
- Did the inquiry inspire thinking about similar issues in other contexts?

Quality Indicator 3: Inquiry Design

Teacher researchers develop an inquiry design that has been thoughtfully planned and carefully articulated. Actions taken by the inquirer (whether to address a problem or to develop a better understanding of a problem) are described in detail. Where appropriate, literature is cited in support of the course of action the teacher researcher took. The inquiry design incorporates flexibility, allowing for adjustments to be made based on new insights that emerged as the design was implemented. As such, if applicable, teacher researchers note and explain any detours taken from their original plan for inquiry. The research is designed and implemented in an ethical manner, acknowledging any collaboration with colleagues and/or AI tools in the design and implementation of the inquiry plan.

Questions to ask when assessing the design of an inquiry:

- Was there a clear link between the study's context and the wondering? Between the wondering and the approach to data collection?

- Were perspectives from multiple stakeholders in the problem of practice sought as part of the design process?

- Was literature consulted in planning the approach to data collection and/or actions taken throughout the inquiry?

- Were the ethics of the inquiry clearly considered? If necessary, were appropriate permissions obtained prior to the start of data collection?

- If used, were the ethics of AI tools clearly considered?

- If any ethical dilemmas arose during the inquiry, did the teacher researcher discuss how these were handled?

Quality Indicator 4: Data Collection

Teacher researchers collect data in alignment with their research design. They employ a variety of data sources, with particular attention to naturally occurring data, to provide a well-rounded investigation of their wonderings. Effective data collection involves not only gathering information from diverse sources but also providing a rationale for the selection of each source and how it contributes to addressing the inquiry questions. A high-quality data collection process ensures that data are collected over a suitable time frame to capture meaningful insights and provide credible evidence.

Questions to ask when assessing the data collection for an inquiry:

- Were data collected from multiple sources to deepen understanding of the wondering (e.g., student work, field notes, interviews, etc.)?
- Were data collected from a variety of different perspectives and/or stakeholders in the problem of practice?
- Was a compelling explanation offered for why each data source was selected and how it contributed to the inquiry?
- Were data collected over a suitable time frame to provide credible insights for the wonderings posed?
- Were sufficient data collected to enable an informed, meaningful response to the wondering?

Quality Indicator 5: Data Analysis

Teacher researchers engage in a thorough analysis of the collected data, both formatively (throughout the inquiry) and summatively (at the close of an inquiry cycle), using methods that enable them to draw meaningful insights related to their wonderings. The teacher researcher keeps track of and reports on the data analysis methods used (i.e., coding, memoing, visual displays, etc.) and how these methods were applied to make sense of the data, citing literature on teacher research methodology when appropriate. A strong analysis also considers any data that do not align with expected outcomes, providing explanations for these discrepancies.

Questions to ask when assessing the data analysis for an inquiry:

- Was a systematic approach to summative data analysis employed (e.g., the four-step process described in Chapter 5)?
- Was the approach to data analysis (including any coding, memoing, or other strategies used) clearly explained, with concrete examples offered to illustrate the approach?
- Were the analytic methods well-suited for both the data collected and for responding meaningfully to the wondering?

- Were descriptions offered of any changes that occurred within the data analysis process throughout the time frame of the inquiry?

- If quantitative data were used, were descriptive statistics reported? If so, were these statistics useful in illustrating the findings?

- If qualitative data were used, were coding and memoing processes used? If so, were these processes clear and transparent?

- Were data displays used effectively during the descriptive and sense-making phases of analysis? Were visual displays provided and the purpose explained?

- Was adequate attention given to patterns and themes in the data?

Quality Indicator 6: Statements of Learning (Findings)

Teacher researchers articulate clear, thoughtful statements about what they learned through summative data analysis (their research findings), taking care to provide evidence from their data to support the learning claims made. Each finding is supported, in detail, by data. If relevant, they may also include data that did not appear to fit with the findings being reported, with possible explanations for the discrepant data. Teacher researchers weave readings and other relevant experiences into the discussion of their findings as the readings and experiences relate to what was learned. Additionally, teacher researchers integrate relevant readings or prior experiences to better understand and contextualize their findings. They reflect on what was learned about the inquiry topic and the teacher research process itself.

Questions to ask when considering the learning (findings) that resulted from an inquiry:

- Is it clear how the analysis linked the statements of learning/findings to the data that were collected?

- Were all claims/conclusions supported by multiple pieces of data?

- Were any claims/conclusions reported that were unsupported by data?

(Continued)

(Continued)

- Were any experiences that were shared connected to the data and analysis? Were experiences used to force data to fit into preexisting beliefs or opinions held prior to the start of the inquiry?
- How were the findings illustrated (through themes, metaphors, vignettes, etc.)? Were these illustrations effective in conveying the key findings?
- Were multiple potential interpretations considered?
- Were unexpected, surprising, or contradictory findings acknowledged? If so, were they addressed thoughtfully?
- Were reflections on what was learned about teaching shared? Were reflections about the process of teacher inquiry shared?

Quality Indicator 7: Implications for Practice

Teacher researchers detail examples of instructional change they have made or will consider making based on what they learned through their research. Changes in practice flow logically from the teacher researcher's findings. In addition, teacher researchers discuss wonderings that they might pursue in the future based on what they learned from their current teacher research.

Questions to ask when assessing the implications for practice of an inquiry:

- Did the inquiry lead to specific actions, planned changes, or recommendations for teaching practice?
- Were the actions or planned changes logical outgrowths of what was learned? In what ways?
- Were the actions clearly connected to data collected through the inquiry? Which specific pieces of data supported the actions taken or changes planned?
- To what extent do the actions taken resonate with others' experiences or teaching practices?
- In what ways might the findings inform or apply to others' classrooms?

What Are Some Ways to Enhance Inquiry Quality?

As previously mentioned, the quality of teacher research can be enhanced simply by taking the time to reflect on and discuss the quality of your work with others and to apply what you learn through these discussions to your next cycle as a teacher researcher. The questions we have provided in the previous section are designed to get you started on these reflections and discussions. In addition to engaging in collaborative reflections on the quality of your teacher research with colleagues, we have found that the coaching teacher inquirers receive throughout the process is directly related to the quality of their work (Dana & Yendol-Hoppey, 2006; Drennon & Cervero, 2002; Krell & Dana, 2012). These coaches might be colleagues in your building with many years of inquiry experience or National Board teachers in your district who have made inquiry a central piece of their teaching practice. You might also solicit help from university partners who specialize in coaching the teacher research process. Whomever you select, involving an experienced coach can greatly enhance the quality of your inquiry, since discussing your wondering with a critical friend will deepen both the process and the knowledge constructed. If you are interested in increasing the quality of teacher inquiry that occurs in your school, district, or teacher education program through careful and thoughtful attention to the development of quality coaching, you might enjoy the companion book to this text, *The Reflective Educator's Guide to Professional Development: Coaching Inquiry-Oriented Learning Communities,* or *The PLC Book,* a text we wrote that seamlessly integrates the inquiry process into the fabric of the ways a Professional Learning Community functions, thereby providing coaching for all learning community members.

Where Do I Go From Here?

In the preface to this text we stated that when teachers inquire, they provide insights "into the power that teacher inquiry holds to transform classrooms and schools to places where teachers' voices contribute to the knowledge generated about teaching and learning." We hope that as you finish this text, you have enjoyed your journey through the basic tenets of the inquiry process, the ultimate goal of which is *not* to produce an inquiry product but instead to adopt a stance toward your teaching and the teaching profession characterized by continuous problematizing of practice, studying of practice, and leading change efforts to improve life and learning conditions for *all* students based on the outcomes of such study. This is the ultimate journey on which we hope you will embark. This is where you go from here—embracing this ultimate journey to empower and guide you throughout the entirety of your professional life.

We believe no other author captures the nature of this ultimate journey as eloquently as William Ayers in the following quote we used at the very opening of this book. Coming full circle, we close our book as we began it:

Teaching involves a search for meaning in the world. Teaching is a life project, a calling, a vocation that is an organizing center of all other activities. Teaching is past and future as well as present, it is background as well as foreground, it is depth as well as surface. Teaching is pain and humor, joy and anger, dreariness and epiphany. Teaching is world building, it is architecture and design, it is purpose and moral enterprise. Teaching is a way of being in the world that breaks through the boundaries of the traditional job and in the process redefines all life and teaching itself. (Ayers, 1989, p. 130)

Through embarking on the inquiry journey, you break boundaries. You redefine life. You redefine teaching itself. Bon voyage!

CHAPTER 8 EXERCISES

1. Table 8.2 summarizes the seven quality indicators in this chapter and the corresponding questions you can use to reflect on and assess the quality of your own work and the work of others. Use this table to review your most recent piece of teacher research. What do you consider to be your strengths as a teacher inquirer? What are some areas you wish to improve on in your next pass though the teacher inquiry cycle?

2. Consider a product of teacher research that you have recently read or heard presented at a faculty meeting, class presentation, teacher inquiry conference, or any other venue where you had the opportunity to hear teacher inquirers share their work. Use the seven quality indicators in this chapter (summarized in Table 8.2) to reflect on and assess the quality and transferability of others' teacher research to your own classroom and teaching context.

DISCUSSION QUESTIONS

1. Which of the quality indicators presented in this chapter do you agree and disagree with and why?

2. What are some additional quality indicators you might add to those presented in this chapter?

3. Which quality indicators present the greatest challenges to novice researchers? Why?

4. How can you create a mechanism for providing honest feedback to peers on their inquiries that both honors and celebrates their work and provides areas for future growth and development as teacher researchers?

5. How can you ensure that discussions with peers about enhancing the quality of their own as well as your own teacher inquiry in future cycles will not negate the value of the research you all have produced?

ONLINE MATERIALS

The following materials designed for assessing inquiry are available for download at **https://companion.corwin.com/courses/ReflectiveEdsGuide5e**:

- **Activity 8.1: The 4 A's Protocol: Understanding the Complexity of Inquiry Stance and Assessing Teacher Inquiry.** Select passages about inquiry from the text you Agree with, Argue with, and Aspire to, as well as articulate Assumptions about the inquiry process made throughout the book's final chapter.

- **Activity 8.2: Self and Peer Evaluation.** Use seven quality indicators to conduct a self and/or peer evaluation of your own and/or others' inquiry presentations or write-ups.

References

Acheson, K. A., & Gall, M. D. (1997). *Techniques in the clinical supervision of teachers: Preservice and in-service applications*. Longman.

Adams, P. (2016). Preparing learning teachers: The role of collaborative inquiry. *Canadian Journal of Action Research*, *17*(1), 20–35. https://journals.nipissingu.ca/index.php/cjar/article/view/241

Allen, B. J. (2018). *Privilege exercise*. http://www.differencematters.info/uploads/pdf/privilege-beads-exercise.pdf

Allington, R. L. (2006). *What really matters for struggling readers: Designing research-based programs* (2nd ed.). Pearson Education.

Almquist, C. (2000, April). *Science tables in first grade*. Paper presented at the Second Annual State College Area School District–Pennsylvania State University Teacher Inquiry Conference, State College, PA, United States.

American Association of Colleges for Teacher Education (AACTE). (2018). *A pivot towards clinical practice, its lexicon, and the renewal of educator preparation: A report of the AACTE Clinical Practice Commission*. Author.

Argyris, C., & Schön, D. A. (1992). *Theory in practice: Increasing professional effectiveness*. John Wiley & Sons.

Aronowitz, S., & Giroux, H. (1985). *Education under siege*. New World Foundation.

Assaf, L., Garza, R., & Battle, J. (2010). Multicultural teacher education: Examining the perceptions, practices, and coherence in one teacher preparation program. *Teacher Education Quarterly*, *37*(2), 115–135. https://www.jstor.org/stable/23479592

Association of Teacher Educators. (2023). *Clinical experience standards* (3rd ed.). https://www.ate1.org/uploads/1/4/5/7/145746398/ate_2023_clinical_experience_standards_final_rev_011524_digital.pdf

Athanases, S. Z., Bennett, L. H., & Wahleithner, J. M. (2013). Fostering data literacy through preservice teacher inquiry in English Language Arts. *The Teacher Educator*, *48*(1), 8–28. https://doi.org/10.1080/08878730.2012.740151

Athanases, S. Z., Wahleithner, J. M., & Bennett, L. H. (2013). Learning to attend to culturally and linguistically diverse learners through teacher inquiry in teacher education. *Teachers College Record*, *114*, 1–50. https://doi.org/10.1177/016146811211400703

Au, W. (Ed.). (2009). *Rethinking multicultural education: Teaching for racial and cultural justice* (2nd ed.). A Rethinking Schools Publication.

Avery, C. (1993). *. . . And with a light touch: Learning about reading, writing, and teaching with first graders*. Heinemann.

Ayers, W. (1989). *The good preschool teacher: Six teachers reflect on their lives*. Teachers College Press.

Ayers, W., Ladson-Billings, G., Michie, G., & Noguera, P. A. (Eds.). (2008). *City kids, city schools*. The New Press.

Baird, M. S. (2018). *Improving the outcome of minority students from a high needs background in an online secondary chemistry class* [Unpublished doctoral dissertation]. University of Florida.

Baker, C. N., Peele, H., Daniels, M., Saybe, M., Whalen, K., & Overstreet, S. (2021). The experience of COVID-19 and its impact on teachers' mental health, coping, and teaching. *School Psychology Review*, *50*(4), 491–504. https://doi.org/10.1080/2372966X.2020.1855473

Barnes, J., Conrad, K., Demont-Heinrich, C., Graziano, M., Kowalski, D., Neufeld, J., Zamora, J.,

& Palmquist, M. (2007). *Generalizability and transferability*. Fort Collins: Colorado State University Department of English. http://writing.colostate.edu/guides/research/gentrans

Barnett, B. G., & Muth, R. (2008). Using action-research strategies and cohort structures to ensure research competence for practitioner-scholar leaders. *Journal of Research on Leadership Education, 3*(1), 1–42. https://doi.org/10.1177/194277510800300101

Barth, R. (1990). *Improving schools from within: Parents, teachers, and principals can make a difference*. Jossey-Bass.

Barth, R. (2001). Principal centered professional development. *Theory into practice, 25*(3), 156–160.

Berger, W. (2014). *A more beautiful question: The power of inquiry to spark breakthrough ideas*. Bloomsbury.

Bernhardt, V. (2004). *Data analysis for continuous school improvement*. Eye on Education.

Biafora, F., & Ansalone, G. (2008). Perceptions and attitudes of school principals towards school tracking: Structural considerations of personal beliefs. *Education, 128*(4), 588–602. https://eric.ed.gov/?id=EJ816945

Bigelow, B., & Peterson, B. (1998). *Rethinking Columbus: The next 500 years*. Rethinking Schools.

Bildstein, P., Kruse-Meek, M., Pohland, J., Snitkey, N., & Welsh, H. (2018, February). *Using teacher inquiry to explore creating community through cultural relevancy*. Paper presented at the Association of Teacher Educators Annual Meeting, Las Vegas, NV, United States.

Bishop, R. S. (1990). Mirrors, windows, and sliding glass doors. *Perspectives, 6*(3), ix–xi.

Blumenreich, M. (2016). Assigning reflective memo blogs to support teacher research data analysis. *Voices of Practitioners, 11*(1), 68–75. https://www.naeyc.org/sites/default/files/globally-shared/downloads/PDFs/resources/pubs/vop_fall_2016.pdf#page=72

Boudett, K. P., City, W. A., & Murnane, R. J. (2005). *Data wise: A step-by-step guide to using assessment results to improve teaching and learning*. Harvard Education Press.

Boyd, T. A. (1961). *Prophet of progress: Selections from the speeches of Charles F. Kettering*. E. P. Dutton.

Boykin, W., & Noguera, P. (2011). *Creating the opportunity to learn: Moving from research to practice to close the achievement gap*. Association for Supervision and Curriculum Development.

Brindley, R., & Crocco, C. (2009). *Empowering the voice of the teacher researcher: Achieving success through a culture of inquiry*. Rowman & Littlefield.

Brown, P. (2010). Teacher research and university institutional review boards. *Journal of Early Childhood Teacher Education, 31*, 276–283. https://doi.org/10.1080/10901027.2010.500559

Bryan, C., & Reilly-Kaminski, K. (2002, April). *Effective parent communication: What does it look like?* Paper presented at the fourth annual State College Area School District—Pennsylvania State University Teacher Inquiry Conference, State College, PA, United States.

Burgin, S. (2007a). A Demo-a-Day in high school chemistry. In N. F. Dana & D. C. Delane (Eds.), *Improving Florida schools through teacher inquiry: Selections from the 2006 Teaching, Inquiry, and Innovation Showcase* (pp. 126–135). University of Florida, Center for School Improvement.

Burgin, S. (2007b, April). *Student perceptions of teacher help outside of class*. Paper presented at the third annual University of Florida Teaching, Inquiry, and Innovation Showcase, Gainesville, FL, United States.

Burns, J. (2024). *Nurturing inquiry stance in teachers: Balancing accountability and inquiry-based practice*. Paper presented at the British Educational Research Association (BERA) Annual Conference, Manchester, UK.

Burris, C. C. (2014). *On the same track: How schools can join the twenty-first century struggle against resegregation*. Beacon Press.

Buss, R. R. (2018). Using action research as a signature pedagogy to develop EdD students' inquiry as practice abilities. *Impacting Education: Journal on Transforming Professional Practice, 3*(1), 23–31. https://doi.org/10.5195/IE.2018.46

Butville, B., Hanrahan, S., & Wolkenhauer, R. (2021). Prepared to take responsibility: Practitioner inquiry for social justice in a professional development school partnership. *School–University Partnerships, 14*(3), 167–190. https://napds.org/wp-content/uploads/2021/08/SUP-143-Butville-et-al.-Article.pdf

Calkins, L. M. (1986). *The art of teaching writing*. Heinemann.

Capobianco, B. M., & Ní Ríordáin, M. (2015). Navigating layers of teacher uncertainty among preservice science and mathematics teachers engaged in action research. *Educational Action Research, 23*(4), 581–598. https://doi.org/10.1080/09650792.2015.1045537

Caro-Bruce, C., Flessner, R., Klehr, M., & Zeichner, K. (2007). *Creating equitable classrooms through action research*. Corwin.

Carr, W., & Kemmis, S. (1986). *Becoming critical: Knowing through action research*. Deakin University Press.

Carter Andrews, D. J., Richmond, G., Warren, C. A., Petchauer, E., & Floden, R. (2018). A call to action for teacher preparation programs: Supporting critical conversations and democratic action in safe learning environments. *Journal of Teacher Education, 69*, 205–208. https://doi.org/10.1177/0022487118766510

Chmielewski, A. K. (2014). An international comparison of achievement inequality in within- and between-school tracking systems. *American Journal of Education, 120*(30), 293–324. https://doi.org/10.1086/675529

Clark, C. (1995). *Thoughtful teaching*. Teachers College Press.

Clark, J. V. (2013). Introduction. In J. V. Clark (Ed.), *Closing the achievement gap from an international perspective: Transforming STEM for effective education* (pp. 3–6). Springer.

Clayton, C., & Meadows, G. (2013). Action research projects in pre-service teacher education. *Teacher Educators' Journal, 20*, 5–18. https://eric.ed.gov/?id=EJ1085619

Cloutier, D., Lilley, B., Phillips, D., Weber, B., & Sanderson, D. (1987). *A guide to program evaluation and reporting*. University of Maine Cooperative Extension Service.

Cochran-Smith, M. (1991). Learning to teach against the grain. *Harvard Educational Review, 61*(3), 279–310. https://doi.org/10.17763/haer.61.3.q671413614502746

Cochran-Smith, M., & Lytle, S. L. (1993). *Inside/outside: Teacher research and knowledge*. Teachers College Press.

Cochran-Smith, M., & Lytle, S. L. (1999). The teacher research movement: A decade later. *Educational Researcher, 28*(7), 15–25. https://doi.org/10.3102/0013189X028007015

Cochran-Smith, M., & Lytle, S. L. (2001). Beyond certainty: Taking an inquiry stance on practice. In A. Lieberman & L. Miller (Eds.), *Teachers caught in the action: Professional development that matters* (pp. 45–58). Teachers College Press.

Cochran-Smith, M., & Lytle, S. L. (2009). *Inquiry as stance: Practitioner research for the next generation*. Teachers College Press.

Colantonio-Yurko, K., Miller, C., & Cheveallier, J. (2017). Rigor and relevance: A teacher research study on using young adult literature in detracked secondary English language arts courses. *Journal of Practitioner Research, 2*(2), 1–24. https://digitalcommons.usf.edu/jpr/vol2/iss2/2/

Cook, G. (2004). Grade inflation reaches new heights. *American School Board Journal, 191*(6), 8. https://digitalcommons.usf.edu/jpr/vol2/iss2/2/

Crawford-Garrett, K., Anderson, S., Grayson, A., & Suter, C. (2015). Transformational practice: critical teacher research in pre-service teacher education. *Educational Action Research, 23*(4), 479–496. https://doi.org/10.1080/09650792.2015.1019902

Crawford-Garrett, K., & Carbajal, D. R. (Eds.). (2023). *Promising pedagogies for teacher inquiry and practice: Teaching out loud*. Teachers College Press.

Creswell, J. W., & Poth, C. N. (2018). *Qualitative inquiry and research design choosing among five approaches* (4th ed.) Sage.

Crisp, T., Knezek, S. M., Quinn, M., Bingham, K. G., & Starks, F. (2016). What's on our bookshelves? The diversity of children's literature in early childhood classroom libraries. *Journal of Children's Literature, 42*(2), 29–42. https://www.proquest.com/scholarly-journals/whats-on-our-bookshelves-diversity-childrens/docview/1837539742/se-2

Crowther, F. (1997). The William Walker oration, 1996: Unsung heroes: The leaders in our classrooms. *Journal of Educational Administration, 3591*, 5–17.

Currin, E. (2018). *Storied stance: An oral history of long-term teacher researchers in the age of accountability* [Unpublished doctoral dissertation]. University of Florida.

Dana, N. F. (1994). Building partnerships to effect educational change: School culture and the finding of teacher voice. In M. J. O'Hair & S. J. Odell (Eds.), *Partnerships in education: Teacher education yearbook II* (pp. 11–26). Harcourt Brace College.

Dana, N. F. (1995). Action research, school change, and the silencing of teacher voice. *Action in*

Teacher Education, 16(4), 59–70. https://doi.org/10.1080/01626620.1995.10463219

Dana, N. F. (1999). *The professional development school story: Assessing the impact of year one (1998–99) of the State College Area School District—Pennsylvania State University Elementary Professional Development Schools*. Research report submitted to The State College Area School District Board of Directors, State College, PA.

Dana, N. F. (2001, April). *Inquiry in the PDS: The thread that ties the content areas together*. Paper presented at the annual meeting of the American Educational Research Association, Seattle, WA, United States.

Dana, N. F. (2013). *Digging deeper into action research: A teacher inquirer's field guide*. Corwin.

Dana, N. F. (2016). The relevancy and importance of practitioner research in contemporary times. *Journal of Practitioner Research, 1*(1), 1–7. https://doi.org/10.5038/2379-9951.1.1.1034

Dana, N. F. (2017). Practitioner inquiry and PDS work: A reflection on 25 years of purpose, problems, and potential. *School–University Partnerships, 10*(4), 5–12. https://napds.org/wp-content/uploads/2020/07/SUP-104-Teacher-Inquiry-Invited-Piece_Dana.pdf

Dana, N. F., & Baker, J. (Eds.). (2006). *Improving Florida schools through teacher inquiry: Selections from the 2005 Teaching, Inquiry, and Innovation Showcase*. Monograph published by the Center for School Improvement and North East Florida Educational Consortium, Gainesville.

Dana, N. F., Bondy, E., Kennedy-Lewis, B., Adams, A., & Ma, V. W. (2016). Exemplifying the dissertation in practice. Carnegie Project on the Education Doctorate (CPED) White Paper Project. http://www.cpedinitiative.org/research-resources

Dana, N. F., Burns, J. B., & Wolkenhauer, R. (2013). *Inquiring into the common core*. Corwin.

Dana, N. F., & Currin, E. (2017). Inquiry for equity: Exploring the impact of practitioner research. *Journal of Practitioner Research, 2*(2), 1–7. https://digitalcommons.usf.edu/jpr/vol2/iss2/1/

Dana, N. F., & Delane, D. C. (Eds.). (2007). *Improving Florida schools through teacher inquiry: Selections from the 2006 Teaching, Inquiry, and Innovation Showcase*. Monograph published by the Center for School Improvement and North East Florida Educational Consortium, Gainesville.

Dana, N. F., Delane, D. C., MacDonald, M., & Mundorf, J. (2017, March). *The role of teacher inquiry in teacher leadership*. Invited keynote address at the International Conference on Teacher Leadership, Miami, FL, United States.

Dana, N. F., & Kilgore, K. L. (2021). Introduction to the special issue: Inquiring into, about, and during Covid-19. *Journal of Practitioner Research, 6*(1), 1–10. https://doi.org/10.5038/2379-9951.6.1.1197

Dana, N. F., Pape, S. J., Griffin, C. C., & Prosser, S. K. (2017). Incorporating practitioner inquiry into an online professional development program: The Prime Online experience. *Professional Development in Education, 43*(2), 212–231. https://eric.ed.gov/?id=EJ1130957

Dana, N. F., & Silva, D. Y. (2001). Student teachers as researchers: Developing an inquiry stance towards teaching. In J. D. Rainer & E. M. Guyton (Eds.), *Research on the effects of teacher education on teacher performance* (pp. 91–104). Kendall/Hunt.

Dana, N. F., & Silva, D. Y. (2002a). Building an inquiry oriented PDS: Inquiry as a part of mentor teacher work. In I. N. Guadarrama, J. Nath, & J. Ramsey (Eds.), *Forging alliances in community and thought: Research in professional development schools* (pp. 87–104).

Dana, N. F., Silva, D. Y., & Snow-Gerono, J. (2002b). Building a culture of inquiry in a professional development school. *Teacher Education and Practice, 15*(4), 71–89. https://eric.ed.gov/?id=EJ675652

Dana, N. F., Smith, J., & Yendol-Hoppey, D. (2011). Teacher research in the PDS: How do we define the quality of this research? In J. Nath, I. N. Guadarrama, & J. E. Ramsey (Eds.), *Investigating university–school partnerships* (pp. 137–152). Information Age Publishing.

Dana, N. F., & Yendol-Hoppey, D. (2006, April). *Facilitating the inquiry of others*. Paper presented at the second annual Teaching, Inquiry, and Innovation Showcase, Gainesville, FL, United States.

Dana, N. F., & Yendol-Hoppey, D. (2008a). *The reflective educator's guide to professional development: Coaching inquiry-oriented learning communities*. Corwin.

Dana, N. F., & Yendol-Hoppey, D. (2008b). Resisting crash diet staff development. *Kappa Delta Pi*

Record, 44(2), 66–71. https://doi.org/10.1080/0228958.2008.10516497

Dana, N. F., & Yendol-Hoppey, D. (2016). *The PLC book*. Corwin.

Dana, N. F., Yendol-Hoppey, D., & Snow-Gerono, J. L. (2006). Deconstructing inquiry in the professional development school: Exploring the domains and contents of teachers' questions. *Action on Teacher Education*, 27(4), 59–71. https://doi.org/10.1080/01626620.2006.10463402

Darling-Hammond, L. (1994). Developing professional development schools: Early lessons, challenge, and promise. In L. Darling-Hammond (Ed.), *Professional development schools: Schools for developing a profession* (pp. 1–27). Teachers College Press.

Darling-Hammond, L. (2013). Inequality and school resources: What it will take to close the opportunity gap. In P. Carter & K. Welner (Eds.), *Closing the opportunity gap: What America must do to give every child an even chance* (pp. 77–97). Oxford University Press.

Davis, E., Flavin, A., Harris, M. M., Huffman, L., Watson, D., & Weller, K. M. (2021). Addressing student isolation during the pandemic: An inquiry into renewing relationships and reimagining classroom communities on remote instruction platforms. *Journal of Practitioner Research*, 6(1), 1–9. https://doi.org/10.5038/2379-9951.6.1.1199

Davis, J., Clayton, C., & Broome, J. (2018). Thinking like researchers: Action research and its impact on novice teachers' thinking. *Educational Action Research*, 26(1), 59–74. https://doi.org/10.1080/09650792.2017.1284012

Davis, K. L., Brown, B. G., Liedel-Rice, A., & Soeder, P. (2005). Experiencing diversity through children's multicultural literature. *Kappa Delta Pi Record*, 41(4), 176–179. https://doi.org/10.1080/00228958.2005.10532067

Dawson, K., & Dana, N. F. (2007). When curriculum-based, technology enhanced field experiences and teacher inquiry coalesce: An opportunity for conceptual change? *British Journal of Educational Technology*, 38(4), 656–667. https://doi.org/10.1111/j.1467-8535.2006.00648.x

Delane, D. C., Dana, N. F., & Steward, M. (2010). *The story of May and her inquiry journey: Creating a positive behavior support system in a seventh-grade science classroom*. Unpublished manuscript.

Delane, D. C., Hooser, A., Richner, M., Wolkenhauer, R., Colvine, S. M., & Dana, N. F. (2017). Practitioner inquiry as the anchor of clinical practice throughout the teacher education program. In R. Flessner & D. R. Lecklider (Eds.), *The power of clinical preparation in teacher education* (pp. 69–86). Rowman & Littlefield Education.

Delpit, L. (2006). Lessons from teachers. *Journal of Teacher Education*, 57(3), 220–231. https://doi.org/10.1177/0022487105285966

Dempsie, G. (1997). Using puppets in a primary classroom: A teacher-researcher's findings. *Teaching and Learning: The Journal of Natural Inquiry*, 11(3), 5–13. https://commons.und.edu/cgi/viewcontent.cgi?article=1182&context=tl-nirp-journal

Dempsie, G. (2000). Can I love you? A child's adventure with puppets and play. *Journal of the Imagination in Language Learning*, 5, 28–36.

Derman-Sparks, L. (1989). *Anti-bias curriculum: Tools for empowering young children*. National Association for the Education of Young Children.

Dewey, J. (1933). *Democracy and education*. Free Company.

Dickinson, V. L., & Young, T. A. (1998). Elementary science and language arts: Should we blur the boundaries? *School Science and Mathematics*, 98(6), 334–339.

Donohoo, J. (2017). *Collective efficacy: How educators' beliefs impact student learning*. Corwin.

Dougherty, C., Mellor, L., & Jian, S. (2006). *The relationship between advanced placement and college graduation* (National Center for Educational Accountability, 2005 AP Study Series, Report 1). National Center for Educational Accountability.

Drennon, C. E., & Cervero, R. M. (2002). The politics of facilitation: Negotiating power and politics in practitioner inquiry groups. *Adult Education Quarterly*, 52, 193–209. https://doi.org/10.1177/0741713602052003003

Dresser, R. (2007). The effects of teacher inquiry in the bilingual language arts classroom. *Teacher Education Quarterly*, 34(3), 53–66. https://www.jstor.org/stable/23478993

Drexler, W., Dawson, K., & Ferdig, R. (2007). Collaborative blogging as a means to develop elementary expository writing skills. *Electronic Journal for the Integration of Technology in Education*, 16, 140–160.

Dvir, B., Rutten, L., Butville, D., & Wilson, E. (2023). Partnering to support K-12 instruction of difficult topics through inquiry-based professional learning. *School-University Partnerships*, 16(2), 101–109. https://www.emerald.com/insight/content/doi/10.1108/sup-03-2023-0017/full/html

Easton, L. B. (2004). *Powerful designs for professional learning*. National Staff Development Council.

Emdin, C. (2016). *For White folks who teach in the hood . . . and the rest of y'all too: Reality pedagogy and urban education*. Beacon Press.

Ermeling, B. A. (2010). Tracing the effects of teacher inquiry on classroom practice. *Teaching and Teacher Education*, 26, 377–388. https://doi.org/10.1016/j.tate.2009.02.019

Escue, C. (2006, April). *Why can't we all get along? If cooperative learning is such a great teaching strategy, why is it so painful at times?* Paper presented at the second annual University of Florida Teaching, Inquiry, and Innovation Showcase, Gainesville, FL, United States.

Farizan, S. (2013). *If you could be mine*. Algonquin Young Readers.

Farizan, S. (2015). *Tell me again how a crush should feel*. Algonquin Young Readers.

Fashola, O. S. (Ed.). (2005). *Educating African American males: Voices from the field*. Corwin.

Ferlazzo, L. (2011). Involvement or engagement? *Educational Leadership*, 68(8), 10–14. https://eric.ed.gov/?id=EJ932180

Fiel, J. E. (2013). Decomposing school resegregation: Social closure, racial imbalance, and racial isolation. *American Sociological Review*, 78(5), 828–845. https://doi.org/10.1177/0003122413496252

Fleet, A., De Gioia, K., & Patterson, C. (2016). *Engaging with educational change: Voices of practitioner inquiry*. Bloomsbury Publishing.

Frank, M. (1979). *If you're trying to teach kids how to write, you've gotta have this book!* Incentive.

Friedrich, L., & McKinney, M. (2010). Teacher inquiry for equity: Collaborating to improve teaching and learning. *Language Arts*, 87(4), 241–251. https://doi.org/10.58680/la20109927

Fullan, M. (2012). *Change forces: Probing the depths of educational reform*. Routledge.

Garman, Q. (1997, Fall). The slap heard 'round the room. *Partnership News (Newsletter of the Pennsylvania State University College of Education)*, 1–4.

Geiger, M. (2022). *Slowing down to speed up: The development of social justice family engagement activities through practitioner research* [Dissertation proposal]. University of Florida.

Glickman, C. D., Gordon, S. P., & Ross-Gordon, J. M. (2007). *SuperVision and instructional leadership* (7th ed.). Allyn & Bacon.

Glogowski, K., & Sessums, C. D. (2007). *Personal learning environments: Exploring professional development in a networked world*. Paper presented at the meeting of Web Heads in Action Online Conference 2007. http://www.webheadsinaction.org/node/168

Goddard, R., Hoy, W., & Woolfolk Hoy, A. (2004). Collective efficacy beliefs: Theoretical developments, empirical evidence, and future directions. *American Educational Research Association*, 33(3), 3–13. https://doi.org/10.3102/0013189X033003003

Grace, J., Simieou, F. III, Lastrapes, R. E., & Decman, J. (2024). Confronting the racism boogeyman: Educational leaders make meaning of the impact of George Floyd. *Education, Citizenship and Social Justice*, 19(1), 124–138. https://doi.org/10.1177/17461979221123014

Greene, M. (1986). Reflections and passion in teaching. *Journal of Curriculum and Supervision*, 2(1), 68–81.

Griggs, T., & Tidwell, D. (2015). Learning to teach mindfully: Examining the self in the context of multicultural education. *Teacher Education Quarterly*, 42(2), 87–104. https://www.jstor.org/stable/10.2307/teaceducquar.42.2.87

Guskey, T. (2018, September 9). How can we improve professional inquiry? [Blog post]. https://blogs.edweek.org/edweek/finding_common_ground/2018/09/how_can_we_improve_professional_inquiry.html?r=1822647756

Haas, B. J. (2020). Bearing witness: Teacher perspectives on developing empathy through Holocaust survivor testimony. *The Social Studies*, 112(2), 86–103. https://doi.org/10.1080/00377996.2019.1693949

Hall, J. (1998). *Organizing wonder: Making inquiry science work in the elementary school*. Heinemann.

Hallman, H. L., Rios, A., Craig, C. J., & Hill-Jackson, V. (2022). Teacher education's moment: From solution to challenge. *Journal of Teacher Education*, 73(2), 127–128. https://doi.org/10.1177/00224871221076906

Hampton, D., & Schickel, B. (2002, April). *Phonemic awareness: A key to kindergarten*. Paper presented at the fourth annual State College Area School District—Pennsylvania State University Teacher Inquiry Conference, State College, PA, United States.

Harris, D. (2023). *The antiracist school leader: What to know, say and do*. Solution Tree Press.

Harris, M. (2015). *The role of the music teacher in collaborating with academic teachers within a professional learning community* [Unpublished doctoral dissertation]. University of Florida.

Hart, A. (2021). *Supporting authentic teacher collaboration by breaking down barriers* [Unpublished doctoral dissertation]. University of Florida.

Hattie, J. (2008). *Visible learning: A synthesis of over 800 meta-analyses relating to achievement*. Routledge.

Hermann-Wilmarth, J. M., & Ryan, C. L. (2015). Doing what you can: Considering ways to address LGBT topics in language arts curricula. *Language Arts, 92*(6), 436–443. https://doi.org/10.58680/la201527391

Hill, A. P. (2013). *Understanding and enacting self-regulated learning with students receiving tier 3 instruction in reading: A practitioner inquiry approach* [Unpublished doctoral dissertation]. University of Florida.

Holly, M. L., Arhar, J. M., & Kasten, W. C. (2009). *Action research for teachers: Traveling the yellow brick road* (3rd ed.). Boston: Pearson.

Hosfeld, A. (2000, April). *Implementing anti-bias curriculum: Addressing the needs and constraints of an elementary classroom*. Paper presented at the second annual State College Area School District—Pennsylvania State University Teacher Inquiry Conference, State College, PA, United States.

Hubbard, R. S., & Power, B. M. (1993). *The art of classroom inquiry: A handbook for teacher researchers*. Heinemann.

Hubbard, R. S., & Power, B. M. (1999). *Living the questions: A guide for teacher researchers*. Stenhouse.

Hubbell, D. (2006). Focus on fractured fairy tales and fluency flourishes. In N. F. Dana & J. Baker (Eds.), *Improving Florida schools through teacher inquiry: Selections from the 2005 Teaching, Inquiry, and Innovation Showcase* (pp. 5–8). University of Florida, Center for School Improvement.

Insana, L., Johnson Mardones, D., Welsh, H., & Johnston-Parsons, M. (2014). Narrative dialogue and teacher leadership for social justice: Re-Storying to understand. In I. Bogotch & C. Shields (Eds.), *International handbook of social [in]justice and educational leadership* (pp. 447–464). Springer.

Jacobs, F. (1992). *The Tainos: The people who welcomed Columbus*. G. P. Putman.

Janicke, K. (2018, September). *Developing a peer tutoring program for a high-school chemistry honors class*. Paper presented at the P. K. Yonge Inquiries and Investigations Teacher Research Symposium, Gainesville, FL, United States.

Jones, A., & Reed, D. (2000, April). *Rethinking Columbus*. Paper presented at the second annual State College Area School District—Pennsylvania State University Teacher Inquiry Conference, State College, PA, United States.

Jones, J. M. (2021). The dual pandemics of COVID-19 and systemic racism: Navigating our path forward. *School Psychology, 36*(5), 427–431. https://doi.org/10.1037/spq0000472

Joseph, P. B. (Ed.). (2011). *Cultures of curriculum* (2nd ed.). Routledge.

Journell, W. (2022). Classroom controversy in the midst of political polarization: The essential role of school administrators. *NASSP Bulletin, 106*(2), 133–153. https://doi.org/10.1177/01926365221100589

Katzenmeyer, M., & Moller, G. (2001). *Awakening the sleeping giant: Helping teachers develop as leaders* (2nd ed.). Corwin.

Kincheloe, J. (1991). *Teachers as researchers: Qualitative inquiry as a path to empowerment*. Falmer.

Kinskey, M. (2018). Using action research to improve science teaching self-efficacy. *International Journal of Science Education, 40*(15), 1795–1811. https://doi.org/10.1080/09500693.2018.1502898

Körkkö, M., Kyrö-Ämmälä, O., & Turunen, T. (2016). Professional development through reflection in teacher education. *Teaching and Teacher Education, 55*, 198–206. https://doi.org/10.1016/j.tate.2016.01.014

Kosciw, J. G., Greytak, E. A., Palmer, N. A., & Boesen, M. J. (2015). *The 2013 National School Climate Survey: The experiences of lesbian, gay, bisexual and transgender youth in our nation's schools*. A Report from the Gay, Lesbian & Straight Education Network. New York: Gay, Lesbian & Straight Education Network.

Krell, D. E., & Dana, N. F. (2012). Facilitating action research: A study of coaches, their experiences, and their reflections on leading teachers in the process of practitioner inquiry. *Professional Development in Education, 38*(5), 827–844. https://doi.org/10.1080/19415257.2012.666052

Kur, J. (2000, April). *Dinosaurs in the primary classroom: From facts and crafts to inquiry.* Paper presented at the second annual State College Area School District—Pennsylvania State University Teacher Inquiry Conference, State College, PA, United States.

Kush, J. M., Badillo-Goicoechea, E., Musci, R. J., & Stuart, E. A. (2022). Teachers' mental health during the COVID-19 pandemic. *Educational Researcher, 51*(9), 593–597. https://doi.org/10.3102/0013189X221134281

Ladson-Billings, G. (1995). Toward a theory of culturally relevant pedagogy. *American Educational Research Journal, 32*(3), 465–491. https://doi.org/10.3102/00028312032003465

Ladson-Billings, G. (2007). Pushing past the achievement gap: An essay on the language of deficit. *The Journal of Negro Education, 76*(3), 316–323. https://www.jstor.org/stable/40034574

Ladson-Billings, G. J. (2005). Is the team all right? Diversity and teacher education. *Journal of Teacher Education, 56*(3), 229–234. http://doi.org/10.1177/0022487105275917

Langrall, C. W. (Ed.). (2006). *Teachers engaged in research: Inquiry in mathematics classrooms, grades 3–5.* Information Age.

Lassonde, C. A., Ritchie, G. V., & Fox, R. K. (2008). How teacher research can become your way of being. In C. A. S. Lassonde & S. E. Israel (Eds.), *Teachers taking action: A comprehensive guide to teacher research.* International Reading Association.

Lesesne, T. S. (2003). *Making the match: The right book for the right reader at the right time.* Stenhouse.

Lessem, D. (1991, May 19). The great dinosaur rip-off. *New York Times.*

Levin, B. B., & Rock, T. C. (2003). The effects of collaborative action research on preservice and experienced teacher partners in professional development schools. *Journal of Teacher Education, 54*(2), 135–149. https://doi.org/10.1177/0022487102250287

Loewen, J. (1995). *Lies my teacher told me: Everything your American history textbook got wrong* (1st ed.). New Press.

Loughran, J. (2010). Seeking knowledge for teaching teaching: Moving beyond stories. *Studying Teacher Education, 6*(3), 221–226. https://doi.org/10.1080/17425964.2010.518490

Love, N. (2004). Taking data to new depths. *Journal of Staff Development, 25*(4), 22–26. https://all4ed.org/wp-content/uploads/2013/09/lovejsdarticle.pdf

Lowenstein, K. L. (2009). The work of multicultural teacher education: Reconceptualizing White teacher candidates as learners. *Review of Educational Research, 79*(1), 163–196. http://doi.org/10.3102/0034654308326161

Lunsford, S. (1998). *Literature-based mini-lessons to teach writing.* Scholastic Professional Books.

Ma, V. W., Dana, N. F., Adams, A., & Kennedy, B. L. (2018). Understanding the problem of practice: An analysis of professional practice EdD dissertations. *Impacting Education: Journal on Transforming Professional Practice, 3,* 13–22. https://eric.ed.gov/?id=EJ1357990

MacDonald, M. (2007). Grade inflation, grade deflation—What can data tell me? In N. F. Dana & D. C. Delane (Eds.), *Improving Florida schools through teacher inquiry: Selections from the 2006 Teaching, Inquiry, and Innovation Showcase* (pp. 51–68). University of Florida, Center for School Improvement.

MacDonald, M. (2016). *The role of differentiation and standards-based grading in the science learning of struggling and advanced learners in a detracked high-school honors biology classroom* [Unpublished doctoral dissertation]. University of Florida.

Malaggese, L. (2001, April). *What is a fair share? And other fractional adventures in a first-grade classroom.* Paper presented at the third annual State College Area School District—Pennsylvania State University Teacher Inquiry Conference, State College, PA, United States.

Masingila, J. O. (2006). *Teachers engaged in research: Inquiry into mathematics classrooms, grades 6–8.* Information Age Publishing.

McAvoy, P., & Hess, D. E. (2013). Classroom deliberation in an era of political polarization. *Curriculum Inquiry, 43*(1), 14–47. https://doi.org/10.1111/curi.12000

McCarty, C., & Poehner, P. (2002, April). *Peer coaching in an elementary classroom.* Paper presented at the fourth annual State College Area School District—Pennsylvania State University Teacher Inquiry Conference, State College, PA, United States.

McClintock, C. (2004). The scholar-practitioner model. In *Encyclopedia of distributed learning* (pp. 393–396). Sage.

Mertler, C. (2024). *Disseminating your action research: A practical guide to sharing the results of practitioner research*. Routledge.

Meyers, E., & Rust, F. (Eds.). (2003). *Taking action with teacher research*. Heinemann.

Middaugh, E. (2019). More than just facts: Promoting civic media literacy in the era of outrage. *Peabody Journal of Education, 94*(1), 17–31. https://doi.org/10.1080/0161956X.2019.1553582

Miles, M. B., Huberman, A. M., & Saldaña, J. (2020). *Qualitative data analysis: A methods sourcebook* (4th ed.). Sage.

Miller, M. (2018, September). *How do students respond to LGBTQ texts in our current political climate?* Presentation at the P. K. Yonge Inquiries and Investigations Teacher Research Symposium, Gainesville, FL, United States.

Mills, G. E. (2014). *Action research: A guide for the teacher researcher* (5th ed.). Pearson Education.

Milner, H. R., IV. (2010). *Start where you are, but don't stay there: Understanding diversity, opportunity gaps, and teaching in today's classrooms*. Harvard Education Press.

Mitchell, K. (2000, April). *How do airplanes fly? (How do I become a more effective science teacher?)* Paper presented at the second annual State College Area School District—Pennsylvania State University Teacher Inquiry Conference, State College, PA, United States.

Munsart, C. A. (1993). *Investigating science with dinosaurs*. Teacher Ideas Press.

Naidoo, J. C. (2014). *Diversity programming for digital youth: Promoting cultural competence in the children's library*. ABC-CLIO.

Nash, J. (2017). *Understanding how to interest girls in STEM education: A look at how LEGO® education ambassador teachers engage female students in STEM learning* [Unpublished doctoral dissertation]. University of Florida.

National Association for Professional Development Schools. (2021). *What it means to be a Professional Development School: The nine essentials* (2nd ed.) [Policy statement]. Author. https://napds.org/wp-content/uploads/2021/05/What-it-Means-to-be-a-PDS-Second-Edition-2021-Final.pdf

National Center for Education Statistics (NCES). (2018) *Fast facts*. https://nces.ed.gov/fastfacts/display.asp?id=28

National Education Association (NEA). (2018). *Code of ethics*. https://www.nea.org/assets/docs/Code_of_Ethics_NEA_Handbook_2018.pdf

National Parent and Teachers Association. (1997). *National standards for parent/family involvement programs*. https://files.eric.ed.gov/fulltext/ED405405.pdf

National School Reform Faculty. (2007). *Frequently asked questions*. www.nsrfharmony.org/faq.html#1

Nessel, D., & Dixon, C. (2008). *Using the language experience approach with English language learners*. Corwin.

Nichols, S., & Cormack, P. (2017). *Impactful practitioner inquiry: The ripple effect on classrooms, schools, and teacher professionalism*. Teachers College Press.

Niebauer, H. (1997, Fall). Learning, not control. *Partnership News (Newsletter of the Pennsylvania State University College of Education)*, 10–11.

Nieto, S. (2000). Placing equity front and center. *Journal of Teacher Education, 51*(3), 180–187. http://doi.org/10.1177/0022487100051003004

Nolen, A. L., & Putten, V. (2007). Action research in education: Addressing gaps in ethical principles and practices. *Educational Researcher, 36*(7), 401–407. https://doi.org/10.3102/0013189X07309629

Oakes, J. (2005). *Keeping track: How schools structure inequality* (2nd ed.). Yale University Press.

Olsen, L. (2003, May 21). Study relates cautionary tale of misusing data. *Education Week, 22*(37), 12.

Pace, J. L. (2022). Learning to teach controversial issues: A path forward. *The Learning Professional, 43*(5), 26–38. https://learningforward.org/wp-content/uploads/2022/10/focus-learning-to-teach-controversial-issues-a-path-forward.pdf

Paris, G., & Paris, A. (2001). Classroom applications of research on self-regulated learning. *Educational Psychologist, 36*(2), 89–101.

Patton, M. Q. (2015). *Qualitative research & evaluation methods: Integrating theory and practice*. Sage.

Perry, G., Henderson, B., & Meier, D. R. (2012). *Our inquiry, our practice: Undertaking, supporting, and learning from early childhood teacher research(ers).*

National Association for the Education of Young Children.

Perry, J. A. (2013). Introduction: Developing stewards of practice. In J. A. Perry & D. L. Carlson (Eds.), *In their own words: A journey to the stewardship of the practice in education* (pp. 1–14). Information Age Publishing.

Perry, J. A., & Imig, D. G. (2008). A stewardship of practice in education. *Change: The Magazine of Higher Learning, 40*(6), 42–49. https://doi.org/10.3200/CHNG.40.6.42-49

Perry, N. (1998). Young children's self-regulated learning and contexts that support it. *Journal of Educational Psychology, 90*(4), 715–729.

Peters, B., & Romig, G. (2001, April). *Let's talk about science*. Paper presented at the third annual State College Area School District—Pennsylvania State University Teacher Inquiry Conference, State College, PA, United States.

Pritchard, I. A. (2002). Travelers and trolls: Practitioner research and institutional review boards. *Educational Research, 31*(3), 3–13. https://doi.org/10.3102/0013189X031003003

Quindlen, A. (1997). *Happily ever after*. Random House.

Ramirez, M. (2007). Differentiating instruction in math in the primary grades. In N. F. Dana & D. C. Delane (Eds.), *Improving Florida schools through teacher inquiry: Selections from the 2006 Teaching, Inquiry, and Innovation Showcase* (pp. 100–106). University of Florida, Center for School Improvement.

Ranschaert, R. (2023). When shutting the door won't do: Teaching with the specter of community backlash and the implications for teacher education. *Journal of Teacher Education, 74*(4), 371–382. https://doi.org/10.1177/00224871231180831

Reiter, A. B., & Davis, S. N. (2011). Factors influencing pre-service teachers' beliefs about student achievement: Evaluation of a pre-service teacher diversity awareness program. *Multicultural Education, 18*(3), 41–46. https://eric.ed.gov/?id=EJ955944

Richardson, W. (2006). *Blogs, wikis, podcasts and other powerful Web tools for classrooms*. Corwin.

Robinson-Wilson, R., Parkinson, M., Wright, N., & Yendol-Hoppey, D. (in press). An approach to designing professional learning for early childhood STEM educators: Integrating frameworks to enhance teacher self-efficacy and motivation. *Action in Teacher Education*.

Rock, T. C., & Levin, B. R. (2002). Collaborative action research projects: Enhancing preservice teacher development in professional development schools. *Teacher Education Quarterly, 29*, 7–21. https://www.jstor.org/stable/23478324

Rotz, L., Kur, J., Robert, M., & Heitzmann, M. (2002, April). *Getting smarter with smart boards: A collaborative project*. Paper presented at the fourth annual State College Area School District—Pennsylvania State University Teacher Inquiry Conference, State College, PA, United States.

Routman, R. (2002). *Conversations: Strategies for teaching, learning, and evaluating*. Heinemann.

Ruddock, J., & Hopkins, D. (Eds.). (1985). *Research as a basis for teaching: Readings from the work of Lawrence Stenhouse*. Heinemann.

Russell, J. L. (2002, April). *Once upon a writer's workshop: Using children's literature to inspire dazzling, complete stories*. Paper presented at the fourth annual State College Area School District—Pennsylvania State University Teacher Inquiry Conference, State College, PA, United States.

Rust, R., & Meyers, E. (2006). The bright side: Teacher research in the context of educational reform and policy-making. *Teaching and Teaching: Theory and Practice, 12*(1), 69–86. https://doi.org/10.1080/13450600500365452

Ruth, A. (1999, May). *The kindergarten writing center: Providing opportunities for an ESL student's language growth and development*. Paper presented at the first annual State College Area School District—Pennsylvania State University Teacher Inquiry Conference, State College, PA, United States.

Ruth, A. (2001, April). *Two journeys of exploration*. Paper presented at the third annual State College Area School District—Pennsylvania State University Teacher Inquiry Conference, State College, PA, United States.

Ruth, A. (2002, April). *Wanted: A new approach to using the minutes between 8:30 and 9:00 a.m. in my classroom*. Paper presented at the fourth annual State College Area School District—Pennsylvania State University Teacher Inquiry Conference, State College, PA, United States.

Rutten, L. (2021). Toward a theory of action for practitioner inquiry as professional development in pre-service teacher education. *Teaching and Teacher Education, 97*, 1–14. https://doi.org/10.1016/j.tate.2020.103194

Rutten, L. (2022). A question-based framework for co-constructing supervision in clinically based teacher preparation. *Journal of Educational Supervision, 5*(1), 68–87. https://doi.org/10.31045/jes.5.1.4

Rutten, L., Butville, D., & Dvir, B. (2024). Leaning into difficult topics: Inquiry communities as teacher professional learning for turbulent times. *Journal of Teacher Education, 75*(3), 292–304. https://doi.org/10.1177/00224871241231543

Rutten, L., Butville, D., Smith, W. L., & Dvir, B. (2023). Practitioner inquiry for turbulent times: Learning to take an inquiry stance toward teaching difficult topics through a teacher inquiry community. *Journal of Practitioner Research, 8*(2), 1–19. https://digitalcommons.usf.edu/jpr/vol8/iss2/5/

Rutten, L., Butville, D., Wolkenhauer, R., & Dvir, B. (2025). When difficult topics bubble up: How K–12 teachers understand unplanned difficult-topics moments. *Action in Teacher Education.* http://doi.org/10.1080/01626620.2024.2430771

Rutten, L., Doyle, S. L., Wolkenhauer, R., & Schussler, D. L. (2022). Teacher candidates' perceptions of emergent teacher leadership in clinically based teacher education. *Action in Teacher Education, 44*(4), 308–329. https://doi.org/10.1080/01626620.2022.2074912

Rutten, L., & Wolkenhauer, R. (2023a). Hero, wanderer, companion, or colleague? Theorizing teacher candidates' orientations toward community during practitioner inquiry-based clinical practice. *Teaching and Teacher Education, 123*, 1–11. https://doi.org/10.1016/j.tate.2022.103938

Rutten, L., & Wolkenhauer, R. (2023b). What's the point? A case study characterizing teacher candidates' purposes for practitioner inquiry. *Action in Teacher Education, 45*(1), 52–67. https://doi.org/10.1080/01626620.2022.2157906

Rutten, L., & Wolkenhauer, R. (2024). Inquiry project or inquiry stance? A continuum of teacher candidate perceptions of knowledge construction during practitioner inquiry-based clinical practice. *Teacher Development, 28*(2), 261–277. https://doi.org/10.1080/13664530.2023.2293893

Schön, D. A. (1983). *The reflective practitioner.* Jossey-Bass.

Schön, D. A. (1987). *Educating the reflective practitioner.* Jossey-Bass.

Schwandt, T. A. (1997). *Qualitative inquiry: A dictionary of terms.* Sage.

Seligman, D. (2002). The grade-inflation swindle. *Forbes, 169*(6), 94.

Sensoy, O., & DiAngelo, R. (2017). *Is everyone really equal?: An introduction to key concepts in social justice education* (2nd ed.). Teachers College Press.

Sergiovanni, T. J., & Starratt, R. J. (1998). *Supervision: A redefinition.* McGraw-Hill.

Shulman, L. (1986). Knowledge and teaching: Foundations of the new reform. *Harvard Educational Review, 57*(1), 1–22. https://doi.org/10.17763/haer.57.1.j463w79r56455411

Shulman, L. S., Golde, C. M., Bueschel, A. C., & Garabedian, K. J. (2006). Reclaiming education's doctorates: A critique and a proposal. *Educational Researcher, 35*(3), 25–32. https://doi.org/10.3102/0013189X035003025

Silva, D. Y., & Dana, N. F. (1999, February). *Cultivating inquiry within a professional development school.* Presentation at the annual meeting of the American Association of Colleges for Teacher Education, Washington, DC, United States.

Sleeter, C. (2001). Preparing teachers for culturally diverse schools: Research and the overwhelming presence of whiteness. *Journal of Teacher Education, 52*(2), 94–106. http://doi.org/10.1177/0022487101052002002

Smith, L. M. (1990). Ethics in qualitative field research: An individual perspective. In E. W. Eisner & A. P. Peshkin (Eds.), *Qualitative inquiry in education: The continuing debate* (pp. 258–276). Teachers College Press.

Smith, S. Z., & Smith, M. E. (Eds.). (2006). *Teachers engaged in research: Inquiry in mathematics classrooms, grades Pre-K–2.* Information Age Publishing.

Snow, J. L., Dana, N. F., & Silva, D. Y. (2001). Where are they now? Former PDS interns emerge as first year teacher leaders. *Professional Educator, 24*(1), 35–48. https://eric.ed.gov/?id=EJ646396

Snow, J., Wenner, J., Dismuke, S., & Hicks, S. (2017). *Novice educator realities: How do new teachers negotiate varied school contexts?* Paper presented at the American Educational Research Association Meeting, San Antonio, Texas, United States.

Somekh, B., & Zeichner, K. (2009). Action research for educational reform: Remodelling action research theories and practices in local contexts. *Educational Action Research, 17*(1), 5–21. Information Age Publishing. https://doi.org/10.1080/09650790802667402

Sunner, N. (1999, May). *Questioning*. Paper presented at the First Annual State College Area School District—Pennsylvania State University Teacher Inquiry Conference, State College, PA, United States.

Tatum, A. W. (2005). *Teaching reading to Black adolescent males: Closing the achievement gap*. Stenhouse.

Taylor, L. A. (2017). How teachers become teacher researchers: Narrative as a tool for teacher identity construction. *Teaching and Teacher Education, 61*, 6116–6125. https://doi.org/10.1016/j.tate.2016.09.008

Temple, C., Martinez, M., & Yokota, J. (2014). *Children's books in children's hands* (5th ed.). Pearson.

Thate, J. (2007, April). *Can culturally relevant literature change attitudes towards reading?* Paper presented at the third annual University of Florida Teaching, Inquiry, and Innovation Showcase, Gainesville, FL, United States.

Thorne, S. (2000). Data analysis in qualitative research. *Evidence-Based Nursing, 3*, 68–70.

Thulin, J. (1999, May). *Meaningful melodies: Reading to the beat of a different drummer*. Paper presented at the first annual State College Area School District—Pennsylvania State University Teacher Inquiry Conference, State College, PA, United States.

Tomlinson, C. A. (2014). *The differentiated classroom: Responding to the needs of all learners* (2nd ed.). Association for Supervision & Curriculum Development.

Tschannen-Moran, M., & Barr, M. (2005). Fostering student learning: The relationship of collective teacher efficacy and student achievement. *Leadership and Policy in Schools, 3*(3), 189–209. https://doi.org/10.1080/15700760490503706

Tyson, K. (2013). Tracking, segregation, and the opportunity gap: What we know and why it matters. In P. Carter & K. Welner (Eds.), *Closing the opportunity gap: What America must do to give every child an even chance* (pp. 169–180). Oxford University Press.

University of North Dakota. (n.d.). *Artificial intelligence (AI)*. https://und.edu/academics/provost/about/ai.html

U.S. Department of Education. (2016). *The state of racial diversity in the education workforce*. https://www2.ed.gov/rschstat/eval/highered/racial-diversity/state-racial-diversity-workforce.pdf

Van Buren, J. (2017). *Culturally responsive teaching in an Algebra I class for repeating ninth graders* [Unpublished doctoral dissertation]. University of Florida.

Van Zoest, L. R. (Ed.). (2006). *Teachers engaged in research: Inquiry in mathematics classrooms, grades 9–12*. Information Age Publishing.

Walter, M., Kukutai, T., Carroll, S. R., & Rodriguez-Lonebear, D. (Eds.). (2021). *Indigenous data sovereignty and policy*. Routledge. https://library.oapen.org/handle/20.500.12657/42782

Wasley, P. A. (1992). Working together: Teacher leadership and collaboration. In C. Livingston (Ed.), *Teacher leaders: Evolving roles* (pp. 21–55). National Education Association.

Weisberg, L., Beckett, B., Dana, N. F., Commeret, M., & Silva, R. (2024). Teacher candidates' engagement in practitioner inquiry within an equity-centered initial teacher preparation program: Illuminating equity's presence and pitfalls. *Journal of Practitioner Research, 9*(1), 1–27. https://digitalcommons.usf.edu/jpr/vol9/iss1/3

Welner, K. G., & Carter, P. L. (2013). Achievement gaps arise from opportunity gaps. In P. Carter & K. Welner (Eds.), *Closing the opportunity gap: What America must do to give every child an even chance* (pp. 1–10). Oxford University Press.

Wenner, J. A., & Campbell, T. (2017). The theoretical and empirical basis of teacher leadership: A review of the literature. *Review of Educational Research, 87*(1), 134–171. https://doi.org/10.3102/0034654316653478

Wetzel, K., & Ewbank, A. (2013). Conceptualizing the innovation: Factors in sequencing doctoral candidates' interventions in the action research dissertation. *Educational Action Research, 21*(3), 392–411. https://doi.org/10.1080/09650792.2013.813402

Wildavsky, B. (2000). At least they have high self-esteem. *U.S. News and World Report, 128*(5), 50.

Willegems, V., Consuegra, E., Struyven, K., & Engels, N. (2018). Pre-service teachers as members of a collaborative teacher research team: A steady track to extended professionalism? *Teaching and Teacher Education, 76*, 126–139. https://doi.org/10.1016/j.tate.2018.08.012

Wolcott, H. F. (1990). *Writing up qualitative research*. Sage.

Wolcott, H. F. (1994). *Transforming qualitative data: Description, analysis, and interpretation*. Sage.

Wolcott, H. F. (2008). *Writing up qualitative research* (3rd ed.). Sage.

Wolk, S. (2008). School as inquiry. *Kappan, 90*(2), 115–122. https://www.pdkmembers.org/members_online/publications/archive/pdf/k0810wol.pdf

Wolkenhauer, R., & Hooser, A. (2017). "Inquiry as confidence": How practitioner inquiry can support new teachers. *Journal of Practitioner Research, 2*(1), 5. https://digitalcommons.usf.edu/jpr/vol2/iss1/5/

Wolkenhauer, R., Rutten, L., Cunningham, A., & Yen, Y. (2022). Making an inquiry community the core of a PDS: Learning together across institutional boundaries and roles. *School–University Partnerships, 15*(1), 64–69. https://eric.ed.gov/?id=EJ1346056

Woolley, R. (2011). Controversial issues: Identifying the concerns and priorities of student teachers. *Policy Futures in Education, 9,* 280–291. https://doi.org/10.2304/pfie.2011.9.2.280

Yazzie-Mintz, T. (2011). Sustaining Indigenous traditions. In P. B. Joseph (Ed.), *Cultures of curriculum* (2nd ed., pp. 174–195). Routledge.

Yendol-Hoppey, D., & Dana, N. F. (2008). Inquiry-oriented mentoring in the professional development school: The case of Claudia. In I. N. Guadarrama, J. Nath, & J. Ramsey (Eds.), *Collaboration in leadership and learning: Research in professional development schools* (Vol. 3, pp. 251–274). Information Age.

Yendol-Hoppey, D., & Franco, Y. (2014). In search of signature pedagogy for PDS teacher education: A review of articles published in school–university partnerships. *School–University Partnerships, 7*(1), 17–34. https://eric.ed.gov/?id=EJ1034140

Yendol-Hoppey, D., Jacobs, J., & Burns, R. W. (2018). Improving teacher practice based knowledge: What teachers need to know and how they come to know it. In S. Zepeda & J. Ponticell (Eds.), *Handbook of Educational Supervision* (pp. 509–532). Wiley-Blackwell.

York-Barr, J., & Duke, K. (2004). What do we know about teacher leadership? Findings from two decades of scholarship. *Review of Educational Research, 74*(3), 255–316. https://doi.org/10.3102/00346543074003255

Zeichner, K. (1986). Preparing reflective teachers: An overview of instructional strategies which have been employed in preservice teacher education. *International Journal of Educational Research, 7*(5), 565–575. https://doi.org/10.1016/0883-0355(87)90016-4

Zeichner, K. (1996). Teachers as reflective practitioners and the democratization of school reform. In K. Zeichner, S. Melnick, & M. L. Gomez (Eds.), *Currents of reform in preservice teacher education* (pp. 199–214). Teacher College Press.

Zeichner, K. M., & Liston, D. P. (1996). *Reflective teaching: An introduction.* Lawrence Erlbaum.

Zimmerman, B. J. (2000). Attaining self-regulation: A social cognitive perspective. In M. Boekaerts, P. Pintrich, & M. Ziedner (Eds.), *Handbook on self-regulation* (pp. 13–39). Academic Press.

Index

AACTE (American Association of Colleges for Teacher Education), 26
AAIMSE (Applications of Artificial Intelligence in Middle School Education), 273
abilities, 22, 24, 66, 72, 80, 86–87, 120, 122, 125, 148–49, 195, 319, 321–22, 325–26, 328
academics, 7, 11, 169–70, 209, 227
accountability, 138, 195, 347–48
achievement levels, 139–40
act, 1, 8, 11, 19, 26, 80, 85, 89, 104, 115–16, 369
action and inquiry cycles, 248
action component, 178–79, 181–82
action planning, 236
action plans, 224–26, 237, 320
action research, 5, 10–11, 25, 32, 72–73, 293, 301, 311, 314–15, 376, 381
action research process, 25, 72, 207
action research project, 221, 369
actions, 29–30, 62, 69–70, 96–97, 101, 104–5, 107, 120–21, 164, 178–88, 192, 227–28, 231–32, 234–35, 287, 372–74, 384, 386, 388–89, 392
    problem children's, 367
actions and learning, 96
Adam, 6, 41, 273–75, 279–80
Adam's requests, 279–80
Adobe Firefly, 101–2, 104
advanced placement (AP), 69–70
adventures, 324, 328, 338
AERA (American Educational Research Association), 294–95
AfL (Assessment for Learning), 222–23, 226
African American, 21, 59–60, 76–77
African American students, 59, 75
African-American students, 143–44
ages, 67, 215, 271, 347–48, 374
AI-generated images, 101, 104
AI-Generated Student Work, 100, 104
Alachua County Teacher, 55–56

Algebra, 66, 69, 138, 140–41, 263
America, 49, 51–52, 54, 167
American Association of Colleges for Teacher Education (AACTE), 26
American Educational Research Association (AERA), 294–95
American Rescue Plan Act (ARPA), 14, 81
Amy, 40, 42–43, 49, 51–53, 106–7, 109, 147, 273–82
Amy's inquiry, 40, 54
analysis process, 137, 283–84
analytic processes, 137
Angela, 289, 292
annual event, 299–300
Anxious Math Learners, 250–51
AP (advanced placement), 69–70
AP classes, 70
Applications of Artificial Intelligence in Middle School Education (AAIMSE), 273
approval, 213–15
architecture, 1, 66–67, 69, 394
ARPA (American Rescue Plan Act), 14, 81
articles, empirical, 176–77
artist, 41, 279–80
Art of Classroom Inquiry, 61
ASCD (Association for Supervision and Curriculum Development), 295
Ashley Pennypacker Hill, 215–16, 246
Assessing Practitioner Inquiry, 383
assessing student learning, 57
Assessing Teacher Inquiry, 395
assessment data, formative, 223–24
Assessment for Learning. *See* AfL
assessment measures, 30, 95, 138, 142–43, 208
assessment practices, 6, 348
assessments, 121, 127, 144–45, 151, 221–22, 224, 226, 238, 240, 289, 379, 382, 386
    formative, 222–25

411

assignments, 46, 67, 200, 214, 218, 224, 329, 339, 382
Association for Supervision and Curriculum Development (ASCD), 295
assumptions, 13, 33, 144, 183, 185, 195–96, 217, 227, 373
attendance, 135–36

barriers, 90, 101, 180–82
beliefs, 30, 38–39, 51, 58, 61–62, 93, 204, 230, 348–49, 367, 373
beliefs and practice, 61–62
benchmark, 65, 238, 318, 321, 324–25, 341
    district's, 65, 316, 318, 324–25
benefit student learning, 6
biology, 59, 140–41, 149–52, 223–24, 347, 349
blogging, 124–26
blogs, 123–25, 145, 262
bottom, 115–16, 245–46
box, formula, 254–56
BR, 147–49
bridge-building project, 119–20
briefs, 199–200, 206
building, 15, 17, 54, 78–79, 90, 189, 197, 289, 293–94, 299, 373

calculate, 251–55, 258
calculations, 251–52, 254–55
calendar, 192, 225
Calkins, 64–65, 317–18, 332, 337–38, 341
candidates, 44, 346, 373
card, index, 275, 277
career, 3, 23, 27, 94, 270, 273, 295, 345, 355, 365
Carlee, 69–70
Carnegie Project on the Education Doctorate (CPED), 28, 162
categories, 39, 232, 242, 259, 261–62, 267–68, 272, 279, 283, 322, 338–39
categories of students, 137, 232
Category, 242–43, 322–23
CD, 147–48
Cell C24, 254–55
cells, 250, 252–55, 257–58
    designated, 254–55
center, 40–41, 106, 167, 274–75, 279–80, 288, 357, 366
CFGs (Critical Friends Groups), 25, 146, 149, 151, 154, 262, 357, 359, 361
Challenge Baskets, 117
challenges, 16–17, 37, 40, 68–69, 180, 203–4, 227, 271–72, 341, 343, 360, 362, 367, 370

change student learning, 151
Charlie, 333, 335–36
chart, 47, 112, 188, 256–58, 283, 325, 365
chart title, 257–58
chatbot, 18, 86, 89–92, 167, 199, 312, 314
ChatGPT, 175, 200, 202, 204–5, 271, 312
checklists, 331, 336, 338
Cheryl, 109, 111–13
child, 38–42, 45, 72–73, 75, 93, 106, 108–9, 132–33, 181, 215–16, 279, 289, 324–25, 327–31, 339
    particular, 43
children, 4–5, 7–9, 31–32, 39–41, 45–48, 56–57, 62, 64–66, 73–74, 98, 104–6, 122–23, 127, 132, 269, 316–30, 336, 341, 359–61, 365
children's literature, 66, 97, 319–21, 336, 360
Christina, 87–88, 352
circle, 31–32, 108, 122, 160, 163, 167, 199, 234, 364, 369–70, 374, 378, 380
claims, 29, 98, 165, 168–69, 185, 269, 313, 322–23, 325, 339, 386
claims/conclusions, 386, 391
class, 46–47, 68–70, 72–73, 77–80, 86–87, 90–91, 112–13, 120–21, 127, 135–36, 139–40, 147–48, 152–54, 222–26, 241–44, 263–64, 267, 295–96, 337–38, 355–57
    chemistry, 136
    particular, 210
classmates, 90–91, 242, 264, 267, 335, 349
class meeting, 117, 154
class member's work, 296
classroom, 1, 8–9, 12–13, 16–19, 40–44, 64, 82–86, 88–92, 95–96, 104–5, 112–15, 117–18, 120–22, 132–34, 178–79, 202–4, 288–89, 316–17, 339–41, 377–78
    particular, 81, 179
classroom-based inquiry, 204
classroom conditions, 241–42
Classroom Inquiry, 61
classroom learning environment, 62, 241
classroom learning experiences, 83, 203–4
classroom management, 62
classroom practice, 8, 11–12, 24, 30, 57, 61–62, 155, 172, 233
    responsive, 263
    teacher's, 10
classroom research, 10, 200, 205, 246
classroom researchers, 183
classroom/school, 95, 187
classroom teachers, 9, 11–12, 88, 95, 114, 177, 218, 223, 250, 370, 377

classroom teaching, 38, 375, 377
classwork, 113, 222
click, 252, 254, 256–58
clinical experiences, 26, 34, 109, 137
Coaching Inquiry-Oriented Learning Communities, 167, 393
Cochran-Smith & Lytle, 3, 10, 15, 72, 193, 195, 218, 270, 376
Coded Data, 277–78, 281
coding, 108, 259, 276–77, 385, 390–91
coding and memoing processes, 385, 391
collaboration, 14–15, 23, 27, 180, 183, 193–94, 196–99, 202, 206, 227–28, 230, 384, 389
collaborative inquiry, 83, 167
collaborative work, 60, 180–82
collaborative work times, 181
colleague feedback, 30, 95, 146, 149, 155, 165
colleagues, 78, 82–84, 146, 150–51, 154–56, 166–67, 172, 183–84, 193–96, 198, 206, 213, 219, 228, 288–89, 294, 304, 372–73, 382–83, 393
collection, 4, 31–32, 72, 80, 137–38, 149, 154, 221–22, 237, 244, 248
collections of teacher research, 4, 72
college, 66, 214, 354, 359–62, 382
Columbus, 49–51
column, 47, 188, 250–51, 253–58
column charts, 250, 256–58
common behaviors and actions in school culture, 372
communication, 58, 82, 132–33, 183, 269
communities, 9, 13–15, 17, 78, 80, 194, 196, 198, 212, 338–39, 342, 354–55, 357
compass, 15, 35–36
Complete formative assessment on learning targets, 225–26
completion, 163, 168, 214, 217, 224, 268, 375, 382
Complexity of Inquiry Stance and Assessing Teacher Inquiry, 395
components
  exhilarating, 190
  individual, 31–32, 159, 365, 370
components of teacher inquiry, 196
conference participants, 296
conferences, 60, 221, 289, 294–96, 299, 333, 343
connect and network groups of professionals, 24
consult, 67, 161, 168–70, 172, 199, 249
contemporary understandings of teacher inquiry, 13
content, 19, 24, 47, 49, 51–52, 54–56, 163, 167, 183–84, 191, 350, 352, 355

content area, 16, 53–55, 57, 271
content knowledge, 30, 38–39, 56–57, 93, 170, 361
  adult-level, 56
contested issues, 16–18, 34
context, 22–23, 38–39, 81–83, 85, 93, 125–26, 154–55, 161–64, 168–69, 171–72, 179, 268, 292, 383–84, 387–88
  classroom/school, 268
continuous problematizing of practice, 393
contribution, 22, 29, 279, 380–81
control, 8, 11, 164, 198, 212, 241, 269, 376
conversations, 25–26, 90–92, 104, 108, 110, 112, 269, 271, 291, 296, 312, 314, 332
  teacher inquirer-chatbot, 199
Copilot, 311–12
coursework, 35, 210, 356–57, 360
CPED (Carnegie Project on the Education Doctorate), 28, 162
creating equitable classrooms, 5, 72
Creating Excel Data Sets, 250
creation, 14, 18, 22, 39, 56, 71, 86, 200, 205, 345–68, 371
credibility, 339, 380–81
Critical Friends Groups. *See* CFGs
cultures, student's, 91
curricula, language arts, 83
curriculum, 6, 8–9, 15–17, 38–40, 47–54, 57, 83–85, 93, 179–80, 197, 201, 361–62, 381, 383
  prepared, 381
curriculum development inquiries, 47, 52
cycles, 97, 100, 178, 180, 284, 287, 290, 305, 345, 347–49, 371, 374–75, 380–83
  individual, 375
  particular, 246

Dakota language, 51–52
Dana's inquiry, 79–80
Darice, 100, 104–5
data
  collecting, 25, 79, 123, 187, 189, 234, 273–74, 280, 369
  entered, 253
  occurring, 37, 88–89, 95, 164, 187, 389
  piece of, 143, 146, 224, 246–47, 265, 274, 350, 386, 392
  raw, 140, 248
  teacher-issued, 140
data analysis, 30–31, 137–38, 220, 231–33, 262–63, 268, 270, 285, 287, 311, 313, 339–40, 342, 385–86, 390
data analysis memos, 262, 267, 285

data analysis process, 191, 220, 246, 272, 280, 282, 284, 385, 391
data collection, 89, 95–157, 161, 187–92, 212–13, 231–32, 236, 366, 370–71, 384–85, 389–90
data collection and analysis, 80, 107, 149, 172, 281, 320, 365
data collection and analysis processes, 137
data collection and data analysis, 137
data collection brainstorming process, 188
data collection in process, 231
data collection plan, 132, 135, 144, 207
data collection process, high-quality, 389
data collection sheet, 274
data collection strategies, 30, 95, 109, 146, 154–56, 159, 181, 187, 306, 356
data set, 244, 248–51, 260, 272, 274–75, 277
data sources, 104, 144, 187–88, 212, 221–22, 236, 240, 269, 274, 385, 389–90
date, 70, 96, 98, 124, 154–55, 189, 191–93, 225–26
dazzling language, 336–37
dazzling words, 336
Debbi, 142, 144–45, 179, 301, 377
Debbi's research, 377
defined problems of practice, 23
Demo-A-Day unit, 121
demonstrations, 120–21
description, 8–9, 11, 160, 168, 171, 245, 247–48, 258–60, 378, 383–86, 391
descriptive statistics, 248–49, 252, 254, 258, 385, 391
descriptive step of data analysis, 262–63
design, 18–19, 67, 70–71, 183–84, 187, 190, 201, 204–5, 306, 311, 313, 384, 389
design process, 384, 389
development, 30, 32, 39, 47–48, 52–53, 64, 70, 79–81, 87, 89, 92–93, 198–200, 316–17, 319–20, 371–72
development of teacher inquiry, 32
dialogue, 15, 25, 61, 86–87, 146, 167, 195–96, 199, 279, 288, 373
Diane, 51–54
Diane's inquiry, 49, 51
DIBELS (Dynamic Indicators of Basic Early Literacy Skills), 142, 238, 301
DIBELS data, 144–45
differences, 11–13, 40, 49, 122, 138–39, 248–49, 255–57, 290, 358, 376, 380
  significant, 203–4
difficult topics, 16–17, 34, 77
dilemmas, 10, 37, 39, 42–43, 49–50, 56, 93, 129, 139
dimensions, ethical, 30, 160, 206, 218–19, 227–28

direction, 36–37, 75, 77, 86, 92, 109, 112, 201, 361
disciplined students, 82–83
discoveries, 51–52, 58–59, 61, 78–79, 129, 167, 183
  true, 49, 51, 54
discrepancies, 187, 386, 390
display, 191–92, 260
distinct groups of students, 136
district, 23, 25, 28, 48–49, 82, 85, 169–70, 213–14, 270, 288–89, 292–94, 299, 316, 381–83, 393
Districtwide Approach, 25
Districtwide Approach to Staff and Student Learning, 25
diverse students, 362, 364
diversity, 6, 57, 69, 355–56, 359–62, 365
doctoral student, 29, 81, 90, 215
documents, 96–98, 104, 118, 138, 177, 186, 218, 261, 264, 267, 361
  electronic, 97–98, 100
Documents/Artifacts/Student Work, 356
Dubuque, 354–55, 359–60
duration of data collection, 161, 189–92
Dynamic Indicators of Basic Early Literacy Skills (DIBELS), 142, 238, 301

education, child's, 132
Educational Action Research, 293
Educational Leadership, 366–67
educational research, 9–10, 33–34, 220, 226, 347
education research, 173–74
educators, 3, 5–6, 14, 18, 21–22, 28–29, 162–63, 165, 183, 200–201, 203–4, 208, 220, 345, 370–71
educators and students, 203
Educators' Beliefs Impact Student Learning, 198
Elementary and Secondary School Emergency Relief (ESSER), 81
elementary school, 49, 52, 290, 299, 326
elements, cultural, 90–91
endings, 65, 318, 321, 324, 328–30, 336
energy, 41, 154, 194, 227–28, 333
engagement, 22, 26–27, 29, 31, 33–34, 164, 184, 203–4, 209–10, 291, 345, 375, 378
  developing home-school, 185
  individual, 29
  individual school districts approach, 213
engagement in group work, 267
engagement in inquiry, 4, 6–7, 11, 22, 26, 86, 270, 289, 345, 378
engagement in inquiry/action research, 29
Engagement in practitioner inquiry, 218
engagement in practitioner research, 378

engagement in teacher inquiry, 26–27, 34, 118, 209–10, 228
English language learners, 174, 354, 357, 361
English language learner students, 174, 274
enter, 28, 101, 176, 212, 251–53, 294, 341, 348, 355–56, 361, 373
equitable school experiences for students, 45
equity, 14, 21–22, 30, 69, 71–72, 79, 81, 93, 345–46, 365–66, 368
    issues of, 22, 39, 367–68
Equity/Social Justice, 38–39, 93, 170
ESE (Exceptional Student Education), 75
ESL students, 8, 40–42
ESSER (Elementary and Secondary School Emergency Relief), 81
ethics, 161, 208–9, 211–12, 217, 219–20, 230, 293, 384, 389
everyday work, 2, 4, 7, 207, 209, 229
evidence, 4, 6–7, 11, 18, 20, 171, 173, 195–96, 323, 328, 343, 373, 378
examples, 22, 28, 30, 32, 39–40, 81, 96, 103, 167, 182, 259–62, 268–69, 277–78, 293, 305–6
examples of student responses, 263–64
examples of teacher inquiry, 306
excel, 249–52, 256, 284, 349, 353, 382
excel worksheet, 250, 252, 257
Exceptional Student Education (ESE), 75
exercises, 30, 32–33, 38–39, 57, 60, 62, 70–71, 160, 163–64, 168, 185–87, 190–92, 198, 200, 282–83
exhilarating components of teacher inquiry, 190
expectations, 66, 68, 122, 148, 263, 267, 269, 319, 323, 325, 327, 330–31, 366–67
experiential learning opportunities, 354–55
explorers, 49–50, 375
extensive review of research on teacher inquiry, 7

faculty, 82, 296, 356, 362, 364, 367
Fairfax County Public Schools, 213, 306
families, 132, 181, 183–84, 367
Family Educational Rights and Privacy Act. *See* FERPA
family engagement activities, designing, 185
farmers, 12–13
favorite parts, 131, 328
    least, 131, 328
FCAT (Florida Comprehensive Assessment Test), 139–40, 147–48, 150, 152
features, critical, 311, 313, 343
feedback, 123, 131, 146, 149, 155, 159, 205–7, 226, 228, 333, 342

female students, 59–60, 151–52, 179–80
FERPA (Family Educational Rights and Privacy Act), 214–15
field experiences, 26–27, 47, 199, 306, 356–57, 362
field notes, 55–56, 104–7, 109, 113–14, 118, 121, 124, 154–55, 273–74, 281, 385, 390
    taking, 105, 108–9, 156, 188
fifth-grade students, 215, 218
Fifth-grade teacher inquirer Wendy Lane Smith, 17
findings, 15, 38, 74, 77–78, 171, 176–77, 196, 231–85, 292–93, 341–43, 361–62, 370–71, 375–78, 385–87, 391–92
findings inform, 386, 392
first semester science grades, 139
fit, 39, 95–96, 136, 156, 245, 261–62, 339, 386, 391–92
Florida, 5, 14, 24, 215–16, 271, 273, 299, 303, 305–6, 311, 355–57
Florida Comprehensive Assessment Test. *See* FCAT
fluency, 142, 179, 182, 301
fluency development, 142, 144, 179, 301, 376–77
focus groups, 30, 95, 117–18, 121, 145, 154–55, 224–25
forces, 103, 114, 129, 261, 302
formative data analysis, 191, 221, 232–37, 240–41, 246, 284
formative data analysis partner, 272
formative data analysis process, 241, 247, 272
fourth-grade students, 50, 90, 118, 144, 250–51, 253
fourth group of students, 136
fraction bars, 116
fractions, 87–88, 112–13, 116
    conceptual understandings of, 115, 117
    equivalent, 115–16
framework, 50, 86, 101, 160, 380
framing, 77, 165–66
functions, 28, 251, 254, 311
futures, 128–29, 201

Gail, 46, 108–9, 228
gaps, 62, 71–72, 169, 223–24, 360–61
gender, 16, 22, 72–73, 80, 86, 139–40, 151, 242, 354
generalizability, 376, 379
Geometry, 59, 140–41, 224
gifted students, 202
givens, 195, 345
goals, 9–10, 24, 26, 28, 64–66, 129, 131, 179–80, 183–85, 208, 248, 258, 316–19, 330, 370
    personal, 218
Google Forms, 137–38, 224–26, 249

grade deflation, 139, 146, 148
grade distributions, 148, 151
grade inflation, 139, 148
grade level, 16, 40, 85, 139, 151, 169, 180, 199
graders
   first, 65, 87
   fourth, 50–52, 54–55, 167, 301
grades, 46, 56, 132, 138–41, 143, 145–48, 151–52, 214, 216, 222, 347–49
group, 67–69, 77–78, 112, 118–19, 121, 146–47, 185–86, 198, 207, 245, 250–53, 255–58, 261, 269, 301, 367–68
   distinct, 136
   dysfunctional, 68
   fourth, 136
   inquiry Critical Friends, 357
   multigenerational teacher inquiry, 5
   network, 24
   particular, 171
   small, 64, 108, 135, 154, 218, 223, 236–37, 317, 331, 344, 373
   students work in, 67, 153
grouping, 242, 245, 261, 267
group members, 67, 118, 146, 207, 274
groups of students, 21, 37, 72, 105, 118, 135–36, 153, 171, 238
groups of students for additional support, 223
group work, 120, 153, 163, 267
growth, 1, 6, 23–24, 41, 125, 128, 162, 165–67, 257, 268, 270, 322, 325
growth students, 40–41
guidance, 38, 96, 154, 159, 181–82, 252, 260
guidelines, 208, 249–50
guide reflection, 220

Hefner, Megan, 234–35, 238–39
help sessions, 135–36, 224, 232
heuristics, 375–76
highlight, 22, 164, 254–58, 261, 314, 339
high school, 70, 73, 81, 139, 143, 152, 299, 348–49, 355
high school biology, 347, 349
high school chemistry teacher Stephen Burgin, 120, 135
high school graduation, 348
high school students, advanced, 202–4
Hilarie, 355–57
Hilarie's inquiry stories, 346
Hillsborough County Public School Research Review process, 214
Hillsborough County Public Schools, 214

historical events, 50–51
Holocaust, 54–56
home-school journals, 133–34
homework, 113, 132, 152, 195, 222, 224, 242–43, 302
honing, 36, 86, 165, 167
Hoppey, David, 235, 238–39

identities, teaching as, 63
IEPs (individualized education plans), 97, 202
images, 11, 13, 102–4, 123, 143, 212, 271, 361, 376
Impactful Practitioner Inquiry, 6
impacting students, 79, 289
impact of inquiry, 6–7, 22
impact student learning, 197–98
implementation plan, 160–61, 172, 178, 181, 190–91, 206, 227
implementing, 52, 74, 81, 120, 151, 179–81, 237, 381
implications, 70, 128, 146, 149, 223, 228–29, 247–48, 269, 283–84, 386, 392
incidents, 42–43, 47, 274
   critical, 43, 47, 70
indicators, 139–40, 149, 383–86
Indigenous peoples, 51–52
individual engagement in teacher inquiry, 29
individualized education plans (IEPs), 97, 202
individual school districts approach engagement in inquiry, 213
inequalities, 21–22, 69, 72, 345
inform, 20, 154, 157, 169–70, 172–73, 177–78, 217, 219, 231, 233–35, 282, 284, 346–47
information, 127, 132, 134, 171, 175–77, 188–89, 194, 210, 214, 299, 302, 387, 389
   hard time processing auditory, 44
innovative school calendars for professional learning, 24
inquirers, 6, 10, 17, 199, 206, 211, 229–30, 311–12, 315, 384, 388
   collaboration teacher, 194
   practitioner, 202, 209
inquirer's problem of practice, 200
inquirer's process, 233
inquirer's work, particular, 282
inquiries to push school administrators, 14
inquiring, 2, 30, 32, 59, 115, 117, 199, 345, 347, 364, 374
inquiry, 2–8, 10–12, 17–37, 52–59, 72–75, 78–81, 83–90, 153–57, 159–61, 163–73, 178–200, 204–15, 227–37, 270–74, 287–96, 303–6, 311–15, 342–49, 368–76, 380–93

inquiry and equity, 346
inquiry-based professional learning programming, 24
Inquiry Brief, 160, 193, 200, 227
Inquiry Brief Example, 221–22
inquiry brief prime time, 203
inquiry brochure, 306
Inquiry Brochure Example Source, 307
inquiry coach, 230, 285
inquiry collaboration, 198
inquiry community, 3, 14–17, 78, 373
   schoolwide, 77
inquiry culture, 294, 299
inquiry cycle, 17, 97, 100, 178–82, 190–91, 231–32, 248, 270, 272, 287, 289, 361, 364
   fifth, 348
   particular, 375
inquiry data, 282–83
inquiry design, 30, 388–89
Inquiry Example, 250–51, 253–54, 257
inquiry experience, 199, 287, 311, 370, 393
inquiry facilitation work, 183
inquiry findings, 269, 360–61, 380
   teacher researcher's, 380
inquiry for equity, 22, 368
inquiry inspire thinking, 384, 388
inquiry journey, 32, 35–37, 88, 95, 154–55, 159–60, 164, 167–69, 189, 192–93, 198, 287–343
inquiry learning community, 78
inquiry passions, 163
inquiry plan, 191, 206, 220, 229, 234, 241, 248, 389
inquiry planning, 146, 159–60, 169, 220, 227, 231
inquiry presentations, 342, 362, 395
inquiry product, 370, 393
inquiry project, 6, 41, 48, 50, 87, 122, 280, 335, 374
   shared, 108, 132
inquiry question, 30, 52, 54, 85, 89–90, 92, 109–10, 165, 167–68, 172, 174, 189, 191
   first, 74–75
   researchable, 373
Inquiry Roundtable Session, 373
Inquiry Scaffolding Seminar, 373
inquiry's focus, 384, 388
Inquiry Sharing Assistant, 312
inquiry's problem of practice, 314
inquiry stance, 2–4, 16–18, 23, 26–27, 29, 40, 69, 86, 159, 369–75, 380–81
inquiry stance in relationship, 369
inquiry stance on teaching, 270
inquiry step, 30
inquiry step by step, 30
inquiry stories, 5, 365, 368

inquiry story, 365–66
inquiry template, 306
Inquiry Template Example Source, 310
inquiry timeline, 160, 189, 191–92, 206, 227
inquiry write-ups, 305–6, 344
insightful pieces of teacher research, 73
insights, 25, 27, 78, 80, 108–9, 153–54, 168–70, 187–89, 209, 231–35, 244–45, 262–63, 272–73, 380–81, 389–90
institutional review boards, 209, 220
instruction, 60, 64–66, 120, 122–23, 126, 180, 202–4, 215–16, 222–23, 235–36, 240, 316–22, 341–42, 349–50, 352
   following, 225–26
instructional actions, 179, 186, 192
instructional activities, 115–16, 223–25, 350
instructional model leverage student learning opportunities, 223
instructional practices, 18, 72, 183, 213, 222–23, 236, 240
instructional strategy, 159, 179, 250
instructional support process, 45
instructional support teachers in addition to students, 114
integration, 92, 106, 197, 203–4, 240
interactions, 19, 37, 39, 42–43, 90, 118, 120, 274, 280, 366
   social, 40, 90, 92, 373
interns, 40–41, 64, 289, 296, 299, 317, 342
intersection, 30, 58, 62, 69, 74, 316
intervention, 8, 144, 176, 186, 236–38, 240, 267, 306
intervention plan, 237
interviewing, 114–16, 120–22, 232
interviews, 6, 114–16, 121, 123, 134, 136, 145, 151, 153–55, 331, 333, 385, 390
   focus-group, 117
   whole-class focus group, 241
IRBs, 209, 211, 215–17, 229
isolation, 13, 97–98, 154, 197
italics, 149–50
iterations, 262–64, 267
iterative processes, 137, 149, 159, 314

journal articles, 169, 174, 378
journal entries, 122, 155–56, 219, 224, 274, 322–23, 326
journaling, 20, 91, 122, 124–26, 155, 157, 202
Journal of Practitioner Research, 32, 73, 293, 305
Journal of Teacher Action Research, 32, 305

journals, 32–33, 73, 80, 122–23, 125–26, 134, 155–57, 171–72, 175, 274, 278, 305, 350
   open-access, 172, 175
   reflective, 156, 356, 361
   researcher, 222, 263–65
journey, 2, 29–32, 35–93, 129, 159–60, 189, 211, 248, 287–88, 341, 347
   ultimate, 393–94
J-Term, 354–55, 357
Julie, 70, 110, 305–6, 316, 319–20, 322, 339
Julie's inquiry, 63, 319, 323, 339
Julie's work, 305, 311
junior year, 356–57, 359–60, 364–65

Kelly, 82, 132, 134, 137
key component of teacher inquiry, 20
knights, 333–34, 337, 341
knowledge, 2–3, 9–10, 27, 56, 59, 61, 124, 169–70, 195, 208–12, 217, 221–22, 367, 378–79, 393
   background, 50, 373
   conceptual, 115, 188–89
   generating, 195, 210–11
   metacognitive, 226
knowledge base, preexisting, 169
knowledge base for teaching, 288, 293, 376, 380–81
knowledge/understanding, 51

language, 51–52, 63, 65, 166, 209, 212, 316, 318, 324, 328–29, 336
Language Experience Approach, 357–58
law, fraction, 115–16
leaders, 28, 70, 362, 372–73
learners, 40, 42–43, 83, 86, 88, 105–6, 179, 323, 325, 348–50, 352–53, 376–77, 381
   particular, 43, 46–47
learning, 1–3, 5–6, 14–17, 19–20, 22–24, 59–62, 96–97, 129–31, 183–85, 202–5, 220–24, 226–27, 270–71, 273, 282–83, 302–5, 322–23, 339–40, 355–56, 386–87
   blended, 223
   cooperative, 57, 60, 68–69, 153
   online, 223
   powerful, 15, 187
   project-based, 24, 181
learning activities, 6, 224–25, 349–50
learning and maximize student, 20
learning communities, 27–28
   inquiry-oriented, 25
   professional, 23–24
learning conditions, 3, 169, 209, 214, 229, 393
learning context, 30, 81
learning environments, inclusive, 367

learning experiences, 19, 71, 202
   equitable, 22, 171, 365
   professional, 180, 292
learning/findings, 386
Learning Forward, 24–25, 295
learning gains, 202–3, 237
learning goals, 223, 352
   particular, 223
Learning Management Systems (LMSs), 97
learning objectives, 35, 159
learning of high school chemistry, 120
learning outcomes, 32, 370
learning process, 9, 56, 114, 120, 291
learning situations, 120, 291
learning targets, 223–26
   self-assessment of, 224–26
learning to address, 16, 77
learning to teach, 1, 26, 364
lesson planning, 159, 220
lesson plans, 52, 159, 220, 228, 320
lessons, 2, 47, 49, 51–52, 58, 74, 109, 112–15, 122–23, 221–22, 259, 265, 319–22, 325–27, 329
letters, 44, 144–45, 236, 238, 240, 250, 301, 357
letter work, manipulative, 237–38
levels, 55, 70, 112, 139–41, 147, 150, 152, 179–80, 199, 201, 357
Lex's thinking, 272
librarians, 170, 172, 176–77, 299
life chances, 2, 22
lifetime, 31
   professional, 93, 369, 374–75
lifetime of professional learning, 31
Linda, 65, 318, 327, 340–41
line charts, 250, 256–58
list, 46–47, 52–53, 57, 60, 80, 85, 155, 174, 176–77, 187–88, 269, 274–76, 331
literacy curriculum, 52
literature, 77, 82, 123, 139, 168–73, 177, 179, 227, 320, 323, 333–34, 336–37, 356, 360–62, 389–90
   published, 337–38
   relevant, 384
literature on teacher research methodology, 227, 390
LMSs (Learning Management Systems), 97
Loras, 354–55, 357, 360, 362, 365
Loras College Teacher Education Conceptual Framework, 363
Loras students, 354

Madison Metropolitan School District's Classroom Action Research Program, 106, 306
Making Inquiry Science Work, 49, 52

INDEX   **419**

Making Meaning, 146, 149–50
marvel, 269–70
materialize, 38, 244
materials, 48, 50, 53, 56–57, 77, 148–50, 152–53, 159, 213, 221–22, 359
   manipulative, 115, 221–22
math, 59–60, 75, 140–41, 147, 149–52, 221, 223, 264
math class, 112–13, 147–48, 150, 174
math concepts, basic, 221
math scores, 139–40, 147, 150
matrix, 250, 271
May Steward, 234, 240–41
mechanism for professional learning, 21, 289
median, 248, 250
Megan, 235–37, 240, 244
memoing, 259, 262, 385, 390
memoing processes, 385, 391
mentor teacher, 29, 42–44, 87, 90, 109, 167, 236–37, 288–89, 299, 306
metaphors, 3, 31, 268, 284, 386, 392
methods, investigation-based teaching, 241
Mickey's work, 138, 149
middle school education, 82, 271
middle school students, 101, 128
Mills, 211, 215, 219, 282, 303–4
mini-lessons, 66, 319, 325, 327, 336–37
minority students, 349
models, 25, 68, 100–101, 153, 169, 223–24, 229, 305–6, 334, 344, 372–73
   scientific, 101
mother, 46, 63, 316, 330
movement, practitioner-inquiry, 217, 346
Multicultural Education, 354–56, 359–61
multiple times, 179, 259, 264, 301
music, 45, 59, 212, 264, 268

NAEYC (National Association for the Education of Young Children), 295
name, student's, 46
NAPDS (National Association for Professional Development Schools), 27–28
NASUP (National Association for School University Partnerships), 28, 295
National Association, 27–28, 295
National Association for Professional Development Schools (NAPDS), 27–28
National Association for School–University Partnerships. *See* NASUP
National Association for the Education of Young Children (NAEYC), 295
National Council of Teachers of English (NCTE), 53, 295

National Council of Teachers of Mathematics. *See* NCTM
National Education Association's (NEA), 208
National School Reform Faculty, 25, 146
National Science Teachers Association (NSTA), 53, 241, 295
native peoples, 49–50
NCTE (National Council of Teachers of English), 53, 295
NCTM (National Council of Teachers of Mathematics), 5, 53, 175, 295
NEA (National Education Association's), 208
network, 32, 293, 299, 305
newsletters, 133, 314
Newton's Laws, 100, 102, 104
Nicole, 346, 357, 360–61, 365–66
NJD, 147–49
North Dakota, 51–52, 81, 211
NSRF, 146
NSTA (National Science Teachers Association), 53, 241, 295
numerical values, 248, 251–52

observations, 42–44, 47, 88–89, 107, 109, 111, 113, 135–36, 148, 151, 219, 221, 224
office, 78–79
Online Journal for Teacher Research, 32, 293
on-task behavior, 112–13
Open-Ended Wonderings, 165
oppression, 16, 184–85
organizing units, 261, 283
outline, 154, 159–60, 173, 192, 269, 283, 314–15, 342
outsiders, 8–10, 12
ownership, 12, 46, 127, 268, 330–31

page, 63–64, 98, 101, 156–57, 199, 234, 237, 268, 270, 301, 303, 314–17, 378, 380, 387
Paige, 346, 359–60, 365–66
painstaking process, 65, 318, 328
paper, 62, 64, 160, 189, 193, 200, 261, 317, 326, 328–29, 332–33, 335, 341
paperwork, 96
paradigm, 8–10, 379
Parental Survey, 133–34
Parent and Teachers Association (PTA), 132
parentheses, 254
parents, 46, 48, 68–69, 75, 83–84, 132–34, 136, 211, 213, 215, 224–26, 348, 353
part, 2–3, 7, 30–32, 91, 95, 102, 113–14, 168–70, 193, 195–96, 198–99, 212–13, 215, 227–28, 244–45, 250–54, 256–57, 262–64, 304, 329–30
participants, 171, 207, 210, 216, 219, 296, 300

participation, 22–23, 80, 127, 133, 174, 216–17, 219, 222, 232, 380
Participation in teacher research, 193
particular class of students, 210
particular cycle of inquiry, 246
particular group of students, 171
partners, 102, 176, 205, 229, 270, 325, 332–33
  student's, 333
partnership work, 28
Part of student instruction, 223
parts of stories, 322, 324, 329, 331
passage, 44–45, 340, 395
passionate, 41, 88, 90, 163, 304
passion exploration work, 167
passion for teaching, 63, 317
passions, 22, 30, 35–95, 122, 160, 163, 165, 167, 184, 316–19, 326
  particular, 30, 180
  personal, 63
patterns, 221–22, 232, 236, 246–47, 253, 261, 268, 272, 276–80, 339–40, 385, 391
PBIS (Positive Behavior Interventions and Supports), 78
PDSs (Professional Development School), 23, 27–28, 34, 198, 288, 295, 299
Pedagogies, 5
Pedagogies for Teacher Inquiry and Practice, 5
peer interactions, 40–42, 210, 273–75, 280
peer-review process, 170
peers, 11, 41, 44, 90–91, 170–71, 174, 264, 274, 276, 279–80, 395
people, 14–15, 17, 53, 55, 71, 75–76, 84, 103, 127, 129, 243, 267, 269, 299–300, 331–32
perceptions, qualitative, 203
person, 63, 70, 107–8, 128, 164, 174, 195, 251–52, 279, 316, 340
personality, 46, 279
perspectives, 49, 53–55, 57, 80, 84, 86, 89–90, 163, 165, 171, 383–85, 387, 389–90
phenomenon, scientific, 101, 104
philosophies, 58, 61–62, 80, 113, 123, 241, 387
pictures, 44, 118, 145, 155, 163, 245–46, 274, 282, 326, 339, 357
  digital, 30, 95, 118, 120–21
piece of action research, 381
piece of teacher research, 380–82, 394
pieces, 160, 170, 172, 244–45, 247, 261–62, 276–77, 323, 327, 335, 339–40
  blue, 245
  half, 116
  insightful, 73

Pintrich, 223, 226
plan, 131, 134, 157, 160, 165, 179, 181, 184–88, 190–93, 205–7, 219, 384, 386, 389
  wondering/inquiry, 235
planned changes, 386, 392
planned reflection time, 20
planning, 87, 92, 154, 159–61, 167, 169, 172, 179, 181, 189, 191–92, 324–25, 384
planning process, 159–60, 199
plants, 12
PLCs (professional learning communities), 23–26, 34, 146, 154–55, 271
policy, 85, 201, 213, 293
ponder, 155, 163–65, 172, 187–88, 190–92, 199, 206, 244–45
  practitioner-inquiry movement, 210
PoP, associated, 164–65, 169, 172
Popplet, 357–58
positionality, 171, 185, 227, 383, 387
  teacher researcher's, 383, 387
Positive Behavior Interventions and Supports (PBIS), 78
Positive relationships, 179, 264
Positive social interactions, 145, 302
possible solution to address, 181–82, 227
posters, 265, 267, 294–96, 300, 311
  student's data, 350
postsurveys, 327–29, 339
posttest, 251–53, 255, 257
posttest scores, 250–51, 253–55, 258
post-unit survey, 129, 131
poverty, 21, 26, 73, 82, 349, 366–67
powerful learning of teacher inquiry, 187
PowerPoint, 311, 315
PowerPoint Slides, 294, 300–301, 311
practical guide, 311, 314–15
practice, 3–6, 9–10, 20–31, 36–39, 61–62, 71–73, 162, 164–65, 169–70, 179–80, 186, 199–206, 228, 236–37, 293–95, 347, 369–73, 384–86, 388–90, 392–93
  clinical, 26, 28
  current, 9, 132, 166
  current teaching, 165, 283
  daily, 37, 40, 218, 220, 233
  educational, 1, 3, 10, 288, 353, 371
  evidence-based, 173, 237
  inequitable schooling, 73
  inform, 173, 214
  new, 196, 386
  reflective, 21, 25, 167, 183
  schoolwide, 372

practicing teachers, 6–7, 21, 27, 29, 32, 35, 38, 40, 86, 88, 299–300, 305
practitioner-inquirer, 202
Practitioner Inquiry, 2–394
 defining, 217
practitioner inquiry dissertation, 200, 205
practitioner inquiry movement, 193
practitioner research, 7, 10, 22, 209–11, 217, 305, 311, 314–15, 369, 378, 382
Practitioner research and institutional review boards, 220
practitioner research and IRBs, 211
practitioner research dissertation, 270
practitioner researchers, 126, 204, 209–10
practitioner research methodology, 172
practitioner research movement, 22
practitioner research process, 125
practitioner research quality, 378
practitioners, 27–28, 32, 173, 210, 262, 293, 299, 315
 inquiry-oriented classroom, 10
prepared curriculum package, 381
preparing, 31, 129, 159, 288, 311–12, 314, 362
presentation, 67, 214–15, 289, 294, 299–300, 311–12, 314–15, 356, 360–61, 365, 369–71
 oral, 31, 300–301, 303, 315, 369, 382
presenters, 207, 296, 300
presurvey, 327–28
pretest, 221, 250–55, 257
pretest scores, 253, 255, 258
pre-unit survey, 130–31
principles, 71, 165, 167–68, 208
Pritchard, 209–11, 220
privacy, 213–14
problematizes, 9
problematizing, continuous, 393
problem description, 236
problems, 9–10, 18, 20, 37–38, 67–69, 75–76, 159–62, 168–70, 179–82, 190–91, 200, 202–4, 206–7, 220–22, 227, 320–21, 323–24, 333–34, 384–85, 388–90
 defined, 23
 inquirer's, 200
 inquiry's, 314
 real-world, 30
 shared, 199
problem solving, 18, 112–13, 357
process, 3–4, 8–10, 13–14, 16–23, 31–36, 44–46, 56–59, 169–71, 197–99, 208–9, 229, 233–36, 244–46, 259, 261–62, 272–74, 288–89, 292–93, 369–72, 377–79
 systematic, 244, 259

process and stance, 16–17, 34
process and stance of inquiry, 17
process and stance of inquiry support, 34
process and stance of teacher inquiry, 16
process for designing research, 220
processing
 auditory, 44–45
 visual, 44–45
process of finding, 40
process of grouping, 245, 261
process of teacher inquiry, 209, 228, 289–90, 292–93, 303, 306, 353, 386, 392
process of teacher inquiry to plan, 292
process of wondering development, 39, 72, 244
process-product, 8–9, 11
process-product paradigm, 8–9, 11, 217, 379
process redefines, 1, 394
products, 4, 14, 31, 120, 123, 180, 304, 369–72, 374–75, 381
profession, 2, 26–27, 29, 33, 203, 288, 292–93, 299, 373, 379, 381
professional development, 23, 25, 27, 34, 132, 167, 201, 222, 270, 292, 304
Professional Development/Learning Programs, 23
Professional Development School. See PDSs
Professional Development Schools, 23, 27–28, 198, 288
professional inquiry, 168
professional learning, 14, 21, 23–26, 31, 35, 209, 213, 218, 220, 289, 292, 375, 378
professional learning communities. See PLCs
Professional Learning Community, 60, 146, 198, 271
professional learning endeavor, 305, 347
professional learning framework, 380
professional learning mechanism, 209, 228
professional learning programs, 24, 198
 inquiry-based, 24
professional learning sessions, 179–81
professional learning time, 292
professional practices, 10, 15, 17, 23, 27, 29, 34, 196, 198, 370, 384
programs, 23, 106–7, 200, 216, 296, 299, 361, 372
 experimental student-teacher-as-researcher, 61
 professional practice doctoral, 23, 28–29, 34, 199, 305
progress monitoring, 235, 237, 240
progress monitoring process, 234, 237
Progress Monitoring Step, 236–37, 240
project, 66–69, 118, 122–23, 210, 214, 216, 319–21, 324–28, 334, 338, 341, 369–70, 381–82
proposal, 217, 229, 343, 355–56
protein synthesis, 350, 352

protocols, 25, 146, 149, 157, 206, 285, 395
PTA (Parent and Teachers Association), 132
public schools, 306, 362
published authors, 306, 320, 323, 338
punishing students, 79, 153
purpose and rationale, 161, 164, 172
purpose of engagement in inquiry by classroom teachers, 11
purpose of teacher research, 377, 380
puzzle, 245–46, 268, 270
puzzle pieces, 245–46, 262

qualitative data, 78, 187, 234, 240–41, 244, 248, 258–60, 282, 373, 385, 391
Qualitative Inquiry, 61, 282
qualitative perceptions and experiences of educators and students, 203
quality, 26, 31, 100, 123, 160, 170–71, 224, 227, 375, 378–87, 393–95
  assessing, 380–81
quality children's literature, 320
quality indicators, 31, 383, 387–92, 394–95
Quality Indicators for Assessing Practitioner Inquiry, 383
quality of teacher inquiry, 393
quality of teacher research, 379, 381–82, 393
quality research, 170–72, 379
quality teacher research, 375, 382
quantitative data, 78, 187, 202–3, 234, 240, 247, 249, 258–60, 385, 391
questioning, 57–59, 61, 123, 347, 369–71
questions, new, 78, 89, 232–35, 269, 280, 304
questions/wonderings, 388
quiz, 70, 121, 136, 224–25, 350
quizzes, short content, 224–25

race, 16, 22, 72–73, 80, 184, 330, 354
range, 6, 64–65, 90, 247, 249, 254–56, 271, 295, 305, 316–18, 331
rate, better student work turn-in, 148
rationale, 161, 164, 168, 172, 385, 389
react, 62, 66, 319, 372
readers, 65, 75–77, 163, 301–2, 304, 316, 318, 322, 335–36, 338, 377–78
reading group, 122, 328, 335, 337
reading group time, 186
Real Evidence-Based Practice, 172–73
real-world problems of practice, 30
Recall Stephen Burgin's inquiry, 232
recording, 105, 107–9, 168
  audio, 107–9, 214

reflections, 19–20, 36–37, 118, 121–24, 126, 199–200, 224–25, 350, 353–54, 368, 370–71, 381, 383, 386–87, 392–93
reflective educator's guide to classroom research, 200, 205, 246
reform, 1, 28–29, 32, 346, 379
relationship, close, 137
Remote Learning Inquiry (RLI), 14
rereading, 142, 144, 258–59, 264
research, 5–13, 27–28, 31–32, 54, 61–62, 76–77, 106–7, 139, 142–44, 169–73, 177, 209–11, 215, 217–19, 293–94, 303–4, 306, 373, 376–79, 382–83
  existing, 172–73
  inquiry/action, 29
  practical, 28
  process-product, 8–9
  qualitative, 282
  teacher/action, 11
  teacher's, 378
  university-based, 6, 11, 13
research activities, 213, 304
research approval processes, 229
  mandatory, 219
research articles, 175, 178
research databases, 175
research design, 282, 389
researchers, 1, 8, 10, 57, 61, 137, 169, 175, 369, 375, 378, 382, 388
research findings, 386, 391
research journeys, 169
research literature, 174, 176
research on self-regulated learning, 215
research paradigm, 8–9, 379
Research Plan, 159, 163–229
research process, 9–10, 19, 168
research projects, 132, 134, 315
  particular action, 374
research purpose, 11, 202
research quality, assessing teacher, 378–79
research questions, 19, 38, 77, 126, 137, 190, 200, 202–4, 256–57, 263, 265
research screening process, 213
research situation, 250, 377–78
research skills, 7, 202, 375, 382
research summaries, 174–76, 380
research traditions, 10–11, 379–80
resources, 49–50, 56–57, 80, 88–89, 159, 166, 174, 177, 290–91, 315, 320
responses, 103, 105, 108, 131, 133, 135–37, 232–33, 236, 242, 260–61, 272, 312, 327, 329
Response to Intervention (RtI), 236

responsibility, 48, 72, 78, 122, 208, 211–12, 283, 304
result in better student work turn-in rate, 148
results, 51–52, 102–3, 132–33, 137–38, 176–77, 179–80, 215–16, 224, 227, 288–89, 292, 294, 312, 314–15, 377–78, 380–81
results of practitioner research, 311, 314–15
review, 50, 54, 102–3, 155, 170, 206, 209, 213–14, 216, 219, 232–33, 312, 314
ripe contexts for teacher inquiry, 34
RLI (Remote Learning Inquiry), 14
role, 9–10, 13, 56–57, 66–67, 74, 180, 183, 185, 203, 205, 211–13, 279, 332, 375, 377
room, 20, 41–42, 113, 207, 242, 276, 280, 323, 332–33, 338, 340–41
Routman, 334, 336, 342
RtI (Response to Intervention), 236
RtI Design Worksheet, 237–38
rubrics, 223, 321, 323, 326, 329–31
Ruth, 41, 273–74, 280–81
 Amy, 40, 106, 156, 275–78, 281
Rutten, 6–7, 13–17, 26, 29, 77

Sarasota, 355–56, 359
SCALE, 140–41
school board policies, 16–17
school calendars, innovative, 24
school community, 40, 82
school context, 181, 247
school day, 19, 58, 126, 128, 145, 155, 189, 218, 228, 289, 380
school district research policies, 161, 213
school districts, 5, 14, 23, 72, 81, 213, 215, 295–96
 public, 14, 81
school funding, 21, 345
school improvement, 305, 346, 375
school improvement efforts, 209, 228
schooling, 8, 26, 62, 195, 247, 269, 284, 289, 345, 347–48, 350
schooling experiences, 21–22, 29, 31
 equitable, 22, 39, 45, 290, 345, 353
schooling system, 347, 353
school learning, 45
school level, 85, 293
school reform, 3, 196
School Reform Initiative, 25, 368
schools, 9, 12–14, 24–28, 51, 72–73, 75–79, 82–85, 96, 133–34, 142–43, 169–70, 180–83, 213, 222–23, 288–90, 292–93, 295, 345–49, 354–55, 366–68
 equitable, 345, 368
 hates, 329, 339
 local, 296
 magnet, 355
 middle, 59, 77, 81, 85, 152, 299
 playing, 63, 316
schools and society, 13, 22
school structures, 292, 294
school types, 355
school work ethic, strong, 150
schoolwork ethic, strong, 148
school year, 24, 47–48, 53, 65, 81, 100, 114, 135, 316, 318, 347–48
science, 48–49, 59–60, 108, 114, 118, 126–27, 129, 147, 150–51, 188–89, 348–49, 352
science center, 181
science classes, 59–60, 139, 151
science curriculum, 48
science learners, successful, 241–42
science learning, 60, 241, 348
science students, ninth-grade integrated, 347
Science Talks, 108, 126–28
Science Talks Enhance Student Understandings, 188
science unit, 48–49, 52, 167
scores, 139–41, 144, 208, 224–25, 248–49, 325, 329–30, 341
 students graph quiz, 225–26
scripted field notes, 105, 323
scripting, 58, 105–6, 108, 114
search, 1, 95, 139, 173–77, 245–46, 336, 394
second graders, 64, 66, 109, 304, 317, 319, 322, 324, 327, 332, 341
segment, 120, 122, 259
self, 372, 374–75, 395
self-regulated learning, 215, 223
self-regulation, 125–26, 215, 218
self-regulation strategies, 215, 218
sequence of steps, 255
Session, 64, 224, 232, 238–39, 296, 299, 317, 324
 concurrent, 296, 299
 extra-help, 135, 232
set, 76–77, 155, 160, 169, 218, 225, 250–52, 254, 256, 373, 383
setting workshop, 321, 326
sexuality, 22, 72, 86, 355
shared inquiry, 28, 224
shared problem of practice, 199
sharing, 2–3, 20, 108–9, 118, 195, 197, 241–42, 287–343, 356, 360, 369
sharing inquiry, 290, 294, 343
sharing phase of teacher inquiries, 315
Sharing Work, 366
showcase, 9, 299–300
 student inquiry, 289

SIGs (special interest groups), 294
skim, 177, 191, 233, 235
slides, 301, 315
small group instruction, 223
SMART Board, 60, 197
SMART Board technology, 197
social justice, 5, 14, 30, 71–73, 86, 93, 185, 270, 345, 355
  issues of, 72–74
social workers, 81, 173
society, 13, 15, 21–22, 72, 171, 205, 208, 345, 368, 387
solutions, possible, 181–82, 227
sound recognition, 236, 239–40
sounds, 4, 43–44, 236, 238, 295, 331
source, 85, 98–99, 104–5, 110–11, 113, 119, 122–24, 133–34, 149, 194, 226–27, 238–40, 275–78, 302–3, 385–86
  multiple, 55, 145–46, 187, 323, 339, 385, 390
  reputable, 168
space, 15, 24, 71, 78, 116, 126, 131, 274, 291, 294, 352
special interest groups (SIGs), 294
spreadsheet, 146–47, 150, 252
SSS, 140–41, 147
stage, 44, 160, 167, 174, 178, 181, 185, 189–91, 193, 261, 267
  five inquiry planning, 160
stages of inquiry planning, 231
stages of planning, 159, 167, 199–200
stance, 2–3, 7, 13–14, 16–18, 22, 31, 34, 217, 220, 369–72, 374, 381–82
stance and process of inquiry, 14, 18
stance of inquiry work, 371
standard deviation, 247, 249–50, 254
standardized test scores, 21, 30, 95, 138–39, 143–46, 156, 347–50, 381
start, 15, 30, 78, 80, 118, 160, 171, 173–74, 189–90, 192, 243, 245–46, 272, 294, 299–300
start of data collection, 384, 389
state, 35–36, 75, 85, 88, 187, 189, 260, 288, 290, 292, 295, 347, 349
statistics, 139, 249, 252–56, 385, 391
  calculated, 252–54
step, 30–32, 149–50, 159–60, 168, 173–74, 176–77, 207, 235, 241, 246–48, 250–52, 254–60, 268–69, 313, 331
  action planning, 237
  first, 35–36, 149, 236, 250, 252, 255, 282
  multiple, 32
  next, 32, 125, 168, 233, 246, 272, 275, 340, 349, 360

summative data analysis process, 31
  timed, 25
Stephen, 120–21, 135, 137, 232
Stephen's subquestions, 135
Steward, 242–43
sticky notes, 106, 168, 265, 267
stories, 41–42, 44, 50, 52, 54, 65–66, 122–23, 279, 300, 302, 318–22, 324–38, 355, 359–61, 365–68
  complete, 66, 319, 321, 324–25, 328
  complete inquiry, 346
stories and practice, 52
story element, 321, 327, 330
strategies, 56, 59–61, 95–96, 117–18, 120–23, 126, 137–38, 156, 173–74, 176, 186–89, 218, 246, 283, 385
student and teacher learning, 73
student artifacts, 225–26, 301
student classroom assignments, 195
student data, 151, 214, 237, 312
student engagement, 37, 153, 165, 267
student feedback, 131, 187, 192
student growth, 40–42, 322, 324
student information, 214
student interviews, 114, 118, 137, 149, 214, 225, 263, 350
student learning, 8, 11, 18, 25, 28, 47, 56, 151, 183, 223, 236
  improving, 384, 388
student learning problem, 236
student motivation, 8, 174
student partnerships, 333
student performance, 46, 138, 148, 237
student population, 82, 163, 203
student reflections, 225–26
student responses, 259–60, 263–64, 272
students, 16–24, 45–53, 55–61, 64–70, 78–86, 88–92, 103–10, 112–18, 120–32, 135–40, 142–45, 147–56, 162–69, 213–19, 221–24, 234–42, 288–93, 315–39, 346–50, 354–62
student's behavior, particular, 43
student selection, 236
students experience, 117, 139, 166
students experience schooling, 289
student's group number, 251
student sharings, 337
students in group, 121, 251
students in math class, 174
students questions, 116, 209
student surveys, 130, 323
student teacher's inquiry, 289

student teaching, 26–27, 43, 129, 131, 189
student teaching experience, 26, 61
student thinking, stimulated, 118
student work, 20, 25, 30, 95–98, 100, 104, 107, 144–45, 153–54, 208, 214, 385, 390
  collecting, 105
  individual, 154
student work completion, 149
student work samples, 89, 104, 219, 263, 350, 356
study context, 383, 387
study sessions, 224–26
  afterschool group, 224
subject areas, 57, 87
subwonderings, 223–24
summary, 178, 240, 306, 314, 382
  executive, 305–6, 344
summative data analysis, 191, 232, 240, 244–48, 262, 270, 273, 280, 284–85, 385–86, 390–91
summative data analysis process, 241, 245–47, 259, 262–63, 273, 280, 284–85
summative data analysis process step by step, 31
Summative Data Analysis Step by Step, 247
supervisor, 109, 274, 277, 304, 321–23, 325, 327
support, 14, 18, 20, 23–24, 27–29, 51–52, 56–57, 59–60, 90, 128–30, 193–95, 197–98, 220, 314–15, 332–33
support student learning, 60, 167
support teacher for students in grades, 56
support teacher inquiry, 22
Support Teacher Research Data Analysis, 262
support teachers, instructional, 114
surveys, first, 133–34
symbols, 276–77
system, 7, 108–9, 114, 117, 260, 271, 292, 320, 347, 353

teach, 1–2, 4–5, 13, 26–27, 45–48, 50–55, 57, 59–60, 66–67, 70–71, 80, 86, 170–71, 208–9, 217–19, 319–20
teacher action research, 32, 305, 377
teacher activity, 54–55
teacher candidates, 6–7, 21–23, 26–27, 29, 31, 34–35, 38, 40, 42, 47, 118, 305–6, 345–46, 354
teacher candidates learning, 27, 364
teacher education, 27, 29, 354
teacher education program, 14, 21, 32, 137, 346, 354, 356–57, 359–62, 364, 372, 393
teacher inquirer pieces, 323

teacher inquirers, 11–13, 30–31, 38, 95–96, 100–101, 106–7, 125–26, 168–71, 193–94, 199–200, 209–11, 215, 219, 227, 268–70, 294
teacher inquirers celebrate problems, 162
teacher inquirer's work, 31
teacher inquiry, 2, 4–9, 13–16, 18–20, 22, 26–30, 32–35, 38–39, 193, 195–96, 209–11, 227–29, 289–96, 369, 378–79, 392–93
  collaborative, 198
  first, 61, 72
teacher inquiry and inquiry communities, 15
teacher inquiry and reading books on teacher research, 43
teacher inquiry communities, 146
teacher inquiry conference, 295, 394
teacher inquiry cycles, 347, 352, 356, 394
Teacher Inquiry Defined, 3–33
teacher inquiry experience, 2, 379
Teacher Inquiry in Professional Development Schools, 28
teacher inquiry journey, 382
  personal, 34
teacher inquiry movement, 10, 34, 217
teacher inquiry project, 365
teacher leaders, 27, 291–92, 294
teacher leadership, 291–92
teacher preparation, 26, 295
teacher research, 4–5, 9–11, 31–32, 61, 72–74, 77, 120–21, 137–38, 217, 292–93, 305, 375–77, 379–83, 393–94
  good, 143, 156
  teacher inquiry, 10
teacher researcher communities, 194, 196
teacher researcher Mickey MacDonald, 248–49, 346
teacher researchers, 4–5, 20, 77, 95–96, 107, 120–23, 144–45, 169–72, 196, 248–49, 258–59, 262, 269–70, 294–95, 305–6, 340, 347–48, 376, 381–93
  longtime, 31
  middle school, 120
  novice, 124, 346–47
  passionate, 270
teacher researchers approach, 179, 381
teacher researcher's classroom, 380
teacher researcher's findings, 392
teacher researcher's work, 380, 382
teacher research findings, 293
teacher research methodology, 227, 390
teacher research process, 172, 376, 381–82, 391, 393
teacher research products, 381, 394
teacher research work, 372

teachers, 1–2, 4–17, 19–27, 52–58, 61–66, 69–74, 78–86, 90–92, 95–98, 114–17, 167–69, 179–85, 193–99, 207–10, 216–20, 288–96, 304–6, 316–19, 354–55, 371–82
   academic, 59–60
   culture, 51–52
   elementary, 14, 46, 54–55, 72
   high school science, 139, 153
   middle school, 75, 153, 241, 271
   preservice, 123
   prospective, 294–95, 299
   responsive, 263, 367
   student, 289, 373
teachers as action researchers, 10
teacher's day, 195
teacher's experience, 380
teachers inquire, 21, 80, 169, 393
teacher's inquiry, 31, 172–73, 176, 306, 370
teacher's inquiry journey, 169
teacher's work, 38, 217, 306, 369
teach fractions, 88
teaching, 1–12, 15–20, 26–30, 39–43, 47–50, 56–64, 69, 80–90, 106, 167–70, 193–96, 208–11, 215–16, 218–19, 226–29, 291–93, 346–47, 369–77, 379–81, 392–94
   ethical, 208–9
   good, 19, 21, 37, 143
teaching and learning and maximize student, 20
teaching and research, 19, 273
teaching careers, 22–23, 72, 270, 345, 355, 360
teaching context, 162, 164, 170, 185, 383, 394
teaching fractions, 87
teaching practice, 36, 39, 163, 165, 171, 173, 217–18, 228–29, 234, 270–71, 273, 375–76, 381–83, 386, 392–93
teaching practice and teacher research, 383
teaching profession, 29, 33, 39, 209–10, 288, 291, 361, 365, 374, 379, 383
teaching strategies, 30, 37–38, 52, 59–60, 89, 170
   list of, 60, 90
Teaching Strategies/Techniques, 39, 93
teaching techniques, 30, 57, 126
teach self-regulation, 215, 218
teach students, 125, 168, 223
techniques, 38, 57, 59–60, 170, 267, 306, 340, 348
technology, new, 60, 197
terms, 3, 10–11, 21, 24, 173, 176, 193, 201, 203–4, 211, 219
text, 10–11, 30, 32–33, 35–36, 84, 123, 125, 147–48, 211–12, 230, 316–17, 357, 362, 393, 395

textbox, 86, 92, 100, 167, 172, 199, 282, 291, 311–12, 366, 372
themes, 47, 221–22, 261–62, 267–68, 272, 280, 289, 359, 364, 385–86, 391–92
theory and practice, 9, 282
theory of action, 30, 101, 161, 181, 183, 185–86, 188, 195, 227
thinking, 86, 89–90, 95–97, 104–5, 115–16, 122–26, 154–55, 167, 199–200, 204–5, 244–45, 267, 288, 303–4, 337–38
   comfortable, 323, 337–38
third-grade students, 123
thought partner, 19, 212, 272–73
thought partner in data analysis, 270, 273
thought processes, 38, 109, 121–22
thoughts, 41, 43, 63–64, 87, 108, 117–18, 124–26, 130–31, 202, 274, 283, 304–5, 316–17, 328–31, 340–43
time, 11, 13–15, 21–22, 40–43, 53–54, 64–67, 73–74, 76–78, 98, 108–9, 123–26, 151–55, 189–94, 220, 233–38, 241–44, 263–65, 274–75, 316–18, 382–83
   finding, 352
   first, 13, 26, 31, 41, 47, 68, 73, 88, 106, 137, 163
   good, 167, 190, 193
   last, 47, 53
   particular, 154
   second, 233, 274
   story, 359
time Adam's group, 274
time constraint, 304
time frame, 385, 389–91
   particular, 190
time intervals, particular, 105
timekeeper, 206–7
timeline, 70, 161, 188–89, 207
timing, 161, 189, 191–92, 248
timing and duration of data collection, 161, 189–92
titles, 3, 188, 258, 296, 324
tools, 18, 101–2, 121–22, 175, 183, 186, 203–4, 211–13, 311–12, 314–15, 347, 380, 383–84, 389
   important, 26, 130–31
topic, 16–17, 35, 39–40, 48, 57, 83–84, 87–88, 155, 161, 163–66, 168–72, 175–78, 180, 190–91, 354–56
   inquiry's, 155
topic of inquiry, 18, 271, 391
topic of inquiry for educators, 18
TR, 147–49

traditions, 11, 51–52
transcripts, 259, 261, 263, 350
transferability, 315, 376–78, 382, 394
transfer self-regulation strategies, 125–26
turbulent context, 15–16
types, 23–24, 93, 95, 108–9, 143, 148, 150, 209, 212, 214, 227, 232–33, 256–59, 314–15, 355–56

ultimate goal of engagement in inquiry, 31, 39, 345
understanding, 22, 50–51, 55–56, 81–82, 95–96, 127–29, 136–37, 143–44, 168–69, 172–73, 208–10, 220–24, 272–74, 293, 362, 372–73
  better, 179–81, 347–48, 388
  informed, 185
understanding students, 92, 108, 117, 120, 204
unit, 47–50, 53, 57, 80, 126, 129, 131, 183–85, 189, 196, 261, 264, 350
  dinosaur, 48
  ecology, 224–26
university, 12, 49, 51, 170, 175, 209, 211, 214–15, 218, 220, 227, 229, 291, 293, 296
university and inquiry, 12
University-Based Research and Teacher Inquiry Comparison, 12
university-based researchers, 6–7, 11, 13
University of Florida, 14, 118, 200, 215–16, 249, 271, 273, 299, 305–6, 311
University of Florida's school partner's website, 306
University of South Florida education student, 214
university partnerships, 28, 295
University researcher, 8–9, 12

value, maximum, 250, 252–54
variables, 251–56
veteran teacher researcher George Dempsie's passion, 288
veteran teachers, 1, 14, 26–27, 35, 47, 86, 89, 294, 299, 382
video, 30, 95, 107, 118, 120–21, 145, 155, 212, 214, 265
video work, 120
voices, 1–2, 5, 17, 32–33, 42, 44, 54, 57, 63, 65, 316, 318, 332, 335–37, 379

Wait Time and Student Responses, 260
websites, 53, 133, 169, 306, 314–15, 368
Wendy, 17–18, 123–24
Wolcott, 282, 303–4, 340
wonderings, 36–37, 39–40, 42, 57–58, 81–82, 86, 88–89, 166–67, 180–81, 319–20, 340–41, 380, 383–85, 387–90, 392
  potential, 93
wonderings and purpose, 384, 388
wonderings in problems, 37
wonderings in problems of practice, 37
words, key, 174, 177
work, 3–4, 11–13, 27–32, 67–69, 95–96, 159–65, 193–99, 217–19, 222–24, 227–31, 287–89, 294–96, 299–302, 304–6, 311–12, 314–15, 340–43, 375–77, 381–83, 393–95
work environment, 163, 169
work of teacher inquiry, 28
worksheet, 250–57
worksheet window, 250, 252
workshops, 42, 64, 142, 153, 316–17, 321–22, 325–26, 328, 330–33, 335–36, 341–42
  complete story, 331
  final, 321
  first, 324–25, 336, 346
  last, 325, 331
work teacher inquiry, 52
work time, 327
world, 1, 3, 56, 64, 73–74, 123, 128–31, 243, 245, 316–17, 394
writers, 63, 66, 303, 305, 316, 319–23, 325, 327–29, 332–33, 335–36, 338–39, 341
  good, 65, 318, 328–29, 339
  second-grade, 64, 317, 331
  young, 64, 317, 330, 338, 341
writer's workshops, 64, 317, 322, 324, 328–29, 332, 334, 336, 344
  final, 324, 338
  last, 337, 340
  series of, 322, 336

YAL (Young Adult Literature), 84, 361
Yonge Developmental Research School, 139, 303
Young Adult Literature. *See* YAL

Education for Educators
Where will your professional learning journey take you?

Choreography of Presenting, Second Edition
Kendall Zoller

The Impact Cycle
Jim Knight

Intentional Moves
Elisa B. MacDonald

Blended Coaching, Second Edition
Gary Bloom
Jackie Owens Wilson

Student-Centered Coaching: The Moves
Diane Sweeney
Leanna S. Harris

Transforming Teaching Through Curriculum-Based Professional Learning: The Elements
James B. Short · Stephanie Hirsh

Assessing Students, Not Standards
Lee Ann Jung

Engaging Parents and Families in Grading Reforms
Thomas R. Guskey

To find these and other best-selling books, visit **corwin.com/PLBooks**

GP241067104

Free Professional Development

WEBINARS
Listen and interact with education experts for an hour of professional learning to gain practical tools and evidence-based strategies—and maybe win some free books!

LEADERS COACHING LEADERS PODCAST
Join Peter M. DeWitt, Michael Nelson, and their guests as they discuss evidence-based approaches for tackling pressing topics that all education leaders face.

CORWIN CONNECT
Read and engage with us on our blog about the latest in education and professional development.

SAMPLE CONTENT
Did you know you can download sample content from almost every Corwin book on our website? Go to corwin.com/resources for tools you and your staff can use right away!

SOCIAL JUSTICE RESEARCH
Takeaways for K–12 from the latest research on advancing educational equity and justice.

corwin.com/resources

CORWIN

To help every educator help every student

We believe   that every single student deserves a great education

We believe   that knowing our impact is both a privilege and a responsibility

We believe   that a fair, stable, and thriving society is built on education

THE PROFESSIONAL LEARNING ASSOCIATION

Learning Forward is a nonprofit, international membership association of learning educators committed to one vision in K–12 education: Equity and excellence in teaching and learning. To realize that vision, Learning Forward pursues its mission to build the capacity of leaders to establish and sustain highly effective professional learning. Information about membership, services, and products is available from www.learningforward.org.